THE WILEY SCIENCE EDITIONS

The Search for Extraterrestrial Intelligence, by Thomas R. McDonough
Seven Ideas that Shook the Universe, by Bryon D. Anderson and Nathan Spielberg
The Naturalist's Year, by Scott Camazine
The Urban Naturalist, by Steven D. Garber
Space: The Next Twenty-Five Years, by Thomas R. McDonough

The Naturalist's Year

24 Outdoor Explorations

Scott Camazine

Cornell University

**With Original Illustrations by
Cynthia Camazine and the Author**

Wiley Science Editions

John Wiley & Sons, Inc.
New York • Chichester • Brisbane • Toronto • Singapore

Publisher: Stephen Kippur
Editor: David Sobel
Managing Editor: Andrew Hoffer
Production Service: G & H SOHO, Ltd.

Library of Congress Cataloging-in-Publication Data

Camazine, Scott.
The naturalist's year.

1. Natural history—United States—Outdoor books.
2. Seasons—United States. I. Title.
QH104.C32   1987   508.73   86-24627
ISBN 0-471-62943-X
ISBN 0-471-84845-X (pbk)

Printed in the United States of America
87   88   10   9   8   7   6   5   4   3   2   1

To all for whom the world of nature is a source of wonder,
an inspiration, and a haven

Source Notes

Pages 7, 14, 20, 22, 35, 43, 60, 71, 74, 82, 86, 96, 98, 105, 108, 117, 127, 134, 136, 138, 148, 161, 163, 169, 173, 185, 189, 195, 202, 204, 214, 224, 231, 242, 247, 252: Cynthia Camazine.

Pages 10, 11, 26 (top), 42, 89, 99, 118, 120, 121, 124, 140, 142, 153, 168, 180, 182, 222, 228, 249: Copyright © 1987 Scott Camazine.

Page 15: Adapted from *The salamanders of New York,* S.C. Bishop, New York State Museum Bulletin, no. 324, 1941.

Page 26 (bottom): From *Migration of Birds,* F.C. Lincoln, copyright © 1952 Double-day and Company, Garden City, NY, p. 39. Reprinted by permission.

Page 32: From *Migration of Birds,* F.C. Lincoln, copyright © 1952 Doubleday and Company, Garden City, NY, pp. 49–52. Reprinted by permission.

Page 36: From *Beekeeping in the United States,* Agricultural Handbook no. 335, U.S. Department of Agriculture.

Pages 37, 106, 145, 170: Scott Camazine.

Page 39: From *Swarm Control,* G.S. Demuth, Farmers' Bulletin no. 1198, U.S. Department of Agriculture.

Page 48: From *A Textbook of Entomology,* 4th Ed., H.H. Ross, C.A. Ross, and June R.P. Ross, John Wiley & Sons, Inc., NY, 1982.

Page 50: From *Insects Injurious to the Household and Annoying to Man,* G.W. Herrick, Macmillan, 1926, and the British Museum of Natural History.

Page 62: From *Life in Moving Fluids,* S. Vogel, copyright © 1981 Willard Grant Press, Boston, MA, p. 257. Reprinted by permission.

Pages 64–65: From *Fresh-water Invertebrates of the United States,* 2d. Ed., R.W. Pennak, copyright © 1978, John Wiley & Sons. Reprinted by permission of John Wiley & Sons, Inc.

Page 78: From *Phytognomonica,* G. Porta, 1588.

Pages 92–93: From *The Natural History of Plants,* A.K. von Marilaun and F.W. Oliver, Blackie & Son, London, 1896.

Page 101: Cynthia Camazine and Scott Camazine.

Page 109: From *Anatomy of Seed Plants,* 2d. Ed., K. Esau, copyright © 1978, John Wiley & Sons. Reprinted by permission of John Wiley & Sons, Inc.

Pages 113–115: From *Anatomy of the Honey Bee,* R.E. Snodgrass, copyright © 1956 Cornell University, Ithaca, NY, p. 12. Reprinted by permission.

Preface

THE NATURALIST'S YEAR is a guide to natural history for inquisitive naturalists. It explores the world of living organisms — the earliest spring wildflowers, edible and toxic fungi, insect defenses, spiders' webs, mating salamanders, migrating birds, and the lives of mammals. It examines animal behavior, adaptations for survival, and natural phenomena, such as blowing winds, drifting snow, the motion of the stars and planets, the formation of fossils, and the crystallization of water into delicate snowflakes.

The Naturalist's Year attempts to provide a greater understanding, appreciation, and respect for the natural world. It is a glimpse of nature aimed at instilling a sense of wonder and awe. Some of you may not yet share my passion for snakes, skeletons, flies, and bats. You may never have watched a spider snare its prey, or captured a swarm of honey bees, or seen salamanders mate. My intent is to kindle your interest, and spark your curiosity. Whether you are a novice or a devoted naturalist, this book will sharpen your skills as an observer, stimulate ideas, and lead to questions that will increase your understanding of the world around you.

Once the name of a plant or animal is known, you have made an acquaintance with whom you are on speaking terms. For the relationship to grow, and to make this organism an intimate friend, you have to learn its personality, its idiosyncrasies, and its behaviors. Field guides introduce you to an organism. Considering that there are over 1,000,000 different insects, 250,000 species of flowering plants, 30,000 fish, almost 9,000 birds, and 4,000 mammals, field guides have a formidable task.

To become more intimate with nature's organisms, another kind of guide is also needed. *The Naturalist's Year* is meant to be such a book.

One need not travel to exotic rain forests to study natural history; fascinating subjects abound in your own backyard. I have chosen 24 explorations, merely a handful of the wealth of subjects available for study. Each exploration provides a detailed discussion of a biological, geological, botanical, or zoological subject. Each chapter includes "hands-on" activities for pursuing your explorations in greater depth because natural history is learned by doing and observing. These investigations are arranged according to season so that you can undertake explorations throughout the year.

My wish is that this book will stimulate the reader to embark on adventures into nature's endless nooks and crannies. Jean Henri Fabre, the famous French school-teacher and naturalist, wrote,

Because I have stirred a few grains of sand on the shore, am I in a position to know the depths of the ocean?

Life has unfathomable secrets. Human knowledge will be erased from the archives of the world before we possess the last word that the Gnat has to say to us. . . .

Part of the thrill of nature comes from realizing that you could spend a lifetime exploring any one of these "unfathomable secrets." Therefore, I have presented my topics not as complete packages, but as explorations with varying levels of completeness and complexity. For some readers, a particular chapter may provide enough information to satisfy curiosity. However, each chapter is intended as a stepping-stone to a vast world of further explorations. Should you become captivated by a topic, you can begin to delve more deeply by referring to the list of references and suggestions for further reading provided at the end of each chapter. My efforts will be truly successful if you choose to venture into the unknown, beyond what could be presented in this book.

I have many people to thank for their advice, suggestions, and support. First, my parents. My mother's interest in natural history, and her encouragement of my childhood interests, provided a conducive atmosphere for a curious young naturalist. I know few mothers who would tolerate the endless procession of snakes, toads, roadkills, spiders, and insects that I brought home. My father, though less enamored of crawling creatures, has always given his unflagging encouragement and support to my endeavors.

I am especially indebted to the naturalists who explained things to me in the field, and to those interested people who accompanied me and listened as I repeated these teachings. I have learned from their questions and comments. For these teachers and pupils, I have written this book.

Illustrations are an essential and integral part of this book. My stepmother, Cynthia Camazine, did nearly all of the original illustrations. In addition to her beautiful artwork, I appreciate her patience.

Many people commented on portions of the manuscript: S. Anderson, W. Bock, B. Camazine, R. Camazine, E. Conlisk, N. Ferrari, R. Gardner, C. Henderson, H.W. Levi, E. Marsden, R.A. Morse, J.C. Ogden, L. Osborn, G. Rowe, P.K. Visscher, and D. Welebit. My special thanks to H. Evans and to my father, who both read the entire manuscript. Everyone's suggestions helped me to eliminate awkward exposition, and occasional inaccuracies. It was a pleasure to work with David Sobel, my editor at John Wiley & Sons. His suggestions made my work easier, and certainly improved the quality of the manuscript. Many others have helped to make this book possible, including Andrew Hoffer and Dawn Reitz at John Wiley & Sons, and Claire McKean at G & H SOHO, Ltd.

As is always the case, the responsibility for remaining flaws lies solely with me. Any corrections or suggestions from my readers would be most welcome.

Scott Camazine
Ithaca, New York

Contents

Introduction   *1*

SPRING

1. Skunk Cabbage: The Warm-Blooded Plant of the Swamps   7
2. Mating of the Mole Salamanders   14
3. The Remarkable Migrations of Birds   22
4. When Honey Bees Swarm   35
5. Creatures in My Home   43
6. Insect Adaptations for an Aquatic Existence   60

SUMMER

7. Herbal Medicines: A Pharmacy in Our Own Backyards   74
8. The Contrivances by which Flowers Are Pollinated by Insects   86
9. The Milkweed Community   96
10. Life in the Arid Desert   105
11. Camouflage and Mimicry: Defense Strategies for a Hostile World 117
12. On the Trail of the Whitetail Deer   127

AUTUMN

13. How Animals Wage Chemical Warfare   138
14. Seed Dispersal: Preparing for the Next Generation   148
15. A Glimpse at Fungi   161
16. Scrutinizing Spiders   173

17. Feasting in the Fields   185
18. Autumn Color and Falling Leaves   195

WINTER

19. Fossils: Stories in Stone   204
20. Explorations of Snowflakes   214
21. Blowing Winds and Drifting Snow   224
22. Unraveling the Mysteries of Skeletons   231
23. Coping with the Cold   242
24. Under the Night Sky: Sights Beyond Our Solar System   252

Appendix A: Common Names and Scientific Names
             of Organisms Mentioned in This Book   265

Appendix B: Sources of Equipment and
             Supplies   273

Index   275

List of Activities by Chapter

CHAPTER 1
Observing skunk cabbages   9
Observing skunk cabbage visitors   11

CHAPTER 2
Observing mole salamanders   19
Observing amphibian development   20

CHAPTER 3
Bird-watching for spring migrants   28
Observing bird migrations   31
Moon-watching for passing migrants   33

CHAPTER 4
Observing a swarm of honey bees   38
How to approach a honey bee swarm   39
Some experiments with a swarm   40
A bee beard   41

CHAPTER 5
Using a key to identify insect orders   51
Microscopes   57
Identifying the common household flies   58

CHAPTER 6
Collecting insects from ponds and streams   70
Setting up a freshwater aquarium   70
Demonstrations of surface tension   71
Making observations of aquatic insects   72

CHAPTER 7
Making a plant collection   81
Identifying plants   83
The anatomy of a flower   83

CHAPTER 8
Observing insects pollinating flowers   90
The piston apparatus of birdfoot trefoil   91
Jewelweed and the nectar thieves   94

CHAPTER 9
Experimenting with the pollination mechanism of milkweeds   100
Observing and collecting milkweed visitors   100

CHAPTER 10
Dissecting an insect   112
Examining plant stomata   115

CHAPTER 11
Close-up photography in the field   123
    Equipment / Depth of field / Lighting

CHAPTER 12
How to observe wild animals and what to look for   132
Tracks and traces of deer   133
Attracting deer   135
Making plaster casts of animal tracks   136

CHAPTER 13
Observing chemically defended invertebrates   145
Making an insect collection   145
    Killing jars / Pinning and labeling specimens /
    Arrangement and care of the collection

CHAPTER 14
Exploring a plant's adaptations for seed dispersal   156
Collecting seed hitchhikers   158
Experiments with flying seeds   158
Animals as seed dispersers   159

CHAPTER 15
How to observe and identify mushrooms   168
    How to look at a mushroom

CHAPTER 16
Collecting spiders   175
Preserving and identifying spiders   177
The care and feeding of spiders   178
Studying and observing common spiders   178
    Jumping spiders / Orb weavers

CHAPTER 17
Sumac lemonade   188
The versatile cattail   188
A taste of fungi   190
    The giant puffball / Shaggy manes / Sulfur
    shelf / Morels

CHAPTER 18
Recording the sequence of changes in the autumn foliage   199
Visualizing leaf pigments   200
    Filter paper chromatography / Separation of leaf pigments
    by chromatography / Extracting anthocyanin pigments
    from plants

CHAPTER 19
Collecting fossils   210
    Equipment
Preparing specimens   212
Organizing your collection   212

CHAPTER 20
Studying and preserving snowflakes   219

CHAPTER 21
Creating a miniature avalanche   229
Experimenting with snowdrifts   230

CHAPTER 22
Preparing skeletons for study   239

CHAPTER 23
Collecting winter creatures and observing their
    survival adaptations   247

CHAPTER 24
Equipment for stargazing   256
    Star maps and star wheels / Binoculars
Star-hopping through the night sky   259
Sightseeing in the celestial sphere   262
    *The Milky Way / Multiple Stars, Clusters, and Nebulae /
    Other Galaxies*

Introduction

EACH CHAPTER OF *The Naturalist's Year* consists of a detailed description of an organism or natural phenomenon that can be easily observed in the United States at a particular time of the year. The introductory material in each chapter presents the important concepts of the topic, enabling the reader to pursue the activities suggested in the remainder of the chapter. By learning about the subject before heading outdoors to explore on your own, you will be able to reap the full benefits of your observations and experiments.

Although the activities complement the chapter in which they appear, many of the techniques described carry over to other chapters of the book. I have attempted to present these general activities — such as collecting and preserving plants and insects, and close-up nature photography — early in the book. Leaf through the book, and pursue whatever activities seem interesting, or that are applicable to the nature studies you are involved with at the time.

COMMON NAMES AND SCIENTIFIC NAMES

In the text, I generally refer to organisms by their common names. I have done this to keep the writing from seeming unduly technical. In addition, throughout much of the book, I refer to groups of organisms, such as spiders, milkweeds, or salamanders, rather than to individual species that are found in more restricted areas of the country.

However, I do not mean to minimize the value of scientific names. In some cases organisms do not have common names (many mushrooms and insects), and in other instances common names are confusing since many organisms have a multitude of common names that vary from region to region. To add to the confusion, different organisms often have the same common name. An example is jimsonweed (*Datura stramonium*). This poisonous plant is also known as thornapple, moon lily, and sacred datura. An unrelated shrub or small tree, with long thorns and with red fruits that make an excellent jelly, is hawthorn. Our regional poison control center recently received a call from a worried mother reporting that her child had just eaten "thornapple." Unaware that hawthorn is also occasionally referred to as thornapple, the mother was advised to make the child vomit to rid his stomach of the poisonous fruit. I was asked to verify the identification of a sample of the "poisonous" plant. The bright red fruits were harmless hawthorn berries, not the prickly green fruit of *Datura*. The story had a happy ending, even though the child had the unpleasant experience of drinking a dose of ipecac syrup.

The serious naturalist refers to an organism by its unique scientific name, consisting of two parts: the generic name, and the specific name. The genus comes first and is capitalized; the species name follows, uncapitalized. Both names are italicized. After a while, the use of scientific names becomes second nature, no more difficult than using common names. Thus the Canada lily is *Lilium canadense*, and the wood lily is *Lilium philadelphicum*. These two species are in the same genus, indicating that they have some characteristics in common. The daylily (*Hemerocallis fulva*) is a less closely related, introduced species. Further discussion of classification and a list of the scientific names of organisms mentioned in this book are included in Appendix A.

SUPPLIES AND EQUIPMENT

As a young naturalist, before I had access to a high school or college biology laboratory, finding equipment and chemicals was one of my greatest frustrations. In many cases your pharmacy or hardware store will have what you need. Check these places first since you will get things quicker, and more cheaply, there than by placing an order with one of the biological supply houses listed in Appendix B.

MEASUREMENTS

The United States is in the process of converting to the metric system. The scientific establishment already uses the metric system; weather reports often give temperatures in both Celsius and Fahrenheit degrees, and many gas stations now pump gasoline by the liter. It is a good idea to start thinking metric. Therefore measurements in the book are given both ways. U.S. measures are listed first, followed by their approximate metric equivalents in parentheses.

REFERENCES

The references and suggestions for further reading included at the end of each chapter are of two types. There are general readings, which are at the same level of technicality as the chapter itself. Especially useful is the list of field guides for the identification of various organisms. In addition, I have listed more specialized references, including scientific journals. I encourage anyone interested in a particular topic to begin with one of the general references, which can be found in your library or bookstore. Many of the journal references can be found in a college library; they have been included because they are the sources I used in writing this book, and because I expect (and hope) that some readers will wish to pursue a topic in greater detail.

BEING A NATURALIST

Being a naturalist means being interested in the world around you. It means asking questions and seeking answers in an attempt to discover the intricacies of nature. No one is as fortunate as the naturalist. The whole world is his workplace, and his work is to explore and learn.

A field trip is the naturalist's starting point. I try to learn the name of at least one new organism, and to observe at least one new thing, on every field trip. I return home with questions and ideas that lead to further study.

Nature can be viewed as a series of solutions to the problems of survival. All organisms have four major concerns: nourishment, protection from environmental extremes, defense, and reproduction. The variety, complexity, and beauty of nature are a result of the nearly infinite number of solutions to these problems. When we look at an organism in the field, we are observing its response to these concerns, its adaptations for survival.

By studying adaptations, we will find that organisms have become adept engineers, physicists, and chemists. Through millions of years of evolution, life has "learned" how to live. Nature has already designed and perfected nearly every device that man has so proudly invented, from the wheel to the rocket.

If we look at nature this way, there is always a mystery to be solved. A walk in the field is often the beginning of an adventure, a search for an answer. How can certain moths fly at temperatures below freezing? How do Canada geese find their way back home each spring? How can kangaroo rats survive in the desert without ever drinking water? Why are some caterpillars hairy?

What's more, once you begin to observe an organism carefully, you discover additional mysteries. Years ago I gathered some maggot-ridden mushrooms. I decided to identify the flies that had deprived me of a meal. I placed the fungi in a plastic container, covered with a pane of glass. Later that afternoon, I found that hundreds of maggots had made their way up the sides of the container. When I lifted the glass, they amazingly began to catapult into the air! How could legless fly larvae jump? Why were they jumping? As I became more familiar with my jumping maggots, I noticed that they always began jumping at sunset, and only in one direction. I discovered that they jumped by curling in a loop, engaging microscopic hooks on their back. No one ever had noticed these hooks, but they were clearly revealed under the microscope.

Eventually I reared some of the larvae to adulthood and found, as I had suspected, that they were fungus gnats. It is thrilling, and humbling, to realize that each organism has the potential for a lifetime of study. The poet William Blake expressed it better than I:

> To see a World in a grain of sand,
> And a Heaven in a wild flower;
> Hold Infinity in the palm of your hand,
> And Eternity in an hour.
> (from *Auguries of Innocence*)

PREPARATION FOR THE FIELD

Everyone has his or her own style. I like to be ready for anything, so I tend to take just about everything when I embark on a day-long field trip. As a result, I often need a strong and willing companion to help carry all my paraphernalia. Lacking a field assistant, I must make do with a sturdy day pack or shoulder satchel. The following is my field trip checklist:

hand lens	field guides
binoculars	notebook and pen
pocket knife	camera equipment
single-edged razor blade	tripod
forceps (tweezers)	canteen
collecting net	compass
vials	topographical map
jars and plastic containers	insect repellent
zip-lock plastic bags	wide-brimmed sun hat
killing jar	folding seat

Each trip has a different goal and destination, making for individual requirements. Choose carefully and take only what you need, for one of the objectives of getting out into the field is to escape the encumbrances of the civilized world. Being weighted down with equipment defeats that purpose.

The bare essentials are proper clothing. I always wear a pair of old jeans, a long-sleeved shirt, and sturdy shoes or sneakers. I did not have to return from many field trips, clad in a t-shirt and shorts, before my bleeding arms and legs taught me that lesson. Unless you are properly dressed, if the catbriers, cleavers, and cut-grass do not get you, the mosquitoes and black flies will.

THE RESPONSIBILITIES OF A NATURALIST

The countryside is a haven from our busy and crowded world. As naturalists, our responsibility is to see that it survives. It is incumbent upon us to preserve our environment, and its helpless creatures, for our future and for the generations to come.

In the field, always keep the following suggestions in mind:

1. Do not litter. Carry a plastic garbage bag for your own and any other litter you find. When you return, you will be happier to have made the effort.

2. Do not disturb the environment. Leave things as they were. Put logs and stones back in the position you found them, and fill in holes that you dig. Before you leave an area, look around; try to remove any sign of having been there.

3. Collect, but only collect what you need. Never collect rare or endangered species.

4. Always ask permission to enter, and collect, on private land.

5. Respect life. Never kill an animal needlessly. Snakes, spiders, bats, rats, and all those often-despised creatures deserve to live just as much as you or I. If you do not like them, avoid them, but do not kill them. And encourage others not to kill them either. To some extent, a naturalist must kill living creatures to learn about life. Our museums contain useful collections of preserved organisms. However, when possible, do your collecting with a camera or a drawing pad. If you kill a creature, make sure you are doing it for a reason. Seek alternatives. For example, roadkills are a source of birds and mammals. Pet shops will often give you animals that die. My cats are always bringing home dead mice, voles, shrews, and moles.

6. In general, you will learn most about an animal by observing it in the wild, under natural conditions. It is difficult to get many animals to behave normally in captivity. If you bring an animal home to photograph or to observe it, return it to the place you found it. Attend to the welfare of any animal you capture, always making sure the animal has food, water, and a proper environment.

7. Always set a good example. When you take others out into the field, they will learn by watching you and following your example.

1

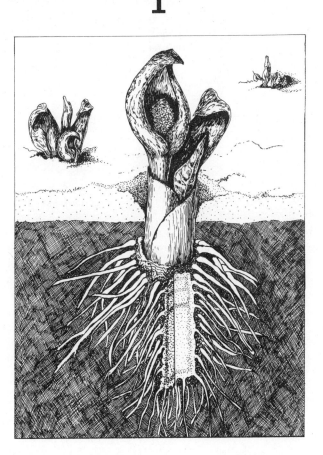

Skunk Cabbage: The Warm-Blooded Plant of the Swamps

LATE FEBRUARY and early March: Cold winds; dustings of snow and sleet intermittently cover the ground; walks through the nearby fields reveal no evidence of the approaching spring.

For a naturalist impatiently awaiting the new season, this is a time of clandestine activity and preparation for a new year. The sap begins to rise in the sugar maples. Striped skunks, chipmunks, and red squirrels are mating in their cozy dens; it will be several weeks before the young are born. The red maple and pussy willow buds have begun to swell, ready to burst forth into leaves and flowers in the first warm days to come. In the midst of all this concealed activity, despite the occasional snowfalls and subfreezing weather, the skunk cabbage has already flowered.

This hardy pioneer pushes up through the thick cold mud of the swamps and makes its way to the surface through several inches of snow. Has nature gone amok?

HOW SKUNK CABBAGES KEEP WARM

Skunk cabbages have peculiar flowers. Instead of whorls of petals and sepals, one finds a single hood, called a **spathe**, about five inches high, in a mottled pattern varying from green to purplish. The spathe, like cupped hands, surrounds a solid, rounded inflorescence, the **spadix**, upon which are borne the stamens and the pistils of the flower cluster.

The flowers die if frozen, yet skunk cabbages survive and bloom when other flowers have not yet dared to break through the surface of the ground. They are protected from a frozen fate. Although the temperatures during February and March may drop far below freezing, the temperature of the flower is maintained at a nearly constant 72° F (22° C).

Astonishingly, the skunk cabbage flower stays warm because, much like a warm-blooded animal, its spadix produces heat and regulates the flower's temperature. When the temperature around the spathe drops from 63° F (17° C) to a chilly 45° F (7° C), the spadix responds by nearly doubling its oxygen consumption, producing heat as a by-product of its increased metabolic activity. According to scientist Roger Knutson, the skunk cabbages are "behaving more like skunks than cabbages."

Where does the skunk cabbage get the energy to fuel its burning furnace for two weeks in the frigid late winter? The huge root, about one foot (30 cm) long and two inches (5 cm) thick, is packed with starch. The skunk cabbage burns this fuel and consumes oxygen at a rate roughly comparable to that of a small shrew or hummingbird, an accomplishment possibly unique among the plants. The heat generated by the spadix is conserved by the thick, spongy spathe, whose texture, much like Styrofoam®, acts as a marvelous insulator surrounding the spadix.

Together, these superb adaptations achieve a near-tropical climate around the flower. However, it is costly for the plant to maintain these high temperatures; throughout the year starch must be synthesized and stored in the massive root for use when the flower blooms. Therefore, we must ask, "What advantage does it serve the skunk cabbage to produce this heat?" Wouldn't it be more economical simply to wait for the warmer days of spring and forego the need to amass the starchy provisions? One would think so, but skunk cabbages continue to stoke their floral furnaces.

A look at the skunk cabbage's cousins may provide an explanation. Skunk cabbages are in the Arum family, and most of its members live in the tropics. They include many well-known house plants — *Caladium*, *Calla*, *Dieffenbachia*, *Philodendron*, and *Anthurium*. The evolutionary origin of the skunk cabbage's heat production may be inferred by examining other Arums. The voodoo lily and the lords-and-ladies give off malodorous scents in a brief period of several hours during which they heat up. In this case the function of the heat is not to warm the plant, but to volatilize odoriferous chemicals that attract insect pollinators. These plants produce chemicals with such descriptive names as putrescine, cadaverine, and skatole. The plants exude these amines and ammonia, producing a scent reminiscent of dung, urine, and decaying flesh. These chemicals are formed from the metabolic breakdown of common amino acids present in the plant. In the case of the voodoo lily and lords-and-ladies, the brief burst of metabolic activity aids in the evaporation of these putrid compounds. From the surrounding countryside, insects such as flies and beetles come, seeking carrion and dung in which to lay their eggs. However, they are deceived by the Arum flowers. The insects are attracted to the odors of rotting flesh and feces but find no suitable place to deposit their eggs. What is worse, some of the Arum plants have evolved intricate devices for trapping the flies and beetles attracted to the odors. Once captured, they are detained until they are covered with pollen. The flowers later release the insects so that they may pollinate other nearby flowers.

Although the skunk cabbage exudes these malodorous scents, it possesses no trap to detain would-be pollinators. Besides, its heat production occurs at a time when few insects are active. Apparently, the course of evolution in the skunk cabbage has emphasized the role of the flower's heating system; the odors remain little more than vestiges of its ancestry as a tropical Arum. What originated as a means of dispersing volatile odors has been converted to a heater to cope with the cold. The skunk cabbage has adapted the heat-producing mechanism to deal with the rigors of a temperate climate. Coming north from the tropics, the skunk cabbage has brought along a heating system, giving it time to flower and set seed at a more leisurely pace. Providing its own warm climate may also give the plant a head start over neighboring flowers, which must wait out the winter.

Whatever the origin and price of this elaborate flowering mechanism, it appears to work quite well, for the skunk cabbage is one of our most successful plants of the swamps.

ACTIVITIES

Observing skunk cabbages

Skunk cabbages are remarkable plants, worthy subjects to lure us into the cold mucky swamps to renew our nature studies after a long winter's respite.

From fall through winter, the skunk cabbage's immature flower buds and leaves are often visible, poking through the ground but unopened. Carefully examine the skunk cabbage spadix in late winter, and then again at intervals in early spring. An immature spadix is a smooth mosaic of crowded flower parts. At this early stage, the pistils and stamens are not yet exposed. Later in the season, you will see that

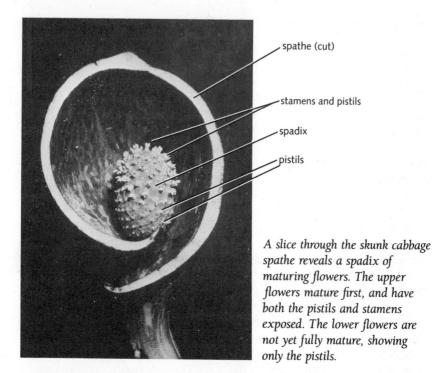

spathe (cut)

stamens and pistils

spadix

pistils

A slice through the skunk cabbage spathe reveals a spadix of maturing flowers. The upper flowers mature first, and have both the pistils and stamens exposed. The lower flowers are not yet fully mature, showing only the pistils.

the flowers mature from top to bottom. First, the female pistils push their way out of little pits on the surface, but the anthers, lying at the base of the pits, have not yet emerged. In order for these upper pistils to be fertilized, they must get pollen from another, more mature flower somewhere else in the swamp. It may be brought by insects if the weather is warm enough, or perhaps may be carried by the wind.

Later, after the pistils of the upper flowers have matured, these same flowers will put forth their pollen-coated stamens. Now the lower flowers have their pistils exposed and can receive pollen from the upper flowers as it is swirled within the spathe by the wind. I've often wondered whether these self-pollinated flowers produce seeds or whether there is self-incompatibility that prevents the pollen from a flower from fertilizing its own ovules.

The leaves of the skunk cabbage do not appear until warmer weather, pushing up through the rich black mud of the swamps in tight coils, which later unfold to the size of large platters. The fruits are already ripening. By midsummer the leaves wither away, leaving only the fruit, as large as a tennis ball, filled with dark seeds the size of peas. These are occasionally eaten by gray squirrels and other rodents. Those seeds that survive will be found germinating on the surface of the soil near the parent plants.

Before we leave this warm-blooded plant of the swamps, let's examine its roots. This will not be an easy task; the root system is enormous. Try to find a plant growing in loose soil or at the edge of a stream bank, where it will be easy to undermine the roots. Carefully dig around the base of a plant. Notice the many thick, lateral rootlets, each about the diameter of your little finger, coursing diagonally downward in a great circle around the main root. These rootlets grow deeply into the soil, and when they are firmly anchored, they contract, becoming wrinkled and ridged on the surface. In so doing, they drag the plant downward into the ground. Year after year this occurs, and although an individual skunk cabbage plant may be more than 75 years old, it never grows upward like a majestic oak or palm. Indeed the skunk cabbage has been described by J. Marion Shull as a plant that "carries on many of its important functions backwards, as compared with the rest of the plant world, flowering in the winter instead of the summer, filling the air with a stench instead of a pleasant odor, growing downward into the earth instead of up into the air."

Observing skunk cabbage visitors

Skunk cabbage visitors can be classified either as casual passersby, hungry herbivores, or expectant mothers. Honey bees are in the first category. In early spring, when hardly any food is available, the queen bee is busy laying eggs. The bees in the colony need an adequate supply of pollen in order to synthesize secretions to feed the newborn larval bees. The foragers at this time of the year are diligently roaming the countryside looking for pollen to bring back to the hive. Occasionally, honey bees will stumble upon a skunk cabbage and begin collecting its pollen. The spathes may also serve as tiny warming huts for the foragers. Bees generally do not fly if the temperature is much below 65° F (18° C), but they have been seen visiting skunk cabbages at air temperatures below 50° F (10° C).

A midge, an early spring visitor, rests on the skunk cabbage spadix. The stamens are fully extended, and the anthers are releasing their pollen.

Other insects reported at skunk cabbages include harvestmen (daddy-long-legs), and various species of spider. *Pachygnatha brevis,* in the genus of thick-jawed spiders, is found near water. Knutson found many of these spiders crawling on the surface of the spathe, perhaps attracted by the warmth. Another observer, writing in the early 1900's, noticed many skunk cabbages with webs spun across the opening of the spathe. It was suggested by R.W. Shufeldt that the spider "possesses a very clear idea of what it is after. It knows that, at this time of the year, many thousands of tiny, black flies swarm about the entrance to the concavity of the spathe—and thus scores of them fall a prey to these artful little arachnids." An interesting observation, but I would object that the author has fallen prey to anthropomorphism.

Concerning the hungry herbivores, few animals eat the skunk cabbage. All portions of this plant, and others in the Arum family, contain sharp pointed crystals of calcium oxalate that make the skunk cabbage unpalatable for most animals. For example, the dumbcane, *Dieffenbachia,* and *Philodendron* are beautiful Arums often used as house plants. A bite of the leaves produces intense pain and swelling of the mouth and throat. The symptoms can be so severe that the victim is unable to speak, hence the common name, dumbcane. The leaves of skunk cabbages vary in their oxalate content. They can be boiled and eaten as a passable wild edible, only slightly peppery in taste. The mature leaves of the plant are often speckled with holes, evidence that invertebrates eat the leaves. These are most likely to be slugs, creatures seldom deterred by any toxic plant.

After blooming, skunk cabbage spathes soon begin to decay, and at this time many flies can be found hovering about the rotting plants. These expectant

VISITORS REPORTED AT SKUNK CABBAGES	
Common Name	Activity at the Plant
moth flies	Breeding in rotting plant
frit flies	Breeding in rotting plant
midges	Breeding in rotting plant
punkies	Breeding in rotting plant
pomace flies	Breeding in rotting plant
gall gnats	Breeding in rotting plant
shore flies	Breeding in rotting plant
beetles	Breeding in rotting plant
booklice	Breeding in rotting plant
springtails	Breeding in rotting plant
honey bees	Gathering pollen
bugs	Casual visitors
spiders	Casual visitors
harvestmen	Casual visitors
slugs	Feeding on leaves

mothers find skunk cabbage a suitable place to deposit their eggs. The decaying plant tissues encourage the growth of bacteria, yeasts, and other fungi, and the maturing fly larvae probably feed on these organisms. In one study, the larvae of 19 species of flies belonging to 7 families were found to feed in rotting portions of skunk cabbage. These included pomace flies, frit flies, shore flies, gall gnats, midges, punkies, and moth flies. In addition to flies, you may be able to find a few species of beetles, springtails, and booklice that also breed in skunk cabbages. Try to see what the skunk cabbages in your region harbor. Bring home the decaying skunk cabbage flowers and place them on damp sand in covered plastic containers. Keep the plants moist, and examine them every few days for emerging insects. Refer to a field guide to identify these insects.

References and Suggestions for Further Reading

Grimaldi, David, and Jaenike, John. 1983. The diptera breeding on skunk cabbage, *Symplocarpus foetidus* (Araceae). *Journal of the New York Entomological Society* 91: 83–89.

Knutson, Roger M. March 1979. Plants in heat. *Natural History* 88: 42–47.

———. 1974. Heat Production and temperature regulation in Eastern skunk cabbage. *Science* 186: 746–747.

———. 1972. Temperature measurements of the spadix of *Symplocarpus foetidus*. *American Midland Naturalist* 88: 251–254.

Meusse B.J.D. July 1966. The voodoo lily. *Scientific American* 215: 80–88.

Shull, J. Marion. 1924. A Methuselah of the plant world—the skunk cabbage. *Journal of Heredity* 15: 443–450.

2

Mating of the
Mole Salamanders

EVEN BEFORE SPRING ARRIVES in the Northeast, spring peepers begin to chorus on the warmer evenings in mid-March. They won't begin to breed until the first week in April, but the first few early arrivals are getting ready for the annual mating season. Surprisingly, even at temperatures below 40° F (4° C) these small amphibians are actively calling. As the high-pitched, almost insectlike sounds fill the rainy nights of early spring, I use their songs as a cue to start my own forays to the swamps in search of several species of salamanders and frogs that may reproduce even before the snows have completely melted.

ABOUT MOLE SALAMANDERS

I am searching for the mole salamanders, members of the genus *Ambystoma*. Due to their secretive behavior, they are seldom seen, making it difficult to believe that they are present year-round. They stay underground for most of their lives, burrowing to a depth of a foot or more, hence the name mole salamander. The best opportunity to find them is during the breeding season when large congregations suddenly appear in ponds, slow-moving streams, and temporary pools. Hundreds may gather to mate, and then, just as quickly, disperse. An occasional salamander may be found under stones or within a rotted log, and you may stumble upon a hungry wanderer during an evening walk in moist woods, but otherwise one would never suspect their presence.

A dozen or so species are found in this country, making it possible to observe at least one species nearly anywhere in the United States. The tiger salamander is widely distributed except in the western deserts, the Northeast, and southern Florida. This giant, the world's largest terrestrial salamander, reaches 13-3/8 inches (33.8 cm), and may live for 12 years. In dry weather it stays hidden in the abandoned burrows of mammals such as ground squirrels, marmots, gophers, or badgers, in cellars, crevices, or in decaying logs. Other mole salamanders are smaller, generally between 3 and 8 inches (8 to 20 cm) long. Eastern naturalists may see several species of mole salamanders: spotted, blue-spotted, or Jefferson's salamanders. Other species are confined mostly to the Northwest and the southeastern portions of the United States. Many are beautifully colored, with contrasting patterns of splotches, rings, and spots. Except for the marbled and flatwoods salamanders, all members of the genus lay their eggs in the water, and even the eggs of these two species must later be covered by water in order to develop.

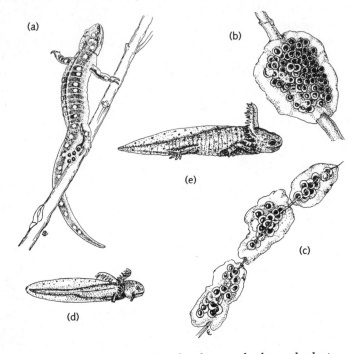

Mole salamander life cycle. (a) A female spotted salamander laying eggs.
(b) Spotted salamander egg mass. (c) Jefferson's salamander egg mass.
(d) Young larva with balancers. (e) Full-grown larva.

The aquatic, larval stages have a long tail fin, external gills behind the head, and, often, small balancers extending outward from behind the mouth. These may help the young larvae keep their gills out of the mucky bottom of ponds. Tadpoles of frogs and toads should not be confused with salamander larvae. Salamanders develop all four legs early in life; they have external gills on the neck, and the head is distinct from the body.

Most mole salamander larvae transform into adults in a single season. They lose their gills, develop lungs and eyelids, and leave the water. However, the larvae of a few species (tiger, talpid, and Northwest salamanders) sometimes grow large, yet retain their gills, and remain permanently aquatic, maturing and breeding without developing all the adult characteristics. This is called **neoteny**, and such individuals are called **axolotls**, a Mexican-Indian name meaning water doll. A deficiency of iodine in the water is believed to prevent the thyroid gland from producing a growth hormone necessary for metamorphosis.

MIGRATIONS AND MATING

In the Northwest, and at high altitudes, the breeding migrations of the tiger salamanders and the Northwest salamanders may be delayed until summer. In New Mexico and Arizona, the tiger salamanders wait for the summer rains. Southern species may mate in the fall.

In the eastern United States, the Jefferson's and the spotted salamander are common. In the Northeast, the first warm rains in April trigger the breeding migrations of Jefferson's and spotted salamanders. If warm, wet conditions persist for several days, dozens, even hundreds, of salamanders can be found marching toward water from sunset until dawn. More often, a day or two of warm weather will be interrupted by cold spells that freeze the surface of the ponds and bring the migratory movements to a temporary halt. However, tiger salamanders, whose range extends into Canada, have been seen traveling over the snow.

Eventually, large congregations of salamanders fill the shallow waters. Jefferson's salamanders usually arrive at the ponds several days ahead of the spotted salamanders, and they have often laid their eggs before the spotteds arrive. Both salamanders are roughly the same size, although the Jefferson's tends to be slightly smaller. They are easily told apart by their coloration. The dingy gray-brown Jefferson's lacks the brilliant, yellowish row of spots located along the back, from head to tail.

The males of all the species tend to arrive first. The sexes look alike throughout most of the year, except during the breeding season when a gland around the male's vent, the opening behind the hind legs, begins to swell. The gland produces the **spermatophore**, a structure containing the male's sperm packet. Males also differ from females by having slightly longer tails and stouter hind limbs.

Once the males and females have arrived, the shallow waters will be alive at night with writhing salamanders performing their nuptial dance. The salamanders swim about, rubbing against each other vigorously, occasionally rising to the surface for air. At times the water seems virtually to boil with activity. The

Jefferson's male takes a direct approach to mating. He embraces a female, grasping her with his forelegs just behind hers. Then, with undulations of the body, and rubbing motions of his chin upon her head and snout, he attempts to stimulate the female. Clasping by males is unusual in *Ambystoma,* occurring only in Jefferson's, blue-spotted, Northwestern, and long-toed species. Spotteds do not clasp the females. They nestle up to their prospective mates, attempting to rub their heads against the female's ventral surface. During this "nosing" process, the females usually remain passive. After this preliminary activity, the males of both species move forward and deposit their spermatophores. These are cone-shaped masses of clear jelly, up to one-half inch (1.3 cm) tall, topped with a milky cap of sperm and seminal fluid. The spermatophores are deposited on leaves and twigs under the water. If a female is receptive, she will advance and cover the spermatophore with her vent. Spreading the lips of the vent, she will take the sperm-laden cap into her cloaca, the opening within the vent that transmits both eggs and wastes. The sperm are stored by the females and used to fertilize the eggs before they are laid. At first glance, this method of reproduction may seem bizarre. For human beings, mating is an intimate affair, involving close contact and the union of the genital organs. Mammals, birds, and insects all mate this way. However, mating is necessarily an intimate affair only on land. Sperm is minute and delicate, subject to instantaneous desiccation. In the water, there are other ways to wed sperm and egg. The least elegant method is utilized by some fish. The female merely ejects her eggs into the water; the male then releases his sperm, or **milt**, in more or less the same vicinity. The mating couple "hope for the best." To compensate for the rather careless way that eggs and sperm are brought together, and for losses caused by predators, these fish produce copious quantities of eggs and sperm. Frogs are slightly more efficient. By clasping the female tightly, the male brings his genital opening in proximity to hers. As soon as the female deposits her eggs, he releases his sperm, providing better opportunity for sperm to meet the eggs. The spermatophore method can be considered a refinement; internal fertilization assures a more reliable union of egg and sperm.

About a week or so after the mating frenzy has begun, the only signs of the salamanders are their eggs and the remains of spermatophores. The adults have returned to the woods just as suddenly as they came. Hiding under logs and stones or buried within the soft earth, they subsist on a diet of earthworms, snails, slugs, spiders, millipedes, and various small insects. They will not return to the waters until next year's mating season.

Egg masses differ from species to species. The spotted salamander lays a large globular cluster of up to 250 eggs. The female grasps a twig or other support with her hind legs and deposits the eggs one by one. The egg mass of a Jefferson's salamander contains fewer eggs (7 to 40), deposited along the length of a twig at a rate of several a minute. A cluster of spotted salamander eggs can be larger than the female herself because the gelatinous layers surrounding the eggs swell enormously within an hour or two after the eggs are laid. Initially the mass is small, about one-half inch (1.3 cm) in diameter.

The eggs and larvae are susceptible to both predation and the rigors of the environment. Studies have shown that the thick gelatinous egg masses are well

		THE RANGE, BREEDING PERIOD,
Common Name	Scientific Name	Range
Northwestern	*Ambystoma gracile*	coastal NW
long-toed	*Ambystoma macrodactylum*	NW
tiger	*Ambystoma tigrinum*	most of U.S., except far west and NE
spotted	*Ambystoma maculatum*	eastern U.S., except FL
ringed	*Ambystoma annulatum*	portions of MS, AR, OK
marbled	*Ambystoma opacum*	SE
small-mouth	*Ambystoma texanum*	SE, except coastal states
talpid	*Ambystoma talpoideum*	portions of SE
flatwoods	*Ambystoma cingulatum*	southern portions of SC, GA, and AL, and northern FL
mabee's	*Ambystoma mabeei*	coastal plain of the Carolinas
Jefferson's	*Ambystoma jeffersonianum*	NE
blue-spotted	*Ambystoma laterale*	NE, north-central U.S.

protected against predators, such as dragonfly larvae, crayfish, minnows, and whirligig and diving beetles, but a spell of freezing weather can wipe out all the eggs. The young larvae are helpless and are eaten by many animals. In the late spring, the temporary ponds begin to shrink, concentrating the larvae into small pools where they become easy prey. In addition, they cannibalistically feed on any kin smaller than themselves. It is no surprise, therefore, that more than a hundred eggs must be laid by each female in order to assure the survival of the species.

Nevertheless, large numbers of eggs are of no avail against other dangers, which are the result of human activity. Increasingly common is the filling-in of temporary ponds and swampy areas in an effort to reclaim land or to cut down on mosquito populations. Nearby, drier land is developed for housing or industry, destroying the areas where the salamanders live. One wonders how large a toll is taken by avid collectors and by passing vehicles that kill salamanders as they cross roads en route to their mating areas. Finally, little is known about the effects of acid rain and pesticides that leach into nearby breeding ponds.

For the present, despite hazards, salamanders continue in their clandestine ways, completing their yearly cycles. Each spring you can find me at their ponds, visiting these secretive creatures.

AND EGGS OF MOLE SALAMANDERS

Breeding Period	Description of Eggs
Jan. to July	globular clusters attached to submerged vegetation (30–270 eggs/cluster)
after the snow melts	variable: singly or in clusters of 5–100 eggs, attached to submerged objects
Mar. to June (in the north and at high altitudes); with summer rains in July and Aug. (in NM and AZ)	loose clusters of up to 100 eggs on submerged objects, such as twigs
early spring (Feb., Mar., Apr.)	globular clusters of up to 250 eggs on submerged objects
autumn	——
autumn	about 100 eggs laid on the ground. Female attends eggs until the area is flooded.
early spring	laid singly or in clusters of up to 25, attached to submerged objects
Jan., Feb.	loose clusters of 4–20 eggs on submerged objects
late autumn, winter	small groups of eggs laid on the ground and left unattended
late autumn to early spring	laid singly or in loose chains of 2–6 on submerged leaves, twigs, etc.
early spring	clusters of 7–40 eggs, attached to submerged twigs
spring	small clusters, attached to submerged vegetation

ACTIVITIES

Observing mole salamanders

Salamander migrations and mating behavior are easy to observe *if* you are at the right place at the right time. In the Northeast, wait for the first warm rainy night after the snows have melted. In upstate New York, where I live, one can expect to find salamanders in the first week of April. For other regions, the timing will be different. Refer to the table above for the breeding period of species in other parts of the country.

The time to search is after dark. Take along high boots and a flashlight or lantern. The salamanders return to the same places year after year to mate. If you are not sure where to find them, visit a variety of ponds, slow streams, and temporary pools. If you have no luck at one place, try another. Once you have found a good spot, you will know where to look in subsequent years. If you find only a few individuals, return every few evenings, especially during a warm spell. The activity may not have reached its peak.

Once you have located some salamanders, sit quietly and observe them with your light. They are usually oblivious to your presence, and with luck you may be able to observe the entire sequence of mating behavior. Be sure to search along the outskirts of the pond, watching for salamanders coming to the water from the nearby woodlands. Examine the undersides of several individuals to determine their sex. At this time of the year, the males will have a conspicuously swollen vent. Make a survey over several nights to see if the number of arriving males and females changes. If you have begun your observations at the beginning of the breeding season, you may find only males arriving. Return to the ponds during the day when it will be easier to find spermatophores and egg masses. It should do no harm to gather a few spermatophores and a dozen or so eggs. Place them in a container of pond water. Look for the egg masses of other amphibians, such as frogs, toads, and newts. Each type of egg mass is distinct. The size of the eggs, the number in each cluster, the substrate upon which the cluster is laid, and its overall shape are clues to its identity.

Observing amphibian development

At home, you can examine the spermatophore and watch the development of the eggs. Living sperm are observed by taking a spermatophore, teasing apart its white cap, and placing a bit on a microscope slide under a cover glass. At 100- to 400-power under a microscope, a myriad of wriggling sperm will be seen. Unlike the sperm of most other animals, that of salamanders does not have a distinct head and tail, so the sperm appears to be an undulating mass of spaghetti.

Next, observe the eggs with a hand lens, or preferably with a low-power stereo-microscope. They pass through a number of stages typical of the developing embryos of most animals. At first the egg is a solid ball, but soon this single

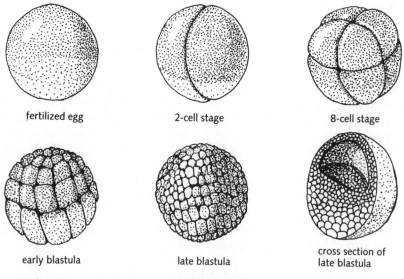

fertilized egg   2-cell stage   8-cell stage

early blastula   late blastula   cross section of late blastula

Early stages in the development of an amphibian egg, showing the cleavage of the fertilized egg into a mass of many cells, and the formation of the hollow blastula stage.

fertilized cell divides into two cells, the two divide into four, and so on, until the egg is a mosaic of smaller cells, or **blastomeres**. Note how long the cells take to divide. This depends in part upon the water temperature. You can demonstrate this by leaving some of the eggs outdoors and comparing their progress with those developing in the warmth of your home. As cleavage continues, the cells arrange themselves on the surface of the sphere, forming a hollow ball, or **blastula**. As the egg develops further, the cells undergo invaginations, foldings, and movements that form all the different tissues of the larvae — skin, nervous system, skeleton, muscles, etc. Finally, a recognizable, wriggling larva can be seen within the egg membranes, ready to break out and wiggle free. It takes about a month for the eggs to develop fully and hatch, and then the larvae take two to three months before they are mature and ready to leave the water. Those of you with more interest in observing the embryonic development of amphibians should refer to one of the general biology references listed below.

References and Suggestions for Further Reading

Barbour, Roger W. 1971. *Amphibians and Reptiles of Kentucky*. University Press of Kentucky, Lexington.

Bishop, Sherman C. 1941. The salamanders of New York. *New York State Museum Bulletin*, no. 324.

Conant, Roger. 1975. *Field Guide to Reptiles and Amphibians of Eastern and Central North America*. Houghton Mifflin, Boston.

Keeton, William T. 1980. *Biological Science,* 3d ed. Norton, New York.

Smith, Hobart M.A. 1978. *Guide to the Amphibians of North America*. Golden Press, New York.

Stebbins, Robert C. 1966. *Field Guide to Western Reptiles and Amphibians*. Houghton Mifflin, Boston.

Storer, Tracy I., and Usinger, Robert L. 1957. *General Zoology,* 3d ed. McGraw-Hill, New York.

Ward, David and Sexton, Owen J. 1981. Anti-predator role of salamander egg membranes. *Copeia* 3: 724–726.

3

The Remarkable
Migrations of Birds

MYSTERIOUSLY TRIGGERED by some quietly ticking internal clock, billions of birds make their way south each autumn to spend the winter in a more hospitable climate. For the youngest birds, this will be their first southbound journey, but when that inner restlessness overcomes them, they unhesitatingly succumb to an irresistible urge to travel and embark on a long hazardous migration into unknown territory. With the same clockwork regularity, these birds travel northward in the spring to mate and rear their young. Year after year, adult birds return to their breeding grounds, often within a few hundred yards of the place where they were born.

What technological feat of man can compare to the flight of a tiny ruby-throated hummingbird crossing the Gulf of Mexico? Weighing about as much as a penny (a tenth of an ounce, or 3 gm), this minute flying machine expends a quarter of its body weight to fuel its lonely 500-mile (800-km), 10-hour, nonstop nighttime voyage. The blackpoll warbler undertakes an oceanic pilgrimage that may take it from Halifax, Nova Scotia, to Antigua in the West Indies. This bird flies nearly four days, covering over 2,000 miles (3,200 km) without stopping. This would be equivalent to a man running 1,200 consecutive four-minute miles. If the blackpoll were fueled on gasoline rather than its reserve of body fat, it would be getting 720,000 miles (1,160,000 km) per gallon!

These journeys have awed naturalists for centuries, yet their complexities are still only partially understood. Research has unraveled a few mysteries and has dispelled several erroneous beliefs. Aristotle, in ancient Greece, reported the autumnal movements of birds to warmer regions, but he also believed that birds hibernate in hollow trees, caves, or even in swamps beneath the mud. Early naturalists substantiated "eye-witness accounts" of flocks of swallows landing in marshes and sinking into the water to hibernate. There were also reports of fishermen catching hibernating swallows along with fish as they drew in their nets.

Scientists and naturalists today have many questions about migration. What are its advantages? How are birds guided on their journey? How do they know when to begin their flights? How do they know when they have reached their destination? How fast, how high, and how far do various species fly?

WHY BIRDS MIGRATE — SOME POSSIBLE ADVANTAGES

For such exhausting and lengthy expeditions to be undertaken, we must assume that migrations serve an important purpose. We have little difficulty in justifying the annual autumn exodus to the south. The harsh approaching winter strips the land of its food supply, killing insects or forcing them into hibernation, and covering seeds and vegetation with snow. Many birds could not survive the northern winters. In spring, however, why should birds leave South America, the West Indies, and the southern United States, with their tropical warmth and seemingly adequate food supplies? It is suggested that the springtime northbound migrations allow birds to take advantage of breeding sites and feeding areas vacated during the winter. As uninhabitable regions become more favorable in spring, the migrants leave the relatively overcrowded southern areas to seek more spacious breeding territories to the north. Others argue that the northern regions provide a longer duration of daylight, enabling the parent birds to feed their young for a few hours more each day. This may serve to speed up the nestling phase when the chicks are especially vulnerable to predation. However, these explanations cannot be the complete answer. Some species of birds have extensive breeding ranges that encompass wide climatic variations. Among the robins for example, individuals in Washington, D.C., head south for the winter and are replaced by the more northern variety of the very same species. They find the abandoned winter homes perfectly suitable for survival. These birds then fly north in the spring, and their places are taken by the southern variety returning to nest. Why do robins migrate if the species is capable of surviving throughout the year in Washington?

HOW BIRDS MIGRATE

Even more perplexing than understanding why birds migrate is understanding how they unerringly find their way. Birds may travel thousands of miles twice each year, often returning to the very same spot to nest; I often get lost on a short afternoon hike through the woods near my home.

The basic ingredients required for orientation and migration are a navigation system that permits the birds to select and maintain the proper flight direction, and the knowledge of which direction to take — in essence, a compass and a map. Both are needed to find your way home. If you are lost in an unknown forest, a compass alone will be of little use. You may be able to select any course you wish, whether north or south-southwest, but you will not be able to find your way without a map that tells you your present location and final destination.

Birds have at least three different biological compasses. Over 30 years ago, it was shown that pigeons could orient to a particular direction by using the sun's position as a compass. Experiments in which the apparent position of the sun was changed with mirrors correspondingly altered the pigeon's orientation. In order to use this sun compass, birds also need an accurate internal clock to compensate for the sun's movement throughout the day. This was demonstrated with starlings trained to use the sun to go in a particular direction for food. When a stationary light was substituted for the sun, the bird's bearing shifted approximately 15 degrees per hour, corresponding to the sun's daily movement through the sky.

Experiments with indigo buntings in a planetarium revealed an astral navigation system. Buntings can use prominent stars and northern constellations — the Big Dipper, the North Star, and Cassiopeia — to get their bearing. Young buntings become imprinted on star patterns in the northern sky, and later use this information to guide their migratory flights. Buntings raised in the laboratory and prevented from seeing the constellations cannot orient by the stars.

On overcast nights, a sun compass or star compass is useless. As a back-up system, some birds can cue in on the earth's magnetic field. A compass has been discovered inside the head of pigeons, consisting of vast numbers of microscopic needle-shaped objects. A pigeon's head contains about 100 million of these tiny magnets made up of the iron-containing mineral, magnetite. Altering the magnetic field by strapping a magnet to its back disorients the bird when it is released far from home on an overcast day. On clear days, the bird simply uses its sun compass.

Birds are sensitive to many other stimuli that may also help them navigate the skies. Unlike human beings, pigeons can sense polarized light, minute changes in barometric pressure, and extremely low-frequency sounds, called infrasounds. Infrasound waves may serve as both an all-weather compass and a map for birds. Mountain ranges, jet streams, ocean waves, thunderstorms, and other physical features produce these low-frequency sounds that can be detected over hundreds, even thousands, of miles. Each geographic region may have its own identifiable infrasound signature, providing the elusive map that scientists have long been seeking. It is possible that birds follow unique patterns of infrasound, which guide them home as reliably as the radio signals used by pilots.

Whatever stimuli birds are using for their compass, their navigational feats are remarkable, and often totally baffling to the scientists eager to understand the mysteries of bird migration. At times, individual birds are capable of homing in on the exact location of their original nesting spot. In one experiment, 18 adult albatrosses were captured on the Midway Islands in the Pacific Ocean. They were taken by plane and released in distant spots, such as the Hawaiian Islands, Japan, the Philippines, and the coast of Washington. Incredibly, 14 of the birds returned to their nests, traveling up to 317 miles (510 km) per day. The longest distance covered was 4,120 miles (6,630 km). How an animal can travel thousands of miles over unfamiliar territory may remain a mystery for many years to come.

BIRD BANDING AS A TOOL FOR STUDYING BIRD MIGRATION

Over the years, the observations of thousands of enthusiastic amateur bird-watchers have contributed greatly to the understanding of bird migration. Barn swallows suddenly disappear from the United States in September and October and are soon found in the sunny South American countries of Colombia, Brazil, Peru, Bolivia, Paraguay, and northern Argentina. Then, as spring approaches, observers have noted their arrival in Louisiana about March 20, in Missouri about April 7, and in North Dakota about April 25. By keeping track of the arrival and departure of groups of birds, we have learned in a general way where and when birds migrate. An even more direct method would be to follow individuals. Although one cannot follow a bird on an actual flight over a long distance, individual birds can be followed indirectly if they are uniquely identified. Loosely fitting aluminum or plastic bands are placed around the bird's leg. Each band has an identification number and an address to which information should be sent if the bird is found. Later, when the bird is captured, killed, or found dead, the number on the band allows two points of the individual bird's journey to be established. Often years will have elapsed between the time the bird was banded and was recovered. The bird may have made several migrations in the interim, but at least it is known that this bird traveled between those two points.

Bird-banding studies yield information about the exact arrival and departure dates of individual birds, the relation between weather conditions and the starting times for migrations, the traveling speed of individual birds, and the regularity with which birds return to their exact summer or winter homes each year. Only by individually labeling birds can such details be learned.

In various studies throughout the world, over 60 million birds have been banded. Birds are often banded after being captured in fine, nearly invisible "mist" nets strung close to the ground. Sometimes fledglings are banded while still in their nests. Very few birds are ever recovered — less than 1 percent of small songbirds — but occasional, fortuitous events allow scientists gradually to build up an accurate picture of the migrations of many species. A barn swallow banded in Massachusetts was found dead two months later, trapped in the sticky asphalt of a tarred roof in Florida, 1,225 miles (1,970 km) away. A purple finch on its northward

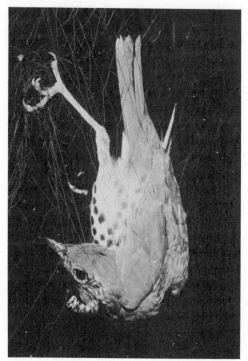

A wood thrush, captured unharmed in a mist net, can be banded and released.

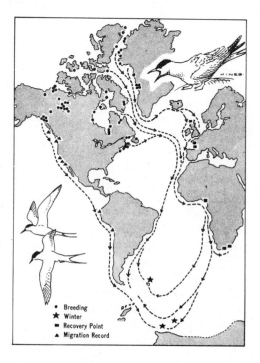

The migration route of the arctic tern. No other species is known to breed abundantly in North America and to cross the Atlantic Ocean to and from the Old World. Its extreme summer and winter homes are 11,000 miles apart (17,700 km), and since the birds take a circuitous migratory route, they probably fly at least 25,000 miles (40,000 km) each year.

• Breeding
★ Winter
▬ Recovery Point
▲ Migration Record

spring migration was banded in central Massachusetts and recaptured three days later in Bar Harbor, Maine, 230 miles (370 km) away. Little tidbits of information give approximate information on migration pathways and flight speeds.

Spectacular migrations have been documented. A lesser yellowlegs, a shore bird, was banded on the coast of Massachusetts on August 28. Six days later it was shot 1,930 miles (3,106 km) away on Martinique in the West Indies. Even if it flew nonstop after being banded and was captured the moment it arrived on Martinique, it would have averaged an impressive 322 miles (518 km) per day.

The arctic terns are the most famous long-distance fliers. One bird was banded as a chick in Greenland on July 8 and was recaptured on October 30, halfway around the world on the east coast of South Africa, 9,500 miles (15,290 km) away, having traveled an average of 100 miles (160 km) a day for 13 weeks.

As an amateur naturalist, you may at some time come across a banded bird. If so, you should carefully note the complete number on the band. If the bird is alive and uninjured, it should be released. If dead, the band should be removed. The date, location, and manner in which the bird was obtained should be reported to the Fish and Wildlife Service, Washington, D.C. The reports will be acknowledged with the name of the bird, the date, and place it was banded.

SOME DETAILS OF MIGRATION

Each bird species has its own schedule and characteristic migration behavior. Most of the secretive insectivorous species, such as flycatchers, sparrows, vireos, thrushes, wrens, warblers, and orioles, migrate at night. So do rails, snipes, sandpipers, and plovers. Nocturnal migration may be a means of avoiding predators, but it also allows small birds to stop and feed by day. After flying all night, they are often nearly exhausted. They spend the day replenishing their food supplies, and resting. In contrast, larger birds — crows, doves, swifts, swallows, herons, geese, ducks, gulls, loons, and pelicans — migrate by day. Wading and swimming birds can feed at all hours, and hawks, swifts, and swallows feed on the wing as they migrate. In addition, the birds of prey can tolerate an occasional day's fast.

The migrants begin their journeys at different times. Many shore birds get the urge to start south as early as July, even though food is still plentiful. Others, such as goshawks, snowy owls, redpolls, and Bohemian waxwings, wait until severe winter weather forces them to leave. Once they get going, species travel at their own pace. A common flying speed for ducks and geese is 40 to 50 MPH (64 to 80 km/hr), while small birds, such as flycatchers, amble along at a leisurely 10 to 17 MPH (16 to 27 km/hr). Herons, hawks, horned larks, ravens, and shrikes travel about 25 MPH (40 km/hr) while the speedier mourning dove may go as fast as 35 MPH (56 km/hr).

Variations in flight speed and the number of hours spent flying each day result in variable migration speeds. Canada geese have a slow but steady migration. They move north at the same pace as the advancing spring. Other birds rush their northbound journey. The yellow warbler leaves the tropics and reaches New Orleans about April 5, when the average temperature is 65° F (18° C). However, it speeds quickly northward, outpacing the season, to arrive in its Manitoba breeding ground in late May when the average temperature is only a brisk 47° F (8° C).

Sometimes males and females migrate at different times. Male red-winged blackbirds, robins, song sparrows, rose-breasted grosbeaks, and scarlet tanagers start out early, probably to stake out breeding territories before the females arrive. The over-energetic long-billed marsh wren may even build several nests before the females arrive, in hope of enticing a mate.

Migrants differ in the altitude at which they fly. Radar studies at sea have shown that the most common altitude for migration is 1,500 to 2,500 feet (457 to 762 m), with only 10 percent of radar echoes coming from above 5,000 feet (1,524 m). Ducks and plovers commonly fly at an altitude of 8,000 feet (2,438 m). Curlews and cranes near Mount Everest have been spotted at 20,000 feet (6,096 m), and geese flying over the Himalayas have been seen at 29,500 feet (8,991 m). At this altitude, the air has only 30 percent of the oxygen concentration it has at sea level.

Birds may fly singly or in groups. The wood warblers often travel in flocks of several species. Similarly, swallows, sparrows, blackbirds, and some shore birds migrate in mixed company. Other species, such as chimney swifts, nighthawks, crows, waxwings, crossbills, bobolinks, and kingbirds, usually travel only with their own kin. Canada geese may even maintain their family groups; they probably migrate with an older bird in the lead.

Sometimes curious migration patterns occur when birds change their geographic distribution. Populations of bobolinks are now found in the Northwest, having extended their eastern range. These birds do not head directly for their wintering spots in South America; they first head directly east to their ancestral flyways rather than take the more direct shortcut across Arizona, New Mexico, and Texas.

Man has sought to unravel the mysteries of animal migration for centuries, attempting to understand the voyages of caribou, seals, whales, sea turtles, newts, monarch butterflies, and birds. However, it seems that nature reveals her secrets begrudgingly; studies will continue for years to come. In the meantime, we gaze in wonder at the flocks of geese passing overhead each spring on their way back to the same small pond on the Canadian tundra that they left last autumn. And even if the day should come when all their mysteries have been disclosed, I will surely continue to be thrilled by the songs of the cackling geese.

ACTIVITIES

Bird-watching for spring migrants

Spring is a time of rapid change. With the arrival of warm weather, wildflowers burst into bloom, hibernating mammals and insects awaken from their winter sleep, and migrating birds arrive from the south. Before you realize it, spring has passed. Wrapped up in my own activities, I too often fail to appreciate the day-to-day changes that are occurring at this time of the year.

Keeping track of migrating birds is an excellent activity for the spring. Start by making a list of the birds that are present in late winter. Once you are familiar with

SOME COMMON YEAR-ROUND RESIDENTS OF THE UNITED STATES

Jay (blue, Steller's, scrub)	Tufted titmouse
Great blue heron	Mourning dove
Flicker	Horned lark
Common crow	White-breasted nuthatch
Red-tailed hawk	Cardinal
Great horned owl	Starling
Downy woodpecker	Cedar waxwing
Hairy woodpecker	House sparrow
Ring-necked pheasant	Evening grosbeak
Ruffed grouse	Slate-colored junco
Black-capped chickadee	American goldfinch
Brown creeper	Pigeon
Mockingbird	Robin

the permanent residents, it will be easier to recognize the migrants as they arrive. Visit different habitats, such as forests, swamps, seashores, lakesides, and open meadows. A six- to eight-power pair of binoculars and a field guide will allow you to make accurate identifications of birds. Often, the best time for birding is early in the morning when the newly arrived migrants are actively searching for food amid the vegetation. Watch for "waves" of warblers, thrushes, and other songbirds temporarily stopped on their northbound journey when they encounter a cold front.

Dress in drab clothing and walk slowly. For some poorly understood reason, you can often encourage small birds to come out from hiding by making a "pishing" sound, by sucking air noisily through your lips. Chickadees, in particular, will often approach within a few feet when they hear this noise. Nearly every state has a local bird club or Audubon group that goes on field trips. You can quickly learn the key markings and songs by "birding" with these experienced naturalists.

Even the heart of big cities offers ample opportunities for bird-watching. Small parks and cemeteries provide shelter, food, and water for migrants. Keep a weekly list of the birds found in your area. With careful observations throughout the year, you can make a graph like the one shown on page 30, indicating the arrival and departure dates of birds in your area. Such a list is an ideal way to learn about the seasonal movements of birds. Update the list yearly, adding as many different species as you can find. The challenge and joy of discovering a new bird will increase as your list becomes more complete. From your data you should be able to predict the arrival of spring migrants. Slight differences in the arrival dates from year to year reflect not only your skill as an observer but also variations in the weather conditions and the availability of food. You will need to be a keen observer to find some species, such as the warblers. Many of these small songbirds breed in the northern part of North America. Warblers such as the blackpoll, bay-breasted,

SEQUENCE OF ARRIVAL AND DURATION OF STAY OF COMMON MIGRATORY BIRDS IN NEW YORK STATE*

Species	Jan	Feb	Mar	Apr	May	Jun	Jul	Aug	Sep	Oct	Nov	Dec	Habitat
Eastern bluebird													DEG
Robin													FG
Red-winged blackbird													CDE
Common grackle													CFG
American woodcock													DE
Eastern phoebe													BFG
Tree swallow													BDG
Hermit thrush													FG
Field sparrow													E
Myrtle warbler													FG
Pine warbler													F
Rufous-sided towhee													EFG
White-throated sparrow													EFG
Yellow warbler													EG
Yellowthroat													CEG
House wren													G
Catbird													EG
American redstart													EFG
Ruby-throated hummingbird													EG
Eastern kingbird													EG
Wood thrush													FG
Magnolia warbler													FG
Scarlet tanager													FG
Baltimore oriole													FG

KEY to Habitats:
A: Lakes, rivers
B: Lake shores, river shores, sand beaches, mud flats
C: marshes, bogs, swamps
D: Open fields, pastures, wet meadows
E: Thickets, hedgerows, forest edges, brushy fields
F: Forests
G: Parks, cemeteries, orchards, suburban areas, feeding stations

* Although these arrival and departure dates refer specifically to central New York, this sequence is applicable to much of the Northeast where these birds are common residents.

(Adapted from O.S. Pettingill, and S.F. Hoyt. 1968. *Enjoying Birds in Upstate New York*, 2d ed. Laboratory of Ornithology, Cornell University, Ithaca, N.Y.

palm, Cape May, and Tennessee can be seen only for the few weeks that it takes them to pass through most of the United States as they head for their breeding grounds.

About 1,780 species of birds live and breed in North America. If you exclude Mexico and Central America, the number drops to about 645 species. Visiting different habitats, a diligent amateur can commonly find 200 to 300 species throughout the year. One's own suburban yard may host more than 50 different species.

Observing bird migrations

Most often you will be aware of migrations by the sudden appearance or disappearance of a new species as the seasons progress. To observe birds as they are actually migrating is more difficult. An obvious exception is the V-shaped flocks of Canadian geese heard squawking noisily overhead, but more often you need to be in just the right place at the right time.

In 1935, Frederick Lincoln described four major migration routes taken by waterfowl over the continent of North America. These flyways are the major avenues used by birds to reach their winter resting spots in the West Indies and in Central and South America. The Atlantic flyway is a route used by about 50 different species of land birds breeding in New England, and by great numbers of ducks coming from their breeding grounds on the northern plains of central Canada. These southward-flying birds are funneled to the Atlantic coast and then to Florida. By island and mainland routes they proceed into the Caribbean and on to South America. The next great flyway converges on the Mississippi valley. This is the longest route in the Western Hemisphere, originating as far north as the Arctic Coast of Alaska, continuing across the Gulf of Mexico to Yucatan, with some birds going as far south as Patagonia in South America. From the mouth of the Mackenzie River to the Mississippi delta — over 3000 miles (4,828 km) — this route provides ample protection, food, and water for millions of migrant ducks, geese, shore birds, blackbirds, sparrows, warblers, and thrushes. Observers in the Mississippi valley at the peak of migration can see more species and individuals than any place else in the world. The central flyway in the vicinity of the Great Plains and the Rocky Mountains, and the Pacific flyway along the West Coast, have similar points of origin in the far north in the Mackenzie River delta, Alaska, and western Canada, and go south paralleling the other flyways. These routes are not as important as the others. The central flyway is used by large numbers of shorebirds, waterfowl such as the pintail, American widgeon, and redhead, and by many small landbirds, such as the golden-winged, the worm-eating, and the Kentucky warblers. The Pacific flyway hosts scoters and other sea ducks, the Canada goose, Ross' goose, and many species of western land birds that nest in Alaska and along the Pacific Coast — western tanagers, black-headed grosbeaks, rufous hummingbirds, Wilson's warblers, and others.

One other flyway is of particular interest because of its great expanse across the ocean. Every fall, more than 100 million songbirds and small shorebirds head out to sea from the eastern coast of North America. They ultimately arrive in the Carib-

(a)

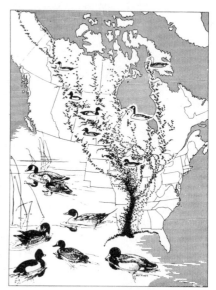

(b)

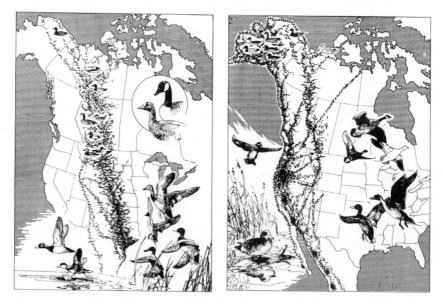

(c)

(d)

Important migratory routes followed by waterfowl. Land birds follow similar, though broader, routes. (a) The Atlantic flyway. (b) The Mississippi flyway. (c) The Central flyway. (d) The Pacific flyway.

bean and South America, a journey of over 1,800 miles (2,900 km). Most of these birds begin their voyage at night after a cold-front weather system has moved southeast over the coast. Aided by the strong northwest wind, the birds head directly southeast over the ocean. Continuing on this constant heading would take the birds far into the Atlantic away from South America, but the birds encounter the northeast trade winds in the area of the Sargasso Sea, and they shift their track southwest. The warblers, sandpipers, godwits, and plovers that use this perilous route are usually brought safely to the continental shore. However, during severe Atlantic storms, hundreds of small songbirds have been seen flying around ships, crashing into masts and rigging. Bird feathers found in the stomachs of deep-sea fishes are further evidence of occasional widespread mortality of these migrants.

Moon-watching for passing migrants

The oceanic migrations of birds were followed with radar each fall for six years in an enormous, concerted effort involving six national governments, four federal agencies, and the Woods Hole Oceanographic Institution. We can make some of our own observations with a smaller budget and far less effort.

Standing on the Cape Cod shore in the evening in late September or early October with a strong wind from the northwest at your back, you should be able to hear throngs of small birds calling to one another as they head southeast out to sea. In other areas of the northern United States, you can also hear these nocturnal migrants, especially on overcast nights when the migrants are more vocal. On clear nights you should peer through a telescope or binoculars at the full moon. Every few minutes birds will be seen flying across the moon's surface. Observers have seen as many as 9,000 birds per hour. Make note of the number of birds you see, and how their numbers change from day to day with the weather conditions. Try to determine what time of evening the birds are most active. If you can make enough observations, you may be able to graph your results and determine when the migrations reach their peak.

It is rather surprising that so much can be learned by this bird-watching technique. After all, the full moon occupies a mere 1/100,000 of the whole sky. Nonetheless, moon-watching has revealed that the maximum number of migrants fly in the middle of the night, and experts can sometimes tell what type of bird is flying past by noting its speed and wingbeat frequency. Regardless of what you may discover, what better way is there to spend a brisk autumn evening than gazing through a telescope at the moon and birds?

REFERENCES AND SUGGESTIONS FOR FURTHER READING

Emlen, S.T. August 1975. The stellar-orientation system of a migratory bird. *Scientific American* 223: 102–111.

Griffen, D.R. 1964. *Bird Migration*. Natural History Press, New York.

Gwinner, E. April 1986. Internal rhythms in bird migration. *Scientific American* 254: 84–92.

Keeton, W.T. December 1974. The mystery of pigeon homing. *Scientific American* 231: 96–107.

Lincoln, F.C. 1952. *Migration of Birds*. Doubleday, New York.

Peterson, R.T. 1947. *A Field Guide to the Birds*, 2d ed. Houghton Mifflin, Boston.

Robbins, C.S.; Bruun, B.; and Zim, H.S. 1966. *Birds of North America, A Guide to Field Identification*. Golden Press, New York.

Williams, T.C., and Williams, J.M. October 1978. An oceanic mass migration of land birds. *Scientific American* 239: 166–176.

4

When Honey Bees Swarm

HONEY BEES ARE remarkable creatures. A single bee, one-fortieth the weight of a penny, flies about 500 miles in her brief lifetime of 35 days. For all her efforts, a bee produces a mere one-third teaspoon of honey. To make a pound of honey on her own, she would have to work all day, every day, for eight years, and in so doing would fly more than 50,000 miles — twice around the earth. Bees are such efficient fliers that two tablespoons of honey would fuel a flight around the world.

As industrious as a single bee may be, the collective endeavors of the entire colony are the key to this insect's success. Bees are the epitome of social creatures, cooperatively working for the health and survival of the colony. The workers make honeycomb, keep the hive clean, feed and care for the maturing bees, gather nectar, guard and protect the inhabitants, and dispose of bees that die in the hive. An average colony has 50,000 worker bees, all of them female. The hive has a single fertile female, the queen, who lays all the colony's eggs and is the mother of all the bees. She is slightly larger than the worker bees, with a longer, more slender

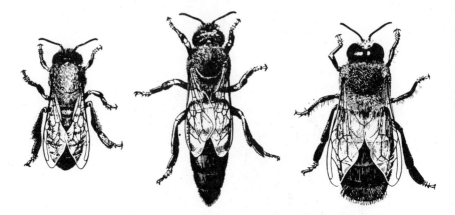

Worker, queen, and drone honey bees.

abdomen, filled with her huge well-developed ovaries. A colony also has several hundred male bees, called **drones**, who contribute nothing to the colony's welfare. Drones do not work; their only function in life is to search for a newborn queen outside the hive, and to mate with her in mid-air. In so doing, the drone dies.

How can we study the ways of bees? In the field we can watch bees working individually, gathering nectar or pollen. However, to truly understand honey bees, we must study them as a colony of interacting creatures.

Observing a swarm of honey bees is an exciting way to study bees in action. Finding my first swarm was certainly one of my most thrilling nature experiences. It is well worth the effort to overcome one's initial hesitation and fear of bees.

WHAT IS A SWARM?

Everyone has heard of swarms of bees, but few people know what a swarm really is. A swarm of bees is not a haphazard horde. Swarms assemble to establish a new colony. When the original colony becomes too populous, outgrowing its home in a tree cavity or man-made hive, the workers sense the population explosion and begin producing a new queen.

When the new queen is born, the old queen departs with a portion of the colony's inhabitants — the colony swarms. For days the bees that leave have been preparing for the exodus by engorging themselves with honey, storing up the food reserves needed to start a new colony. The honey is kept in a small dilated sac of gut, the honey stomach, located between the esophagus and the true stomach. The honey of all these bees (about 11 oz., or 300 gm) and the bees themselves constitute the sole resources of the queen. With these she undertakes the task of creating a new colony.

Swarming generally occurs once a year, in late spring and summer (from mid-May to mid-July) when the hive is rapidly growing. This brief event is easily missed. Within moments, the bees stream from the colony and are gone.

The bees usually alight near the parent colony and prepare to find a new home. A small proportion of the bees, perhaps 5 percent, act as scouts. They leave the swarm and fly off in all directions, searching for a suitable cavity in which to live. When a bee finds a potential spot, she will carefully examine it, crawling about the inside and outside of the cavity.

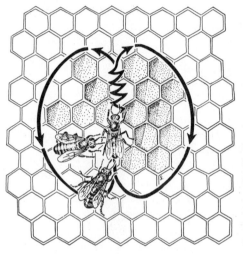

The waggle dance is used to indicate food (or a nest site) more than 330 feet (100 m) from the hive. Two worker bees are following the dancer. By dancing straight up on the comb, as illustrated, the bee indicates food is in the direction of the sun.

When the examination of a potential nest site is over, the scout returns to the swarm to make her report. To communicate the location of nectar or a potential new home, a scout bee uses dancing movements. Landing on the surface of the cluster, the scout bee will begin performing the **waggle dance** to tell the other scouts the location and quality of the cavity that she found. The better the potential site, the more lively and rapid will be the dance. Nearby bees follow the dancer closely, reading the message in her motions. The location of the site is indicated symbolically by the configuration of the dance. The bee moves in a semicircle on one side, then runs in a straight line back to where she began. Next she turns around and moves in a semicircle to the other side, thus completing the circle. Again she will retrace the straight-line portion of the dance, running back to the original starting point. During this straight run, the bee vigorously wiggles her abdomen from side to side, thus the name waggle dance. The direction of the straight run, in relation to a vertical line, indicates the location of the site. For example, if the potential nest site can be reached by flying directly toward the direction of the sun, then the straight run of the dance will be straight up on the surface of the swarm. If the site is in the opposite direction from the sun, then the straight run is downward. Directions in between, to the right or the left of the sun, are indicated by comparable angular deviations to the right or left of the vertical.

This same dance is used by foraging bees in the hive to guide their nestmates to nectar-producing flowers.

When the scouts finally agree on a site for the new home, they will all be dancing in the same direction. Soon the bees' behavior will change. Frantically, the scouts will begin to bore their way into the swarm, vibrating their abdomens and producing a high-pitched sound, perceptible if you place your ear very, very close to the bees. Suddenly, the cluster will begin to "dissolve," leaving loose strings of bees that appear to drip from the swarm as they take to the air. About 100 bees lead the swarm, flying quickly toward the new nest site. Repeatedly, these leaders return to the edge of the flying swarm and again fly ahead, as if guiding the main mass of bees to its new home as far as several miles away.

ACTIVITIES

Observing a swarm of honey bees

I would recommend that all the activities in this chapter be done, at least at first, with someone experienced with bees. The most difficult aspect of this activity will be locating a swarm. If we knew the location of a hive and were willing to sit by its side all day long from May to July, we would most likely see a swarm depart. But that is rather impractical, as well as boring. To find our swarm we will take advantage of two facts. First, after the swarm departs the old colony, it finds a temporary resting spot from which to reconnoiter. There it may stay for several days until it finds, and decides upon, a new permanent home.

The second fact deals not with bees, but with man's habitual fear of animals that sting or bite. When the honey bee swarming season begins in May, the phones at the local fire departments, police stations, and university entomology departments begin to ring. Frantic people can be heard: "A huge swarm of bees just landed in my yard. I'm allergic to bees, and I'm sure I will get stung." If you want to find a swarm of bees, begin by asking the fire and police departments what they do when they receive a swarm call. Often they will contact a local beekeeper who is willing to capture such swarms.

Another way to locate a swarm is by advertising. For a few dollars you can put an advertisment in your local newspaper offering a reward for information leading to the capture of a swarm. I've found that a jar of honey is usually reward enough. In this manner, you should be able to locate a swarm with the help of local bee lovers and bee haters. I've rarely come upon a swarm accidentally, but I've received many phone calls asking me to fetch swarms off parking meters in the center of town, on mailboxes, and in neighbors' trees.

Next, find yourself a beekeeper. You might begin by looking up "Beekeepers' Supplies" in the yellow pages of your phone book. Beekeepers are a friendly group of people, eager to talk about bees, to help a novice beekeeper, and to show the public that bees are really wonderful animals to work with, well worth the occasional sting they inflict. I learned how to handle bees from an old, sun-shriveled beekeeper in Greece who spoke hardly a word of English. I'll never forget the thrill (and initial fear!) I felt when he handed me my first frame of bees clustering on their comb. I took it hesitantly, certain I would be stung, but I was too embarrassed to refuse. The bees had no intention whatever of stinging me. At that moment I knew I had to have my own colony of bees.

How to approach a honey bee swarm: proper attire and behavior

Let's assume you have just received a phone call alerting you to the whereabouts of a swarm. Grab your friendly beekeeper and hurry over to the location. You'll need a bee veil and proper attire, light-colored pants and a long-sleeved shirt. Bees are much more likely to sting someone wearing dark, woolen clothing. Perhaps dark, furry clothes are reminders of skunks and bears that prey upon bees and honey. I also bring along a pair of rubber dish-washing gloves, just in case I need to protect my hands. These are the bare essentials. A bee smoker is sometimes useful. The smoker is a metal chamber attached to a small bellows. It is filled with burning leaves or hay, and is pumped a few times to waft smoke at the bees. For some reason, the smoke will calm the bees if they become disturbed. This apparatus, as well as the others, can be purchased at a beekeeping supply shop. Most towns have one.

An experienced beekeeper shaking a swarm of bees into a basket. From there the bees can be transferred to a permanent home in a wooden hive. Most swarms are gentle enough so that the beekeeper needs only a bee veil.

Actually, one rarely needs a smoker, gloves, or even a veil when dealing with a swarm in warm weather. Swarming bees are generally very docile. Occasionally, when the weather turns bad after a swarm has departed its original hive, the swarm will be trapped for a few days at its temporary resting site. The bees are unable to forage in the inclement weather, and their food reserves dwindle. Such "dry swarms" may be aggressive. If the weather over the previous few days has been rainy, leave that swarm, or get the assistance of an experienced beekeeper, who will use the smoker to calm the bees and safely hive the swarm.

At the site of the swarm, put on your veil and tuck your pant legs into your socks. If your pants are tucked in, bees will simply crawl up the outside of your pants where they can be gently brushed away with your hand or a blade of grass.

Approach the swarm slowly but confidently. Usually, it will be in a shaded spot on a tree or bush. If you are lucky, it won't be too high up, making it difficult to observe. Look at the swarm carefully. Although it appears to be just a mass of bees, there is much more going on than meets the eye. Biologists who have spent years studying swarm behavior still don't have all the answers.

Some experiments with a swarm

One of the difficulties in understanding what's happening in a swarm arises because there are so many bees, and they all look alike. Studies have shown that the average swarm has 12,000 bees. Think of the problem as follows: Imagine yourself to be an alien in a spaceship from Mars, hovering above New York City. It's rush hour, and thousands of tiny human beings are scurrying below, crossing streets, entering buildings, milling about in chaotic, apparently random, motion. You would understand much more if you could single out one person and follow him through the day: He enters a building at 9:00 A.M., sits at a small wooden structure covered with papers until 10:00, ingests a small quantity of hot dark liquid, returns to the desk until noon, shuffling papers and holding a piece of white plastic pressed against the ear, then leaves the building at noon, returns at 1:00 P.M., and so on, until 5:00 P.M. The routine of an office may be tedious, but at least it has a pattern.

Identifying and observing individuals is one of the key techniques of biology, whether placing a band on a bird's leg, making note of the unique pattern of scars on the fluke of a particular whale, or dabbing a spot of colored paint on the back of a bee. Much can be learned by carefully observing single individuals.

Marking bees is very simple. With a bottle of nail polish, and a bit of dexterity, you can paint a small spot of polish on the thorax of a bee. Use just a tiny bit, taking care to avoid the wings. Don't worry, the bee won't sting you. If you get a bit too much polish on her back she may get a bit riled up and begin to furiously clean herself, but even so, she will not sting.

Mark one bee and follow her activities. What does she do? Does she stay in one spot? Does she fly away? If so, how long does it take before she returns? Can you find the same bee an hour later?

Look closely at the swarm. You may not realize it, but the cluster of bees has a distinct structure. There is a compact outer shell of bees, about three bees thick, and a loose inner part, consisting of chains of bees connected to the shell. The shell provides protection, warmth, and mechanical strength for the swarm. By marking bees in the outermost portion of the shell, it has been demonstrated that the bees in the shell are constantly changing places. Most likely this allows the bees on the surface to keep warm by snuggling up to the bees deeper in the swarm. In one study, two-thirds of the bees on the surface of the shell changed places with those bees on the inside portion of the shell over a period of ten minutes. It might be interesting to try to demonstrate this yourself. Mark about 50 bees that are on the surface of the swarm and see where they go over the next half-hour. Another very dramatic way to see how the outer shell of bees protects those within the core is to observe the swarm during a rain shower. In a sudden downpour, the bees on the surface cling tightly to their neighbors just above. The bees' wings are held flat over their bodies and act as an umbrella. The bees align themselves so neatly that the whole swarm looks like a carefully shingled roof. It's a marvel of behavior, organization, and altruism.

Since we can't control the weather, you might want to try the following simple experiment. Get a spray bottle, the kind used to squirt a fine mist on house plants. Fill it with clean water and gently spray the swarm from a distance of a foot or two. They won't become alarmed. For them, it will be merely a brief sun shower. Notice how the bees hold their wings and how they cling to one another. After the rain, with a small stick, gently spread the shell to see if you can appreciate the looser structure of the core.

Another feature of the swarm that you cannot readily visualize is the division of labor within the cluster. From experiments with marked bees of known ages, it has been demonstrated that the scout bees searching for a new homesite are over 21 days old. They are the oldest, most experienced bees, having previously been the bees that spent their time foraging for nectar in the fields. The bees in the shell are slightly younger, 18 to 21 days old. Those inside the shell are younger yet. This makes sense. The older bees are most likely to receive casualties, either scouting for a new home, or serving as the outer protective shell for the swarm, and they are the most expendable. The younger bees within are physiologically best able to care for the young larvae the queen will soon be producing at the new colony site. Aside from the queen, they are the swarm's most precious resource.

A bee beard

It's difficult to describe the excitement of hearing and seeing thousands of bees flying all around you, bumping into you, and crawling over your clothing. You expect to get stung but find that the bees are heedless of your presence—not a single sting. Although I would not recommend performing the following demonstration without considerable beekeeping experience, fashioning an elegant "bee beard," like the one shown, clearly demonstrates the docile nature of a well-fed honey bee swarm. It's a little trick that beekeepers sometimes do to show off.

If you take the queen from the swarm and place her in a little screened cage, you can tie the cage under your chin with a piece of string, making a necklace. The bees in the swarm will begin looking for their queen, and when they find her, they will begin to cluster around your chin, arranging themselves into a bee beard. The sight of a bee beard, with thousands of bees calmly resting on your face, dramatically illustrates how a little understanding of animal behavior enables man to interact quite amicably with his fellow creatures.

The author sporting a bee beard.

REFERENCES AND SUGGESTIONS FOR FURTHER READING

Dadant and Sons (eds.) 1949 and 1979. *The Hive and the Honey Bee.* Dadant and
   Sons, Hamilton, Illinois.
Fell, D.F., et al. 1977. The seasonal cycle of swarming in honeybees. *Journal of
   Apiculture Research* 16: 170–173.
Frisch, K. von. 1967. *The Dance Language and Orientation of Bees.* Harvard Univer-
   sity Press, Cambridge, Mass.
Morse, R.A. 1975. *Bees and Beekeeping.* Cornell University Press, Ithaca, New York.
Seeley, T.D. October 1982. How honeybees find a home. *Scientific American* 247:
   158–168.

5

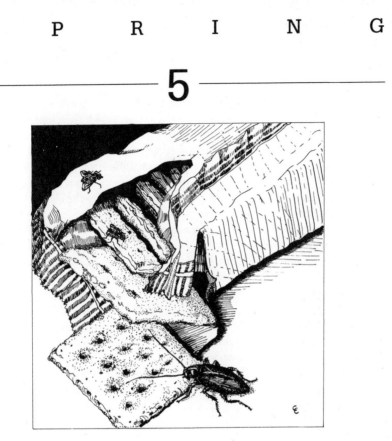

Creatures in My Home

THE OUTDOORS is the best place to pursue one's natural history interests. However, when the ground is covered with snow, or if rain is pouring from the sky, I often retreat to the warm, dry refuge of my home. That's the ideal time to get acquainted with the myriad housemates that share our living quarters. To the disgust and amazement of many tidy housekeepers, nearly every home harbors a varied fauna of tiny boarders. Some merely seek refuge from the harsh elements, while others search for a free meal. Some prey upon the other household denizens, but a few even prey upon us. Sometimes we are unaware of these unwelcome house guests; they often manage to remain well hidden. Other intruders, such as the flies, are quite conspicuous, but we probably know very little of their life and ways. This chapter will give you a chance to rummage about the nooks and crannies of your house, and will allow you to discover the habits of the many squatters that share your home.

THE FRENZIED FLIES

No home is free from the invasion of flies. A tiny hole in a window screen or the momentary opening of a door provides sufficient access for these obnoxious and detrimental trespassers. Their loud buzzing, tireless flight, and persistent habit of landing on one's face or dinner plate are enough to drive anyone mad.

Most people do not realize that there are many different types of flies found in the home, and that distinguishing one species from another may not be easy. Most commonly encountered are the lesser house fly, the face fly, the cluster fly, several types of blow flies, as well as the house fly itself.

Musca domestica has rightfully earned the name the house fly. In 1900, a publication with the unsavory title "A contribution to the study of the insect fauna of human excrement" documented that 99 percent of 23,087 flies collected in dining rooms across the country were none other than *Musca domestica*. However, times change, and each neighborhood is different, so we should not assume that every fly we find will be the common house fly. For example, in 1900, the face fly could not be found in the United States, but since its introduction to Nova Scotia from Europe in 1952, it has become a frequent household inhabitant throughout much of Canada and the United States.

Like all flies, the house fly undergoes complete metamorphosis with distinct egg, larval (maggot), pupal, and adult stages. The life cycle is similar to that of the other household flies. The female fly lays about half a dozen batches, each of more than 100 eggs. She prefers horse manure and human excrement but will settle for any kind of decaying vegetable matter. In the warmth of summer, eggs hatch in half a day. The larval stage lasts five days. The mature maggots then crawl away from their feeding places to seek a more protected spot in the soil or under debris. The soft white maggot then surrounds itself with a hard brown oval case, the **puparium**, in which it stays for another four or five days to complete its adult development. Once it is mature, the fly needs a special device, called a **ptilinum**, to free itself from the puparium. This weird structure is a membranous balloon that protrudes from a slit in the head. As the fly increases its internal body pressure, the ptilinum fills up with body fluids and pops open the lid of the puparium. Then, alternately expanding and contracting this sac, the adult fly opens a passageway through the soil to the surface. The ptilinum is then withdrawn into the head and is used no more. All that remains of this bladder is a narrow slit in the head that gives this group of flies its name, the **Schizophora**.

With a total of ten days from egg to adult insect, about a dozen broods are possible during the warm summer breeding season. At this rate, flies could be wildly prolific if they had an unlimited food supply. The following calculation is often quoted. "A pair of flies beginning operations in April may be progenitors, if all were to live, of 191,010,000,000,000,000,000 flies in August. Allowing one-eighth of a cubic inch to a fly, this number would cover the earth forty-seven feet deep." Obviously, populations never get that out of hand, being kept in check by competition for food supplies, bad weather, disease, predation, and fly swatters.

If the temperature is maintained at 60° F (16° C), the flies can breed throughout the year, but in colder climates they overwinter as adults within the walls of houses, in cracks and crevices in the basement or attic, or outdoors in protected spots. Adults generally stay within a couple of miles of their birthplace, but studies with radioactively labeled flies have shown that they can disperse up to 20 miles (32 km).

Flies are well designed for life in the home. These devilishly agile fliers perform aerobatics that constantly frustrate our attempts to pulverize them into oblivion. Certain details of their acrobatics were only recently discovered. For example, flies have no problem zipping through a room and then deftly alighting on the ceiling. Think of it. How can an insect fly belly downward and then suddenly land belly up on the ceiling? For a long time it was assumed that a fly executed a barrel roll in mid air, coming to a screeching halt upside down. In fact, flies perform a more elegant maneuver. They fly close to the ceiling in a normal position, reach backward over their heads until their feet touch the ceiling, and then somersault upside down into position.

In addition to their strong flight and dexterous maneuvering, flies possess elegant landing gear. The tips of their feet are equipped with a pair of claws for clinging to rough surfaces, and two pads, called **pulvilli**, for gripping smooth surfaces. The pulvilli bristle with hundreds of tiny hairs that secrete an oily fluid; this fluid allows the insect to adhere to the sleekest surface, yet pull away at will, without sticking.

The final gadget in the fly's toolbox is a retractable mouth called a **proboscis**, equipped at its end with two fleshy lobes. Each has a series of transverse hollow channels through which the fly sponges up liquids. Although the fly uses the proboscis to drink, it does not use this "tongue" to taste. Its taste receptors are on its toes (**tarsi**). As a fly walks along, the moment its foot touches food its proboscis is automatically extended.

In order to consume foods, the fly has the rather disgusting habit of salivating all over its meal in order to partially dissolve and predigest solids before lapping them up. A series of minute teeth on the underside of the lobes allow the fly to rasp its food slightly, but a fly is still incapable of swallowing any solid particles. Unlike mosquitoes and black flies, house flies cannot bite.

These tiny insects are not only engineering marvels, but they are also efficient carriers of disease organisms. One study showed that an average fly carries over a million bacteria. In its restless wandering, a fly accumulates pathogens on its feet and proboscis, as well as internally in its digestive tract. Germs can be spread as the fly walks about, wiping its feet, regurgitating food, and depositing blackish specks of infected feces. A partial list of over 100 pathogenic organisms recovered from flies includes the causative agents for amebic dysentery, typhoid fever, cholera, salmonellosis, anthrax, leprosy, polio, hepatitis, and infantile diarrhea. Flies also can carry the eggs of pinworm, whipworm, hookworm, tapeworm, and roundworm. Needless to say, flies are undesirable household guests, but in their defense it must be pointed out that they carry only the pathogens that are available nearby. With proper sanitation and careful disposal of sewage, there are no pathogens to spread. Indeed, after the end of World War I, prior to the era of antibiotics, sterilized blow fly maggots were intentionally introduced into infected wounds to clean out the dead infected tissues.

Fannia canicularis, the lesser house fly, appears early in the season, in May and June, before the common house fly, whose numbers do not peak until late summer. Because *Fannia* looks like a small *Musca domestica,* many people mistakenly believe that little flies grow into big flies. However, all insects stop growing once they become adults. Thus the butterflies, beetles, wasps, and flies one sees are all full-grown. They come in one size only, give or take a tiny bit, depending upon how well they ate as children.

Fannia's breeding habits and life cycle are essentially the same as those of its larger relative, although the maggot is quite different, being flattened and adorned with rows of spines. Unlike the common house fly, *Fannia* rarely settles on food; it flies about in the center of a room, hovering without landing, executing straight flights, punctuated by zigzags that bring the fly back to its starting point. Often several males will be flying about together until a female enters the room and is pursued. The circling behavior of the males is thought to be part of the mating activities, similar to the activities of large swarms of male flies that one sees outdoors hovering, or slowly rising and falling, over some stationary landmark such as a bush. *Fannia,* however, generally uses an overhead marker, such as a lighting fixture in the center of the room.

The face fly, *Musca autumnalis,* is a newcomer to the United States, but it is rapidly becoming an important pest. Except for its slightly larger size, it is nearly identical to its close relative *Musca domestica.* For most of the year it lives outdoors in pastures, where the females lay their eggs on cow manure and swarm over the faces of livestock to feed on mucous secretions around the nose and eyes. They spend the night resting on vegetation. Male flies are found on fence posts and trees, rarely on animals. In the fall, with colder weather, the flies seek the refuge of houses. Large numbers of unmated adults hibernate together in crevices and between the walls, emerging in early spring or occasionally on warm winter days. This fly has been accused of transmitting the cattle infection pinkeye and is a possible source of human pathogens.

The three previous flies were all members of the family **Muscidae**, house flies. The bluebottle or greenbottle flies are blow flies in the family **Calliphoridae**. Their loud incessant buzzing, large size, and shiny color make them unmistakable. One does not think of a fly as a beautiful creature, probably because we generally see them up close only in a two-dimensional mashed state. But next time you instinctively reach for the fly swatter, take a moment to capture a fly intact. Under a hand lens, a greenbottle or bluebottle fly is a marvelous creation. The body shimmers with brightly polished metallic colors, punctuated over the surface with carefully aligned rows of stout bristles. Transparent wings, reinforced with a network of veins, and large geometrically patterned eyes make the design of this tiny creature as elegant and "high tech" as the fanciest sports car.

Unfortunately, these flies have rather disgusting habits, breeding in carrion, excrement, garbage, and the open sores of living animals. They, too, can spread disease. Most of the time they are outdoors, but they often enter houses in late spring, searching for shelter and a place to lay their eggs. They are probably less of a health hazard than the house fly because they are not particularly interested in landing on our food. They spend most of their time relentlessly flying back and forth in a room, from one window to the next, in what appears to be an urgent effort to escape. One authority suggests that flies are frantically searching for a suitable place to lay their eggs. I do not agree; I think they do it just to be a nuisance!

Cluster flies are in the same family but have quite different habits from all the other household flies. They are not attracted to food and pose no health hazard. In the early 1900's, it was discovered that cluster flies are parasitic on a single species of earthworm, *Allolobophora rosea*. Their eggs are laid in the soil, and the young, active maggots penetrate the bodies of earthworms, where they live as internal parasites for 13 to 22 days before pupating. The pupal period lasts two weeks, making the entire life cycle up to 39 days, much longer than that of the housefly.

Throughout the summer the flies live outdoors on vegetation, but they enter houses in autumn searching for snug retreats in which to hibernate. At times thousands of flies will cluster behind curtains and in the corners of rooms. They do not fly very much but crawl lazily about. They enter buildings one by one through seemingly insignificant cracks and crevices. One friend described in horror how hundreds of flies crept into the house from behind the walls, through tiny chinks around the baseboards, electrical outlets and the plumbing. Since the fly breeds in earthworms, it would be undesirable, if not impossible, to eliminate their breeding places, so one may be forced to spray the outside walls of the house to discourage the hordes of flies from seeking entry to the house.

SCURRYING COCKROACHES

Next to flies, cockroaches are the epitome of insect household invaders. They are the bane of all conscientious housekeepers. One study of low-income apartments in the southeastern United States found that 97.5 percent were roach-infested, with an average of 33,600 roaches per dwelling! Four species are commonly found in buildings, the German, the oriental, the American, and the brown-banded cockroaches. Although the first three have names suggesting countries of origin, all four are widely distributed throughout the world's temperate areas. The names may indicate the location where they were first found, but they more probably reflect our penchant for slandering our neighbors. No one cares to admit that his own homeland could be the source of so unwelcome a creature as a roach, so everyone quickly blames the pestilence on the neighbors. Thus the German cockroach was called the Prussian roach by the Russians, the Russian roach by the Prussians. It is much like the vehement and slanderous nomenclature that surrounds that embarrassing social disease, syphilis. It was the French disease to the English, the Spanish disease to the Italians, the Italian disease to the French, the Polish disease to the Russians, and the Portuguese disease to the Indians and the Japanese.

Although roaches may not be as bad as syphilis, they are nonetheless perceived as highly repulsive. Growing up in a very proper suburban neighborhood, I remember how upset my mother became when a roach was discovered one evening in the kitchen, wandering over an otherwise spotless Formica® counter top. A series of regular visits from the exterminator ensued until the "plague" was finally eradicated. The mysterious origin of the pestilence was not determined until some months later when another stowaway roach was found hidden in a bunch of bananas brought home from the grocer. My mother wanted to complain to the store manager and probably would have filed a lawsuit against the supermarket, but we managed to calm her down. In the end we instituted a policy of searching all incoming groceries.

Roaches have several features that distinguish them from other insects. Their oval, flattened shape allows them to hide in all sorts of crevices. Except for long filamentous antennae, the head is nearly concealed under a shield on the thorax called the **pronotum**. They usually have long brownish wings and spiny legs. At the end of the abdomen are a pair of appendages called **cerci** that sense air movements, ground vibrations, and sound. In essence, the cerci act as ears.

These household residents are easily distinguished. The American cockroach is the largest, up to 1-1/2 inches (4 cm) long, with reddish-brown wings. The German cockroach can be recognized by the two dark longitudinal stripes on the pronotum. All roach eggs are enclosed in a capsule called an **ootheca**, but the German roach has the curious habit of carrying her egg case around with her until her offspring hatch. Nearly the size of the female's abdomen, it is readily visible, protruding from the end of the body. The adult oriental cockroach is shiny black, about an inch in length. The female has only stubs of wings, while the male's short wings cover only a portion of the abdomen. As the name suggests, the brown-banded cockroach has stripes. The two light bands are most noticeable on the body of the wingless young, but they can also be seen on the wings of the adults. The two sexes are different; the male is more slender with longer wings.

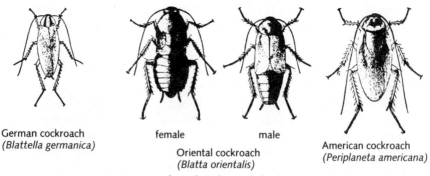

German cockroach
(*Blattella germanica*)

female   male

Oriental cockroach
(*Blatta orientalis*)

American cockroach
(*Periplaneta americana*)

Some cockroaches that invade the home.

I have often heard people speak of water bugs or water beetles invading their home. Knowing something of insect habits, I could not imagine what insect they were describing, since water bugs are not found in the house. I finally learned that these are common names for cockroaches, but they avoid the stigma of having a roach-infested household. The use of scientific names avoids the confusion of having several common names for a single species. The German roach got its nickname, the Croton bug, for another reason. It was first associated with the water system of New York City that is supplied by the Croton aqueduct.

The life cycle of all four roaches is similar. The shiny brown ootheca contains 16 to 48 eggs, depending upon the species. The eggs are in two neat rows within the egg case, and the young hatch several weeks later through a seam along the side. They undergo a long period of development, varying with the temperature and the species. The German cockroach may reach maturity in a little over 100 days, while the oriental roach may take over 2 years. Metamorphosis is simple, meaning that the young, called **nymphs***, grow progressively larger but essentially look like miniature versions of the adult, except for their lack of fully developed wings.

Cockroaches are extremely catholic in their tastes, consuming practically anything digestible. Unlike the house flies, roaches have well-developed chewing mouthparts. In addition to all the foods we eat, cockroaches have been known to eat paper, ink, shoe polish, bookbindings, dead insects, their own cast-off skins, excrement, sputum, and even the toenails of sleeping people.

It is possible to have a house full of roaches without ever being aware of their presence. They shun the light, quickly retreating out of sight the moment lights are turned on. I once discovered an infestation in the laboratory because all the stamps in the secretary's office were mysteriously losing their glue. I returned one evening after dark and quickly opened the desk drawer, sending the villains scurrying for cover. It was months before I could lick a stamp without feeling that I was kissing a cockroach.

Roaches are pests mostly because of their indiscriminate tastes and the unpleasant roachy odor they exude. They have been implicated in the transmission of disease, but not to the extent of the more mobile filth-loving flies. However, in one case, a *Salmonella* epidemic in a pediatric hospital ceased immediately after the nursery was treated with DDT to kill the bacteria-laden roaches. The mere presence of roaches is disturbing, regardless of the actual damage they cause; I must admit that even I find them somewhat loathsome.

A FEW OTHER VISITORS

Many more visitors to our home deserve mention, if only briefly. Silverfish and firebrats are very primitive, wingless insects. The silverfish prefers cool damp situations, while the firebrat likes warm spots around furnaces and steam pipes. Both eat all sorts of starchy materials, such as bookbindings and wallpaper glue. The tiny book lice (0.1 inch long, or 3 mm) are also wingless, found in the same situations as silverfish. They, too, feed on moldy books and debris.

---

* Nymph refers to the immature stage of an insect that has gradual metamorphosis. **Larva** refers to the immature stage that undergoes complete metamorphosis; that is, with a distinct larval, pupal, and adult stage.

silverfish

booklouse

earwig

cricket

bedbug

saw-toothed
grain-beetle

saw-toothed
grain-beetle (larva)

worker termite

webbing clothes moth

red ant

carpenter ant

webbing clothes moth (larva)

black carpet beetle

black carpet
beetle (larva)

carpet beetle

Other household pests (not shown to scale).

Earwigs get their name from the old superstition that they crawl into people's ears, another silly example of people's entomophobia. These nocturnal insects are scavengers found in damp cellars. The pincerlike cerci at the tip of their abdomen can give a slight pinch, but they are otherwise harmless.

A few insects attack household products and can be troublesome pests. Two species of clothes moth are commonly found. The webbing clothes moth has a half-inch (1.3 cm) wingspread. Its tiny larva spins a silken webbing or tube upon which it crawls while feeding. It attacks woolen fabrics, furs, feathers, and the bodies of dead insects. The case-making clothes moth has similar tastes but different larval habits. It builds itself a neat tube of silk and fabric fragments. As it outgrows its case, it makes a slit up one side and fills in the triangular opening with a swath of material. It repeats the process on the other side and then turns around within its retreat and enlarges the diameter of the other end. The tube is then lengthened with additions at both ends. The work of this tiny seamstress can be elegantly demonstrated by transferring the larva to different colored fabrics as it grows, resulting in a calico patchwork hideaway.

Perhaps more destructive than the clothes moths are the family of **Dermestid** beetles. Their common names include carpet beetles, larder beetles, and hide beetles. They eat all sorts of animal and vegetable products, including wool, feathers, hides, hair, meat, flour, grain, and furniture upholstery. They can destroy museum displays and insect collections. In Chapter 22 (Unraveling the Mysteries of Skeletons), I describe how these voracious insects are used to clean animal carcasses for the study of bones.

One unusual house guest is a fly that usually appears only in the bathroom. For years I never knew why. The moth fly is completely clothed in hairs, making it look just like a tiny moth. I finally discovered that its maggots develop in the bit of sludge in the U-shaped bend of pipes beneath the sink. Unseen, the adults mysteriously appear from the sink drains and are often found on bathroom walls.

So far I have mentioned only insect housemates. Pillbugs (also called sowbugs or woodlice), millipedes, centipedes, and spiders are not insects but related arthropods with more than six legs. They, too, find their way into our homes.

Finally, we should not forget that man himself supports a varied fauna. A number of creatures live or feed on man. These parasites include fleas, lice, scabies mites, bedbugs, and mosquitoes. One tiny mite, *Demodex,* lives in the hair follicles of the eyelashes. And within man himself one finds pinworms, hookworms, tapeworms, and roundworms.

Although scrupulous housecleaning and careful personal hygiene are the best measures against the invasion of all these household creatures, remember that their presence attests more to the ubiquity and superb adaptability of these pests than to our own lack of cleanliness.

ACTIVITIES

Using a key to identify insect orders

One of the first things you need to know about an organism is its identity and how to distinguish it from other organisms with similar appearances, life cycles, or

COMMON INSECTS FOUND IN THE HOME

Common Name	Scientific Name	Order	Diet
silverfish	Lepisma saccharina	Thysanura	bookbindings, starchy materials
firebrat	Thermobia domestica	Thysanura	bookbindings, starchy materials
American cockroach	Periplaneta americana	Orthoptera	practically everything
German cockroach	Blatella germanica	Orthoptera	practically everything
brown-banded cockroach	Supella supellectilium	Orthoptera	practically everything
oriental cockroach	Blatta orientalis	Orthoptera	practically everything
house cricket	Acheta domesticus	Orthoptera	clothing, most human food
termite	Reticulitermes flavipes	Isoptera	wooden buildings
earwig	Forficula auricularia	Dermaptera	decaying materials
booklouse	Liposcelis divinatorius	Psocoptera	moldy books and papers
bedbug	Cimex lectularius	Hemiptera	human blood
carpet beetle	Anthrenus scrophulariae	Coleoptera	wool, feathers, animal products, grain, etc.
larder beetle	Dermestes lardarius	Coleoptera	wool, feathers, animal products, grain, etc.
hide beetle	Dermestes maculatus	Coleoptera	wool, feathers, animal products, grain, etc.
black carpet beetle	Attagenus unicolor	Coleoptera	wool, feathers, animal products, grain, etc.
furniture beetle	Anobium punctatum	Coleoptera	wooden houses and furniture
powder-post beetles	Lyctus spp.	Coleoptera	wooden houses and furniture
confused flour beetle	Tribolium confusum	Coleoptera	flour and grain products
saw-toothed grain beetle	Oryzaephilus surinamensis	Coleoptera	flour and grain products
drugstore beetle	Stegobium paniceum	Coleoptera	practically everything
webbing clothes moth	Tineola bisselliella	Lepidoptera	woolen fabrics, feathers, fur, etc.
casemaking clothes moth	Tinea pellionella	Lepidoptera	woolen fabrics, feathers, fur, etc.

COMMON INSECTS FOUND IN THE HOME *(continued)*

Common Name	Scientific Name	Order	Diet
Indian meal moth	*Plodia interpunctella*	Lepidoptera	flour and grain products
Mediterranean flour moth	*Anagasta kuehniella*	Lepidoptera	flour and grain products
house fly	*Musca domestica*	Diptera	excrement, garbage
face fly	*Musca autumnalis*	Diptera	excrement, garbage
lesser house fly	*Fannia canicularis*	Diptera	excrement, garbage
bluebottle fly	*Calliphoria vomitoria*	Diptera	excrement, garbage, carrion, wounds
bluebottle fly	*Lucilia caesar*	Diptera	excrement, garbage, carrion, wounds
greenbottle fly	*Phaenicia sericata*	Diptera	excrement, garbage, carrion, wounds
cluster fly	*Pollenia rudis*	Diptera	parasite of earthworms
moth fly	*Psychoda alternata*	Diptera	sludge in household drains
fruit fly	*Drosophila melanogaster*	Diptera	rotting and fermenting fruit
mosquito	*Culex pipiens* and others	Diptera	blood
cat flea	*Ctenocephalides felis*	Siphonaptera	blood of humans and pets
dog flea	*Ctenocephalides canis*	Siphonaptera	blood of humans and pets
human flea	*Pulex irritans*	Siphonaptera	blood of humans and pets
carpenter ant	*Camponotus pennsylvanicus*	Hymenoptera	excavates, but does not eat wood
pharaoh ant	*Monomorium pharaonis*	Hymenoptera	sweet foods
little black ant	*Monomorium minimum*	Hymenoptera	sweet foods

behaviors. This is taxonomy, the study of the classification of organisms, and as naturalists we spend much time trying to figure out what's what. Each known organism has a single scientific name, used by biologists all over the world, so that everyone knows exactly which creature is being discussed. Carolus Linnaeus encouraged the use of a hierarchal classification system in the 1700's, aimed at bringing some order to the chaotic jumble of natural history data. Each organism was given a two-part name, indicating its **genus** and **species**, such as *Homo sapiens* for man, or *Musca domestica* for the house fly. Every organism is also part of larger and larger groupings that contain related creatures of similar evolutionary origin. The house fly is classified as follows:

Kingdom — **Animalia**
Phylum — **Arthropoda**
Class — **Insecta**
Order — **Diptera**
Family — **Muscidae**
Genus — *Musca*
Species — *domestica*

This tells us that the house fly is an animal with jointed legs (an arthropod), three pairs of legs, three body parts (a head, thorax, and abdomen — an insect), and two wings (a fly, **Diptera**). It is in the family of house flies (**Muscidae**).

With over a million species of insects alone, it can become rather tricky to identify each individual. Often we will have to be satisfied to identify the family of an organism, or refer the specimen to a specialist. To identify organisms, biologists often use keys. These are like road maps that help us find our way. To show how it works, use the following key to identify some animals you might find in the house.

1a. With 2 legs 2
1b. With more than 2 legs. 3
2a. Body covered with feathers . . . . .Birds
2b. Without feathers . . . . .Man
3a. With 4 legs 4
3b. With more than 4 legs. 5
4a. With retractable claws. . . . . .Cats
4b. Without retractable claws . . . . .Dogs
5a. With 6 legs and 3 body parts . . . . .Insects
5b. With 8 legs and 2 body parts . . . . .Spiders

To use the key, you begin at 1. and make a choice between the two alternatives presented, 1a or 1b. For each alternative, you go to the number indicated at the end of the line, and then continue to make choices from there. Using this key to identify your cat, begin by deciding whether it has two legs or more. From there you jump to 3, which gives you a choice of four legs, or more than four. Next you go to 4. Here, you must determine whether the animal has retractable claws; since it does, it must be a cat.

You may have realized that keys can have their drawbacks. For example, if you had a pet rabbit, this key might lead you to believe it to be a dog. Keys can also be tedious and silly to use if you are already familiar with the plants or animals you are studying. You would never use a key to identify your pets. You recognize your dog as a dog without even thinking about it. Also, you can readily distinguish a butterfly from a fly and from a grasshopper, even though you may not be able to describe how you tell them apart. However, keys are a very useful way to identify organisms you are not familiar with, and a good way to learn the important characteristics of each group of organisms. Many biology books and field guides have keys, so it is important for the serious naturalist to know how to use them.

Our survey of household inhabitants yielded an impressive array of different insects. Our first step in organizing this collection is to identify the various orders to which they belong. Try using the following key to identify insects in or around your home.*

1a. Insects with wings. 2
1b. Insects without wings, or with only inconspicuous
    vestiges of wings 17
2a. Insects with only one pair of wings, and tiny
    knobbed structures (**halteres**) in place of the sec-
    ond pair of wings; sucking, lapping, or piercing
    mouthparts well developed . . . . .DIPTERA
2b. Insects with 2 pairs of wings. 3
3a. The 2 pairs of wings unlike in structure (the first
    pair thick and horny, as in beetles, leathery at the
    base with membranous overlapping tips, as in the
    true bugs; or leathery and with veins, as in the
    grasshopper) 4
3b. The 2 pairs of wings of similar structure, with
    about the same degree of thickness as in bees,
    butterflies, and dragonflies. (One pair is often col-
    ored and could thus differ from the other in trans-
    parency, but not in thickness; or one or both may
    be covered with scales or hairs.) 7
4a. First pair of wings of hard, hornlike substance,
    meeting in a straight line down the back 5
4b. Wings not as in 4a. 6
5a. With a prominent pair of pincerlike parts at tip of
    abdomen (earwigs). . . . . .DERMAPTERA
5b. Without large pincers at the end of the abdomen
    (beetles) . . . . .COLEOPTERA
6a. Front wings leathery at their base, membranous,
    overlapping at their tips; mouthparts a tube for
    sucking, usually extending from underside of head
    in a backward direction (true bugs) . . . . .HEMIPTERA
6b. Front wings leathery, with veins; hind wings folded
    lengthwise when at rest. Mouthparts for chewing
    (crickets, cockroaches, katydids, mantids, etc.) . . . .ORTHOPTERA
7a. Wings covered with scales (in a few species there
    are bare transparent areas). Mouthparts a coiled
    tube (moths and butterflies). . . . . .LEPIDOPTERA
7b. Wings thin, not covered with scales, usually trans-
    parent or thinly clothed with hairs, sometimes col-
    ored (bees, mayflies, dragonflies, etc.) 8
8a. Mouthparts a tube for sucking, attached to hind
    part of the lower surface of the head. Wings when
    at rest slope down and outward from the center,

* Adapted from H.E. Jacques, 1947. *How to Know the Insects*. Wm. C. Brown, Dubuque, Iowa, pp. 47–63. Reprinted by permission.

like a roof (cicadas, leafhoppers, treehoppers, aphids, etc.) ....HOMOPTERA

8b. Not as in 8a.................................9

9a. Slender, mothlike insects, with long slender antennae (as long as body or longer); no evident mouthparts except a pair of slender **palpi**. Wings frequently hairy; usually broadest beyond the middle (caddisflies) ....TRICHOPTERA

9b. Not as in 9a................................10

10a. Wings with few cross veins or none, as in the bees. 11

10b. Wings with several to many cross (vertical) veins, as in dragonflies, lace wings, etc. 12

11a. Front wings the larger; hind wings frequently hooked to front wings. (Often mistaken for one pair in casual observation.) Mouthparts for chewing, or for both sucking and chewing (bees, wasps, ants)......................................HYMENOPTERA

11b. Very small, slender insects. Wings very narrow and margined with bristly hairs; mouthparts for piercing, and sucking (thrips)..................THYSANOPTERA

12a. Front wings much larger than hind wings. Wings when at rest held vertically above body. Two or three long, fragile, threadlike tails — outer two, "cerci"; all three, "caudal filaments" (mayflies)......EPHEMEROPTERA

12b. Not as in 12a 13

13a. Head prolonged into a trunklike beak with chewing mouthparts at its tip. (scorpionflies).....MECOPTERA

13b. Not as in 13a 14

14a. Antennae short and inconspicuous; long slender insects with long narrow wings (damselflies, dragonflies) ....ODONATA

14b. Antennae readily seen 15

15a. Abdomen usually with two rather short tails (cerci). Back wings broader than front wings and folded lengthwise (stoneflies) ....PLECOPTERA

15b. Not as in 15a 16

16a. Without cerci. (The males of some species have conspicuous claspers.) Tarsi with 5 segments (ant lions, lacewings, dobsonflies, alderflies, etc.) ....NEUROPTERA

16b. Wings equal in size and with indistinct veins. Prothorax smaller than head (termites).........ISOPTERA

17a. Narrow-waisted antlike insects; no cerci (ants, velvet ants, etc.)........................HYMENOPTERA

17b. Not narrow-waisted........................18

18a. Antlike but with wide waist and two short cerci. Not flattened. Usually light-colored (termites) ....ISOPTERA

18b. Not as in 18a 19

19a. Small, flat-bodied insects with head as wide as body or nearly so. Chewing mouth parts 20
19b. Not as in 19a 21
20a. Antennae of many segments. Found in old papers, etc. (book lice, bark lice, psocids). . . . . . .PSOCOPTERA
20b. Antennae short; two to five segments. Found mostly on birds, a few on mammals (bird lice). . . .MALLOPHAGA
21a. Small soft-bodied insects with small heads and plump bodies. Two short tubes usually extending from back of abdomen. Found sucking juice from plants (aphids) . . . . .HOMOPTERA
21b. Not as in 21a 22
22a. Small, broad, and flat across back; legs each have a single hooklike claw for grasping hairs; jointed, sucking beak. Parasites found on mammals (sucking lice) . . . . .ANOPLURA
22b. Not as in 22a 23
23a. Small narrow insects, flattened on the sides; sucking mouthparts; hind legs for jumping; five tarsal segments (fleas) . . . . .SIPHONOPTERA
23b. Not as in 23a 24
24a. Very delicate insects with chewing mouthparts and long, jointed, threadlike tails and antennae (silverfish, bristletails) . . . . .THYSANURA
24b. Delicate insects with six or fewer abdominal segments. Underside of abdomen has a sucker and pair of more or less fused appendages for leaping (springtails) . . . . .COLLEMBOLA

Microscopes

The **stereomicroscope** is a wonderful tool, transporting the naturalist to whole new worlds of observation—the barbs on a porcupine quill, the compound eye of a fly, life in a drop of pond water, and the creatures abounding in leaf litter. A 10x hand lens will suffice for many observations, but the stereomicroscope, as the name implies, gives you a true three-dimensional view. These instruments are also called binocular, or dissecting, microscopes. They are an expensive piece of equipment, but a must for the serious naturalist. They usually have a variable magnification from 10x to 60x, and will reveal details of plants and small animals that you can barely see with the unaided eye. They are ideal for dissecting insects or frogs, or for watching the development of salamander eggs. For observations with a stereomicroscope, you will need a bright lamp. Some models come equipped with heat-absorbing filters for prolonged viewing of sensitive organisms.

The compound, or light, microscope provides much greater magnification than a binocular microscope—in the range of 100x to 1000x. This instrument is useful for viewing individual cells on the surface of a leaf, or for examining blood corpuscles. Objects to be viewed must be thin and nearly transparent because they are illuminated with light passing through the specimen. Thick objects, such as plant stems, must be sliced in very thin sections and mounted on a glass slide.

Identifying the common household flies

When I began this chapter, I assumed that it would be a simple task to explain to the reader how to distinguish among the half-dozen or so flies that commonly find their way into the home. Several frustrating days later, after comparing my specimens to those in the university's enormous collection, and after peering through the stereomicroscope, I understood why most of the field guides carefully gloss over the subject entirely. After wending my way through complicated keys of the diptera, I am now proud to say that I can recognize **hypopleural** and **pteropleural** **bristles**, a **plumose arista**, a well-developed **postscutellum**, **calypters**, and the various meanderings of wing veins, with cryptic names such as 3A, 2A, R_5, and M_1. If all this seems rather trivial, you may be right, but this is the way taxonomists identify flies. In the study of classification, seemingly trivial details are of paramount importance. The serious student of diptera might begin his education with *A Field Guide to the Insects* by Borror and White.

The key features of the common household flies are as follows: The bluebottle and greenbottle flies are readily distinguished by their bright metallic colors. The cluster fly has curly golden yellow hairs on its thorax, easily seen with a magnifying glass or binocular microscope. Cluster flies are slightly larger than a house fly and appear longer and narrower because they hold their wings closer together so that the outer edges are almost parallel to the body.

The face fly looks very similar to the house fly, but is generally a bit larger; the abdomen of the female is black on the sides, in contrast to the yellow coloration in the house fly. Unfortunately, the abdomen of the male face fly also has yellow spots, but his eyes are larger than those of other flies, practically touching each other on top. The face fly also appears in great numbers later in the fall, when house flies are dying down, and leaves houses before the house fly has reappeared for the summer.

If any vagrant flies besides those just mentioned happen to wander into your home, they may present some taxonomic dilemmas. However, with a good field guide to insects, a magnifying lens, and some patience, you should be able to identify whatever comes your way.

REFERENCES AND SUGGESTIONS FOR FURTHER READING

Borror, D.J., and White, R.E. 1970. *A Field Guide to the Insects*. Houghton Mifflin, Boston.

Chu, H.F. 1949. *How to Know the Immature Insects*. Wm. C. Brown, Dubuque, Iowa.

Dethier, V.G. 1962. *To Know a Fly*. Holden-Day, San Francisco.

Headstrom, R. 1977. *Adventures with a Microscope*. Dover, New York.

Herrick, G.W. 1926. *Insects Injurious to the Household and Annoying to Man.* Macmillan, New York.

Jacques, H.E. 1947. *How to Know the Insects.* Wm. C. Brown, Dubuque, Iowa.

James, M.T., and Harwood, R.F. 1969. *Herm's Medical Entomology.* Macmillan, London.

Oldroyd, H. 1964. *The Natural History of Flies.* Norton, New York.

Pfadt, R.E. 1985. *Fundamentals of Applied Entomology.* Macmillan, New York.

6

Insect Adaptations for an Aquatic Existence

LIFE EVOLVED IN THE WATER, but eventually some aquatic animals abandoned the seas to colonize the land. Among them were the insects who made their debut 400 million years ago. Eons later some insects returned to the water. Having lost their original aquatic adaptations, they were forced to redevelop devices to cope with life in the water.

Regardless of where an organism lives, it has four survival problems. The four F's (Feeding, Freezing, Fighting and Finding a Mate) are a mnemonic to help remember. Each organism requires nourishment, protection from environmental conditions, and defense against predators. This effort is directed toward the ultimate goal of reproduction.

The aquatic environment is a vast realm covering 72 percent of the earth's surface. However, insects inhabit only a fraction of it. Very few insect species have colonized the oceans. No one knows for certain why. It is not that the oceans are too salty for the insects. The larvae of certain shore flies (family **Ephydridae**) live in the Great Salt Lake, which is 22 percent saline, much greater than the ocean's 3.5 percent. The ocean's great depth, its turbulence, and its relative lack of vegetation are factors in the small insect numbers, but the main reason is probably that their relatives, crustaceans (lobsters, shrimp, crabs, and the like), beat the insects to it. They remained in the oceans when the insects ventured onto land, successfully occupying all the available ecological niches. The remaining watery habitats, lakes, streams and ponds, are the principal homes of the aquatic insects.

THE ADVANTAGES OF BEING AQUATIC

In terms of the four F's of survival, aquatic life has certain advantages. The water abounds with plant and animal life, presenting ample opportunities for procuring a healthful meal. There is less competition from the hordes of insects inhabiting the land, since only 3 percent of insects live in the water. Bodies of water are fairly stable habitats since water warms up and cools down more gradually than the air. In a submerged existence, insects are not threatened with desiccation as they are on land.

PROBLEMS CONFRONTING AQUATIC INSECTS

Nonetheless, aquatic living is hardly carefree. Insects may have left behind some devilishly efficient predators, but they have merely traded birds, bats, spiders, and insects for enemies just as voracious — swarms of frogs, fish, and different insects.

An aquatic existence presents some interesting physical problems. Water offers much greater resistance than air, making locomotion more difficult. Aquatic organisms hasten their progress with sleek streamlined bodies, and with legs modified into oars. Human oarsmen minimize water resistance by lifting their paddles from the water on the recovery stroke. Insects do not have that option, but they achieve the same result in a different way. The hind legs of the predaceous diving beetles (family **Dytiscidae**) are elongated, flattened, and fringed with hairs. On the power stroke, the broad surface of the leg presses against the water and the hairs splay out, providing an additional propulsive surface. On the recovery stroke, the leg segments twist on a ball-and-socket joint, so that the fringe of hairs falls back and lies sleek against the leg; thus, the effective area of the appendage is decreased to reduce resistance and drag. Whirligig beetles (family **Gyrinidae**) use a more elegant device. Instead of a row of hairs, the leg is equipped with a series of flattened blades. During the power stroke, these blades open and overlap like Venetian blinds, presenting a broad continuous surface. On the return stroke, the blades and distal leg segments collapse like a fan, decreasing the exposed leg area by about 30 percent. As is so often the case in nature, the modification and evolution of existing body parts provide solutions to the problems of adaptation.

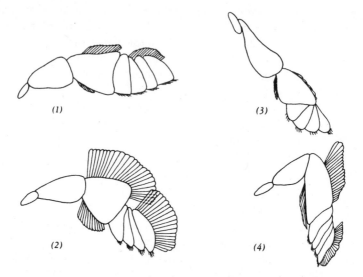

The hind leg of a whirligig beetle during swimming. A series of flattened blades opens like a fan during the power stroke (1) and (2), and folds back on the recovery stroke (3) and (4).

Surface tension results from the greater attraction of water molecules to each other than to the air above. This creates a tough elastic film on the water's surface that presents a new challenge to insects attempting to exploit the aquatic environment. Such insects as water striders glide effortlessly on this surface layer, but unprepared insects are fatally imprisoned. Water insects have evolved special adaptations that allow them to pierce through the surface film without becoming trapped. Mosquitoes and midges spend the early portion of their lives in the water. As adults they would drown if their wings touched the water's surface. Floating pupal cases act as rafts to support the newly emerged flies until their delicate wings expand and enable them to fly. The water-repellent (**hydrophobic**) bodies of creatures that live on the surface film enable them to resist getting trapped. Sometimes only portions of an insect's body are hydrophobic. Water springtails have a hairy hydrophobic cuticle that keeps them from getting wet. However, they are so tiny that they would easily be blown about, were it not for a wettable ventral suction disk (the **collophore**) that extends from the first abdominal segment and anchors them to the surface. Their claws are also wettable, allowing them to grasp the tough elastic water film. Water striders have a velvety coating of nonwettable hairs that permits them to race upon the water's surface, merely dimpling the elastic film. Even if accidentally submerged, they pop back to the surface, buoyed up by the air trapped among the hairs.

On land, staying in one place is relatively easy. Gravity and a good foothold generally keep an insect firmly on the ground. Water, however, is much more buoyant than air. Insects such as predaceous diving beetles, water scavenger beetles, whirligigs, and water boatmen carry an air supply that makes them lighter than water. They must swim strenuously to stay submerged, and they must grasp onto vegetation when they stop in order to keep from popping to the surface like a cork.

In swift currents, staying put is more difficult. Insects have three solutions, a flattened, streamlined body shape, attachment devices, and heavy sinkers. As their name suggests, larval water-penny beetles are brown, flat, and disk-shaped, offering little resistance to the water. They keep from being washed away in rapidly flowing water by clinging tightly to the underside of stones, their flattened bodies presenting little resistance to the flowing water. The larvae of long-toed water beetles and riffle beetles are similarly oval and flat. Mayfly nymphs that live in swiftly flowing water have flattened bodies and widely spread legs.

Suction cups provide a solution for other aquatic insects. The larvae of net-winged midges live in fast-flowing streams and have a series of ventral suckers keeping them firmly anchored. Black-fly larvae have a single disk at the tip of the abdomen, equipped with dozens of tiny hooks. They also use a sticky salivary secretion to anchor themselves in place. Heavy sinkers are the caddisfly larvae's solution. They build portable cases of various materials, held together with glue or silk. The cases are distinctive for each species, and those made of stones both protect and weigh down the larvae in swift streams.

Egg-laying, or oviposition, is not difficult on land, but it presents problems for aquatic insects that spend their early lives in the water, and then must return to the water to lay their eggs. Their delicate wings and terrestrial bodies prevent them from entering the water. As always, insects have evolved imaginative solutions to their problems. *Aedes* mosquitoes lay their eggs in dry places that are likely to be flooded. There they remain until accumulations of water permit hatching and development. *Culex* mosquitoes deposit a floating raft of 150 to 300 eggs on the water surface. Certain horse flies, dobsonflies, alderflies, and caddisflies place their eggs on branches or stones overhanging the water so that the larvae merely fall in when they hatch. The dragonflies fly over the water, dipping their slender abdomens and depositing eggs individually. Stoneflies and mayflies drop the entire egg masses into the water.

A potential disaster for an aquatic insect is a summer drought. Strong-flying beetles and water bugs take off in search of another pond. Many larval insects develop rapidly, reaching maturity before their homes dry up. Others bury themselves in the mud and patiently wait for wetter times. Most mosquitoes spend the winter hibernating as eggs, and may remain desiccated for several years before hatching.

HOW AQUATIC INSECTS BREATHE

The most challenging problem of a watery existence is obtaining oxygen. The ancestors of insects lost their gills when they invaded the land, and they evolved a novel respiratory system designed to breathe air. A network of thousands of tiny

springtail
(Podura aquatica)

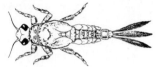

mayfly nymph
(Ephemerella excrucians)

stonefly larva
(Nemoura venosa)

adult stonefly
(Isoperla confusa)

adult mayfly
(Potamanthus sp.)

nymph of dragonfly
(Macromia magnifica)
dorsal view

adult dragonfly
(Macromia magnifica)

damselfly nymph

lateral view
with labium extended

rat-tail maggot, the larva of
the syrphid fly
Eristalis sp.

black fly larva
(Simulium venustum)

pupa showing
respiratory filaments

Common aquatic insects (not shown to scale).

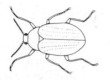

adult water penny beetle
(*Psephenus* sp.)

dorsal view
of larva

ventral view
of larva

whirligig beetle
(*Dineutus* sp.)

head of
whirligig beetle
showing divided eye

predaceous diving beetle
(*Dytiscus* sp.)

caddisfly larvae
and their cases

Phryganea sp.

caddisfly adult
(*Rhyacophila* sp.)

Nectopsyche sp.

water strider adult
(*Gerris* sp.)

backswimmer
(*Notonecta* sp.)

water boatman

water scorpions

Ranatra sp.

Nepa apiculata

giant water bug
(*Belostoma fulminea*)

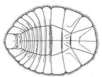

tubes, **tracheae**, permeates every portion of the insect's body. These tubes connect to the outer atmosphere by means of a row of holes, called **spiracles**, along each side of the body. As the insect expands and contracts its body like a bellows, air is pumped in and out through the system. It works fine, but only on land. In returning to the water, insects have had to devise clever means to compensate for their terrestrial heritage. They, too, have invented snorkels and scuba gear, as well as a few other contraptions.

Many different groups of insects have independently returned to the water, and it has been necessary for each to devise its own solutions to the problems of an aquatic existence. Although many are quite similar, more fascinating is the diversity of contraptions, each a logical solution to the same problem.

The aquatic insects can be divided into two groups, semiaquatic and truly aquatic species. The semiaquatic insects breathe air and must return to the surface at regular intervals to replenish their supply. Their tracheal systems have spiracles open to the atmosphere. In these respects, they are just like the terrestrial insects.

Many semiaquatic insects have breathing tubes, snorkels, with which they pierce the water's surface to obtain oxygen. There are different types of snorkels. Water scorpions have two long filaments at the tips of their abdomens that fit together to form a tube. The scorpions rest quietly on vegetation while the siphon pierces the water's film. Among most mosquito larvae, only the posterior spiracles remain functional, being drawn out into a short snorkel. Mosquito pupae do things the other way around, with anterior spiracles developed into two earlike appendages that penetrate the surface. The most unusual snorkel is that of the rat-tailed maggot, the half-inch (1.3 cm) larva of the syrphid fly. Its posterior spiracles are drawn out into a telescopic siphon that can extend almost three inches (7.6 cm). The maggot rests on the bottom mud, extending its retractile snorkel to reach the surface.

Snorkels are not simple tubes like soda straws. These respiratory siphons have special modifications so they do not readily fill with water when submerged. Fly larvae have small glands surrounding the tip of the spiracles that secrete an oily, water-repellent substance, which keeps the tube from being flooded. In addition, the end of the snorkel is encircled with hairs or flaps, which act like a valve to shut the snorkel when the insect dives. When submerged, the flaps come together like the petals of an unopened daisy, preventing the entry of water. When the siphon pierces the surface film, the outer surfaces of the flaps are attracted to the water, and they swing open, exposing the spiracle to the atmosphere. The action is involuntary, depending entirely upon the surface tension forces. One simple means of killing mosquito larvae takes advantage of this principle. A light oil, spread upon the surface of a pond or swimming pool, is not repelled by the oily spiracles. The oil seeps into and blocks the spiracular opening, asphyxiating the larvae.

Certain semiaquatic insects have taken snorkels one step further. Rather than come up to the surface, some fly and beetle larvae use their respiratory siphons to pierce the air-filled cavities of aquatic plant roots. In the mosquito, *Mansonia*, the tip of the snorkel has two sets of teeth. One anchors the larvae in place; the other saws its way into the plant tissue to tap the oxygen supply.

Some semiaquatic insects take a supply of air like a scuba tank down with them, allowing them to stay submerged for longer periods. The diving beetles keep an air bubble beneath the **elytra**, the hard outer wing covers. The water boatmen and backswimmers store air beneath their wings, but they also have a coat of short, hydrophobic hairs that retains a thin film of air around their bodies. These bubbles and coatings of air clinging to the insect appear as gleaming silvery mirrors when the insect is submerged. The air supplies are in contact with the spiracles and are gradually taken into the insect's tracheal system.

Insect divers can stay submerged for much longer than one would expect, based upon the size of the air supply they carry. The amount of oxygen in the bubble would allow an insect only a 20-minute dive, but an interesting bit of physics lets the insects stay down for up to 36 hours, extracting oxygen from the surrounding water like the gills of a fish. Air contains oxygen and nitrogen. The insect consumes the oxygen in the bubble and gives off carbon dioxide, which rapidly diffuses into the surrounding water because of its greater solubility. Nitrogen is not consumed. The oxygen pressure in the bubble dwindles, and the nitrogen pressure increases. As a result, oxygen diffuses into the bubble from the surrounding water and nitrogen is forced out. This effect is enhanced by the fact that oxygen is able to diffuse into the bubble three times as fast as nitrogen diffuses outward. Eventually, all the nitrogen diffuses out of the air bubble, and the bubble must be replenished by a quick visit to the surface. This elegant mechanism occurs through no effort or ingenuity on the part of the insect. It is made possible by the differential solubility and diffusion of the gases. Because this mechanism is based upon the physical properties of the gases, it has been called a **physical gill**.

An added feature of the carried air supply is the buoyancy it provides. When the insect stops swimming or lets go of its grasp on the vegetation, it pops to the surface. Once there, the location of the air supply helps the insect maintain the proper orientation to quickly renew its air supply. Diving beetles, for example, break the water's surface tail-first so that more air rushes under its elytra from the tip of the abdomen. The spiracles are located beneath the wings rather than along the sides of the body, making the system more efficient.

A refinement of the physical gill is **plastron respiration**. The plastron, meaning breastplate, is a thin air film that communicates with the spiracles. The air is held in place by a thick pile of specially shaped hydrophobic hairs or scales that maintains its volume constant, unlike the air supply of the physical gill, which is eventually depleted. The plastron can act as a permanent gill provided there is adequate oxygen dissolved in the water. The water bug, *Aphelocheirus,* and the beetle, *Elmis,* can remain submerged indefinitely.

The truly aquatic insects have a closed tracheal system. Their spiracles are not open to the atmosphere, so oxygen must diffuse across the cuticle from the surrounding water. In order to make such a system effective, the body wall must be very thin and have a large surface area for diffusion. In waters high in oxygen, such as fast-flowing streams, these special adaptations are sometimes unnecessary. Some mayfly nymphs can absorb sufficient oxygen through their fairly thick body wall cuticle. However, in most cases, insects rely on gills. **Tracheal gills** are leaflike or filamentous structures that form outpockets of the body wall. They are well supplied with tracheae and their finer branches, **tracheoles**. There are many variations on this theme. The damselfly larvae have three taillike appendages at the end of the abdomen. Mayfly, alderfly, and dobsonfly larvae have pairs of feathery, filamentous, or leaflike gills along the abdomen. These gills are kept in a rhythmic vibration that passes fresh oxygenated water over their surfaces. Among the stoneflies, the gills can be found on the neck, legs, thorax, or abdomen.

You would never know it, but dragonfly larvae have gills. They are neatly tucked away inside the rectum, and are aerated as water passes in and out over the gills by muscular pumping. In many aquatic fly pupae, the spiracles are drawn out into a long hollow tube that functions as a gill. These structures are found in crane flies, black flies, net-winged midges, mountain midges, and dance flies.

In very stagnant water, low in oxygen, gills may be inadequate. Like vertebrates, a few insects resort to hemoglobin to extract and carry oxygen. The larval *Chironimus* midges are called bloodworms. They live in burrows of mud, poor in oxygen, and survive because their hemoglobin absorbs 30 times as much oxygen as water.

BREATHING ADAPTATIONS OF AQUATIC INSECTS

Insects using a respiratory siphon to pierce the water's surface

Common Name	Genus	Family	Order	Life Stage
shore fly	*Ephydra*	Ephydridae	Flies	larva
mosquito	*Culex*	Culicidae	Flies	larva, pupa
rat-tailed maggot	*Eristalis*	Syrphidae	Flies	larva
waterscorpion	*Ranatra*	Nepidae	True Bugs	all
waterscorpion	*Nepa*	Nepidae	True Bugs	all

Insects using a sharp siphon to pierce air-filled spaces in aquatic vegetation

Common Name	Genus	Family	Order	Life Stage
long-horned leaf beetle	*Donacia*	Chrysomelidae	Beetles	larva
mosquito	*Mansonia*	Culicidae	Flies	larva

Insects using a portable air supply

Common Name	Genus	Family	Order	Life Stage
predaceous diving beetle	*Dytiscus*	Dytiscidae	Beetles	adult
whirligig beetle	*Gyrinus*	Gyrinidae	Beetles	adult
water scavenger beetle	*Hydrophilus*	Hydrophilidae	Beetles	adult
water boatman	*Corixa*	Corixidae	True Bugs	all
backswimmer	*Notonecta*	Notonectidae	True Bugs	all

BREATHING ADAPTATIONS OF AQUATIC INSECTS *(continued)*

Insects using plastron respiration

Common Name	Genus	Family	Order	Life Stage
water bug	*Aphelocheirus*	Naucoridae	True Bugs	all
riffle beetle	*Elmis*	Elmidae	Beetles	adult

Insects using tracheal gills

Common Name	Genus	Family	Order	Life Stage
damselfly	*Calopteryx*	Calopterygidae	Dragonflies	larva
dobsonfly	*Corydalus*	Corydalidae	Nerve-winged insects	larva
alderfly	*Sialis*	Sialidae	Nerve-winged insects	larva
mayfly	*Heptagenia*	Heptageniidae	Mayflies	nymph
stonefly	*Acroneuria*	Perlidae	Stoneflies	nymph
water-penny beetle	*Psephenus*	Psephenidae	Beetles	larva
whirligig beetle	*Dineutes*	Gyrinidae	Beetles	larva
crawling water beetle	*Peltodytes*	Haliplidae	Beetles	larva
caddisfly	*Rhyacophila*	Rhyacophilidae	Caddisflies	larva
lily-leaf caterpillar	*Nymphula*	Pyralidae	Butterflies and Moths	larva

Insects using spiracular gills

Common Name	Genus	Family	Order	Life Stage
crane fly	*Tipula*	Tipulidae	Flies	pupa
black fly	*Simulium*	Simulidae	Flies	pupa
net-winged midge	*Blepharocera*	Blephariceridae	Flies	pupa
mountain midge	*Deuterophlebia*	Deuterophlebiidae	Flies	pupa

Insects using rectal gills

Common Name	Genus	Family	Order	Life Stage
dragonfly	*Aeshna*	Aeshnidae	Dragonflies	nymphs

Insects using hemoglobin to extract oxygen from the water

Common Name	Genus	Family	Order	Life Stage
bloodworm	*Chironomus*	Chironomidae	Flies	larva

ACTIVITIES

Collecting insects from ponds and streams

Collecting aquatic insects is like going on a treasure hunt. You never know exactly what you will find, but there is always something new and exciting to discover. A sturdy net and a collecting bucket are the only equipment necessary. A pair of boots or hip waders will let you go into deeper water. I usually walk right in with just an old pair of sneakers.

In a quiet pond, sweep the net, skimming the bottom occasionally until you get a good load of mud, plants, roots, and algae. Empty the contents on the shore or, even better, into a shallow enameled pan with a white bottom. Pick through the muck and plants, searching for insects, and place them in your bucket. Do not overlook creatures concealed in the mud or camouflaged within cases of various sorts. A kitchen strainer is another useful tool for separating insects and worms from the muck in which they hide.

In faster moving water, there is a better technique. Have a partner lift stones while you hold a net just downstream so that any dislodged animal will be swept into it by the current. Also be sure to look on the bottom of stones for many clinging insects.

Setting up a freshwater aquarium

Setting up an aquarium is the best way to observe aquatic insects. The glass walls of the tank permit you to watch the animals performing all their normal behaviors. An aquarium can be a simple, temporary affair, such as a gallon jar filled with a few plants and insects, or a fancier 20-gallon tank with all the accoutrements.

If you plan to keep your aquarium set up for more than a day or so, you should try to make it a balanced, functioning ecosystem. Remember that animals give off carbon dioxide and need oxygen, while plants consume carbon dioxide and give off oxygen. The most common problem encountered is an excess of animals, which will consume the oxygen and fill the water with too much carbon dioxide. The most sensitive insects will begin to die of asphyxiation. Even under the best of circumstances, insects such as stonefly nymphs, which live in fast-moving, well-oxygenated water, will not survive in an aquarium for more than a few hours.

To set up a balanced aquarium, you will need to provide water plants that produce oxygen. Unless you have only a few insects, you will also need an air pump with a bubbler to aerate the water and provide additional oxygen. These can be obtained in any pet shop.

Get a watertight tank or gallon jar and fill it with water from the stream or pond where you collected. Put some mud at the bottom and anchor a few water plants in place. Add a few rocks to provide the inhabitants with nooks and crannies in which to escape from predators. Place the end of the bubbler at the bottom of the tank to aerate the water.

It is a good idea to collect animals besides insects. Snails are useful scavengers to have in an aquarium, since they eat all the organic debris that accumulates. Tadpoles, fish, leeches, amphipods, crayfish, and the like will add a little variety.

You should be able to keep the aquarium active for months. Place it in a well-lit area to keep the plants healthy, but out of direct sun so that the water does not overheat. Put a glass cover on the tank to keep the water from evaporating and also to prevent the inhabitants from escaping.

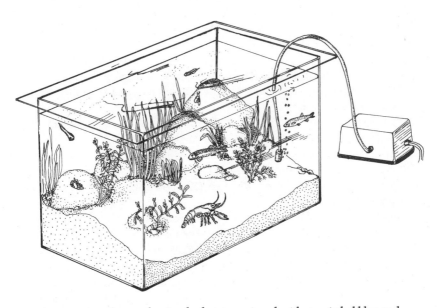

An aquarium for pond animals that is equipped with an air bubbler and aquatic plants.

Demonstrations of surface tension

I have mentioned the importance of surface tension in the life of aquatic insects without thoroughly explaining what it is. A couple of simple kitchen experiments will give you a better idea. Take a clean, dry needle and lightly coat it with a bit of salad oil. Fill a clean bowl with water up to the brim, and lay the needle across the tines of a fork. Gently, gently lower the fork into the water. If you are very careful, the needle will float on the strong elastic surface film of water, dimpling the surface. A water strider, much lighter than a needle, effortlessly glides along the water's surface without falling through. The needle (and the water strider) will suddenly sink if you touch the surface of the water with a bit of dishwasher detergent, which reduces the surface tension. You can demonstrate changes in surface tension by lightly dusting a uniform layer of cinnamon on the surface of a bowl of water. Then, with a tiny drop of detergent on a toothpick, touch the water's surface. The cinnamon will rush away from the toothpick. The soap reduces the surface tension at the tip of the toothpick, and the relatively greater surface tension on the other side contracts the surface and pulls the cinnamon along with it.

Making observations of aquatic insects

If you have a stereomicroscope or a good magnifier, you will be able to make many interesting observations of aquatic animals. First, identify the insects you have collected by referring to the figures or to one of the field guides listed at the end of the chapter. About 5,000 species, representing ten orders of insects, spend some or all of their lives in the water. Try to observe the following distinctive features of each insect order and their common representatives:

Springtails (*Collembola*). Minute (less than 0.2 inches, 0.5 cm) and wingless, with a forked appendage on the underside, which they use to catapult themselves on the water's surface.

Mayflies (*Ephemeroptera*). Nymphs have rows of leaflike gills along the abdomen, three feathery tail appendages, and a single claw on each foot.

Stoneflies (*Plecoptera*). Nymphs differ from mayflies in having a flatter body and two claws on each foot, adaptations for clinging to rocks in swift water. They also have longer antennae and two tail appendages. Tracheal gills, when present, are on the thorax.

Dragonflies and damselflies (*Odonata*). Both have a peculiar **labium**, or lower lip, cunningly adapted for catching prey. When not in use, it is folded under the head, but it can be everted rapidly to grab prey with its clawlike lobes. It extends about a third of the body length, making the insect a treacherous predator. The damselfly nymphs are delicate, with three leaflike gills attached to the tip of the abdomen. Dragonfly nymphs are stouter-bodied, and their gills are hidden away in their rectum. By taking water into the hind end of the digestive system and rapidly squirting it out, dragonfly nymphs use jet-propelled locomotion to escape from predators.

Nerve-winged Insects (*Neuroptera*). Most of the aquatic larvae are predatory with strong jaws and pairs of lateral gill filaments.

True Bugs (*Hemiptera*). This order derives its scientific name from the character of the front wing, half membranous and half thickened. They all have jointed sucking beaks, usually used to suck the body juices from their prey. Be sure to observe the shimmering film of air on the underside of the water boatmen and backswimmers. Take a waterscorpion and gently separate the two filaments that make up its respiratory siphon. You will see that they are held together with rows of hooks.

Beetles (*Coleoptera*). Adults have hard front wings (**elytra**). Most of the larvae are long and slender with biting mouthparts and with lateral gill filaments on the abdomen. Observe the eyes of whirligigs, each divided into two parts so that the insect can see above and below the water simultaneously. Examine the flattened and oarlike hind legs of the whirligigs and diving beetles.

Caddisflies (*Trichoptera*). Most larvae live in cases constructed from leaves, twigs, pebbles, or other debris, glued together with juice from their salivary glands. Two tail hooks hold them in the case. They usually have filamentous gills on the abdomen. Adults are slender and mothlike.

Flies (*Diptera*). The aquatic larvae are mostly legless and wormlike. Look at the valve at the tip of the respiratory siphon of mosquitoes. Search for blackfly larvae in fast-moving streams. Note how they cling to the rocks with the hooks on their posterior disc. The fanlike structure at the front end filters food from the water. Try to find the bright red bloodworms in the mud of stagnant ponds.

Moths (*Lepidoptera*). A few moth larvae live in the water, under nets of silk or in silk-lined cases built of leaf fragments. Some have threadlike gills along the abdomen.

REFERENCES AND SUGGESTIONS FOR FURTHER READING

Borror, D.J., and White, R.E. 1970. *A Field Guide to the Insects of America North of Mexico.* Houghton Mifflin, Boston.

Chapman, R.F. 1971. *The Insects: Structure and Function,* 2d ed. American Elsevier, New York.

Frost, S.W. 1959. *Insect Life and Insect Natural History,* 2d ed. Dover, New York.

Klots, E.B. 1966. *The New Field Book of Freshwater Life.* Putnam, New York.

Reid, G.K. 1967. *Pond Life.* Golden Press, New York.

Richards, O.W., and Davies, R.G. 1970. *Imm's General Textbook of Entomology,* 9th ed. Dutton, New York.

7

Herbal Medicines: A Pharmacy in Our Own Backyards

PEOPLE HAVE ALWAYS used plants as medicines. Through trial and error, each culture has amassed its own herbal recipes to combat disease. In North America, the early settlers learned how the Indians used our native plants. They also experimented on their own, developing new remedies. In other parts of the world, man's use of herbal remedies has been preserved in written records thousands of years old. The first known medical text, the Egyptian Kahun papyrus, was written around 1900 B.C. In China, *Recipes for 52 Kinds of Diseases* was found in a tomb dating from 168 B.C. Of the thousands of detailed prescriptions handed down from generation to generation, some are still employed today in modern medicine's campaign against disease.

A good example is foxglove. Two species are the mainstays of heart disease therapy; *Digitalis purpurea* is one of the commonest English wildflowers, and *D. lanata* grows along the Danube River and in Greece. Welsh physicians, writing in 1250, described how the foxglove could be used internally and topically to treat a variety of illnesses ranging from epilepsy to skin ulcers. In 1785, William Withering published his famous book, *An Account of the Foxglove and Some of Its Medical Uses: with Practical Remarks on Dropsy and Other Diseases.* Dropsy is the old, outdated term for congestive heart failure, the ailment for which digitalis finds its most important use.

The bark of the South American cinchona tree is another herbal remedy with a long, colorful history. Its use was described in a religious book of 1633, written by an Augustinian monk named Calancha, of Lima, Peru. A popular, though possibly apocryphal, story relates how the bark was used in 1638 to treat Doña Francisca Henriquez de Ribera, the Countess of Chinchón, wife of the viceroy of Peru. Her miraculous cure resulted in the introduction of cinchona to Spain. Although there is no evidence that the countess used the remedy, the plant bears her name. By 1640 the drug was being used to treat fevers in Europe. The Jesuit priests were the main importers and distributors of cinchona in Europe, hence the name Jesuit bark. Many looked upon the drug with suspicion because the Jesuits used it. Other conservative medical groups objected to the new remedy because its use did not conform to the teachings of the ancient Greek physician, Galen. As a result, this extraordinary drug fell into the hands of charlatans who dispensed it in the form of secret remedies. The first official recognition of the drug came in 1677, when it was included in the *London Pharmacopoeia,* under the name *Cortex Peruanus,* Peruvian bark. It was nearly 200 years before scientists isolated the active principle, quinine, which became the main treatment for malaria until the 1930's when synthetic antimalarials were developed.

Many other ancient plant drugs with demonstrated pharmacologic bases could be added to this list. Ephedrine is extracted from a plant the Chinese call Ma huang. It was used for over 5,000 years before being introduced into Western medicine in 1924. Ephedrine reduces the bronchospasms of asthma, and acts as a nasal decongestant.

Reserpine is obtained from *Rauwolfia serpentina,* a plant in the dogbane family, indigenous to India. It was used in primitive Hindu medicine for snakebite, hypertension (high blood pressure), insomnia, and insanity. Today, tablets made from the powdered root are effective for hypertension and for psychotic states such as schizophrenia. The list goes on and on.

Scientists continue to peruse the ancient medical literature, finding new remedies to add to our armamentarium against disease. Annual wormwood is a weed introduced to the United States from Asia. In China, it is known as Qing hao, and was described in the *Zhou Hou Bei Ji Fang* (Handbook of prescriptions for emergency treatment) of 340 A.D. as an antipyretic, a remedy to reduce fevers. Its active ingredient, artemisinin, has been used successfully for several thousand malaria patients in China, and it appears to be active against strains of malaria that have developed resistance to other antimalarial drugs.

Garlic has been widely touted for its medicinal properties since ancient times. The Ebers papyrus, a medical document dating to about 1500 B.C., mentions garlic as a remedy for heart problems, headache, bites, worms, and tumors. Among the early Greeks, Aristotle, Hippocrates, and Aristophanes praised the curative effects of garlic. In Rome, Dioscorides, chief physician to the Roman army in the first century A.D., advocated the use of garlic as a vermifuge, or expeller of intestinal worms. In 1858, Louis Pasteur demonstrated garlic's antibacterial actions, and during both world wars garlic was used as an antiseptic to prevent the gangrene of wounds. Recent studies have shown that one component of garlic, ajoene, is as potent as aspirin in preventing blood clots.

DRUGS DERIVED FROM PLANTS

Drug	Plant Source	Use
Steroidal hormones	*Dioscorea* spp. (Mexican yams)	Oral contraceptives, corticosteroids
Digitoxin, digoxin	*Digitalis purpurea, D. lanata* (foxglove)	Cardiac medications
Belladona alkaloids (atropine, hyoscyamine, scopolamine)	*Atropa belladona, Datura stramonium* (jimsonweed)	Parasympatholytic agents
Opium alkaloids (codeine, morphine)	*Papaver somniferum* (opium poppy)	Analgesics
Reserpine	*Rauwolfia serpentina*	Antihypertensives, psychotropic agents
Vincristine, vinblastine	*Catharanthus roseus* (Madagascar periwinkle)	Anticancer agents
Physostigmine	*Physostigma venenosum* (Calabar bean)	Parasympathomimetic agent
Pilocarpine	*Pilocarpus* spp.	Parasympathomimetic agent
Quinine, quinidine	*Cinchona* spp.	Antimalaria agent, antiarrhythmic
Colchicine	*Colchicum autumnale* (autumn crocus)	Antigout agent
Curare	*Strychnos* spp., *Chondodendron tomentosum*	Muscle relaxant
Etoposide	*Podophyllum peltatum* (mayapple)	Anticancer agent
Cocaine	*Erythroxylon coca*	Local anesthetic
Anthraquinone cathartics (senna, cascara sagrada)	*Cassia* spp., *Rhamnus purshiana* (buckthorn)	Laxative
Psyllium	*Plantago psyllium* (plantain)	Laxative

These examples underscore the indispensable role of plants in modern medicine. From 1959 to 1980, drugs derived from plants accounted for one-quarter of all prescriptions dispensed in the United States. In 1980, Americans paid $8 billion for prescription drugs derived from plants. The accompanying table lists important drugs in use today that are prepared from plant sources.

ANOTHER SIDE OF HERBAL MEDICINE

Although many of our most powerful drugs originated from traditional herbal remedies, we must approach the use of herbal medicines with a critical attitude. In earlier times, when these remedies were developed, the physiology and pathology of disease processes were not known. Remedies evolved for reasons other than their proven ability to cure disease. While there can be no doubt that trial and error occasionally yield effective treatments, such serendipities are rare.

The plant remedies of the American Indians point out some of the fallacies of herbal therapy, and suggest how some of these remedies may have developed. The Zuni Indians of New Mexico ascribe a medicinal use to over 100 plants growing in their region. Most of the plants they use are common throughout the western United States.

Sunflower, gumplant, white horsenettle, gaura, milkvetch (locoweed), and doveweed are used for rattlesnake bites. Numerous compounds have been isolated from these plants, but none is effective against snake venom. However, this remedy does have a rational basis. To treat a snakebite, the medicine man chews the root of one of these plants, and then sucks the wound to extract the poison. If done promptly, this will remove some venom. Furthermore, when a poisonous snake bites its victim, 20 percent of the time no venom is injected. In the case of these "dry" bites, any remedy would be effective. In this case, the use of plants is superfluous, but since the victim is often "cured" by the medicine man, the plants are mistakenly believed to be effective.

Such erroneous cause-and-effect relationships are the basis of many herbal remedies. The resinous gum of the pinyon pine is used to treat abscesses. Typically, an abscess is opened and sprinkled with the dry powdered resin, or the sticky gum is mixed with lard and packed into the open wound. Pine resins contain volatile oils such as pinene, the main ingredient of turpentine. In a study of common antiseptics, turpentine was shown to be effective in killing *Staphylococcus aureus,* a major skin pathogen. However, more important than any pharmacologic action of the pine resin is the Zuni practice of opening the abscess. Incision and drainage of infections is standard medical practice today, and this procedure is usually all that is required for a complete cure.

For the treatment of the venereal diseases, gonorrhea and syphilis, the Zuni Indians of the Southwest have used doveweed and thistle. The patient drinks a tea prepared from one of the plants, then runs rapidly in the hot sun over a distance of about a mile. When he returns, he bundles himself in blankets to further increase the sweating. The physiological basis of this remedy is probably the elevation of body temperature induced by vigorous exercise. Studies of healthy athletes have shown that a three-mile (5 km) run in less than 15 minutes can raise the runner's temperature to 106° F (41° C). Before 1943, when penicillin was introduced, fever therapy was an accepted treatment for these diseases. Body temperature was increased to as much as 106° F (41° C) with injections of typhoid vaccine or malaria organisms, and by mechanical devices such as infrared heat boxes, electric blankets, and hot baths of 112 to 115° F (44 to 46° C). Both the gonorrhea and syphilis bacteria rapidly succumb to elevated temperatures.

For these ailments, the folk remedies probably have a beneficial effect. The fallacy lies in believing that the particular plant is important. However, since these remedies were developed long before the causes of disease were known, the treatments are remarkable achievements.

For other illnesses, a naive conception of disease mechanisms has resulted in remedies without any effect. A widely held belief in many cultures is that the characteristics of a plant suggest its use in treating a particular illness. This is the **doctrine of signatures**, which suggests, for example, that heart-shaped leaves are useful in treating cardiac ailments, or that plants with yellow juice should be used to treat jaundice.

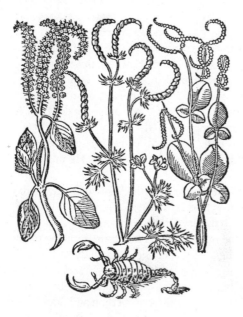

Herbs of the scorpion from the Phytognomonica *of Giambattista Porta, published in 1588, demonstrate the widely held belief that "like cures like." In this case the long, pointed shape of the flowers suggests a scorpion's tail, and hints at the flowers' use as a remedy for the animal's venomous sting.*

On a visit to New Mexico, I asked several Zuni diabetics how they treat their illness. Several prepare a tea from the roots of wild licorice, presumably because the sweet root is thought to be efficacious in treating an illness that results in an excess of sugar in the blood. Similarly, the leaves and roots of various species of spurge are eaten by postpartum mothers to promote lactation. The plant's milky juice is believed to encourage the flow of milk.

Perhaps we find these remedies amusing, but herbal medicines with as little validity are being sold today in every town across the country. Herbal remedies gleaned from antiquated sources are being promoted as genuine cures, and thousands of people are taking these potions. I imagine that this is often done out of ignorance. The promoter probably believes that his treatments are effective. Most illnesses are self-limited. Colds, fevers, headaches, and sprains resolve spontaneously because of the body's natural healing ability. Of the many people who take a herbal remedy, a few will always feel better soon after and will attribute the improvement to the treatment. In this manner, the validity of a remedy is "proven," and acclaimed.

The current back-to-nature sentiment has elicited an increase in the use of herbal remedies. There is an unfounded belief that a natural product is better than a chemical. But all drugs are chemicals. Ephedrine was originally obtained from plants. Now, chemists have learned to synthesize the identical molecule in the laboratory, more easily and cheaply. Vitamin C from rose hips is indistinguishable from vitamin C prepared synthetically.

As both a medical doctor and a naturalist, I find the attitude toward herbal medicine disturbing. People should be made aware of the amazing properties of plants. Nature is the world's most sophisticated chemist, capable of synthesizing compounds that man has never dreamed of or been able to create. However, it is unrealistic to expect herbal medicines to cure all man's ills, and it is heartless to raise the hopes of those who are suffering from illnesses for which we have no cures as yet.

Desperate, frustrated victims will try almost any potion or palliative, hoping that it may work, and rationalizing that, if not, at least it will do no harm. Thus herpes sufferers are applying seaweed, earwax, snake venom, peanut butter, watermelon, ether, baking soda, bleach, yogurt compresses, and carburetor fluid to their sores. Herbal remedies are being sold that purport to cure every illness from cancer to herpes. A recent *Consumer Reports* (May 1985) presented many examples of the frauds foisted upon the public. One product was an extract from a South American shrub that was claimed to eliminate cancerous growths in one week. Another was a "Tibetan herbal food supplement," recommended for the treatment of angina, poor circulation, and senility. According to the House Subcommittee on Health and Long-term Care, quackery is a $10 billion-a-year business in the United States.

The consumer needs to unravel fact from fallacy in order to avoid worthless remedies and costly frauds. It is also important to realize that many herbal remedies do not cure a disease, but can alleviate unpleasant symptoms. Personally, I try to avoid any kind of medication, and even refrain from taking an aspirin. When I get a cold, I simply "tough it out." Nature takes its course, and my body generally cures itself after a few days. For others, it may be comforting to know that something can be done to make them feel better. For them a variety of traditional herbal remedies can offer symptomatic relief.

Many herbal teas are soothing to the throat, and help relieve congestion. When I was a child, I remember inhaling the steam of a vaporizer laced with Vicks Vaporub®. Many American Indian tribes have their own herbal version of this popular remedy. The wormwoods and mugworts are aromatic weeds common

COMMON PLANTS WITH REPORTED MEDICINAL USES

Common Name	Scientific Name	Ailment Treated, Use, or Action
bayberry	*Myrica cerifera*	diarrhea, fevers
bloodroot	*Sanguinaria canadensis*	pneumonia, diphtheria, emetic, laxative
blue flag	*Iris versicolor*	earaches, colds, diuretic, emetic
boneset	*Eupatorium perfoliatum*	fever, arthritis, gout, stomachaches, colds
dandelion	*Taraxacum officinale*	heartburn, chest pain, diuretic
dock	*Rumex crispus*	sores, rashes, skin infections, laxative
dogwood	*Cornus* spp.	malaria, fever, hemorrhoids, diarrhea
doveweed	*Croton texensis*	venereal disease, stomachaches
elderberry	*Sambucus canadensis*	analgesic, burns
evening primrose	*Oenothera hookeri*	swellings
fleabane	*Erigeron* spp.	insect repellent, menstrual problems, colds, headaches
gumweed	*Grindelia* spp.	snakebites, poison ivy, venereal disease, colds, colic
hepatica, liverleaf	*Hepatica acutiloba*	cross-eyes, cough, hepatitis
jack-in-the-pulpit	*Arisaema triphyllum*	laxative, tuberculosis, coughs, asthma, headache
jewelweed	*Impatiens capensis*	poison ivy, eczema, rashes
jimsonweed	*Datura stramonium*	analgesic, gout, tetanus, asthma, insect bites
milkweed	*Asclepias* spp.	asthma, syphilis, dysentery, tapeworms
mullein	*Verbascum thapsus*	dysentery, sore throat, asthma, headache, cough
mustard	*Brassica* spp.	colds, emetic, laxative
pinyon pine	*Pinus edulis*	abscesses
poplar	*Populus* spp.	snakebite, dysentery, fractures, sprains, fevers
Queen Anne's lace	*Daucus carota*	diuretic, stimulant, diabetes, worms
sagebrush, wormwood	*Artemisia* spp.	colds, stomach ailments
thistle	*Cirsium ochrocentrum*	diabetes, burns, skin sores, syphilis
white horse-nettle	*Solanum elaeagnifolium*	toothache, snakebites

throughout the United States. The Zuni, Navajo, Paiute, Shoshone, and other tribes make a tea from this plant for treating colds, sore throats, and nasal congestion. Wormwoods contain eucalyptus oil, camphor, and bornyl acetate. Over-the-counter cold remedies contain menthol, camphor, eucalyptus oil, and turpentine oil. I recently came across a bottle of Dr. Thacher's Old Fashioned Mutton Suet Salve. This once-popular remedy contained nearly identical ingredients — menthol, camphor, thymol, turpentine, and eucalyptol. All these compounds are aromatic, essential oils derived from plants. They produce a pleasant, warm sensation, and have a mild local anesthetic action on the skin and mucous membranes.

For most of us, a cold provides an acceptable excuse to take an occasional day off from work or school, when we need a brief respite from the drudgeries of our daily routines. A cold allows us to be sick, but not too sick, and to reap the benefits of being cared for by our parents, spouse, or children. Herbal teas, chicken soup, and thermometers are a part of the necessary paraphernalia that attends this universal ritual.

WHY PLANTS MAKE DRUGS

Have you ever stopped to think why plants make drugs? Plants certainly do not synthesize their chemicals for our benefit. The compounds used as drugs tend to be present in limited groups of plants, and in small concentrations. These chemicals are called secondary compounds because they have no known function in the plant's primary metabolic processes. They are not the proteins, fats, and carbohydrates that are essential and common to all living organisms. Secondary compounds have ecological roles, serving as attractants for pollinating insects, chemical adaptations to environmental stresses, and chemical defenses against microorganisms, insects, herbivores, or competing plants. The pungent compounds in onions and garlic not only make us cry, but also inhibit fungal decay and ward off hungry insects and mammals. Atropine from jimsonweed, and nicotine from tobacco are insecticidal.

ACTIVITIES
Making a plant collection

Whether gathering plants for herbal teas, food, or nature study, the first step is accurate identification. A worthwhile activity is to prepare a permanent reference collection of pressed plants. Only a few supplies are needed.

On your field excursions, take along plastic bags and a small trowel. Dig up the entire plant, including the roots. (Be sure to gather specimens only where collecting is permitted, and never take rare or protected plants.) Specimens must be kept fresh until pressed; keep them in plastic bags until you return home.

A plant press is simply made from two boards of one-fourth-inch (0.6 cm) plywood, 12 × 18 in. (30 × 45 cm), sheets of corrugated cardboard of the same dimensions, newspaper, and two straps with buckles. The basic idea is to flatten and dry the plants as quickly as possible so they will not rot or discolor. Arrange each plant neatly on a sheet of newspaper so that all its key features will be visible on the pressed specimen. The number of flower parts, and both surfaces of the leaves should be shown. Cover the plant with several sheets of newspaper and a sheet of cardboard. Continue sandwiching plant specimens between layers of newspaper and cardboard, building up a stack. When all the plants have been laid out, place the plywood on top and bottom, and strap the layers tightly together. Store the press in a warm, dry spot. The newspaper absorbs moisture from the plant, and the layers of corrugated cardboard permit sufficient ventilation to dry the plants. Depending upon the temperature and humidity, the plants will dry in one to several weeks. With thick, fleshy plants or a damp environment, you may need to open the press from time to time and exchange the damp sheets of paper and cardboard for dry ones.

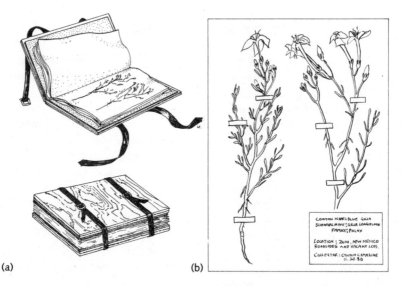

(a)   (b)

How to make a plant collection. (a) A plant press, open and closed. (b) A page from a botanical collection showing a plant mounted and labeled on an herbarium sheet.

Dried, pressed plants are mounted on sheets of white paper with cellophane tape or glue. Standard museum herbarium sheets of heavy white paper are 12 × 18 in. (30 × 45 cm). These can be obtained from supply houses, or you can use paper bought at stationery stores. Each sheet should have a label indicating the plant's common, scientific, and family names, the date collected, the locality, and the habitat. Include a brief description of the size and shape of the plant, and the arrangement, color, and characteristics of the leaves and flowers. These details will greatly improve the teaching value of your collection, and will make it much easier to identify a plant from the pressed specimen.

Your plant collection should be stored flat in a dry cabinet. Dermestid beetles and other pests will destroy your collection if given a chance. A sealed cabinet stocked with mothballs will deter the insects.

Identifying plants

There are numerous field guides to wildflowers, covering various regions of the country. Most are arranged by flower color. While this is the easiest way for a beginner to identify flowers, the serious naturalist should learn to recognize plant families and think in terms of the botanical classification of flowers. Each plant family has characteristic features, such as the numbers and arrangements of the flower parts and leaves. By learning the key features of the plant families, you will be able to identify an unknown flower more easily. To begin classifying plants, you need to learn the basic anatomy of a flower.

The anatomy of a flower

To dissect a flower, you need a hand lens, a forceps, and pins to manipulate the floral parts. A convenient tool is a dissecting needle, made from a small dowel (the diameter of a pencil) to which a needle is attached, point outward. This is easier to handle than a pin.

Dissecting a flower provides an opportunity to learn the botanical terminology necessary to read descriptions of flower anatomy with a minimum of confusion. As in any technical field, botany has its own jargon and shorthand way of describing things. Have you ever seen a 5-merous, zygomorphic, spurred flower with a syncarpelous gynoecium? Certainly; it's a violet!

Begin with a simple flower, as shown in the figure. Notice four whorls of flower parts, **sepals**, **petals**, **stamens**, and **carpels** (also called **pistils**), all attached to the **receptacle**. The sepals, the outermost whorl, enclose the other flower parts. Collectively, they constitute the **calyx**. After noticing how and where they are attached, remove them with your forceps, or spread them aside with the dissecting needle. Next are the petals, usually conspicuously colored, forming the **corolla**. The term **perianth** refers to the combination of calyx and corolla; it is frequently used to describe flowers, such as tulips, in which the petals and sepals are indistinguishable. In such cases, the individual parts are called **tepals**, since you cannot tell sepals from petals.

The stamens form a whorl inside the corolla. Each consists of a **filament** topped by an **anther**, which opens to release pollen. In the center of the flower is a cluster of carpels. Each carpel has an expanded basal portion, the **ovary**, within which is a single **ovule**, which will become a seed. There is also a stalk, called the **style**, capped by the **stigma**, which receives the pollen.

Search at the base of the petals for small depressions, the **nectaries**, which are filled with a sugary solution to attract pollinators. They are not present on all

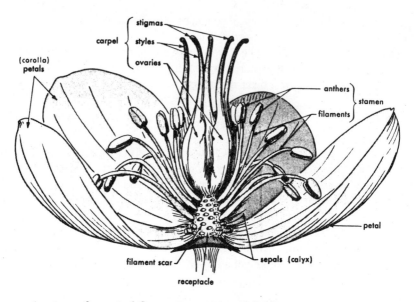

stigmas

carpel { styles

(corolla) petals

ovaries

anthers } stamen

filaments

petal

filament scar

sepals (calyx)

receptacle

Anatomy of a typical flower. From Botany, *6th Ed., T.E. Weier, C.R. Stocking, M.G. Barbour, and T.L. Rost, copyright © 1982 by John Wiley & Sons, New York, p. 270. Reprinted by permission.*

flower species. The four whorls of flower parts are attached to the receptacle, the thickened end of the flower stalk or **pedicel**.

This is the basic plan of a flower. However, through the course of evolution, numerous modifications have occurred, resulting in variations in the number of flower parts and their arrangement.

Other features that are important in the identification of plants are the arrangement of the flowers on the stem, and the shape and arrangement of the leaves. These topics are presented in the field guides and botany books listed on the next page.

A NOTE OF CAUTION:

My goal in writing this chapter was to examine the wonders of plant medicine, another aspect of nature's complexity and beauty. To the discerning reader, it should be evident that plant drugs span the range from miraculous to worthless. Too vigorous an insistence on self-treatment can be unwise, and an uncritical acceptance of unproven remedies can lead to disaster. The information presented here is not intended to be used in the treatment of illnesses.

REFERENCES AND SUGGESTIONS FOR FURTHER READING

Camazine, Scott. 1986. Zuni Indian medicine: Folklore or pharmacy, science or sorcery? In Richard P. Steiner, ed. *Folk Medicine: The Art and the Science.* American Chemical Society, Washington, D.C.

Craighead, John J.; Craighead, Frank C.; and Davis, Ray J. 1963. *A Field Guide to Rocky Mountain Wildflowers.* Houghton Mifflin, Boston.

Fieldler, Mildred. 1975. *Plant Medicine and Folklore.* Winchester Press, New York.

Harrington, H.D., and Durrell, L.W. 1957. *How to Identify Plants.* Ohio University Press, Athens, Ohio.

Lewis, Walter H., and Elvin-Lewis, Memory P.F. 1977. *Medical Botany.* John Wiley & Sons, New York.

Millspaugh, Charles F. 1892. *American Medicinal Plants, An Illustrated and Descriptive Guide to Plants Indigenous to and Naturalized in the United States which are Used in Medicine.* Vols. 1, 2. John C. Yorston, Philadelphia. Reprint, 1974. Dover, New York.

Newcomb, Lawrence. 1977. *Newcomb's Wildflower Guide.* Little, Brown, Boston.

Niehaus, Theodore F., and Ripper, Charles L. 1976. *A Field Guide to Pacific States Wildflowers.* Houghton Mifflin, Boston.

Peterson, Roger T., and McKenny, Margaret. 1968. *A Field Guide to Wildflowers of Northeastern and Northcentral North America.* Houghton Mifflin, Boston.

Vogel, Virgil J. 1970. *American Indian Medicine.* University of Oklahoma Press, Norman, Oklahoma.

Weiner, Michael A. 1972. *Earth Medicine — Earth Foods.* Collier, New York.

8

The Contrivances by which Flowers Are Pollinated by Insects

SOME MAY RECOGNIZE that this chapter's title was paraphrased from Charles Darwin's book, *On the Various Contrivances by which British and Foreign Orchids are Pollinated by Insects*. This masterpiece of natural history observation provided important evidence to bolster the theory of evolution.

Darwin argued that self-fertilization was not the best strategy for the long-term survival of a species, because the offspring produced have genes from only a single parent. Such populations of self-fertilized plants do not maintain sufficient genetic variation to cope with changing environmental conditions.

The alternative is cross-pollination, in which the pollen from one flower fertilizes a different flower of the same species. Although genetically advantageous, it poses the problem of transporting pollen from one plant to another. Orchids, like many plants, rely on insects to carry their pollen. They have evolved an incredible variety of "contrivances" to coax, coerce, and deceive their visitors into shuttling grains of pollen from flower to flower.

What fascinated Darwin and provided evidence for evolution was the realization that orchids manufacture their intricate pollination devices from common floral components. The various levers, traps, and mazes have all been fashioned from the available petals, sepals, and other standard flower parts, modified to suit a new purpose.

Although Darwin chose exotic orchids to make his point, one need merely step outside to the garden or roadside to witness interactions equally captivating. In this chapter we will examine a few of the many means by which insects pollinate flowers.

Let's begin with a brief introduction to flowers and their pollination. The two main tasks of plants are growth and reproduction. Green leaves house the photosynthetic factories where food is produced to nourish the plant. Stems and branches provide the structural framework that permits the plant to rise up into the sunlight to tap solar energy. The plant's life culminates in the production of flowers. The beauty and fragrance of flowers might tempt us to believe that they evolved for human enjoyment, but, in fact, flowers exist for only one purpose, reproduction. The goal of a flower is the production of seeds. To accomplish this task, the flower must transfer its pollen, the male contribution of the plant, to the female reproductive structures.

Flowers were not always as beautiful, alluring, and complex as they are today. When flowering plants first evolved, their pistils and stamens were simple wind-pollinated leaflike structures; for haphazard wind pollination, no attractive devices are needed. A microscopic pollen grain has to be carried by the wind and must reach a minute, distant target. It has been estimated that in order to be reasonably assured of being pollinated, every square foot of a plant's habitat must receive about 100,000 pollen grains. What a waste of pollen! No wonder a single birch catkin produces about 5-1/2 million pollen grains.

It was not until the Cretaceous period, about 100 million years ago, that both flowering plants and insects underwent startling evolutionary modifications and diversifications. The success of these organisms has been largely attributed to increasingly specialized relationships between flowers and their insect pollinators. How did this occur? One can only speculate. A possible scenario is as follows.

The earliest flowering plants were passively pollinated by the wind. The female parts, the ovules, on the surface of leaflike structures, were freely exposed to pollen carried by air currents. These reproductive structures were eventually discovered by insects, probably beetles, which fed on leaves, stems, and flowers. They found the ovules covered with a nutritious sticky sap that helped capture wind-borne pollen grains. Beetles are believed to be the first plant pollinators because they evolved prior to the bees, wasps, butterflies, and moths that are the most important pollinators today.

This initial crude pollination by crawling insects was more effective than the vagaries of wind pollination. It set the stage for the evolution of mutualistic interactions between insects and plants. The more attractive the plants were to the beetles, the more seeds they produced, provided that the hungry insects did not eat the ovules and destroy the seeds. Insect pollination became a success, and plants gradually began to evolve further adaptations to perfect this relationship with their insect visitors.

The basic strategy for a successful flower was to get a particular pollinator or group of pollinators to reliably carry pollen from one flower to another of the same species. The more distinctive cues a flower could provide for its pollinators, the more easily and reliably could an insect find that flower, making it more likely that the insect would consistently visit that flower. The shape, color, and fragrances of flowers all evolved in response to insect pollination. Indeed, if insects did not have color vision, flowers would be drab, and if insects could not detect odors, flowers would have no fragrances.

These mutually beneficial adaptations reached their zenith with the evolution of the bees, the most important pollinators today. Many specialized strategies have evolved. In some cases the flower has perfected its accommodations for a single insect visitor, so that the plant and the pollinator are dependent upon each other. This type of very exclusive arrangement is epitomized by the orchids. In one orchid the flower manufactures a fragrance that mimics the scent given off by the female wasp to attract males. To complete the ruse, the flower parts look like the female wasp. The deception is so perfect that the flowers are visited only by male wasps of one species. The amorous male futilely attempts to copulate with the flower; in so doing, he finds that two sacks of pollen, called **pollinia**, have been stuck to his back, as if in mockery. The pollinia are transferred from flower to flower as the wasp continues to search for a mate.

This is an extreme example. Most pollination devices are not this sophisticated or exclusive. Most flowers have several pollinators, avoiding the risk of relying on a single insect species.

Typically the color of the flowers matches the visual sensitivity of the insect pollinator. Bees cannot see the color red. In Europe, where there are no bird pollinators, there are no native pure red flowers, such as columbines, fuschias, and hibiscus.

At the other end of the spectrum are flowers that reflect ultraviolet. Many flowers that appear uniformly yellow to us have distinctive ultraviolet patterns at the base of their petals. These patterns act as "nectar guides," marking the route to the flower's interior in the same way that painted stripes direct pilots on an airplane landing strip.

Other enticements have evolved to attract insect pollinators. Insect-pollinated flowers generally have a more rigid structure, making it easier for the insects to land and hang onto the flower. The more primitive radial symmetry of flowers has given way to more complicated floral structures, in which certain of the petals are expanded to form landing platforms on which the bees can alight. The stamens and pistils are also more rigid, providing firmer contact with the insect's body and more reliable pollen transfer. In contrast, the wind-pollinated flowers typically have pendulous, flexible catkins, which sway in the wind to release their pollen.

Characteristic odors are another means of making a flower distinctive and more easily found. Bees and moths readily cue in on odors. Many white flowers, such as species of tobacco (*Nicotiana*), have strong fragrances emitted only after sunset, characteristics ideal for flowers pollinated by nocturnal moths.

Certain structural features of pollen make insect pollination more reliable than wind dispersal. Insect-dispersed pollen is often angular, elliptical, or ornamented with bumps, ridges, or spines. In some species it is coated with a sticky oil or gooey threads. These adaptations enable the pollen to cling to the bodies of insects so that a generous load can be transferred to the stigma. Because the carpels are fused and each contains many ovules, a single visit results in multiple fertilizations. In contrast, wind-dispersed pollen is dry, smooth, and dusty, so it may be easily carried in the breeze, pollinating ovules one by one.

Along with adaptations to attract desirable pollinators, there developed adaptations to exclude unwelcome intruders that visit the plant, help themselves to a free meal, and depart without transferring any pollen. The typical bee-pollinated flower has fused petals forming a narrow corolla tube, with special glands at the bottom that produce nectar. With their long tongues, bees can reach the sugary reward, but most other insects are excluded. It is an elegant relationship. By excluding nonpollinators, the plant does not waste its nectar on unreliable and unwelcome intruders who dine and depart without making any contribution. Sometimes insects will try to break in anyway, biting a hole at the base of the floral tube or sneaking in between the base of the petals to steal nectar. These are

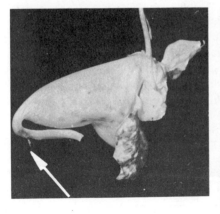
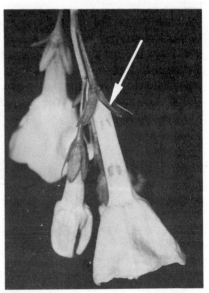

(a) (b)

Flowers that have been robbed by insects. Note the holes at the base of the corolla. (a) Jewelweed. (b) Virginia bluebells.

generally flying insects, especially certain bumblebees and carpenter bees with their powerful jaws. Their proboscises are not long enough to reach to the bottom of certain long tubular flowers, especially those designed for the long coiled proboscises of butterflies. Flowers such as pinks (*Dianthus*) attempt to keep out these unbidden guests by thickening the base of the corolla, encircling it with a leathery calyx, fortifying it with a sheath of tough bracts. The beautiful orange tiger lilies have petals that curve backward to cover and conceal the base of the flower where the nectar is stored. The balloonlike, inflated calyces of campions prevent a thief's proboscis from reaching the nectar, even if the blossom is perforated at the base.

An equally important group of thieves to contend with are wingless pilferers, such as ants, caterpillars, and slugs, that crawl up the stems. There are various safeguards to prevent their invasion: moats of water, sticky obstacles, and barricades of hairs.

The water lilies, arrowheads, water plantains, and other plants growing out of the water are safe islands that cannot be reached by insect pedestrians unable to swim. Even the teasel growing on dry land has devised a temporary moat, using pairs of opposite leaves that encircle the stem to form a little bowl that catches rainwater.

Sticky secretions are more common defenses. Glandular hairs covering the pedicel, bracts, or calyx provide an adhesive, impenetrable barrier to the passage of smaller insects attempting to reach the flowers. The descriptive names of these flowers would surely repel potential thieves, if only they could read: gumweed, night-flowering catchfly, *Rhododendron viscosum* (swamp honeysuckle), *Senecio viscosus* (stinking groundsel), *Ribes viscosissimum* (sticky currant). Heedless invaders can often be found glued to the plants.

A final obstacle consists of impenetrable jungles of bristles and hairy tufts, which may line the corolla or adorn the stamens and pistils. The tangle of hairs is easily bypassed by the proboscis of a long-tongued pollinator, but it impedes crawling insects. Examples of plants with hairy barricades are bearberries and several of the honeysuckles.

I have outlined the general strategies and adaptations of plants for interacting with insect pollinators. With this in mind, we are prepared to make our own observations in the field.

ACTIVITIES

Observing insects pollinating flowers

We are now ready for some flower watching. Bring along a magnifying glass, a small forceps, a butterfly net, a keen eye, and a bit of patience.

When you enter a patch of flowers, you may disturb the insect visitors, so sit quietly and comfortably among the blossoms and await their return. Unfortunately, just as one's bread always falls jam-side down, insects always visit a flower just out of sight, so be patient. Make a note of which insect species visit the flower. Does each enter the flower the same way? At the end of each observation session, capture a few visitors in a net and examine each carefully with your hand lens. Do the bees have pollen baskets filled with pollen? Are their hairy bodies dusted with pollen grains? Are the flies and butterflies also covered with pollen? Is the pollen only in one place, or is it scattered randomly over the body? Understand how each flower works. Dissect the flower; make note of the number of flower parts and how they are arranged. Consult a botany text for descriptions of the flower's anatomy.

Watch how the insects work the flowers. How does the insect manipulate the petals? Where does it land and hold onto the flower? Does it come into contact with the stamens and stigmas in receiving or depositing pollen? Using your forceps to enter the blossom, pretend to be that insect yourself.

Do not forget to look at the simpler types of insect-pollinated flowers, such as buttercups, anemones, thimbleweeds, poppies, geraniums, brambles, and raspberries. Their radially symmetric, cup-shaped flowers are all similar in construction, but there are differences worth observing. Some have nectaries while others just offer pollen rewards. They demonstrate different means of assuring cross-pollination. Sometimes the anthers mature first and cover the stigmas so they cannot receive pollen until later. In other cases, the stigmas are exposed and receptive before the pollen is released. There are many little details that are crucial for the proper pollination of the flower. Nearly any flower you choose to observe will offer its rewards.

The piston apparatus of birdfoot trefoil

You can find this common plant of fields and roadsides throughout much of the United States. It is a perennial, a member of the pea family, and it is sometimes grown for hay. I'm embarrassed to admit that I passed by this ubiquitous weed for years before I learned of its ingenious pollination mechanism.

Many flowers in the pea family have a rather complicated bilateral, rather than radial symmetric, structure. The five flower petals, because of their unusual morphology, are given special names. The uppermost petal, the **standard**, or **banner**, is folded back and held above the flower. Just below are two **wings** that come together and enclose two fused petals called the **keel**. The keel, as the name suggests, looks like the bottom of a boat. It forms a hollow chamber in which ten stamens are fused together at their bases to form a sheath, which surrounds the pistil with its long style.

Looking at the flower, you have to wonder how the pollen is released, for it is stored out of sight like cargo in the hold of a ship. Spread apart the wings and examine the tip of the keel. There is no sign of the pollen or anthers, only a minute opening. The mystery is revealed by dissecting the flower throughout its development. The ten anthers **dehisce** (release their pollen) in a seemingly ill-timed and pointless act even before the flower opens. But it is all part of the plan. Then five of the ten filaments elongate and become club-shaped, forming a snug plug that keeps the discharged pollen packed toward the conical tip of the keel.

The stage is now set for action. A bee, the main pollinator, comes along and straddles the wings. As she inserts her proboscis at the base of the petals in search of nectar, she presses on the wings. They are tightly interlocked with the keel.

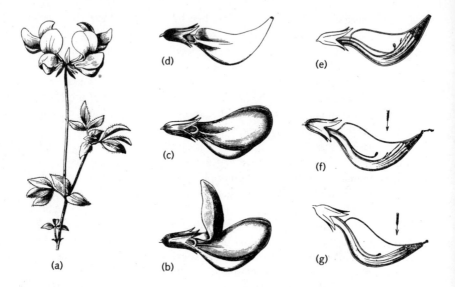

Pollen transfer by means of a piston apparatus. (a) Birdfoot trefoil. (b) Single flower, enlarged. (c) The same flower with the standard removed. (d) The same flower with both the standard and the wings removed to expose the keel. (e) A portion of the keel removed to show the stamens, half of which are club-shaped and form a plug in the conical tip of the keel. This conical cavity is filled with discharged pollen, and the flower's style and stigma. (f) When the keel is depressed, as indicated by the arrow, the thickened stamens pump pollen out of the orifice of the cavity. (g) When the keel is depressed even further, the stigma is extruded and can receive pollen carried on the underside of a visiting insect.

Pressure on the wing is transmitted to the keel and both move simultaneously. This movement pumps the keel up and down. The column of stamens acts like a piston inside a pump, or like a hypodermic syringe, except that the plunger (the thickened stamens) remains stationary, and the barrel (the keel) is moved. A pasty ribbon of pollen is extruded through the pore at the tip of the keel. This ribbon of pollen adheres to the abdomen of the bee, ready to be carried to the next flower. When the bee departs, the keel slides back into its original position. After about eight pumps, all the pollen has been extruded. Now the keel is more easily depressed, causing the stigma tip to emerge and receive pollen from any arriving bee.

Lupines and several other members of the pea family use the same unlikely, yet highly effective, pollination contraption.

Now that we are familiar with the structure of a pea flower, we should look at other members of the same family, alfalfa, broom, or milk-vetch. These flowers have explosive pollination mechanisms that work like a mousetrap. When the mechanism is triggered, a bee is slapped so soundly that the insect often flies away in fright.

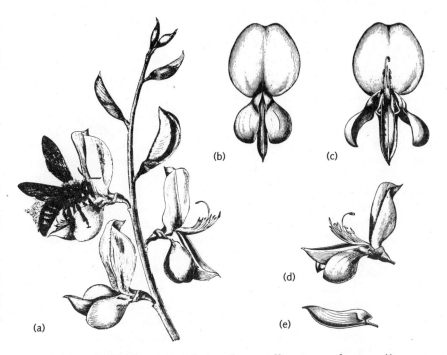

*Transfer of pollen by means of an explosive pollination mechanism. (a)
Broom inflorescence. In the lowest flower, the keel is still closed. The next
flower above has had its keel depressed, and the stamens have sprung
up. The third flower is being visited by a carpenter bee and is ejecting its
pollen onto the undersurface of the insect's body. (b) Enlarged view of an
unsprung flower. (c) Same flower with the keel open; the stamens and
style previously concealed there have sprung up. (d) Side view of the
sprung flower. (e) One of the two petals of the keel, seen from within,
showing a knob at the base of the petal that holds the stamens in place
under tension.*

The structural difference between the flowers of birdfoot trefoil and alfalfa is
that the petals making up the keel of alfalfa are not fused along their upper edge as
are the trefoil's. The keel still encloses the column of stamens, but in this case it is
held under tension by a little knob that protrudes into the chamber of the keel.
When a bee visits the flower, she dislodges the stamen column, letting it snap
upward and strike the belly of the bee, dusting her with pollen. The stigma pops up
as well, receiving any pollen that the bee may have brought from another flower.
The process takes place so fast that you will have to watch it over and over again to
realize what happens. You do not have to wait for a bee each time. The flowers are
easily tripped by wiggling a toothpick in the base of the petals, as if you were a bee
searching for nectar. Once triggered, the stamens and pistil of these exploding
flowers have served their purpose and do not return to the keel.

Jewelweed and the nectar thieves

The best laid schemes o' mice and men
Gang aft a-gley. (Robert Burns)

The careful evolutionary plans of flowers are often foiled. Many flowers fail in their attempts to keep out unwanted intruders.

Visit a patch of jewelweed in August. The flowers are a marvel of engineering design. The gorgeous blossom of fused petals and sepals hangs pendulously from a long narrow pedicel, which discourages crawling insects from attempting a passage. The recurved lips of the flower also hinder pedestrian visitors. The nectar is tucked away at the tip of a narrow tubular spur. The opening of the flower has a landing platform that perfectly accommodates bumble bees, and its dimensions just admit the bee's head. Its tongue is just long enough to reach into the spur for the nectar. The anthers are cleverly designed as a fused cap that surmounts and conceals the stigma. They mature first and rub against the back of any bee that enters the flower. A day later, the wilted anther cap falls off, exposing the receptive stigma. Bees, coated with pollen, arrive from other flowers and readily deposit grains upon the stigma.

It is an ideal contrivance, until unscrupulous short-tongued bumble bees get involved. They are not satisfied to visit flowers that suit their own proportions. Try as they may to reach the nectar spur through the front door, they are unsuccessful. No matter. The rewards are great, the obstacles trivial. They simply go around in back of the flower and bite a hole in the tip of the spur, draining the nectar in moments. Once the back door is open, everyone in the neighborhood takes advantage of the situation. Honey bees, which previously were forced to crawl deeply into the blossom to compensate for their own short tongues, now fly around back, hang onto the spur, and steal a quick meal. For some reason, honey bees do not, or perhaps cannot, pierce the spur themselves.

There is havoc in the jewelweed patch. At times nearly every blossom is pillaged. Nonetheless, the flowers must be adequately pollinated by insects making legitimate visits. Returning weeks later, you will find that hundreds of explosive capsules have matured, discharging their seeds at the slightest touch. This delightful seed-dispersal mechanism gives the jewelweed its other common name, touch-me-not.

Wander through your garden and fields. You will be surprised to find how many flowers have been perforated by the strong jaws of the bumble bees and carpenter bees. Most other insects cannot bite through the petals themselves, but quickly take advantage of the larger bees' work. Virginia bluebell, bleeding heart, andromeda, comfrey, daffodil, and columbine are all subject to nectar thievery. Other flowers have safeguards against pilferers.

These are just glimpses at the variety of pollination mechanisms available for study on any summer's day. Volumes have been written on this popular topic. Spend time out in the fields observing, and refer to some of the references for further details. Some flowers that you should not miss are sage, lady's slipper, orchis, the louseworts, Dutchman's breeches, and the violets. Each is a pleasure and a challenge to understand.

REFERENCES AND SUGGESTIONS FOR FURTHER READING

Faegri, K., and van der Pijl, L. 1979. *The Principles of Pollination Ecology*. Pergamon, New York.

Gould, S.J. 1982. *The Panda's Thumb*. Norton, New York.

McGregor, S.E. 1976. *Insect Pollination of Cultivated Crop Plants*. Agricultural Research Service, U.S. Department of Agriculture, Washington, D.C.

Proctor, M., and Yeo, P. 1972. *The Pollination of Flowers*. Taplinger, New York.

Raven, P.H., and Curtis, H. 1970. *The Biology of Plants*. Worth, New York.

9

The Milkweed Community

EACH SUMMER milkweed makes a grand display near my home, filling abandoned fields and roadsides with dense clusters of pinkish-purple flowers. Looking out over a large field, one sees many individual patches containing dozens of milkweed plants. This pattern of growth occurs because the perennial milkweed propagates itself by means of an underground root called a **rhizome**. Extending in all directions, the rhizome sends up a multitude of flowering stalks. Thus, each colony of milkweed in a field may actually be a single clone of plants growing from a common root system.

Milkweeds are found from the Southwest deserts to the Rockies and across eastern portions of North America. Fields, meadows, waste areas, and roadsides are their homes. The milkweed genus *Asclepias* comprises nearly 100 species, mostly natives of the New World. The name *Asclepias* comes from Asklepios, the Greek god of medicine, so it should be no surprise that milkweeds have been used for a multitude of ailments, such as asthma, dysentery, heart disease, stomachaches, snakebites, ringworm, warts, tapeworms, and even syphilis. Its popularity as a medicine may be related to the copious supply of bitter, milky latex produced in a special system of tubes that branch throughout the plant. The latex contains substances called **cardiac glycosides**, which, in small doses, cause nausea and vomiting, but in larger doses act as heart poisons to vertebrates. For the plant, the latex serves as a defense, oozing profusely from the leaves when they are damaged. On exposure to air it quickly dries and becomes sticky, gumming up the mandibles of insects. Vertebrate herbivores are repelled by the latex's toxicity.

However, as is always the case in nature, for every defense, there exists a counterdefense. Very few insects can tolerate the milkweeds, but several are specialized feeders on the plant, eating nothing else. These specialists have evolved a means of coping with the plant toxin. They don't deactivate it, but they incorporate it into their blood so that it permeates every portion of their body, making them distasteful to their predators. These insects are now in a splendid position. They have very little competition from other insects because the food they eat is poisonous, and with every bite they take, they are building up a powerful defense against their enemies. To top off their clever defensive strategy, these toxic insects advertise their unpalatability by flaunting a distinctive color pattern that predators easily learn. The bright stripes of the monarch caterpillar, the orange and black pattern of the adult butterfly, and the red and black pattern of the milkweed beetle are all warning colorations. A young blue jay will heedlessly eat a monarch butterfly if it has never tried one before. The unfortunate bird soon begins to vomit, but is much wiser for the experience. In the future the blue jay will avoid monarchs, or any butterfly that looks like one. The viceroy butterfly, which is not poisonous, has evolved a coloration that closely mimics the monarch's. Although the viceroy is quite palatable, it is avoided by predators because of its resemblance to the toxic monarch.

With all this talk of poisons, one might expect that man has no use for this weed. However, it is one of our more palatable wild foods. Simply boiling the young stalks, flower buds, or firm young pods in several changes of water dispels the bitter, toxic principles. The unopened flower buds can be eaten like broccoli; the young shoots make a tolerable substitute for asparagus; and the immature pods can be prepared like okra. After the plant matures, it has other non-nutritional uses. As material for their nests, goldfinches gather the silky seed hairs, and orioles strip fibers from the stalks. The early pioneers gathered the silk as a stuffing for pillows and mattresses.

MILKWEED POLLINATION

What fascinates me most about milkweed is its unusual pollination mechanism, more reminiscent of exotic tropical plants than the mundane flowers of the temperate United States. Milkweeds have a remarkable relationship with a diversity of bees, moths, and butterflies, which eagerly seek out the flowers in search of sweet nectar.

Each individual flower is an exquisite engineering marvel designed to assure pollination. Most of the species have attractive flowers, colored either white or deep pastel shades of pink, red, purple, or orange. As the flower matures, its five petals swing back to expose a structure called the **corona**, which, as the name suggests, resembles a crown. This corona consists of five little cups, each called a **hood**, filled with a sugary nectar. As an insect visits a plant to reap a sweet reward, it wanders eagerly over the flower clusters and dips its tongue deeply into one or another of the five hoods. In its haste, a slender leg will often slip into a slit in the stigma. The unsuspecting insect then lifts its foot in an effort to extricate itself, only to find that the slit narrows at the top, catching the insect's leg. When the insect makes a determined effort to yank its foot free, it finds that the leg is now tightly wedged to a small clip, called a **corpusculum**, located directly above the slit. The corpusculum is hard and looks like a miniature coffee bean. It also has a narrowing slit. Further tugging only serves to permanently wedge this clip onto the tip of the insect's leg. When the startled insect attempts to fly away, the clip is dislodged from its chamber and the insect is forced to carry it off. This, however, is only the beginning of the adventure.

In most flowers, the pollen is borne on the tip of slender stalklike stamens, the male portion of the flower. The pollen is powdery and is shed in single grains. The female part of the flower is usually an elongated pistil, consisting of the ovary at the base and a long style capped by a sticky stigma. When a grain of pollen lands on the stigma, it grows downward to the ovary and fertilizes the ovules within.

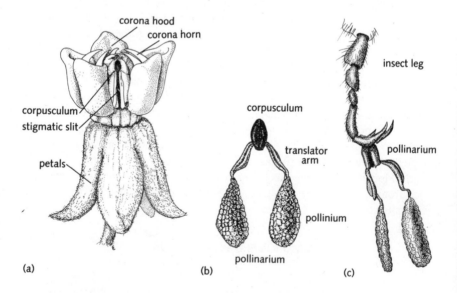

The pollination mechanism of milkweed. (a) Enlarged view of the flower showing the hoods of the corona, the clip of the pollinarium, and the slit of the stigma. (b) A pollinarium consists of a clip, two handles called translator arms, and two sacks of pollen, called pollinia. (c) An insect leg with an attached pollinarium.

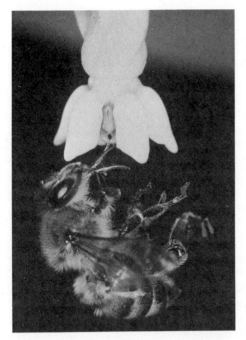

A honey bee with its proboscis caught on the clip of a pollinarium. Unable to escape, this bee perished.

Things are not so simple with the milkweed. The corpusculum, tightly clamped to the insect's leg, is part of a wishbone-shaped structure called a **pollinarium**. The entire pollinarium consists of the clip, two handles called **translator arms**, and two minute sacks of pollen called **pollinia**. These pollinia are unusual structures among plants. Many grains of pollen are packaged together in a waxy coating. Within minutes after an insect yanks a pollinarium from a flower, the translator arms twist, rotating the pollinia by 90 degrees so that they are perfectly oriented for insertion into the lower end of the stigmatic chamber of the next flower the insect visits. The hapless insects with pollinia attached to their legs act as involuntary insect "pony express" riders, carrying "saddlebags" of pollen from plant to plant.

This pollination system is remarkably efficient and mutually beneficial to the plant and the pollinator. Flying insects visit the fragrant milkweeds in great numbers and receive a meal of nectar as inducement for their services as pollen couriers. Without this amazing device and the insect couriers, no milkweeds would be fertilized. Among milkweeds, self-pollinated flowers are rarely fertile. When a flower receives a pollinium from a flower on the same plant, the pods that begin to form usually abort early in development. Since flowers in the same patch are genetically identical clones, flowers fertilized from other members of the patch suffer the same aborted fate. Thus, milkweeds rely completely upon insects that travel from patch to patch, carrying pollinaria from unrelated plants.

There is no need to travel to lush tropical rain forests to study exotic pollination mechanisms. The lowly milkweed, denizen of city lots, roadsides, and abandoned fields, offers an exciting reward for observant nature watchers throughout North America.

ACTIVITIES

Experimenting with the pollination mechanism of milkweeds

I never understood how this bizarre pollination mechanism worked until I carried a few pollinia from flower to flower myself. So, pretend to be a bee, and let a few pollinaria hitch a ride from flower to flower. Start by taking a small watercolor paintbrush or even a single hair from your head. With a magnifying glass select a newly opened milkweed flower that still has its pollinarium in place. You can tell by looking for the dark clip, the corpusculum, at the top of the stigma. Slide the paintbrush into the stigmatic slit of the flower with an upward motion. If you do it just right, you should easily be able to snag the corpusculum and extricate the pair of pollinia from their chamber. The corpusculum will be firmly clasped onto one of the hairs. See if you can observe how the translator arms twist, rotating the pollinia into position. Now "fly" off to another flower with your entrapped saddlebags of pollen, and try to slide the pollinia into the stigmatic slit of the flower. One of the translator arms will snap, leaving a pollinium in the stigmatic chamber. If you continue to gently slide the remaining piece of the pollinarium out of the slit, the broken translator arm will often catch the corpusculum of the resident pollinarium that lies hidden in the chamber. Once you have snagged this pollinarium, you can gently lift it out of the flower. You will now have the beginning of a chain of pollinaria consisting of two clips and three pollinia. Continuing the process in this manner, long strings of pollinaria are built up. At this time of year, I often see honey bees returning to their hive adorned with long chains of pollinaria attached to their feet and proboscises.

Next, see whether you can successfully pollinate a milkweed by transferring a few pollinia from one patch of newly opened flowers to those of a different clone. Cover the flowers with a fine-meshed mosquito-net bag to keep out any other insects. This way you will know that all the flowers were hand-fertilized. Wait a few weeks to see how many milkweed pods form.

Observing and collecting milkweed visitors

Milkweeds harbor many creatures, not only pollinators, but also visitors seeking nectar, predators on the prowl, scavengers, parasites, and others looking for refuge from the rain. This community is an ideal microcosm for the study of the interactions among organisms.

After observing the activities of the animals on milkweeds, try diagramming the relationships among the inhabitants, with arrows connecting organisms that affect one another. The resulting tangle of lines is called a **food web**. Its starting point, and source of energy, is the sun. Plants manufacture their own food from sunlight and raw materials, such as carbon dioxide, water, and soil nutrients. Plants are therefore referred to as **autotrophs**, meaning self-nourishers. In contrast are the **heterotrophs**, animals that obtain their food by eating plants or other animals. In the milkweed food web, these plants fuel the system. Then herbivores eat the milkweed leaves and seeds, the predators eat the herbivores, parasites attack both the predators and the herbivores, and the scavengers take advantage of the left-overs. The result is the interconnected web of interactions linking all the organisms. Try collecting as many different milkweed visitors as you can find. Be sure to look at different times throughout the day and during the entire milkweed season. You should have little problem finding at least 20 different species. Identify each visitor, and note its activity on the plant. Make a display that shows the web of relationships among the species. Mount one of each visitor on a large board with a pressed milkweed plant in the center. Use arrows to show whether the visitor eats the leaves, gathers nectar, or preys upon other visitors.

Among the pollinators there are the honey bees and many species of bumble bees. These strong fliers readily detach pollinaria from the flowers, transporting them on their mouthparts as well as on their legs. Other potential pollinators are

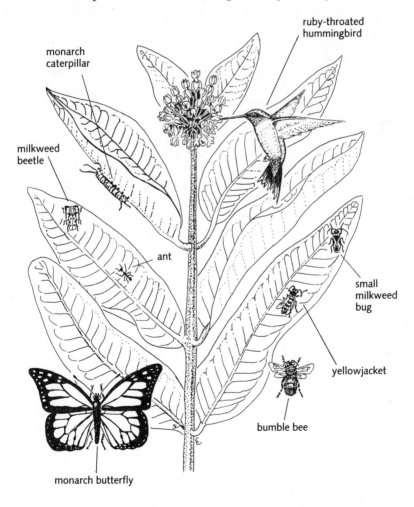

A few common visitors to milkweed.

wasps and butterflies. During the daytime, monarchs, skippers, swallowtails, ctenucha moths, hawkmoths, and hairstreaks are common. Capture some of the insect pollinators and examine them with a magnifying glass or stereomicroscope. You will see that the clips and their tiny translator arms remain firmly attached to the insect. At times, the insects are unable to yank the pollinaria free, so one commonly finds bees and moths dangling from the milkweed blossoms exhausted, sometimes dead in their vain attempts to extricate themselves.

Be sure to include a nighttime visit to a patch of milkweed, armed with a small headlamp or flashlight covered with red cellophane. (Insects don't see red light, and thus won't be disturbed by your nighttime observations.) Studies have shown that as many as 25 percent of the flowers are pollinated at night by moths. The drab brown noctuids are most common.

Other visitors come to gather nectar but don't act as pollinators. They range from minute flies and mosquitoes to the ruby-throated hummingbird. Ants steal nectar, depleting the flowers of their sugary rewards.

Several milkweed inhabitants rely on the plant as their only food source. These are the brightly colored insects that incorporate the milkweed toxins into their body fluids. Early in the season, the milkweed tiger moth caterpillars rapidly consume the leaves. The tiger moth larvae feed as a group of up to 20 caterpillars. They stay on the underside of a leaf and rapidly skeletonize it, eating the soft portions of the leaf and leaving a meshwork of veins.

The monarch caterpillars, especially the older stages, are bolder feeders, often starting at the leaf tip and chewing it all the way down to the base. If you watch carefully from start to finish, however, you will observe a very curious behavior. When the caterpillar first arrives at a leaf, it often gnaws its way partially through the large central vein. The leaf will droop and ooze its milky latex. Only then will the caterpillar crawl out to the end of the leaf and begin to feed. This behavior is a counterdefense against the latex in the plant. The caterpillar severs the pipeline that carries the sticky latex before it begins to feed on the end of the leaf. Even though the caterpillar consumes the toxic leaves, it apparently prefers not to have a constant flow of sticky latex to contend with. Later in the season, the milkweed beetle arrives and uses a very similar ploy. It crawls along the leaf underside and makes a series of bites through the leaf veins. Then it moves to the leaf edge and begins its meal. A careful examination of a leaf allows you to determine who has been there.

Other herbivores are specialized in their feeding habits. The milkweed bugs eat the seeds in the late fall. Aphids insert their proboscises into the plant's vessels to obtain plant juices. Toward the end of the season, with the onset of colder weather, slugs often nibble on the leaves in the evenings.

Some visitors have no interest in nectar, but come to prey on those who do. The predatory crab spider, *Misumena vatia,* with its cryptic coloration, hides among the flowers, camouflaged as a milkweed blossom. It waits patiently, with its outstretched front legs ready to grab an insect meal. The constant insect activity provides ample food for the spider. One study showed that the female spider can increase its weight tenfold in two weeks. Two-thirds of this weight goes into producing an egg mass, which is deposited in a silken sac on the underside of a leaf. She guards the clutch of eggs until they hatch.

To add another dimension to the milkweed community food chain, there are predators of the predators, and also parasites. The spider wasps capture spiders and paralyze them with their sting. The spiders are then carried off to the wasp's nest. An egg is laid on the victim and when the wasp larva hatches, it consumes the living but immobile spider. Spiders are also vulnerable before they are born. Wasps, such as the ichneumons, parasitize the spider eggs, and tachinid flies parasitize monarch caterpillars.

Finally there are the harvestmen or daddy longlegs, close relatives to the spiders. Spiders have two distinct body parts. The **cephalothorax** is the combined head and thorax, to which are attached the jaws and the legs; the other body segment is the abdomen. The harvestmen have a single round body part consisting of the head,

SOME COMMON MILKWEED VISITORS AND THEIR ACTIVITIES AT THE PLANT

Name	Activity
monarch caterpillar	leaf-eater
milkweed tiger caterpillar	" "
milkweed beetle	" "
slug	" "
aphids	plant sap-feeder
large milkweed bug	seed-eater
small milkweed bug	" "
monarch butterfly	nectar-gatherer, pollinator
bumble bee	" " "
cuckoo bumble bee	" " "
yellowjacket	" " "
skipper	" " "
Ctenucha moth	" " "
hawkmoth	" " "
hairstreak butterfly	" " "
geometrid moth	" " "
noctuid moth	" " "
ant	nectar-gatherer
ruby-throated hummingbird	" "
crab spider	predator
phymatid bug	"
mud dauber	parasite of spiders
spider wasp	" " "
tachinid fly	parasite of monarch larvae
harvestman, daddy-long-legs	scavenger

thorax, and abdomen all joined together. They are the clean-up crew of the milkweed, gathering the carcasses of insects discarded by other predators. They also occasionally consume nectar and will prey on small insects and spiders if they can capture them. They are most active at night.

REFERENCES AND SUGGESTIONS FOR FURTHER READING

Morse, D.H. July 1985. Milkweeds and their visitors. *Scientific American* 253: 112–119.

Peterson, L. 1978. *A Field Guide to Edible Wild Plants.* Houghton Mifflin, Boston.

Stokes, D., and Stokes, L. 1985. *A Guide to Enjoying Wildflowers.* Little, Brown, Boston.

10

Life in the Arid Desert

THE DRY, SUN-DRENCHED DESERT is often depicted as most inhospitable, littered with the bleached skeletons of animals who have succumbed to its perils. However, regardless of the environment, all living organisms must cope with the same familiar set of problems: feeding, reproduction, defense from predators, and protection from environmental extremes. In diverse habitats, one or another of these problems may take priority. The desert offers intense sunlight, excessive heat, low humidity, desiccating winds, and a dearth of rainfall. To survive the rigors of this environment, organisms have become adept physicists, chemists, and engineers, evolving special adaptations for gaining and conserving water, and for preventing overheating.

On this excursion through the Southwest deserts, we will explore some general ideas concerning adaptation and learn how organisms manage in this formidable habitat. We will also collect a few specimens to examine more closely in our home laboratories. From San Diego to San Antonio, or from Moab to Tucson, the Southwest is generally hot and dry, and the inhabitants have evolved similar solutions to the problems of survival.

PHYSIOLOGY, MORPHOLOGY, AND BEHAVIOR: TRICKS OF THE TRADE

Adaptations fit into three major categories: physiological mechanisms, morphological specializations, and behavioral ploys. These devices are employed in concert, as a diverse armamentarium evolved to cope with the problems of survival. Surprisingly, we will discover that desert animals and plants have often arrived at nearly identical solutions. This makes sense, since many of the biological constraints of living organisms are the same for active animals as for immobile plants rooted to the ground.

There are only a certain number of ways to accomplish a task. For example, to fly, an organism needs a structure with a large surface area—a wing. This applies to birds, butterflies, and bats, and also to the fruits of maple, basswood, and tulip trees. The same physical laws pertain.

With these ideas in mind, we set out into the desert!

A SCARCITY OF WATER: HOW TO MINIMIZE LOSSES

A major problem in the desert is water balance—preventing water losses and promoting gains. Animals lose water by evaporation from the body surface, by the exhalation of moist air, and by the elimination of wet waste materials. To some extent these losses can be controlled.

Evaporation from the body surface

The darkling beetles, in the tenebrionid family, are common insects of the Southwest. The genus *Eleodes* alone has over 100 species. They are usually brown or

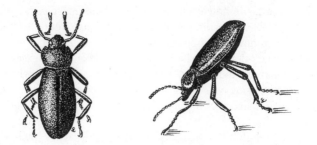

The darkling beetle, Eleodes, *a common desert inhabitant. Top view (left) and defensive "headstand" posture (right).*

black, up to about and inch and a half (3.5 cm) in length, with smooth, more or less shiny bodies. They hide under loose bark and debris by day, and wander about eating plant matter in the cooler early morning or late evening. When disturbed, they often exhibit the curious habit of standing on their heads, emitting a foul-smelling dark liquid from the tip of the abdomen.

Unlike most beetles, many of these desert tenebrionids are wingless. The hard outer wing covers, the **elytra**, are fused together, and they partially wrap around the underside of the abdomen. They form an impermeable jacket for the beetle, minimizing water loss. Furthermore, the insect's exoskeleton is admirably de-signed to keep water in, comprising multiple layers of waterproof waxes, **lipids** (fatty substances), proteins, and **chitin** (the hard cuticle that makes up most of the insect's armor).

The surface of desert plants exhibits similar structural features: resinous coat-ings and thick layers of wax and lipids. The wax coating of the stems of Candelilla (*Euphorbia antisyphylitica*), found in northern Mexico and southwestern Texas, is collected commercially for use in sealing wax, electrical insulators, and waterproof boxes.

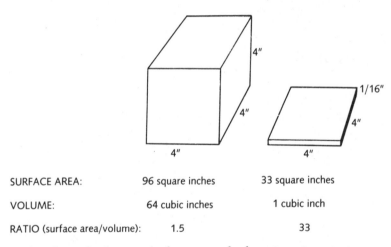

SURFACE AREA:	96 square inches	33 square inches
VOLUME:	64 cubic inches	1 cubic inch
RATIO (surface area/volume):	1.5	33

The relationship between surface area and volume is an important biological concept. Thin objects, such as leaves (here depicted as a flat square plate), have a much greater ratio of surface area to volume than thicker objects, such as a barrel cactus (depicted as a cube).

Plants utilize additional mechanisms to prevent excessive evaporative losses. Water within the whole volume of a plant evaporates from its surfaces. Thus, water losses can be kept to a minimum by reducing the available surface area of the plant in relation to its volume. A sphere has the smallest possible surface area in relation to the volume that it encloses. Consider a flat leaf and a squat round cactus as two extremes in shape. The leaf, depicted for simplicity as a thin square plate, has broad upper and lower surfaces but encloses relatively little volume. The cactus, depicted as a cube of the same dimensions, has a greater surface area because of its greater thickness, but it also encloses a much larger volume. The ratio between the surface area and the volume is much greater for thin leaves than for squat leafless stems. This simple morphological ploy packages a greater plant volume within a smaller surface covering. It explains the robust, spherical, or cylindrical shapes of cacti, as well as their absence of leaves. Other desert plants make compromises. They grow leaves, but roll them up or fold them periodically to prevent water loss. In times of severe drought, the leaves are shed entirely, and the green chlorophyll-laden stems are utilized for photosynthesis.

Cacti are well adapted for life in the arid desert. The spherical or cylindrical shape of the barrel cactus (left) has a low surface area-to-volume ratio, minimizing water loss. The old man cactus (right) is covered with a layer of dense hairs, a means of conserving water in the face of desiccating winds.

Another morphological specialization of the plant surface is a covering layer of dense hairs that provides a barrier to the evaporation of water in dry winds. Many desert cacti, such as the old man cactus in the genus *Cephalocereus*, use this adaptation. It may seem counterintuitive to bundle up in a thick coat in the desert, but it prevents excessive water loss. Bedouins roaming the desert cover themselves with ample loose-fitting clothing for the same reason. Stranded in the desert, a man may lose over 15 pounds (7 kg) of water in a day.

Respiratory losses

Insects do not have lungs, nor do they breathe through their mouths. Special openings called **spiracles** are located along both sides of the body, connecting to thin tubes called **tracheae**, which branch repeatedly and end in an enormous number of the very finest of tubes, called **tracheoles**. A silkworm may have 1,500,000. These carry oxygen throughout the body, and expel carbon dioxide, saturated with water. This helps to explain the desert beetle's curious fused elytra. Wrapping around the body, they cover the spiracles and inhibit water loss. Moist air from inside the insect's body must pass through the spiracles, then through the entire cavity beneath the fused elytra, before reaching a small aperture at the tip of the abdomen. This slows evaporation by creating a zone of humid air around the body. The simple morphological strategy of covering the spiracles and making a humid subelytral cavity helps conserve precious water.

Other desert arthropods don't employ a device as elegant as a humid subelytral cavity. However, their spiracles tend to be smaller or sunken in the surface of their bodies. The same mechanisms are used by plants. The surface of a leaf is riddled with openings, called **stomata**. They permit gas exchange, but are a potential source of water loss. A single square inch (6.45 square cm) of leaf surface may contain over 300,000 of these pores. So numerous are these stomata that a single corn plant may lose more than a gallon (3.8 liters) of water a day. To prevent water loss, desert plants often "bury" their stomata in depressions on the leaf surface, a means of sequestering moist air from drying winds.

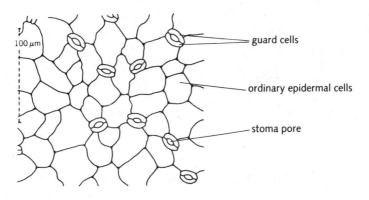

The leaf epidermis showing stomata. Each stoma consists of two guard cells plus a pore.

The stomata are normally opened during the daylight hours when photosynthesis occurs. Another clever adaptation is to close the stomatal pores at times when water loss is great. The cacti store large amounts of water when it is available, and conserve it for times of drought. Their stomata are kept closed during the hot daylight hours, and open only at night when it is cooler and the relative humidity is greater. Carbon dioxide is taken in at night, although it cannot be utilized in the darkess. It is stored in a chemically combined form until the following day, when it is converted back to carbon dioxide for use in photosynthesis, a novel physiological mechanism.

Conserving excretory losses

Desert animals are also thrifty in their elimination of wet waste materials. Birds and insects excrete nitrogen as crystallized uric acid, rather than as urea dissolved in water. In addition, the urine of desert mammals is more concentrated than that of their nondesert relatives, and their feces are dry. Kangaroo rats are so efficient in their water balance that they can survive without ever drinking. They can produce a urine with a 7 percent salt concentration, twice that of seawater. A man stranded at sea hastens his death by drinking seawater because his kidneys can only concentrate urine to 2.2 percent; water is wasted in removing the excess salt from his body. A kangaroo rat forced to drink seawater is unharmed.

The cactus wren, a common inhabitant of the Southwest deserts, even utilizes the water in the feces of its young. In hot weather, the fecal sacs are left in the nest cavity allowing their moisture to evaporate, both cooling the nest and increasing the humidity therein, and reducing respiratory water loss. Adult roadrunners actually eat the fecal sacs of their young! Presumably their adult kidneys have greater concentrating powers than do their offspring's, allowing them to extract a bit of precious desert water. A simple behavioral ploy is used in conjunction with a physiological mechanism.

Sweating is another avenue of water loss. When an animal overheats, it is cooled by the evaporation of sweat. Kangaroo rats do not sweat. They are nocturnal, avoiding the desert heat by foraging at night. Camels reduce sweat losses by tolerating elevated body temperatures. They let their temperature rise to almost 106° F (41° C) before sweating. Although most animals die of dehydration if they lose as much as 20 percent of their body water, a camel tolerates a 40 percent loss without becoming ill, and when it comes time to replenish its losses, it can drink one-third of its body weight in ten minutes!

HOW TO MAXIMIZE WATER GAIN

No adaptation is perfect. Compromises must always be made. In order to exchange gases to breathe, organisms inevitably lose some water vapor. These losses must be offset by comparable gains. Successful strategies to maximize gains include absorption of water from the soil, atmospheric uptake of water, and the production of metabolic water.

Absorption from the soil

Plants obtain nearly all their water from the ground, using two main strategies in the spatial distribution of their roots. Species such as salt cedar and mesquite are guaranteed a continuous water supply by a penetrating taproot, commonly 30 to 50 feet (10 to 15 m) long. When the Suez Canal was built, salt cedar roots were found at a depth of almost 100 feet (30 m). Cacti and many annuals use a different strategy, growing an extensive network of shallow roots close to the soil surface that quickly absorb water from brief sporadic rainfalls and surface runoff.

Atmospheric uptake of water

In some desert areas of the world, such as the Atacama Desert of northern Chile, it may not rain for years. Here, desert plants cannot find any water in the soil.

However, the proximity to the sea allows fog to form when the moist sea air cools. In this region, drops of water can be found at dawn, adhering to the vegetation. This is an important water source for these plants. Even more unusual is the behavior of certain tenebrionid beetles in the Namib Desert of Africa. These beetles use a remarkable strategy to extract minute amounts of moisture from the air. They walk along the desert sands constructing shallow trenches three feet (0.9 m) or more in length, perpendicular to fog-laden winds. These trenches catch moisture in the fog. As the beetles return along the trenches they made, they take up the precious water.

Metabolic production of water

When food is broken down, two of the by-products are carbon dioxide and water. For some animals, such as the kangaroo rat and certain insects that consume only dry foods, this metabolism may be their only source of water. They can survive without ever drinking water.

WHEN THE GOING GETS (TOO) TOUGH

Before leaving the topic of water balance, there is one additional adaptation to mention. In some respects, one might consider it a "nonadaptation." Some organisms simply are not well-adapted for life in the desiccated environment of the desert. Certain primitive plants, such as mosses and lichens, and amphibians, such as frogs and toads, have limited ability to regulate water losses. Unlike moisture held within the relatively impermeable epidermis of desert plants and insects, water evaporates freely through the skin of frogs. Such organisms simply cannot cope. The mosses and lichens shrivel and dry up during times of drought, appearing lifeless. But with the rains, their cells take in water and they return to a functioning state as long as they remain moist.

With the heat and lack of water, the spadefoot toad undergoes a resting state akin to hibernation, called **estivation**. The toad may remain in its burrow for more than three months during times of drought. To survive in its underground tomb, it utilizes a simple morphological device, a cocoon, formed from a layer of dried, shed skin that surrounds the animal and reduces water loss.

When the rains come, these amphibians emerge in great numbers. I witnessed the emergence of many thousands of spadefoot toads in Zuni, New Mexico, when the summer rains filled a large parched reservoir. Within 48 hours, a shallow lake appeared, cluttered so thickly with mating, chorusing frogs that a single scoop with a net captured a dozen or more. The eggs soon hatched, filling the water with tadpoles.

It has been reported in the desert areas of western Australia that the number of frogs emerging after rains has been so great as to interfere with the passage of trains; they are unable to maintain traction on the rails made slippery with thousands of crushed frog bodies. Such is the "bust or boom" existence of many organisms.

In today's hectic, time-conscious society, we admire the hard-driving individual who ever forges onward through adversity. "When the going gets tough, the tough get going." But Nature's organisms are on a different schedule. Perhaps there is something to be learned from the amphibians who wait patiently, protected deep within the soil, for their day in the rain. They deal with adversity by letting it pass them by. When the proper time comes, they seize the moment, explosively mating and reproducing before the drying sun again forces them to retreat below ground to await the next cycle.

RETURNING HOME

We have been lucky during our long day in the desert. Walking along in the hot desert sun, sweating profusely to keep cool, we have been able to drink copiously to replenish our water loses. We can afford to be wasteful with our water, but the other desert inhabitants are not so fortunate. Evaporative cooling is a wonderful way to dissipate heat, but it works contrary to the need to conserve precious body water. For everything you get, you must give up something.

Returning home, we can reflect upon what we've seen. Utilizing principles of physics, chemistry, and engineering, organisms devise physiological, morphological, and behavioral strategies to cope with the world around them. The solutions to their problems of survival are a series of adaptations, evolved over millions of years.

The desert environment presents a unique set of conditions with which the animal must cope as it feeds, reproduces, and defends itself. From the frigid Arctic to the scorching desert, and from the deepest ocean to the tallest habitable mountain peak, each environment presents its own special challenges. The myriad adaptations to the intricacies of each environment result in the diversity of life, a source of endless wonder for the observant naturalist.

ACTIVITIES

Dissecting an insect

You can do this dissection with any large insect. The bigger the insect you can find, the easier it will be to see the anatomy. If possible, try to find one of the black desert darkling beetles in order to appreciate their unusual adaptations for desert life. The accompanying illustrations show the anatomy of a honey bee, which is similar to that of most insects.

Take the insect and place it in a killing jar or freeze it overnight. With a 10x magnifying glass or a stereomicroscope, examine the sides of its abdomen, looking for tiny openings, spiracles, through which the insect breathes. If you look at a grasshopper or a cricket, for example, you will find a series of holes on both sides

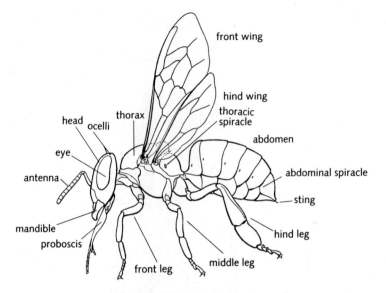

The basic external anatomy of an insect, a honey bee.

of the thorax and abdomen. However, on the desert darkling beetle, the spiracular openings are hidden by the elytra, which partially wrap around the underside of the beetle's abdomen. Using a forceps and a pair of fine scissors, remove the elytra. Note how they are fused along the midline. In other beetles the two elytra readily separate to expose the wings. In these beetles there is a hollow space beneath the elytra that minimizes water loss and insulates the sensitive tissues of the abdomen from the heat of the sun. Find the pairs of abdominal spiracles hidden beneath the elytra. They are pinpoint openings on the sides of the body, connecting to the tracheae, the breathing tubes that penetrate and permeate the beetle's body. To see these structures, you will need to open up the insect's body.

The most convenient way to dissect an insect is to place it in a small dish whose bottom has been coated with a quarter-inch layer of melted paraffin (candle wax). This way you can hold the insect in place by pushing straight pins through the insect into the wax. Place the insect right side up in the dish. Push several pins through the edge of the insect into the wax. Cut off the wings at their bases. Then carefully clip around the edge as if you were opening a can. The entire upper surface of the abdomen can be removed in one piece, like a cover, exposing the tracheal system. If you fill the dish with water, covering the insect, the tracheae will appear as a beautiful network of silvery tubes because the air-filled tracheae act as mirrors, reflecting the light. In addition to tracheae, many insects have thin-walled air sacs filling portions of the body cavity. They appear white and flimsy. It is best to examine this preparation under a stereomicroscope to observe the delicate structure of the tracheal system.

Gas exchange in insects is carried out through this system of internal tubes. Mammals and other vertebrates oxygenate their blood as it passes among the tiny

(a)

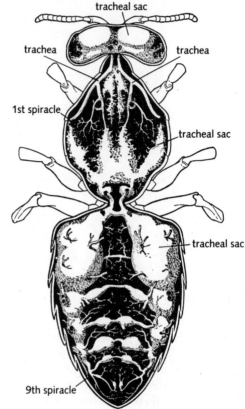

(a) The respiratory system showing tracheae and tracheal sacs.

The internal anatomy of the honey bee, shown after the removal of the upper (dorsal) surface.

air-filled spaces of the lung. The blood, saturated with oxygen, is then pumped throughout the body. The insects use a different mechanism. The tracheae keep branching into finer and finer tracheoles, which ramify throughout the entire body. Thus oxygen is carried directly to the insect's tissues, and the blood is not involved with gas transport. Insects do not inhale and exhale, but a kind of ventilation occurs through movements of the body wall. If you examine living insects, you will see that rhythmical contractions of the body occur. In some insects, such as beetles and grasshoppers, these contractions flatten the body dorsoventrally (from top to bottom), while in insects such as flies and wasps, telescopic movements of the abdominal segments occur. In order to keep the tracheae from collapsing during ventilation, spiral thickenings, called **taenidia**, reinforce the walls. These ridges encircling the tracheae look very much like those on the hose to a vacuum cleaner, and serve the same purpose. After you have examined the respiratory system, you might wish to delve a bit further into insect anatomy. Pick away the tracheae and air

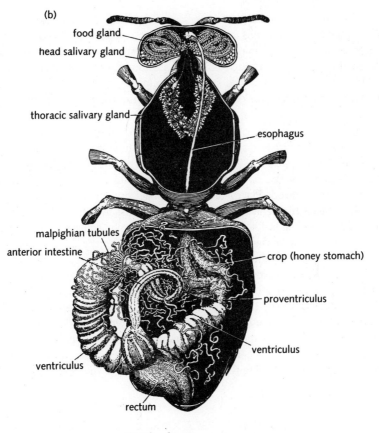

(b)

food gland

head salivary gland

thoracic salivary gland

esophagus

malpighian tubules

anterior intestine

crop (honey stomach)

proventriculus

ventriculus

ventriculus

rectum

(b) The digestive system.

sacs, and remove the upper portion of the thorax to expose the digestive system running the length of the body. This long tube can be moved to one side to reveal the nervous system. In contrast to vertebrates, the nerve cord of insects is on the ventral (belly) side of the animal. Refer to the figure above and on page 114 to identify as many structures as you can.

Examining plant stomata

The stomata of a plant are analogous to the spiracles of an insect, regulating the inward and outward flow of gases. The word stoma is from the Greek word meaning mouth. Stomata are beautiful structures. However, they are less than 25 microns (0.001 inch) in diameter, invisible to the naked eye. You can easily see them under the microscope at a power of about 100x. To make a preparation, carefully peel the surface off the underside of a leaf. This thin translucent layer is the epidermis. Flatten it out and place it on a microscope slide, with a cover glass and a few drops of water. The leaf surface appears as an interlocking mosaic of epidermal cells, as shown on page 109. Interspersed among these cells are pairs of sausage-shaped cells with their ends touching to form an elliptical opening between them. These are the guard cells that control the opening and closing of the stomata. When the cells contain much fluid and are turgid, the outer wall of each cell buckles outward, opening the stoma and allowing gaseous exchange to occur. When it becomes dark, the cells lose water and become flaccid, thereby closing the stoma.

A permanent collection of leaf stomata can be prepared as plastic replicas of the leaf surface. You will need small pieces of acetate film, about one inch square, and about an ounce of acetone. Sheets of acetate film can be obtained in an art supply store. Acetone can be obtained at a hardware store or pharmacy. Nail polish remover will also work. Place a drop or two of acetone on the plastic film, and let it remain for a few moments until the film partially dissolves and softens. Then place the acetate over the leaf surface and apply pressure by squeezing the preparation firmly between your thumb and forefinger. Don't let the film slip on the leaf surface. After several minutes the acetate will dry and can be peeled from the leaf. What you have is a plastic replica of the leaf surface, capturing its minutest details. These impressions can be examined under the microscope. The stomata will be clearly visible. Compare the size and quantity of stomata of plants adapted for the desert and those of more humid enviroments. Examine both the upper and lower plant surfaces. Another method of preparing replicas is to paint a thin layer of Duco® cement on a surface, let it dry, and then peel it off. Try making a replica of your fingerprint by coating the tip of your finger with the glue.

REFERENCES AND SUGGESTIONS FOR FURTHER READING

Bentley, P.J. 1966. Adaptations of amphibia to arid environments. *Science* 152: 619–623.

Gates, David M. December 1965. Heat transfer in plants. *Scientific American* 213: 76–84.

Hadley, Neil F. 1972. Desert species and adaptation. *American Scientist* 60: 338–347.

Lee, A.K., and Mercer, E.H. 1967. Cocoon surrounding desert-dwelling frogs. *Science* 157: 87–88.

Leopold, A. Starker. 1962. *Life Nature Library: The Desert.* Time, New York.

Ricklefs, R.E. 1983. *The Economy of Nature,* 2d ed. Chiron Press, New York.

Seely, M.K., and Hamilton, W.J., III. 1976. Fog catchment sand trenches constructed by tenebrionid beetles, *Lepidochora,* from the Namib Desert. *Science* 193: 484–486.

Tributsch, H. 1982. *How Life Learned to Live: Adaptation in Nature.* MIT Press, Cambridge.

11

Camouflage and Mimicry: Defense Strategies for a Hostile World

FOR THE SMALLER CREATURES of the world, life can be cruel and dangerous. The words of Tennyson, "Nature, red in tooth and claw," summarize their plight. Predators abound, and many animals find themselves relatively defenseless. Hunters such as lions and eagles essentially have no enemies except for man, the cruelest predator of all. They are well equipped with muscles, fangs, and talons for protection. But what of the fawn, the whip-poor-will incubating her eggs, and the plump garden caterpillar? They, too, need defenses. Circling hawks, fierce shrews, insatiable toads, and stealthy spiders are ubiquitous. The fragile claws and diminutive jaws of insects are impotent against these overpowering predators. Many birds and mammals, though larger, cannot contend with voracious carnivores. Nonetheless, nature's more delicate creatures employ an array of imaginative and effective survival strategies.

HOW TO DISAPPEAR

One ploy is to remain as inconspicuous as possible; camouflaging shapes, patterns, and colors conceal creatures among the leaves of plants and upon the forest floor. Nature's hide-and-seek is a game of life and death. The loser forfeits his life, and an unsuccessful predator may die of starvation. Through millennia of encounters, evolution selects the optimum disguises for the prey, while honing the hunter's perception and predatory skills.

Masters of illusion, many potential victims vanish into the surrounding leaves, twigs, tree bark, and lichen-covered rocks. Cryptic coloration conceals the green caterpillar on a leaf, the ruffed grouse on the forest floor, the moth motionless on tree bark, and the horned toad on the desert sand. The effectiveness of these disguises is based upon principles of vision.

Disruptive coloration obscures an animal's outline. The irregular contrasting patches in shades of tan, ochre, and beige make it difficult to perceive the whip-poor-will's contour on the leaf-strewn forest floor. The shape of its body is broken up into a hectic patchwork that blends imperceptibly into the equally chaotic background of dry leaves, sticks, stones, shadows, and dappled light. Even the hawk's keen eye fails to appreciate the silhouette of a tasty meal.

With its disruptive coloration in varying shades of green and gray, the treefrog is well camouflaged in vegetation.

Contrasting stripes help keep a predator's eye from perceiving the body outline of its prey, a common ploy of moths, caterpillars, and frogs. Often, coloration on different portions of the body contributes to the overall pattern. When the leopard frog comes to rest with its legs folded snugly against the body, its markings align themselves into a striped pattern. Similarly, the broad-banded designs of noctuid and underwing moths become apparent only when the insect lands and adjusts its wing posture. The stripes are often in strongly contrasting tones that further deemphasize the animal's contour and prominent features. Fish, frogs, turtles, snakes, and salamanders often have a stripe that passes through the eye region, since the eye is a conspicuous (and vulnerable) feature of the head that readily attracts a predator's attention.

The underwing, or catocala, moths have another trick to confuse predators. Beneath their brown, mottled forewings are conspicuously colored hindwings. When disturbed, the moth flees, flashing its hindwings like a banner, until it suddenly stops on a tree trunk with its hindwings folded under the drab forewings. A confused predator in pursuit searches in vain, unaware that the moth has made a sudden switch from conspicuous display to camouflage. Certain grasshoppers use the same ploy, flourishing bright yellow or red hindwings beneath brown speckled forewings that blend with the ground when the grasshopper lands.

Appropriate behaviors are crucial accompaniments to all these camouflages. The most perfect disguise is easily detected if an animal moves. Whip-poor-wills, nighthawks, and fawns lie motionless by day. The walking stick's slender brown body is not enough; a rigid immobile posture with outstretched front legs is needed to complete its disguise. Certain inchworms and geometrid moth caterpillars act out a similar charade. They grip a twig with their hind legs and extend themselves into the air. Their bodies are decorated with bumps and speckles that bear a perfect resemblance to the leaf scars, lenticels, and other irregularities of a twig. The head and front legs can hardly be distinguished from an unopened bud. These caterpillars feed at night, resting immobile by day. Interestingly, caterpillars often select a resting spot away from the leaves upon which they have been feeding. This behavior appears to be adaptive, since damaged leaves could easily alert a bird to a caterpillar's presence. Similarly, the feeding habits and coloration of certain caterpillars appear to minimize the apparent leaf damage. These caterpillars resemble the leaf edge upon which they feed. As they eat, they fit themselves into the space they have consumed. Other caterpillars feed symmetrically upon a leaf, chewing first on one side, then the other, again minimizing the apparent leaf damage. Several underwing and sphinx moth caterpillars have a better means of concealing evidence of their feeding. After eating, they clean up after themselves, clipping off a partially eaten leaf by chewing through the leaf's stalk. The biologist Bernd Heinrich calls these caterpillars "artful diners" and comments that, for them, "table manners are a matter of life and death."

Dark shadows can ruin the best camouflage, so they are often concealed. Moths press their bodies close to the bark of trees to avoid casting a shadow. Caterpillars that crawl along twigs often have flaps, flanges, or tubercules along their feet that obscure their cylindrical body shape and cast reduced shadows. Shadows can be obliterated by correctly orienting the body; some butterflies tilt their wings perpendicular to the sun. Certain ground-nesting birds keep swiveling toward the sun, reorienting their bodies to diminish their shadows.

An artist utilizes shading to make figures in his drawings appear lifelike and three-dimensional. Countershading has the opposite effect, hiding an animal by obscuring its three-dimensional shape, making it appear flat. An object lit from above has a dark undersurface, clearly revealing its volume and contour. Many birds, mammals, fish, and caterpillars are darker on their upper surfaces, so that light shining on the animal from above produces the effect of a uniformly shaded, flat object; a predator has difficulty in distinguishing the animal from its surroundings.

Some creatures are not born with their disguises, but create their own costumes. The *Synchlora* caterpillar vanishes into its surroundings by cutting out portions of flower petals and sewing them with silk to spines upon its back. Regardless of where it feeds, it can fashion a perfect masquerade. The disguise is marvelous, but the caterpillar is apparently unaware of its own appearance. I have seen a larva, foolishly displaying conspicuous attire, mistakenly plucked from an adjacent flower of contrasting colors.

The maple leaf cutter caterpillar begins its life as a leaf miner, tunneling between the upper and lower surfaces of maple leaves, safely hidden for its first two weeks. It eventually outgrows its haven. Rather than feed in the open, it cuts two oval pieces out of a leaf and sandwiches itself between them, using silk. The upper section is slightly larger than the lower, allowing the caterpillar inconspicuously to eat the surface of the leaf as it crawls along carrying its case.

An animal need not disappear to avoid attack if it can convince a predator that it is something inedible. Many insects spend most of their lives on plants, so an effective ploy is to resemble the foliage upon which they feed or hunt. The leaf mimicry of these insects is perfect down to the finest details. The wings of many grasshoppers, katydids, praying mantises, and moths are decorated with imitations of leaf veins, white fungus spots, jagged edges and holes where caterpillars have eaten, and brownish blotches of dead leaf.

Hairstreak butterflies are found throughout the United States, darting from flower to flower gathering nectar. They are by no means cryptically colored, but

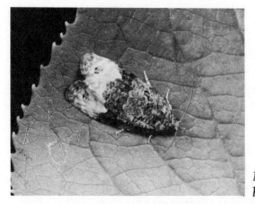

Moths such as this one look like bird droppings.

The tiger swallowtail caterpillar uses two defense tactics, cryptic green coloration and menacing eyespots.

they effectively deceive their predators by simulating a false head at the wrong end of their body. They hold their wings closed when they alight, displaying the wings' undersides. The end of each hind wing has a small dark spot that resembles a head, and a hairlike tail that looks like an antenna. At rest, the butterfly slides its wing surfaces past each other, waving its false antennae to divert the enemy's attention from its real head. Eyespots on the hind wings of many moths also focus a predator's attention on less vulnerable parts of the body. A survey of these moths and butterflies in the field reveals many with damaged hind wings, nonlethal injuries received from birds that pecked in the wrong place.

A perverse scatological inclination causes me to delight in the mimicry of certain other woodland moths and caterpillars. Although most moths flutter through the woodlands and come to rest concealed on the leaf litter or on the bark of trees, these moths behave differently. They rest conspicuously on the upper surfaces of leaves. Disguised as a bird dropping, these insects confidently flaunt their presence. Even the hungriest bird would not be tempted to eat its own feces. One portion of the moth's wing is colored white, like crystals of uric acid excreted by the avian kidney. The rest of the wing is darkly mottled like feces.

The tiger swallowtail caterpillar also employs this fecal artifice, but as it matures into a two-inch long caterpillar, its deception is no longer plausible. Small birds flitting through the woodlands never leave such large droppings, so, as the caterpillar grows, it dons a new disguise. After its initial molts, it takes on a light green coloration, embellished with two menacing eyespots. Sudden confrontation with these false eyes presumably startles a predator into retreat, an innate avoidance response to large eyes.

The larva of the green lacewing treacherously imitates its prey. The insatiable predator wanders among woolly alder aphids, pierces their soft bodies with its sharp hollow mandibles, and sucks them dry. The aphids, as their name suggests, are covered with white waxy tufts secreted by glands on their body. Clusters of aphids are attended by ants, which receive excreted droplets of honeydew in return for guarding the flock. However, the lacewing larva manages to wander freely through the herd, unnoticed by the vicious ant shepherds. The assassin plucks the wool from the aphids and arranges it on its back, thereby escaping the ant's detection. A veritable wolf in sheep's clothing, it devours its prey. If you remove the lacewing's fleecy coat, these denuded hunters are soon discovered, grabbed by the ants, and either tossed from the alder branches, or carried off.

Some insects lack their own defenses but resemble their well-protected relatives, thereby deceiving predators. This is known as **Batesian mimicry.** Certain syrphid flies, robber flies, and the locust borer beetle show a nearly perfect resemblance to venomous bees or wasps. Some have hairy beelike bodies; others have the black-and-yellow striped abdomens of yellow jackets. The clearwing moth has portions of its wings devoid of scales, improving its hymenopteran appearance. These actors often complete their performances with convincing buzzes and wriggling movements of the abdomen, which simulate attempts at stinging. Once a frog or bird experiences a painful sting from an actual wasp or bee, it avoids all similar prey in the future, demonstrating that predators readily learn from their mistakes.

The study of camouflage and mimicry permits us to better understand the visual and mental capabilities of predators. From experiments with stinging wasps, researchers have shown how birds learn, that they see colors, and that they have a keen appreciation for patterns. That a camouflaged animal fools a predator just as

COMMON INSECTS THAT USE CAMOUFLAGE AND MIMICRY AS A DEFENSE

Name	Defense	Scientific Name
ambush bug	camouflaged on flowers	*Phymata fasciata*
brown lacewing	covers itself with debris	*Hemerobius* sp.
tortoise beetle larva	covers itself with feces and molted skins	*Cassida pallidula*
geometrid moth caterpillar	sews flower petals to its back	*Synchlora* sp.
evergreen bagworm caterpillar	builds camouflaged case of leaves and twigs	*Thyridopteryx ephemeraeformis*
underwing moth	camouflaged on tree bark	*Catocala* sp.
Io moth	displays eyespots	*Automeris io*
treehopper	thorn mimic	*Thelia* sp.
geometrid caterpillar	twig mimic	*Prochoerodes transversata*
locust borer beetle	yellow jacket mimic	*Megacyllene robiniae*
flower fly	honey bee mimic	*Eristalis tenax*
robber fly	bumble bee mimic	*Laphria sacrator*
bumble bee sphinx moth	bumble bee mimic	*Hemaris diffinis*
clearwing moth	wasp mimic	*Sanninoidea exitiosa*
katydid	leaf mimic	*Pterophylla* sp.
praying mantis	leaf mimic	*Tenodera aridifolia sinensis*
tiger swallowtail caterpillar	bird-dropping mimic	*Pterourus glaucus*
hairstreak butterfly	false head	*Strymon* sp.

it fools us suggests that the predator sees the world much as we do. For example, if birds did not see colors, then the cabbage butterfly caterpillars hidden in my garden would not be the precise greenish shade of broccoli leaves, nor would the stripes of harmless flies and beetles precisely match the colors of yellow jacket wasps.

ACTIVITY

Close-up photography in the field

It is a challenge to ferret out the camouflaged animals hidden before our eyes. Once they are found, the best way to record your discoveries is through photography. Close-up or "macro" photography transports the naturalist into the realm of the minute. Under each stone, among the nooks and crannies of tree bark, or in a stagnant pool of water one finds worlds teaming with life. Capturing these microcosms on film is an exciting challenge, and it trains the photographer to be a more observant student of nature.

For me there is another benefit of nature photography; it offers the perfect solution to my collecting cravings. Rather than bring everything home to mount, or pin, or press lifelessly, or to pack into jars of alcohol, I simply collect their living portraits. I also learn more about my subjects because I spend more time stalking my "prey" and observing its behavior, rather than snatching it and putting it into a jar where all it can do is demonstrate how it struggles.

EQUIPMENT

If this is your first endeavor in macro photography, you may need to purchase some equipment. A 35mm single-lens reflex (SLR) camera is the most useful camera. The normal 50mm lens purchased with the camera permits you to get within about three feet of the subject, so a special macro lens designed to focus within inches of the subject is needed.

In macro photography, the subject should fill the viewing frame. A portrait of a friend standing at the far end of a football field would make her appear a mere speck in the viewfinder. Similarly, without a macro lens, shooting a moth camouflaged on a lichen-covered tree trunk results in a picture in which the moth will hardly be visible. You must get closer to your subject.

For close-up photography of flowers, I often use a 55mm macro lens. Its short **working distance** means that I have to get quite close, perhaps four inches away, to focus on the subject. You can get that close to a flower, but many insects will be scared away. A telephoto macro lens (about 105mm) is ideal. This short telephoto close-up lens makes it much easier to stalk an insect because you can focus farther away.

We must digress for a moment to explain some terminology. When we think of magnification, we generally imagine 5x or 10x, the kind of magnification produced by a small hand lens. In macro photography we tend to think in more modest terms, magnifications of 3x or smaller. Macro lenses generally permit a maximum

My basic setup for close-up photography consists of a 35mm camera with a macro lens, and two flash units mounted on a bracket. Other variations and equipment are described in the text.

magnification of one-half life-size (0.5x). A magnification of 0.5x doesn't really magnify a subject. The lens produces an image on the film that is one-half the actual life-size of the object. When you hold a slide of an inch-long bee up to the light to view with the naked eye, the image of the insect is half life-size, or one-half inch long. When you project the image on the screen it obviously becomes much larger, but that is not the magnification we are speaking of.

There is a world of animals, flowers, and fungi that will keep you occupied for many seasons without more magnification than 0.5x. Once you're addicted to macro photography, you are likely to find yourself wanting more magnification. There are a number of ways to proceed. An extension tube inserted between the lens and your camera can move you into the life-size range (1x). A supplementary lens can be screwed onto your lens to double the magnification. Greater magnification will require fancier equipment. A bellows unit serves as a long variable-length extension tube, allowing magnifications of 2x or greater. The wide-angle lens, used for scenic panoramas, can be reversed, front to back, for an entirely different purpose. Attached to the camera by means of an adapter ring, it becomes a good macro lens. Combined with extension tubes or bellows, such setups will often yield magnifications of up to 5x. Experiment with all your lenses, reversed, with and without extension tubes or bellows. You'll be surprised at what you can accomplish. The references listed below will provide ideas and more technical information.

But beware! The price of high magnification is paid for in terms of two formidable problems: shallow depth of field and inadequate lighting.

DEPTH OF FIELD

Depth of field refers to how much of your subject is in focus at a time. As magnification increases, depth of field decreases, so it may be impossible for the entire subject to be in focus at one time. When photographing an animal, be sure to keep its eye sharply focused. Some blurriness is tolerable at the edges of a head, but the viewer's gaze is always drawn to the subject's eye, so crisp focus is crucial here. Under the best of circumstances, it will be difficult to have a fat bumble bee completely in focus at a magnification of 0.5x or more, but you can at least make sure its head is sharp. To obtain the greatest depth of field, use the smallest possible aperture (f stop). I always use f11 or smaller. Many 35mm single-lens reflex cameras have a preview button that closes down the diaphragm to the selected aperture, allowing you to view your depth of field before shooting. Compare f5.6 and f16. There will be an enormous difference at magnifications of 0.5 or greater when viewing any object that isn't flat.

LIGHTING

With the diaphragm closed down to a small aperture, notice how dark the subject becomes at an f stop of f16 or smaller. This demonstrates the second problem encountered in macro photography — how to obtain adequate lighting.

As you decrease the size of the aperture, you also decrease the amount of light that reaches the film. This problem is compounded by long lenses and extension tubes, which further diminish the amount of light reaching the film. To make matters worse, when you work close up, your camera often casts a shadow on the subject.

The ideal solution is electronic flash. Generally you cannot mount the flash directly on the camera because it isn't angled properly to illuminate your subject. You can either handhold the flash, or you can mount it on a special bracket attached to the camera with extension cords, to provide the connection between the flash units and camera. Using two flashes simultaneously will provide enough light to use the smallest aperture your camera allows and will provide even, shadowless illumination. Another option is a ringflash, which mounts on the end of the lens and provides even, circumferential illumination.

The final detail to contend with is proper exposure. If you use one of the modern cameras with TTL (through-the-lens) light metering, everything is done automatically. The camera will shut off the flash unit when enough light reaches the film. TTL metering makes macro photography much simpler. The alternative is to make a series of test exposures, making careful note of the f stop, distance from the camera to the subject, and the distance of the flash from the subject. Keep a 3 × 5 card with the proper exposure information for each lens you use.

The final thrill of macro photography is to see your subject projected on a screen for others to view, framed on the wall of your home, or published in a book or magazine. Suddenly, you are transported back to the field, lying on your belly, remembering the moment you clicked the shutter.

REFERENCES AND SUGGESTIONS FOR FURTHER READING

Blaker, Alfred A. 1976. *Field Photography: Beginning and Advanced Techniques.* W.H. Freeman, San Francisco.

Cott, H.B. 1940. *Adaptive Coloration in Animals.* Methuen, London.

Edmunds, M. 1974. *Defence in Animals.* Longman, New York.

Heinrich, B. June 1980. The artful diners. *Natural History* 89: 42–51.

Lefkowitz, Lester. 1979. *The Manual of Close-Up Photography.* Amphoto, New York.

Portmann, A. 1959. *Animal Camouflage.* University of Michigan Press, Ann Arbor.

Shaw, J. 1984. *The Nature Photographer's Complete Guide to Professional Field Techniques.* Amphoto, New York.

Wickler, W. 1968. *Mimicry in Plants and Animals.* McGraw-Hill, New York.

12

On the Trail of the
Whitetail Deer

DRIVING ALONG THE HIGHWAYS and back roads of America, I've become familiar with the diamond-shaped deer-crossing signs that display a black silhouette of a leaping buck. I often mumble to myself that deer obviously cannot read, since I have yet to see a deer crossing at these spots.

Nevertheless, the whitetail deer is the most widespread and best-known big game animal in North America, and unless you spend considerable time observing animals in the field, this may be the only hoofed animal you will see in the wild.

Whitetails can be found throughout most of North America, from Canada southward all the way to Bolivia in South America. They are not found in most of California and Utah, or in portions of Colorado, Arizona, and New Mexico, but here their cousin, the mule deer, is common.

Deer are in the family **Cervidae** which is in the order **Artiodactyla**, hoofed animals having an even number of toes. Other Cervids found in the United States are elk, moose, and caribou. Except for the caribou, only the males possess antlers, and in all species they are shed each year.

Antlers are bony outgrowths of the skull, covered by a furry vascular skin called velvet that provides the antlers' blood supply. They grow rapidly during the spring and summer and by late August have attained their full growth. At this time, their blood supply begins to dwindle, causing the velvet to shrivel and die. The bucks then rub their antlers against trees and saplings, fraying off the velvet in long hanging shreds, until the antlers are smoothly polished. The antlers remain until after the rutting (mating) season when the level of the male hormone, testosterone, begins to drop, causing a narrow zone of bone at the antlers' base to be reabsorbed. With their attachment weakened, the antlers fall off sometime between mid-December and March.

As a buck ages, its antlers generally become larger each year, with more points or tines, so that, by the third or fourth year, they usually have eight points. With the buck's maturity at age seven or eight, the number increases to twelve. Despite this generality, you cannot tell the age of a buck with certainty by the number of points on his antlers. Although the diameter and weight of the antlers do tend to increase until maturity, with old age or poor nutrition the number of tines decreases to the point where an old buck may have only two tines on each antler. Patterns of wear on the teeth are the best indicators of age.

In contrast to the antlers of deer, the horns of buffalo, bighorn sheep, mountain goats, and our domesticated cattle are permanent structures consisting of bony cores covered with horny sheaths that continue to grow from the skull throughout life. The horn itself is hardened skin material with the same structure as our fingernails.

The other distinctive feature of the Cervids is their complex digestive system with its four-chambered stomach. Like the cow, these animals are ruminants, vegetarians who chew their cud. The food they gather is swallowed rapidly, with little chewing, and ends up in the first two stomach chambers, where it is mixed with digestive juices and reduced to a pulp. Later, when the animal is resting, the food is regurgitated to the mouth in small masses, is properly chewed, and is reswallowed for complete digestion in the other stomach compartments.

DESCRIPTION

The whitetail deer is named for its luxurious tail, almost a foot in length, with a striking white underside that the animal displays as it bounds through a field in alarm. Whitetails reach a height of 3-1/2 feet (1.1 m) at the shoulder, with males weighing up to 400 pounds (181 kg) and females 250 pounds (113 kg). Whitetails are agile runners, attaining speeds of 40 MPH; they can jump 30 feet (9 m) horizontally and 8-1/2 feet (3 m) vertically. With long slender legs, they seem to fly, effortlessly clearing farmers' fences.

Like most mammals, deer change their coats twice a year in preparation for the changing seasons. The summer dress, worn from June to September in the north, is mostly reddish, with some white on the underparts and around the eye. Fine short hairs lie sleek and close to the body. This coat is replaced by a drabber winter coat with a blue-gray cast, consisting of a warmer layer of coarse bristles up to two inches thick. Each of these winter hairs is hollow and filled with air, providing a perfectly insulated coat to protect the deer from the vicious cold of northern winters. It even allows the deer to bed down in the snow without melting it.

Whitetail populations are steadily increasing, so much so that I'm beginning to think they can be found anywhere. For example, on the evening of March 31, 1982, an American Airlines DC-10 flew to Phoenix from Chicago's O'Hare Airport. During takeoff, it hit and killed a large buck. In America's busiest airport, surrounded on all sides by highway traffic, densely populated suburbs, and bustling industrial parks, deer had found a cozy, yet dangerous, foraging ground.

In the United States, the whitetail census has fluctuated greatly. From a low of about 1/2 million in 1900 (when the animals were hunted to extinction in many areas) to 5 million in 1935, deer now number nearly 15 million. Many of their predators, wolves, coyotes, bobcats, lynxes, and cougars, have been all but eliminated. The population explosion has been further fueled by the great expanses of forest that have been cleared for timber and farming; the more open areas that have replaced dense forests provide a better habitat for deer.

Motorists account for about 150,000 roadkills a year, and hunters shoot over a million animals, yet deer are now their own worst enemy. If they are unchecked by natural predators, overpopulation and disease may result in enormous winter-starvation death tolls.

REPRODUCTIVE CYCLE

Breeding (rutting) takes place in the fall and early winter. The bucks develop thick swollen necks as they spar with their adversaries and exercise their muscles, carrying their heavy antlers. The battles between the males are usually formalized, with the weaker bucks withdrawing uninjured. Rarely, the antlers of two animals will become entangled and locked, resulting in the starvation and death of both contenders.

Bucks search for female does, locating them by scent. These odors are believed to originate from skin glands. A pear-shaped tarsal gland is found on the inside of each hind leg at the hock joint, the joint corresponding to the ankle in man. It is covered by a tuft of hairs that can be erected, perhaps aiding the spread of its secretion. Other glands are located in front of the eyes, and on the outside of each hind leg, between the hoof and the hock. The interdigital glands, located deep between the toes of each foot, give off a strong-smelling waxy substance that marks the animal's trail. These glands are found in both sexes, and may be especially important during the rutting season.

Although bucks are polygamous, they have only one mate at a time, staying with a doe for days or weeks until she reaches estrus. The does are in heat for only 24 hours. If they are not fertilized at that time, they will come into heat three or four more times at monthly intervals. Although matings can therefore be spread over several months, most fawns are born in late May or June. Generally, young females mate late in the season since they were only seven or eight months old and sexually immature during the normal rut in early winter.

A fawn requires 205 days to develop within its mother's womb. They weigh about five pounds at birth. After a few hours, they can take a few wobbly steps on their spindly legs, but it will be weeks before they are agile runners. Their defense at this time is concealment and camouflage. Odorless at first, the fawns remain mostly hidden for the first month of their life, lying perfectly still with their feet folded beneath their bodies. Their brownish-red coats splattered with white dots allow them to blend unnoticed into the sun-dappled forest floor. If there is more than one fawn, each is hidden separately during the day, visited by the doe at two- to three-hour intervals for nursing. The fawns are silent except for a loud bleat that they utter when picked up. One to four fawns are born at a time; twins are most common.

HABITS AND BEHAVIORS

The most well-known behavior of these animals is the habit of raising their white tails like a flag when alarmed. The older literature I consulted explained this as a signal of danger to other nearby deer. When one deer snaps his tail upright, flashes its white underside, and bounds off into the woods, you can expect all the other deer to follow. More recent studies suggest that this alarm signal may communicate with the predator as well. The message seems to say, "Look! I've spotted you. Do not waste your energy trying to chase me. I'm already on my way." It's just as well that the predator takes heed, for it is unlikely to be able to overtake its swift prey.

I was surprised to learn that whitetails are also excellent swimmers, taking to the water to escape dogs and insects. They have been known to swim as far as six miles.

There is little vocal communication among deer. A deer may snort when startled by man or predators, and bucks occasionally bellow during the rutting season. Young fawns may communicate with each other with "mewing" sounds, like a catbird, and does occasionally bleat for lost fawns.

For an animal as large as a deer, the home range in which it travels is surprisingly small, rarely more than a mile across. Individuals may remain for their entire life in a lowland cedar swamp, well protected from the wind. One buck and doe observed for several seasons in New York seldom moved more than a quarter-mile from a small knoll upon which they frequently rested. An individual is familiar with each tree and landmark in its home range and travels it on a regular schedule. A buck can almost invariably be found at the same spot at the same time day after day, using the same trails with little variation. This explains why deer-crossing signs make sense. Where a deer trail happens to cross a roadway, you can expect regular whitetail traffic.

Deer do not travel in large herds. In the summer, the bucks are generally solitary, traveling alone or in small groups of two to four. However, these groups break up prior to the mating season. The basic social unit is the doe and her fawns. Through the winter, a typical group of two bucks and four or five does with their fawns will inhabit an area of about one-half square mile. Sometimes with heavy snowfalls, animals congregate in "yards" where the snow is kept well packed. In the northern states, large numbers of deer may occupy small yards with a good cover of thick evergreens, whose branches catch the snow and block the biting winds. Even with abundant food less than a mile away, deer may starve in these areas rather than enlarge their range.

Deer are browsers, eating an enormous variety of vegetation. Over a thousand different plant species have been recorded in their diet, although only about 100 are preferred. Their favorite foods are the foliage and twigs of blackberry, raspberry, greenbrier, elderberry, maples, oaks, aspens, ash, choke cherry, sassafras, dogwood, and wild rose. Added to these are some more tender morsels, such as water lilies, sedges, currants, grapes, algae, and ferns. Among the flowering plants, goldenrod, jewelweed, lamb's quarters, nettles, and asters are favorites. In the fall, acorns, beechnuts, apples, and mushrooms are delicacies. Each day a 200-pound deer needs ten pounds of food to stay healthy. In the summer and fall, this is seldom a problem. As food gets scarce in winter, "beggars can't be choosers." Deer will begin to feed on evergreen needles, sprouts of spruce, balsam, and white pine, and dry grasses and leaves. Among the evergreens, white cedar, yew, and hemlock are most palatable. Pines are less preferred, and spruces and tamaracks are eaten as a last resort. Ironwood, slippery elm, box elder, mountain laurel, and rhododendron are avoided. Most likely, various chemicals in the foliage make these plants unpalatable.

Deer have been known to develop some bizarre tastes. There are reports of deer eating fish left on the banks by fishermen, or hanging up at a campsite. A whitetail may even go fishing herself, striking at fish in the water until one is maimed. Large trout may be eaten, still alive and wriggling, chewed and swallowed headfirst.

Sighting a big animal in the wild is always an exciting experience. No other large animal in the United States will provide such an opportunity for observation and behavioral studies. A short ride from almost any city will be likely to bring you into whitetail territory. As with any nature exploration, greater understanding and enjoyment will come with a bit of background knowledge, a lot of patience, enthusiasm, and a keen eye. Do not forget always to be searching beyond those diamond-shaped deer-crossing signs.

ACTIVITIES

The key to observing deer and many other wild animals is coordinating your schedule with theirs. Deer are twilight creatures, with peaks of activity at dawn and dusk. In the very early morning or evening, they can frequently be seen browsing in the open. At about midnight they are inactive again, resting until dawn.

Search for whitetails in mixed habitats where immature woods and brushy areas are interspersed with open fields and meadows. Old New England pastureland, abandoned decades ago, provides a rich, reliable assortment of plants and adequate cover. The edges of forests and swamps and along stream banks are favorite locales. In the winter, look for spots having the least amount of snow. Evergreens, such as spruce, hemlock, fir, and pine, intercept the falling snow so that only a fraction of it reaches the ground. These stands of trees also block cold northerly winds. Steep, south-facing slopes receive the most sun and do not accumulate much snow. If these hints do not help you to find deer, check with local hunters, farmers, and conservationists. They may be able to point out some good observation spots.

How to observe wild animals and what to look for

Any movement is likely to scare away wary wild animals. Deer have an excellent sense of smell, so approach them from downwind so your body odor is not blown in their direction. If you come across them while driving your car, it is best to remain inside and observe them through binoculars, an indispensable item for all field naturalists. (For information about choosing a pair of binoculars, see the Activities section of Chapter 24.)

Blinds, small enclosures that conceal the observer, are useful for more serious, long-term observations. A free-standing nylon tent is ideal, but expensive. More bulky tents, anchored to the ground with tent poles and lines, are cheaper and work fine, especially if you want to leave them up for several days of observation. As a child, I often set up large cardboard boxes, used to package refrigerators. They work great until the first big rain. I cut holes on all sides to fit my binoculars and camera, and had a chair inside to make my viewing comfortable. A makeshift hiding place can also be assembled from piles of branches.

Set up your blind a few days before you are ready to make your observations, so the wildlife will get accustomed to it. Choose a spot that you know the animals frequent. Arrive before they do. For nocturnal mammals, such as deer, raccoons, and opossums, set yourself up during the daylight hours. For birds, come before dawn. Do not forget a notebook, pencils, and a supply of your favorite cookies (in case you get hungry). It helps to have bait set up days in advance in a place where the animals have been used to feeding. Be patient, and wear extra clothes. I can remember being forced to flee my blind one cold early morning many years ago because my hands were too numb to hold my binoculars or click the shutter of the camera.

What should you look for when watching deer? Make careful notes of your observations indicating the date, locality, and weather conditions. Here's a partial list of things to observe and make note of:

1. How many deer are in the group? Can you get an idea of their approximate age and sex? Does the group structure change at different times of the year? If you

observe the same group for several days, try to recognize each animal individually. Do any members have distinctive identifying marks or behaviors to help you distinguish individuals?

2. How do the animals interact with each other? Do any behaviors appear aggressive or cooperative? Does one animal lead the group?

3. What are they eating? Visit the spot when the animals are not there, and make a survey of all the plants that are nibbled and the extent of damage to each species. Light browsing on preferred foods, such as white cedar and maples, indicates adequate food reserves or low deer populations. Heavy browsing on less palatable vegetation, such as beech, spruce, and balsam fir, indicates that the area is becoming overpopulated.

4. How do deer react to disturbance? (Do this at the end of your observation session!)

Tracks and traces of deer

Most wild animals are extremely shy and secretive. Since it may be difficult to find the animal you wish to observe, you may need to become a detective, gathering clues and traces of an animal's recent presence. If you are clever, this will allow you to piece together an entire story of the animal's activity and behavior. Where did the animal walk, when did it pause to feed, to speed up and gallop away? How many individuals were traveling together? The complete tale can be read through a careful examination of the evidence.

The whitetail deer is a perfect subject for your detective work. Even if deer are common in your area, you can more easily find traces of their presence than find the deer themselves.

To locate an area where deer have been, bundle up early in the morning after a rain or a light snowfall and set out into the fields. At this point the "slate" is wiped clean, and you will know that all the tracks you find are freshly made. Remember those roadside deer-crossing signs. That is a good place to start. Try edges of forests and swamps and places with plentiful low vegetation. Old abandoned apple orchards are ideal.

Deer tracks are unmistakable, probably the only hoofed prints you are likely to come across in most areas of the country, unless you are on a cattle ranch. Deer footprints show the two toes about three-and-one-half inches (9 cm) long and two-and-one-half inches (6 cm) wide. On softer surfaces, the toes will be spread apart to give the animal more support. In deeper snow, the two small dewclaws further up the leg will leave small spots behind each foot. When deer move, they leave a pattern of tracks in nearly a straight line. This is characteristic of deer, as well as of dogs and cats. As a deer walks, it places its hind foot right on top of the print of the front foot. When the tracks overlap a bit, this sometimes obscures the shape of the print. In deeper snow, deer will drag their feet, further obscuring their tracks. Prints will be found in various sizes. The front feet are slightly larger than the hind feet because of the extra weight of the animal's head and neck. In addition, the tracks of bucks are larger than those of the does and younger animals.

When deer gallop, the pattern changes slightly. The hind feet are swung far out ahead of the front feet, as with the gallops of rabbits, squirrels, and mice. The length between successive prints increases from about 15 to 20 inches (38 to 51 cm) during the walk to as much as 6 feet (1.8 m) for the gallop. This measurement, from print to print, is called the **stride**, and it is most important in determining how fast the animal was traveling. The width of the trail is called the **straddle**. It does not change much with different gaits, making it useful in identifying different species.

We are all familiar with animal tracks, but deer also leave other evidence of their presence. How many of these deer signs can you find?

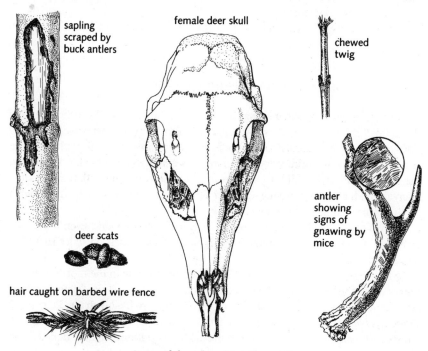

sapling scraped by buck antlers

female deer skull

chewed twig

antler showing signs of gnawing by mice

deer scats

hair caught on barbed wire fence

Signs of deer found in the woods.

1. Buck rubs. In the fall, the bucks will begin to remove the velvet from their antlers by lowering their heads close to the ground and scraping their antlers against saplings and small trees, leaving long, smooth worn spots and shreds of loose bark on the trees.

2. Shed antlers. Antlers are shed annually. Considering the millions of bucks in the United States, there should be twice that many antlers dropped each year. What happens to them all? They are seldom found. An excellent source of calcium, minerals, and protein, many are eaten by rodents, such as squirrels, mice, rabbits, and porcupines. Most of the antlers you do find will show evidence of gnawing in the shape of parallel incisor marks.

3. Scats. These are the feces or droppings of animals and can be quite characteristic of a particular species. In the winter, or when feeding on a dry diet,

whitetails leave piles of small black droppings. Each pellet is about one-half inch (1.3 cm) long and has a small point at one end. In the summer, when the deer feed on succulent green vegetation, the individual droppings are clumped together in piles about two inches (5 cm) wide.

4. Fur. Traveling through the brush or passing by barbed wire fences, deer will often leave bits of their fur. In order to be certain that the fur you collect is actually from a deer, it is useful to make a collection of many types of fur gathered from different road-killed animals. Carefully label your specimens to permit you to identify hair samples found in the field. Get samples of deer fur at different seasons to observe the fine summer hairs and the coarse, insulating winter hairs.

5. Bedding-down spots. During the day, deer will lie down in secluded, protected spots, leaving an impression of their bodies in the snow or thick vegetation.

6. Feeding damage. Deer have no upper incisors to cut their food; they rip and shred the vegetation as they eat. In the winter when other forage is unavailable, the deer mainly subsist on woody growth, such as twigs and buds formed the previous summer. In overpopulated woods, a definite "browse line" may be seen about five feet (1.5 m) off the ground, above which the animals cannot reach. Do not confuse deer-feeding damage with the gnawing of twigs and limbs done by rabbits, porcupines, and mice. The teeth marks of the front incisors are usually quite apparent. Rabbits use their front teeth to chisel clean cuts in the twigs at a 45 degree angle.

7. Rutting grounds. During the rutting season in late fall and early winter, the bucks will begin to joust and battle with each other. During these encounters, they will rush at each other, lock horns, and shove each other around. A half-acre of ground may be ploughed up by their hooves during these contests.

8. Skeletal remains. The skulls and bones of animals endure long after death. Here again, the rodents may beat you to your finds, but enough usually remains to figure out whose skeleton you have found. Try to figure out the sex and the age of the deer. In immature animals, the teeth will not show as much wear, and the heads of the leg bones will not be fused to the shaft. The skull of the buck will have a knob where the antlers attached.

Make a display of as many of these deer signs as you can find, mounting them all on a large sheet of cardboard or a piece of plywood. Fur and scats can be dried, then placed in clear plastic boxes or bags and glued to the board. Branches with buck rub or feeding damage can be clipped or sawn from the plant and wired in place. A cast-off antler, a weathered skull, or even a picture of a deer will look fine in the center of the display. Take photographs of bedding-down spots or buck battle-grounds, and mount them on the board. Finally make a plaster cast of a deer track to add to the display (see "Making plaster casts of animal tracks," on page 136). Label each object with a brief description and the date.

Attracting deer

If you still have trouble finding deer in an area that you know they inhabit, you can try to attract the deer to you. If your backyard abuts a wooded area, you might even be able to watch deer while you eat breakfast. Deer are especially fond of apples and can be tempted out of the woods if you spread some around. Deer, like cattle, also need more salt than they commonly get in their diet. Salt blocks or "salt licks" can be bought from farm-supply stores and placed in your potential observation area. You can also put out a supply of hay.

Making plaster casts of animal tracks

You will need a plastic container, some plaster of Paris, water, and a cylindrical mold or form to place around the track while you pour the wet plaster. The simplest mold is a strip of cardboard or heavy paper, rolled into an open cylinder so that it forms a "collar." The ends can be held together with tape or a paper clip. A more permanent mold, which I prefer, can be made from a small plastic container, the kind that soft margarine comes in nowadays. Cut out the bottom of the container and you are all set. After cleaning around the print, press the form firmly into the ground over the track. Mix up a batch of plaster to the consistency of heavy cream and gently pour it into the mold. Allow it to harden completely (about a half hour) before removing it and cleaning off the attached dirt with an old toothbrush.

How to make plaster casts of animal tracks.

Believe it or not, you can even make a cast of tracks made in the snow. Get a bottle with a nozzle that sprays in a fine mist. On a cold, subfreezing day, find some perfect tracks pressed into the snow. Gently spray a fine mist of water over a track. Let it freeze. Repeat several times until a thin layer of ice coats the track. Do not spray too much water or you will obscure the details of the print. Now, place the form around the track and pour in plaster, just as you did for tracks in the mud.

You can make a positive cast of the animal's footprint by greasing the surface of your plaster cast with some Vaseline® and placing a cardboard collar around it. Then fill this mold with plaster. When it dries, the two can be separated to reveal a new cast that shows the sunken impression of the animal's foot, just as it appeared in the field. Make a reference collection of the animal tracks found in your area. As with all nature collections, be sure to label each object with its identity, locality, and the date.

REFERENCES AND SUGGESTIONS FOR FURTHER READING

Alcock, J. 1979. *Animal Behavior: An Evolutionary Approach*. Sinauer Associates, Sunderland, Massachusetts.

Banfield, A.W.F. 1974. *The Mammals of Canada*. University of Toronto Press, Toronto.

Burt, W.H. 1964. *A Field Guide to the Mammals*. Houghton Mifflin, Boston.

Cahalane, V.H. 1961. *Mammals of North America*. Macmillan, New York.

Caras, R.A. 1967. *North American Mammals: Fur-bearing Animals of the United States and Canada*. Meredith Press, New York.

Doutt, J.K.; Heppenstall, C.A.; and Guilday, J.E. 1977. *Mammals of Pennsylvania*. Pennsylvania Game Commission, Harrisburg, Pennsylvania.

Hamilton, W.J., Jr. 1939. *American Mammals: Their Lives, Habits, and Economic Relations*. McGraw-Hill, New York.

Murie, O.J. 1975. *A Field Guide to Animal Tracks*. Houghton Mifflin, Boston.

13

How Animals Wage Chemical Warfare

CAMOUFLAGE AND MIMICRY are nonaggressive defenses that enable animals to avoid confrontations with potential predators. Another alternative is to take an offensive stance and actively battle an enemy. Defenses such as claws and jaws are the weapons of some animals; small animals require other means to deter large predators. The invertebrates have perfected the nefarious art of chemical warfare.

We are all familiar with — and fearful of — animals that inject venoms into their enemies. The stingers of scorpions, bees, wasps, and ants, the mandibles of centipedes, the fangs of snakes, and the **chelicerae** of spiders are forms of hypodermic syringes that animals often use, not only for defense, but also to subdue their prey. Another type of chemical defense is not injected but is sprayed, oozed, or wiped upon the surface of the assailant. These chemical defenses of invertebrates are the topic of this chapter.

Most of us do not realize that toxic defenses are extremely prevalent. Overturn any stone, and you will be likely to find ground beetles (family **Carabidae**). Many of them discharge odorous chemicals. The brightly colored polydesmid millipedes can be found slowly crawling along the woodland floor. If grabbed or roughly handled, they release cyanide from a row of pores on either side of the body. The toxin's characteristic odor of almonds is easily detected. Although insufficient toxin is released to harm a human being, enough is produced to kill insects placed in a sealed jar with a polydesmid.

Defensive secretions can be irritating to the mucous membranes of the mouth, nose, and eyes, although none are particularly caustic to the thick epidermis of the hand. It is perfectly safe to pick up these insects, provided you wash your hands before rubbing your eyes. If you have not smelled these compounds, it is a fascinating olfactory experience to wander through the fields, sampling the smorgasbord of exotic and pungent odors.

Whereas camouflaged insects test the observer's visual acumen, chemically protected insects will challenge the olfactory sense. I keep a series of small vials containing samples of all these compounds, gathered from dusty shelves in the chemistry department. The collection is my olfactory library, to which I can refer when I discover a new insect.

THE TYPES OF DEFENSES AND HOW THEY WORK

The variety of toxins and their myriad modes of deployment will provide the curious naturalist with many seasons of observations. Numerous invertebrates have tiny membranous sacs tucked away in the recesses of their bodies. These glands are filled with noxious fluids that are discharged when the invertebrate is provoked. When handled roughly or lightly pinched on a leg, stink bugs release a burst of hexanal from glands along each side of the body. In the Southwest, whipscorpions, commonly called vinegaroons, can be found under logs and debris. At the base of their long tail is a mobile body segment that the animal rotates in order to aim its acrid spray, consisting largely of acetic acid, or vinegar. (See illustration of a whipscorpion at the beginning of this chapter.)

Other invertebrates use glues to entangle their attackers. Slugs produce a viscous slime when irritated. If a predaceous beetle bites the slug, the slug's mucus coagulates and gums up the beetle's mandibles. Green, maggotlike syrphid fly larvae feed on aphids, and often encounter ants guarding the aphids, as described in a previous chapter. If attacked, they release a gluey liquid from their salivary glands that immobilizes the ants. Stone centipedes emit a sticky material from their posterior legs, which also entangles ants, spiders, and other attackers.

The beetles are the master chemists of the insect world, concocting an incredible variety of nasty brews. Ground beetles alone produce an impressive array of chemical weapons, including formic acid, acetic acid, benzaldehyde, decane, butyric acid, salicylaldehyde, quinones, and phenols, to name just a few. The arthropods have over 300 different chemicals included in their arsenal.

In general, invertebrates are economical in their use of toxins. These chemical weapons are undoubtedly costly and time-consuming to produce so it pays to use them wisely. In the simplest cases, the secretion merely oozes from the gland opening onto the integument. Many beetles improve upon this delivery system by using their legs to smear the toxin more evenly over the body surface. However, this is rather sloppy and wasteful. The swallowtail caterpillars have a better technique for discharging their poisons. Behind the head is a forked gland called an **osmeterium**, invaginated in the body. When the caterpillar is attacked, the gland is everted, turning inside out. Its inner surface, now exposed to the outside, is coated with a pungent, repulsive compound, called isobutyric acid. The caterpillar swings its head around and wipes its secretion against the attacker. When the battle is over, the gland is reinverted into the body, conserving unused secretion.

The anise swallowtail caterpillar everting its scent gland, the osmeterium, which gives off a strong, disagreeable odor.

Millipedes do not discharge all their glands at once, only those on the side of the body under attack. Organisms with a single pair of glands generally discharge only a fraction of the stored contents. A bombardier beetle can fire its quinone secretion more than a dozen times before exhausting its supply. Over the course of several days, more chemicals will be synthesized to replenish the losses.

Another means of conserving precious compounds is to deploy several lines of defense in sequence, culminating with the release of secretions as a last resort. The tiger swallowtail caterpillar is an excellent example. It rests upon the foliage, camouflaged with its green coloration. From a distance, it relies on this cryptic defense. If discovered, it will turn its head, attempting to threaten a predator with its large eyespots. If that fails, it will regurgitate a droplet of intestinal fluid and smear it on the attacker. If the assailant persists, only then will it brandish its osmeterium, its ultimate and most costly weapon.

The skunk goes through similar antics before it wastes its putrid spray. When threatened, it erects its tail and stamps its forefeet on the ground. The spotted skunk may even do a handstand, displaying its conspicuous black-and-white back to the attacker. Very often, a predator will get the point, and retreat.

APOSEMATISM: THE IMPORTANCE OF GOOD ADVERTISING

The skunk demonstrates that advertising is an important way to avoid wasting chemical defenses. A predator, warned that its potential prey is inedible, may not bother to attack. Therefore, many invertebrates with chemical defenses are **aposematic**, that is, they display warning coloration. This conspicuous approach is an entirely different strategy from the reticent manner of cryptic animals.

To signal their inedibility, aposematic animals use bright colors, contrasting patterns, powerful odors, characteristic sounds, and special behaviors. Cryptic caterpillars are always found singly, but chemically defended caterpillars often form dense aggregations. The unpalatable milkweed tiger moth has showy tufts of black, yellow, and white hairs. Colonies of individuals feed together, plainly visible on the surface of milkweed leaves.

For aposematism to be effective, the unknowing predator must sample the prey, find it unpalatable, and learn from the experience to avoid all similar prey. It is important to make the learning process as effective as possible so that few individuals are sacrificed to train the predator. Aposematic animals tend to be slow, making them easy to notice and capture. Contrasting patterns of stripes or dots appear to be particularly common and effective warning signals. The best examples are black-and-yellow wasps. In addition to their coloration, a buzzing wasp provides an auditory cue to help warn potential predators. A whole slew of insects use contrasting stripes or dots in black, white, yellow, and orange colors. The caterpillars of the monarch butterfly, the milkweed tiger moth, and several swallowtails, ladybug beetles, Mexican bean beetles, and the Colorado potato beetle are a few of the insects masquerading in these aposematic outfits. The advantage of having several insects share a similar pattern is that a naive predator has to sample only one individual in order to learn to avoid many different species. In this manner fewer prey have to be sacrificed each generation in order to teach the predators. This convergence of similar patterns and colors by toxic organisms is called **Müllerian mimicry**. As you may recall, Batesian mimicry, mentioned in a previous chapter, involves perfectly harmless animals that take advantage of a predator's learned avoidance by resembling toxic organisms.

THE ORIGIN OF DEFENSIVE COMPOUNDS

The defensive compounds of invertebrates originate from several sources. Many of the chemicals are synthesized in glands, from raw materials and enzymes present

in the animal's body. In other cases, the toxins are appropriated from plants the
animal eats. Sawfly larvae feed communally on pine needles. When disturbed,
they curl up their front end, and emit a droplet of dark greenish fluid from the
mouth, which is smeared upon the enemy. The pungent fluid is regurgitated pine
resin, which the insect retains in two pouches coming off the esophagus. As the
sawflies eat pine needles, the resin is shunted to these diverticuli, and the edible
portion of the needles passes to the gut. In essence, the insects are storing
turpentine, appropriated from the trees. The pines use these compounds as protection from various disease-causing microorganisms and herbivores. The sawflies
are immune to the resin and use it for their own defense.

The monarch caterpillar also obtains toxic defenses from its food plant. Milkweeds contain cardiac glycosides, bitter toxins that affect the heart and cause
vomiting. The caterpillar tolerates these compounds, and incorporates the toxins
into its blood as it feeds. The poisons protect not only the caterpillar but also the
adult butterfly, which retains the poison during metamorphosis. Naive blue jays,
having never tasted a monarch, readily attack and eat the butterfly. However,
minutes later they become ill and vomit. From then on, the blue jay avoids
monarchs. The nearly identical viceroy butterfly, a palatable Batesian mimic, is
rejected as well.

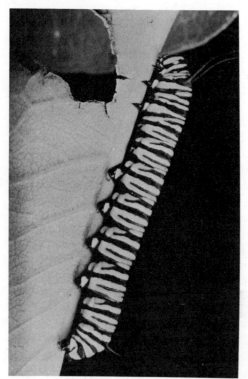

*The monarch caterpillar obtains
toxins from its food plant,
milkweed, and incorporates them
into its blood.*

THE PROBLEM OF AUTOTOXICITY

How to make a poison without poisoning yourself

One obvious concern for a toxic organism is to avoid poisoning itself, to keep its chemical weapons from backfiring. How does an invertebrate store potent irritants inside its body without injuring itself? How are toxins that inhibit physiological processes manufactured without damaging the organism? One solution is immunity. The cyanide-producing polydesmid millipede is unusually resistant to cyanide, even though this chemical is one of the most potent, rapidly acting poisons.

Such immunity is particularly important for organisms that store their toxins free in the blood. When disturbed, ladybug beetles, blister beetles, and Mexican bean beetles "autohemorrhage," oozing droplets of toxin-laden blood from their leg joints.

Glandular products are easier to store, since they are segregated from contact with the body in impermeable cuticle-lined sacs. In some cases the toxins are also stored in an inactive form. The glands of the polydesmid millipede, *Apheloria corrugata,* consist of two chambers. The larger chamber is a reservoir containing an inactive precursor chemical. A smaller compartment, the vestibule, is connected to the reservoir by a duct, which is normally closed. The vestibule contains an enzyme that can rapidly break down the precursor, forming toxic cyanide gas and benzaldehyde. At the moment of attack, the millipede opens the passageway between the two compartments and squeezes the contents of the reservoir through the vestibule to the outside. The enzyme mixes with the precursor, releasing the poisons.

Of all the chemical defenses known, that of bombardier beetles in the genus *Brachinus* may be the most spectacular. Like the millipede, the bombardier beetle has a two-chambered gland. The reservoir contains hydroquinones and hydrogen peroxide. When these ingredients come in contact with the enzymes in the vestibule, a violent reaction takes place, oxidizing the hydroquinones to quinones, and decomposing the peroxide to oxygen and water. The components boil in the process, and the pressure of the oxygen gas explodes the mixture out of the gland with an audible pop. The hot, acrid quinones deter most predators.

However, no defense is foolproof. For each defense, a counterdefense exists; for each ploy, a counterploy. The conspicuous black desert beetle, *Eleodes,* slowly and conspicuously ambles along the white sands of the Southwest deserts. When disturbed, it stands on its head in warning display, advertising its quinone chemical defense, stored in glands at the tip of its abdomen. However, grasshopper mice readily grab the insect. Jamming the beetle's rear end into the ground, the mouse calmly munches its prey as the beetle ineffectively discharges its secretion into the soil.

Chemical Defenses of Common Invertebrate Animals

Animal	Type of Defense	Chemical Used	Scientific Name
slug	glands	sticky mucus	*Arion* spp., *Limax maximus*
polydesmid millipede	two-chambered reaction gland	hydrogen cyanide, benzaldehyde	*Apheloria corrugata*
glomerid millipede	glands	sticky glue fortified with alkaloids	*Glomeris marginata*
lithobiid centipede	glands	sticky glue	*Lithobius* spp.
harvestman	gland	quinone	*Vonones* spp.
whipscorpion	gland	acetic acid	*Mastigoproctus giganteus*
swallowtail caterpillar	evertible osmeterium	isobutyric acid	*Papilio* spp.
monarch caterpillar, adult	blood toxin derived from milkweed	cardiac glycosides	*Danaus plexippus*
milkweed tiger moth caterpillar	blood toxin derived from milkweed	cardiac glycosides	*Euchaetias egle*
milkweed bug	blood toxin derived from milkweed	cardiac glycosides	*Oncopeltus* spp., *Lygaeus* spp.
pentatomid stink bug	glands	tridecane	*Euschistus servus, Nezara viridula*
earwig	gland	quinones	*Forficula auricularia*
syrphid fly larvae	salivary secretion	proteinaceous glue	*Syrphus* spp.
milkweed beetle	blood toxin derived from milkweed	cardiac glycosides	*Tetraopes tetraophthalmus*
ladybug beetle	toxic blood	coccinelline and other alkaloids	*Coccinella* spp.
firefly	toxic blood	steroidal pyrones	*Photinus* spp.
blister beetle	toxic blood	cantharidin	*Epicauta ruficeps* and others
bombardier beetle	two-chambered reaction gland	hot quinones	*Brachinus* spp.
darkling beetle	glands	quinones	*Eleodes* spp.
caterpillar hunter beetle	glands	salicylaldehyde, methacrylic acid	*Calasoma* spp.
lubber grasshopper	tracheal glands	frothy mixture of many substances	*Romalea microptera*
grasshopper	regurgitation of gut fluids	plant juices	many species
sawfly larvae	regurgitation of gut fluids	pine resin from needles	*Neodiprion* spp.

ACTIVITIES

Observing chemically defended invertebrates

One way to study the chemical defenses of invertebrates is to go into the field to observe these animals. Pick up each creature with your fingers or a forceps, and see what happens. Many insects become wet with the secretion they discharge. Smell each insect carefully. Ideally one would like to observe these animals behaving normally in the field, but it is difficult to observe natural encounters. However, you can bring the animals home and set them up in jars or small terraria, where they can be fed and watched. Try feeding chemically protected insects to predators such as frogs and spiders to observe the effectiveness of these defenses.

Making an insect collection

In addition to studying live insects, you can also make a collection of preserved specimens. A well-labeled display is beautiful and instructive. Except for soft-bodied insects, such as fly larvae, caterpillars, and many aquatic animals, most insects are simply pinned and mounted in boxes. Once dried, they keep indefinitely.

KILLING JARS

Insects must first be killed. Killing jars can be purchased from biological supply houses, or you can make your own. The fumes from ethyl acetate, chloroform, or

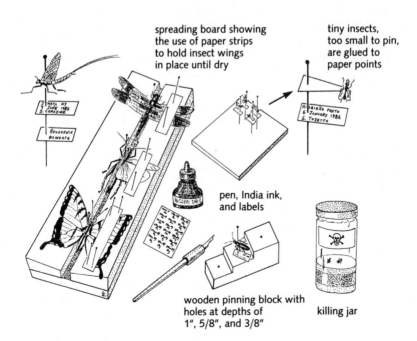

spreading board showing the use of paper strips to hold insect wings in place until dry

tiny insects, too small to pin, are glued to paper points

pen, India ink, and labels

wooden pinning block with holes at depths of 1", 5/8", and 3/8"

killing jar

How to mount insects.

carbon tetrachloride will kill insects. A killing jar is made from a wide-mouthed jar with something absorptive on the bottom. The easiest method is to put a few drops of the killing fluid on a piece of cotton or paper towel, and place it in the jar. A more permanent killing jar is made by mixing plaster and water, and pouring a layer on the bottom of the jar. After it has set, a few drops of ethyl acetate or other poison can be added to the dry plaster, which will absorb it completely so that insects added to the jar will not get wet.

A cyanide killing jar lasts longer without needing to be recharged. They are safe to use if certain precautions are observed. To make a cyanide killing jar, place a one-quarter-inch layer of sodium or potassium cyanide crystals on the bottom of a dry, wide-mouthed, screw-cap jar. A half-inch layer of dry sawdust is laid over that, then a half-inch layer of wet plaster is added and allowed to set. These jars slowly release poisonous hydrogen cyanide gas. Remember that cyanide gas is extremely toxic to human beings and animals, and is released in dangerous quantities if the chemical comes in contact with water. If you do not have experience in handling toxic chemicals, seek the assistance of an expert, or purchase a killing jar ready-made. Cover the outside of the jar with tape to prevent breakage, and dispose of a broken jar carefully, preferably by burying it. All killing jars should be labeled POISON.

PINNING AND LABELING SPECIMENS

After the insects are killed, they must be pinned and labeled. Common sewing pins are too thick and short, and they will rust. Insect pins in various sizes can be purchased from supply houses. As shown in the figures, most insects are pinned vertically through the thorax. Grasp the insect between the thumb and index finger of one hand and insert the pin with the other hand. The insects and their labels should be mounted at a uniform height on the pin. This is accomplished easily with a pinning block, a cube of wood with three small holes drilled to different depths, serving as guides. After the insect is placed on the pin, the pin is inserted into the deepest hole in the block until it touches the bottom, pushing the insect up to the proper height. Small rectangular paper labels are also attached to the pin at uniform heights, using the other holes as depth guides. The upper label has the locality, date, and collector's name. A second label is used for the insect's name, or for other information, such as the habitat or food plant.

Before the labels are placed on the pins, it is best to let the insect dry thoroughly in position. The abdomen of a freshly killed insect will often sag. It can be held in place with two crossed pins, or with a piece of stiff paper placed temporarily on the pin beneath the insect's body. Specimens should be allowed to dry for at least a week. You can determine whether they are ready by very gently touching the abdomen. If it is entirely stiff, the insect is dry. Dry specimens are extremely brittle and must be handled with care to avoid breaking legs, wings, and antennae.

Specimens with long legs or large wings (moths, butterflies, dragonflies) need to have these appendages neatly arranged. A special spreading board is used for large-winged insects. Care must be taken in handling moths and butterflies in order not to rub off the wing scales. Always use a forceps to manipulate the wings. Minute insects are glued to small triangular pieces of paper cut from index cards.

If the insects are pinned shortly after they are killed, they will be soft and can be handled without damaging them. If they have dried out, the specimens must be relaxed. Place the insects in a wide-mouthed jar with some wet sand on the bottom. Add a few drops of phenol or detergent to prevent the formation of mold. After a day or two the insects will be relaxed enough to pin.

ARRANGEMENT AND CARE OF THE COLLECTION

A neatly arranged, carefully labeled collection can be quite useful. Most collections are arranged taxonomically, with all the same types of insects placed together. A label with the insect order or family can be placed at the top of the box and all the insects in that group mounted below. More specialized collections can be made illustrating ecological relationships. You might want to group together all the insects found on a particular food plant, such as milkweed, or all insects found in the desert.

Dermestid beetles and ants are the bane of any insect collection. They can quickly destroy all your specimens. You must place naphthalene flakes or para-dichlorobenzene balls in every box of your collection. Tiny cardboard boxes filled with the repellent should be firmly fastened in the corners of the collection. Special insect boxes can be purchased to house your specimens. They have tight-fitting lids and are lined with cork or Styrofoam® for easy pinning. A variety of homemade boxes can also be used. Cigar boxes work fine. A Riker mount is a short, glass-topped box about an inch high, filled with a layer of cotton. They are ideal for displaying large butterflies.

Collecting insects will keep you busy for a lifetime, wherever you may be. With over a million insect species, new specimens are lurking under every stone.

REFERENCES AND SUGGESTIONS FOR FURTHER READING

Blum, M.S. 1981. *Chemical Defenses of Arthropods.* Academic Press, New York.

Borror, D.J., and White, R.E. 1970. *A Field Guide to the Insects.* Houghton Mifflin, Boston.

Edmunds, M. 1974. *Defence in Animals.* Longman, New York.

Eisner, T. 1970. Chemical Defense Against Predation in Arthropods. In E. Sondheimer, and J.B. Simeone, eds., *Chemical Ecology.* Academic Press, New York.

Milne, L., and Milne, M. 1980. *The Audubon Society Field Guide to North American Insects and Spiders.* Knopf, New York.

14

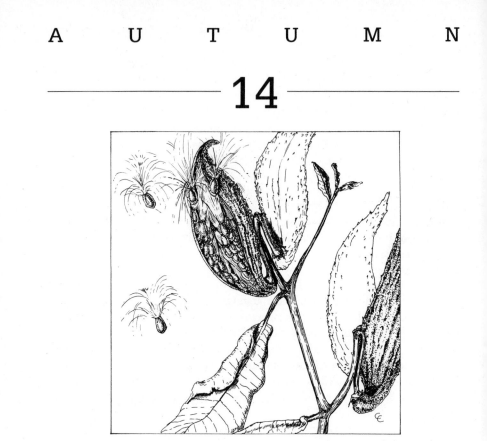

Seed Dispersal: Preparing for the Next Generation

EARLIER THIS SUMMER, flowers were in their peak bloom. In our studies of plant pollination, we learned about relationships between flowers and insects. We watched honey bees carry milkweed pollinia from plant to plant, and we observed the devices by which flowers dust insect visitors with pollen.

Now, as autumn approaches, millions of mature seeds are the fruit of these interactions. Plants are now ready for the next step in the process whose ultimate goal is the creation of offspring. That next step is the dispersal of the seeds to sites suitable for germination and growth.

WHY BOTHER?

Seeds have such an intriguing variety of dispersal mechanisms that we could spend days in the field marveling at their intricacies. It makes me think that it must be very important for the plant to scatter its seeds across the countryside. No adaptation is created on a whim, so the fact that so many different seed-dispersal mechanisms have evolved hints at their importance. We are, therefore, forced to ask ourselves, "Why bother?" Why do all these adaptations for seed dispersal exist?

Common sense tells us that young seedlings need to get out from underneath their parents' feet in order to survive. A tiny acorn would have too much competition for food and sunlight trying to grow among the roots at the base of a tall oak tree. In addition, predators are much more likely to discover seeds or seedlings directly beneath the parent plant. Insects, rodents, and birds may decimate populations of seeds that fall near the parent. In one study conducted on suburban lawns, the seedlings of an elm, growing directly beneath the tree, suffered nearly 600 times greater mortality from leaf beetles than seedlings only meters away. The piles of cracked walnut shells at the base of the trees attest to the fate of nuts that are not dispersed. Seed dispersal, even a few feet from the parent, may be a crucial factor in enabling seedlings to escape mortality. When squirrels cache walnuts beneath the ground for later use, not all are eaten. Many survive to germinate.

What other advantages might there be for seed dispersal? Habitats are unstable. Fires rage, and areas are swept clear of plants by floods and erosion. Plants living in precarious, changing environments may find that the best strategy is to constantly move on, utilizing new habitats. Trees age and fall, and short-lived annuals and biennials die, leaving fertile gaps in the environment waiting to be colonized by opportunistic pioneers. The seeds that get there first have an ideal location to start a new life. The ability to exploit rapidly new habitats may help assure the spread, and ultimate survival, of a plant species.

SOME DIFFICULTIES THAT SEEDS ENCOUNTER

Seed dispersal is no simple task. The goal of a seed is to reach a suitable environment in a viable state, but along the way are many obstacles and blind alleys.

Many adaptations for seed dispersal have evolved, but none is foolproof. Some seeds are deposited in unsuitable environments where they may desiccate, rot, or be consumed by predators. Seeds may lack sufficient light or soil nutrients to grow. Each of these dead ends represents wasted energy on the part of the plant, and must be minimized to assure the long-term survival of the species. The burs clinging to my pants when I return from a field trip usually end up in the trash, unlikely to reach a promising spot of fertile soil. Many of those burs are also hosts to insect larvae that devour the plant embryo. After all, the seed contains valuable food supplies that may nourish a predator as well as the plant embryo.

In response to problems such as these, seeds have evolved a variety of strategies. One solution is to make a seed so small and insignificant, so lacking in any appreciable quantity of food that it wouldn't pay for a predator to eat it. The seeds of orchids are so fine they appear as dust. A single capsule may produce more than a million seeds; 100,000 weigh less than a gram. By producing vast quantities of seeds, the plant also "hedges its bets," increasing its chances of finding a suitable site for a few of them. Another ploy is to produce a larger seed with plenty of nutrients for the growing plant, but to protect it. The seed may be surrounded by a hard shell, or be packaged with poisons to deter predators. Black walnuts have both a rock-hard nut and a thick, bitter husk. The seeds of yew, rosary pea, castor bean, horsechestnut, buckeye, and jack-in-the-pulpit are toxic to human beings and other animals. Acorns taste of astringent tannins. Obviously this defense doesn't always work, since many acorns are consumed by squirrels. Nonetheless, sufficient acorns escape detection or are never retrieved after being buried for later use.

TO EACH HIS OWN

The many ways that plants scatter their seeds

Lacking mobility, seeds avail themselves of every imaginable means of getting about. They sail in the wind, ride water currents, hitch rides with insects, rodents, and birds, and explosively propel themselves through the air.

Plants that rely on air currents have several strategies to keep their seeds aloft and prevent them from falling to the ground too quickly, too close to their parents. The fluffy hairs of milkweeds and the plumes of dandelions act as parachutes, which increase the surface area of the seed so that the slightest breeze is sufficient to carry it off. By hovering and drifting in the air, the seed has a greater opportunity to catch a ride in the wind. Extremely minute seeds, like those of orchids, do not need hairs or fancy structural modifications to catch the wind. The gentlest puff of wind carries them off, like dust.

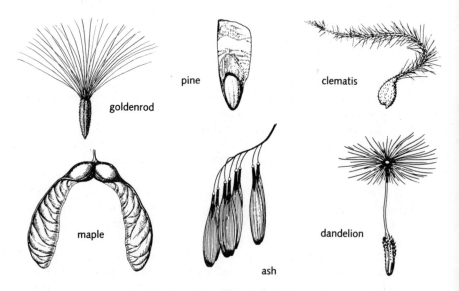

goldenrod

pine

clematis

maple

ash

dandelion

Common wind-dispersed seeds. In part, from Botany, *6th Ed., T.E. Weier, C.R. Stocking, M.G. Barbour, and T.L. Rost, copyright © 1982 by John Wiley & Sons, New York, p. 320, and* Biology of Plants, *4th Ed., Raven, Evert & Eichorn, 1986, copyright © Worth Publishers, New York. Reprinted by permission.*

Maple, ash, and basswood seeds use a different aerodynamic approach — twirling blades and helicopterlike rotors. Again, the strategy is to keep the seed as light as possible and to increase its surface area. In addition, these fruits, called **samaras**, produce aerodynamic lift as they sail downward through the sky. The asymmetrical profile of an airplane wing causes air to flow faster over the top of the wing than the bottom. According to a well-known principle of physics, **Bernoulli's law**, this increased velocity creates a region of lower pressure above the wing, producing an upward force called **lift**. Flying samaras take advantage of Bernoulli's principle, but they achieve their lift in a somewhat different manner. If you have ever watched a tulip tree or ailanthus seed fall, you've noticed that it rotates on its long axis as it descends. This rotation also produces lift, sending the samaras flying gracefully downward instead of just plummeting to earth.

Tumbleweed also takes advantage of the wind, but in a rather crude way. Rather than devise a method of delicately keeping its seeds airborne, the entire plant breaks off at the base and is blown across the prairies, scattering its seeds as it tumbles erratically on its way. Nature has no concern for grace, only utility. If it works, do it.

Water is the other inanimate disperser, carrying seeds in ocean currents, rivers, or the runoff from rains. To make the most of their aquatic journeys, water-borne seeds often possess flotation devices, such as hairy coatings, and tissues with corky air- or oil-filled spaces. The giant coconut fruit and the cranberry both readily float.

Other seeds are small and take advantage of surface tension, with unwettable surface coatings that allow the seeds to rest on the water's surface membrane. A number of plants, such as purple loosestrife, arrowhead, and woundwort, have floating seedlings buoyed up by their lightweight airy **cotyledons** (the embryo leaves in a seed). Spring rains and flooding carry these little travelers on long journeys.

Animals are excellent seed dispersers. Many eat the seeds along with their edible outer coating, passing them through their gastrointestinal tracts unharmed. Others eat the fleshy seed coats and discard the hard pits. Hackberry, occurring throughout much of the United States, has fruits (drupes) with a thin, fleshy pulp covering a hard stone that contains the seed. They are an important winter food source for cedar waxwings, robins, mockingbirds, and yellow-bellied sapsuckers. Wild cherries are among our most widespread and important wildlife food plants. With bitter cherry in the Northwest, black cherry in the East, pin cherry in the Northeast, and choke cherry throughout much of the country, this fruit feeds grouse, grosbeaks, robins, starlings, thrushes, cedar waxwings, bear, rabbits, raccoons, fox, chipmunks, and mice.

In most cases, the larger animals eat the fruits whole. The seeds may germinate better after being exposed to intestinal fluids or after having their seed coats slightly abraded in the gut or gizzard. They are also deposited right in the midst of a pile of fertile manure.

Mammals such as squirrels, chipmunks, and mice carry seeds to nests and underground burrows, where they are cracked open and eaten. However, a few may be carelessly lost or forgotten, and may have the opportunity to germinate. Acorns, hickory nuts, walnuts, cherries, grapes, beechnuts, and hazelnuts are dispersed this way. In one study in Virginia, 50 blue jays cached 150,000 acorns in 28 days. Quite interesting was the observation that the jays were selecting sound nuts to cache. By holding or rattling the acorns in their bills, the birds were able to discriminate between viable and unsound nuts, and they dropped the latter beneath the trees.

Other animals inadvertently pick up hitchhiking seeds that attach themselves to an animal's fur with barbs, hooks, or spines. Seeds are also picked up on animals' feet, along with the muck and mud from swamps. Ducks and raccoons may disperse seeds in this manner.

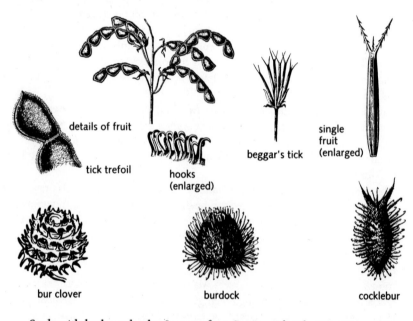

details of fruit

tick trefoil

hooks
(enlarged)

beggar's tick

single
fruit
(enlarged)

bur clover

burdock

cocklebur

Seeds with barbs or hooks. In part, from Botany, *6th Ed., T.E. Weier, C.R. Stocking, M.G. Barbour, and T.L. Rost, copyright © 1982 by John Wiley & Sons, New York, p. 320. Reprinted by permission.*

We are all familiar with seed dispersal by birds and mammals, but there is another disperser, often no bigger than the seed itself. Ants have evolved a curious mutualistic relationship with some flowers. Certain seeds possess edible outgrowths or appendages called **elaiosomes**. They are generally white and oily and quite attractive to ants, which grab the elaiosomes along with the attached seeds and carry them back to their nests where the nutritious knobs are eaten. The seeds themselves remain, often quite hard, smooth, and spherical, now difficult to grasp since their handles have been consumed. The seeds aren't eaten. If possible, the ants may carry them out of the nest. Otherwise they are forgotten, remaining below ground where some may eventually germinate.

An ant carrying a seed of wild ginger that has a fleshy, attractive appendage called an elaiosome.

One might argue that ants don't really carry seeds far enough to be effective seed dispersers, but distance is not the crucial factor. Quick removal and burial, even nearby, effectively shield the seeds from destruction by seed predators, such as mice and birds. Some of our most common and admired flowers appear to have entered into this cooperative bargain with the indefatigable ants. Many of the early spring wildflowers — trilliums, violets, squirrel corn, hepatica, bloodroot, twinleaf, and wild ginger — have elaiosomes. These seed appendages have no known function except to serve as attractants and food for ants.

The final category to consider is dispersal by the plant itself. Although lacking mobility, plants have evolved active explosive or shooting devices, and a number of more passive means of ejecting their seeds.

In various ways, the fruits build up tension internally, providing the force to blast their seeds remarkable distances. In many species, as the fruit matures, dries, and contracts, tension develops. In the vetches and other legumes (members of the pea family), the two valves of the pod split and explosively curl, ejecting the seeds. Witch hazel capsules contract, sending the seeds as far as 50 feet. Similar mechanisms occur in the maturing fruits of violets, castor beans, wood sorrels, and cranesbills.

In other cases, tension develops in the living fruit wall. The lightest touch causes the valves of jewelweed capsules to split and coil like a stretched rubber band, sending the seeds flying. Its other common name, touch-me-not, is quite appropriate.

Dwarf mistletoe is a parasitic plant that grows on tree branches and causes great forest damage in the western United States. Hydrostatic pressure builds up in the fruits, blasting the seeds at speeds of up to 60 miles per hour! This is believed to be one way the seeds are spread from branch to branch and tree to tree. The seeds also have a viscid coating, so that when they land, they stick and germinate in place.

Passive mechanisms rely not on internal tension to eject the seeds, but on the action of an external agent to provide the energy for propulsion. Many of the plants in this category have long, slender, elastic stalks that swing, sway, or snap back, broadcasting the seeds from their capsules. The most familiar contraptions are the "salt-shaker" fruits of the poppies. The globular capsules have pores at the top from which the seeds are shaken free as the stalks swing to and fro in strong winds. Less

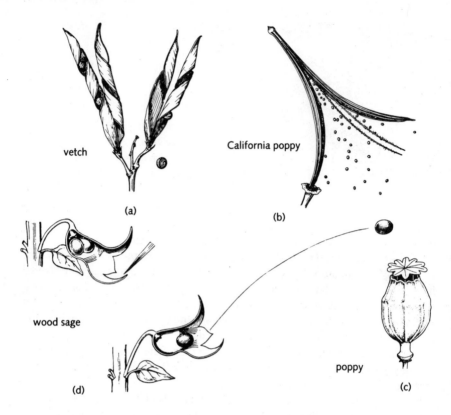

Seeds that shoot or catapult themselves. Seeds of vetch (a) and California poppy (b) are dispersed when the seed capsules dry and suddenly snap open. The "salt-shaker" capsules of poppy (c) have pores at the top from which the seeds are shaken free. When the dry calyx of mints such as wood sage (d) is snagged by a passing animal, it catapults its seeds. In part, from Botany, 6th Ed., T.E. Weier, C.R. Stocking, M.G. Barbour, and T.L. Rost, copyright © 1982 by John Wiley & Sons, New York, p. 320, and Biology of Plants, 4th Ed., Raven, Evert & Eichorn, 1986, copyright © Worth Publishers, New York. Reprinted by permission.

specialized yet efficient capsules are found in the irises and evening primroses. Although their mechanism of seed dispersal may seem rather feeble, measurements show that seeds of the opium poppy can be catapulted up to 45 feet.

Other plants combine an open-ended fruit containing loose seeds with some mechanism to momentarily grip passing animals, bending the stalk and allowing it to spring back into position, ejecting the seeds. Many of the mints, such as motherwort and sage, have flower heads shaped like globular balls, consisting of a whorl of calyces. Each calyx (the remains of a single flower) is a cuplike container edged with five sharp teeth, which briefly snag a passing animal or curious naturalist, then snap back, rocketing the seed through the air.

One could spend chapters describing all the intricate adaptations that have evolved to perfect the process of seed dispersal. What is most important, however, is that we each learn to see with a questioning eye, asking why each stem, fruit, seed, and flower part is shaped the way it is, and how it contributes to the function and success of that particular plant. There are no accidents in nature's design of organisms. Each structure represents a step toward the solution of a particular problem. Viewed in this manner, the fields and woodlands are a classroom where we may learn about the adaptations and the evolution of organisms.

For example, what might be the advantages and disadvantages of a parachuting versus a gliding, winged seed? We've seen that they both fly quite well. One problem with the fluffy, buoyant seeds is that they have weight restrictions and can't afford to pack much food into the seed. The samaras carry a much larger seed with more food, giving the seed a better chance of survival. An advantage of a plumed seed, however, is the greater distance it covers. Winged seeds invariably descend, even though they sometimes glide downward at a fairly shallow angle. The fluffy plumes are often lifted in the updrafts and carried far from the parent plant.

In this analysis, we must also consider the nature of the plant. Only tall trees can be used by the relatively heavy samaras because they need a considerable height from which to take off and begin to spin. The plumed seeds are prevalent in plants of open areas, such as roadsides and recently cleared fields. These open areas have a free flow of wind and many available sites in which to germinate. Here, the strategy is to produce a great number of smaller seeds and to scatter them as widely as possible.

In contrast, the samaras are typically found among trees of woodlands and forests, where there may be less wind and fewer habitable spots. The samaras don't rely on gusty breezes, but produce their own aerodynamic lift as they spin down from the tall trees. The seeds don't travel far, relying more on the chance opportunity to find a small sunlit clearing on the forest floor.

Walking through a field of flowers, dried and shriveled, ready to disseminate their offspring, we can learn the names of a few dozen plants, and remember the type of seed each has and how it is dispersed. However, it is important to look beyond these details and to understand the underlying processes that fashioned all these wonderful and peculiar contraptions and contrivances. Patterns emerge. Nature has designed a great variety of different dispersal mechanisms, but they are often derived from similar floral parts. The fruit's ovary wall can be fashioned into a hairy plume, a delicate wing, or a series of barbs. On the other hand, there are many similar dispersal mechanisms, all constructed from different floral parts. Fluffy parachutes are derived from seed coat hairs, sepals, or from the ovary wall. Nature is an inventive and opportunistic builder, gathering haphazardly the available spare parts of an organism, using whatever is available to suit the purpose. Through the gradual modification of existing structures, new contrivances evolve that add to the organism's individual success. There is no master plan, no grand design, that has been followed in the construction of these seed dispersal adaptations. Here is a lesson to be learned about all of nature, not just the means by which seeds are scattered.

COMMON SEED-DISPERSAL MECHANISMS

SEED DISPERSAL BY WIND

Seeds with parachutes and plumes that increase surface area/volume ratios

Common Name	Scientific Name	Family
milkweed	*Asclepias* spp.	Milkweed
cattail	*Typha* spp.	Cattail
fireweed	*Epilobium angustifolium*	Evening Primrose
sycamore	*Platanus occidentalis*	Sycamore
dandelion	*Taraxacum officinale*	Daisy
goat's beard	*Tragopogon pratensis*	Daisy
goldenrod	*Solidago* spp.	Daisy
thistle	*Cirsium* spp.	Daisy
thimbleweed	*Anemone virginiana*	Buttercup
virgin's bower	*Clematis virginiana*	Buttercup

Seeds with wings that increase surface area/volume ratios and provide aerodynamic lift

Common Name	Scientific Name	Family
maple	*Acer* spp.	Maple
elm	*Ulmus* spp.	Elm
basswood	*Tilia americana*	Linden
tree of heaven	*Ailanthus altissima*	Ailanthus
catalpa	*Catalpa* spp.	Trumpet Creeper
pine	*Pinus* spp.	Pine
birch	*Betula* spp.	Birch

ACTIVITIES

Exploring a plant's adaptations for seed dispersal

Now that we've seen how wind, water, and animals help to disperse seeds, let's wander to the fields to see these devices in action. Before we begin, we should pause for a brief explanation of some botanical terminology. In the previous discussion, I have used terms such as seed, fruit, pod, capsule, and samara. Each describes something different. Most people think of a fruit as a fleshy structure filled with seeds, like an apple or an orange. To a botanist, a fruit is the ripened ovary with its enclosed seeds, plus any other structures closely associated with it. Pea pods, maple samaras, and poppy capsules are fruits. The so-called seeds of sunflowers, maples, or dill, kernels of corn, and nuts, such as acorns and walnuts, are all fruits. The seed itself is the matured ovule within the fruit. It consists of a small plant embryo and a food supply to initiate its development.

COMMON SEED-DISPERSAL MECHANISMS *(continued)*

ANIMAL DISPERSAL

Seeds with barbs, hooks, and spines that cling to an animal's fur

Common Name	Scientific Name	Family
burdock	*Arctium minus*	Daisy
cocklebur	*Xanthium strumarium*	Daisy
beggar's tick	*Bidens* spp.	Daisy
sweet cicely	*Osmorhiza claytoni*	Carrot
tick trefoil	*Desmodium* spp.	Pea
agrimony	*Agrimonia* spp.	Rose
avens	*Geum* spp.	Rose
enchanter's nightshade	*Circaea quadrisculata*	Evening Primrose

SELF-DISPERSAL

Plants using a variety of contrivances to shoot or catapult their seeds

Common Name	Scientific Name	Family
wild bergamot	*Monarda fistulosa*	Mint
wood sage	*Teucrium* spp.	Mint
violet	*Viola* spp.	Violet
wood sorrel	*Oxalis* spp.	Wood-sorrel
castor bean	*Ricinus communis*	Spurge
jewelweed	*Impatiens capensis*	Touch-me-not
vetch	*Vicia* spp.	Pea
birdfoot trefoil	*Lotus corniculatus*	Pea
storksbill	*Erodium cicutarium*	Geranium
spring cress, bittercress	*Cardamine* spp.	Mustard

First, we'll do some careful observations. Look at each plant you come across and try to figure out all the details of how its seeds are dispersed, remembering that even in the most obvious cases there are new things to learn. Think of how all the parts of the plant conspire to achieve optimal seed dispersal. Consider the habitat in which the plant grows. Is there anything about the terrain or associated vegetation that makes the plant's dispersal mechanism particularly suited to that environment? For example, dandelions and milkweeds both have plumed seeds, but notice how the milkweed plumes are packed tightly into the pod. The milkweed needs an efficient means to get its 100 or 200 seeds out and exposed to the breezes. The pod is a fruit called a **follicle**, which means that it splits along a single seam, unlike peas in which the pod opens on both sides. When the follicle dries and opens, the seeds are broad and flattened to catch the wind. When one seed is finally yanked free, it catches the hairs of the next seed, so that each comes out in sequence like the tissues in a box. This process is gradual, and it may take many weeks for every seed to be dispersed. In contrast, the dandelion has its seeds already well exposed to the wind, carefully laid out in a spherical pattern, ready to be plucked by the lightest breeze. Its seeds are generally carried off within a day or two of maturation.

Choose a plant, and try to make a list of as many of its seed-dispersal adaptations as you can. How high off the ground are the flower heads? How stout is the stem? Does it persist all winter, like that of the teasels, evening primroses, and mulleins? What proportion of the seeds remain in early autumn, late autumn, and winter? Are some seeds still on the plant in the spring? What shape is the seed? The poppies and mints have rounded seeds, which roll and easily catapult free from their capsules.

Make a reference collection of seeds and dried flower stalks. Envelopes or clear plastic boxes are convenient for storing seeds. A piece of wood, such as a two-by-four with holes drilled along its length, makes a convenient stand in which to place dried flower stalks. As always, be sure to label your collection.

Collecting seed hitchhikers

Collect some seed hitchhikers by running through a field and dragging different types of cloth (or by wearing clothing of various materials). How many different kinds of seeds cling to the cloth? Try this at weekly intervals to discover when the various seeds mature. If you have a pet dog, comb through its hair to see how various seeds become attached. Examine each seed carefully. How many different attachment devices can you discover? One type, found in burdock and agrimony, acts like Velcro®. How do the seeds of beggar's tick and sweet cicely cling to their victims?

On a wing and a prayer — Experiments with flying seeds

The winged and plumed seeds cast their fate to the wind, in "hope" that their aerial voyage will finally land them in a propitious spot.

For the following observations and experiments, gather as many varieties of wind-dispersed seeds as you can find. First, let's compare the flight pattern of each. Find an elevated spot, such as an upper-story window, a tall ladder, or a rooftop. Release each seed and record how far it travels, how long it stays aloft, and the angle at which it glides to the ground. Try making a diagram of its flight path. Which seed wins the distance contest, landing farthest from its point of release? Which seed is most buoyant, taking longest to reach the ground?

With the naked eye, it may be difficult to observe some of the intricate acrobatics of the winged seeds as they spin and spiral rapidly to earth. Studies using stroboscopic lights have allowed scientists to get a better picture of what is happening. The samara of a maple can revolve 13 times per second, while the smaller seed of the Norway spruce spins 20 times per second, far too fast for the human eye to appreciate. Even at these speeds, you should be able to see that the motion of maple samaras is different from samaras of the ash or tulip trees. The maples spin downward in a uniform helix, while the tulip and ash samaras stop spinning about their vertical axes at regular intervals, drop several inches, and then start spinning again.

It is easier to experiment with these samaras by building large cardboard models of each. The models will spin and rotate slower, enabling you to get a better idea of what's going on. You can also modify the models, adding weights to different areas and snipping off portions of the wings to see how the changes affect the flight of your model samaras.

Tape pennies to the spot on the model where the seed is located. How heavy a load can a cardboard maple samara carry before it simply plummets from the sky? Tape weights on the end of the wing, opposite to where the seed is located. Will this abnormally weighted samara fly? How much of the wing can you remove before the samara won't glide or spin? Can you construct a novel kind of samara that will fly as well as nature's own designs?

Gather some plumed seeds of milkweed or dandelion. If you have enough patience, try counting the number of hairs on different species of seeds. Does each seed have approximately the same number of hairs, or do the larger seeds have more? Can the seeds remain aloft with a portion of their hairs removed, or with the hairs cut half as short?

Animals as seed dispersers

Animals inadvertently transport seeds over the countryside. Human traffic, especially international travel, has dispersed plants throughout the world. We can begin to appreciate the extent of this seed dispersal with a few backyard experiments. Tramp along the edge of a pond or stream, then collect some of the muck clinging to your boots. Get some sterile potting soil, or bake some garden soil to kill any viable seeds it may contain. Mix this dirt with the mud you have scraped from your boots, wet it thoroughly, and place it in a tray covered with a plate of glass to keep the soil moist. Set it in a warm, shady spot for a few weeks. How many seeds germinate? Can you grow them to the stage where you can identify them?

Seeds are also carried in the guts of animals, to be deposited later in their droppings. Gather some scats (droppings) from a variety of different seed-eaters, such as birds, raccoons, and opossums. (There are various field guides to animal tracks and signs that will help you identify the source of your finds.) Try germinating them as you did the seeds from your muddy boots. How many seeds are still viable? Do the seeds gathered right from the plants germinate as well as those that have passed through the animal's gastrointestinal tract?

REFERENCES AND SUGGESTIONS FOR FURTHER READING

Brown, Lauren. 1977. *Weeds in Winter.* Houghton Mifflin, Boston.

Howe, H.F., and Smallwood, J. 1983. The ecology of seed dispersal. *Annual Review of Ecology and Systematics* 13: 201–228.

Johnson, W.C., and Adkisson, C.S. October 1986. Airlifting the oaks. *Natural History* 95: 40–46.

Lampe, K.F., and McCann, M.A. 1985. *AMA Handbook of Poisonous and Injurious Plants*. American Medical Association, Chicago.

Martin, A.C.; Zim, H.S.; and Nelson, A.L. 1951. *American Wildlife and Plants, A Guide to Wildlife Food Habits*. Dover, New York.

McCutchen, C.W. 1977. The spinning rotation of ash and tulip tree samaras. *Science* 197: 691–692.

Murie, O.J. 1975. *A Field Guide to Animal Tracks*. Houghton Mifflin, Boston.

Peterson, R.T., and McKenny, M. 1968. *A Field Guide to Wildflowers*. Houghton Mifflin, Boston.

Pijl, L. van der. 1982. *Principles of Dispersal in Higher Plants*. Springer-Verlag, Berlin.

Vogel, S. 1981. *Life in Moving Fluids*. Willard Grant Press, Boston.

15

A Glimpse at Fungi

FUNGI HAVE an awful reputation. Perhaps the very few deadly species of mush-rooms have given them all a bad name. Historically, mushrooms have had a prominent place in the folklore of black magic and of witches' brews. Ancient potions and poisons usually contained a toadstool or two along with the requisite lizard's tail and raven's claw. Whatever the reason, Americans have acquired a severe case of mycophobia—fear of mushrooms. Perhaps this chapter will provide the antidote. What follows is a glimpse at the world of fungi. I hope it will whet your appetite.

Mushrooms are so unpopular that most do not have common names. You will have to bear with tongue-twisting scientific names in this chapter.

WHAT ARE FUNGI?

The larger organisms of this planet can be divided into three groups, or kingdoms: the animals, the plants, and the fungi. Traditionally, the fungi have been regarded as plants lacking the green chlorophyll necessary to carry on photosynthesis, but this definition did not give them the status they deserve.

Fungi have characteristics in common with both plants and animals. Fungi are plantlike in their lack of mobility, but are animallike in their nutrition; they do not produce their own food but must obtain it from dead or living organisms. In addition, the main component of their cell walls is not cellulose, as with plants, but **chitin**, the same tough material that makes up the hard skeleton of insects. Unlike both plants and animals, the cells of fungi are not separate, discrete units. The partitions between adjacent cells are generally incomplete or absent, so that the **cytoplasm** (cell sap) is continuous through the organism. Fungi reproduce by means of microscopic seeds called **spores**. These produce filamentous (threadlike), branching structures called **hyphae**, which form a mass called a **mycelium**. What we think of as a mushroom is just the fruit of this mycelium. Hidden beneath the ground, ramifying through soil and rotting logs, are tangled webs of mycelium, which intermittently send up a fruiting body called a mushroom. The mushrooms we eat are thus analogous to the apples on a tree.

THE MAJOR GROUPS OF FLESHY FUNGI

To begin your study of mushrooms, the first thing you should do is familiarize yourself with the two major groups of fungi. They differ in the type of cell that bears the spores, and the shape of the spore-bearing surface. In the **ascomycetes**, the spores develop inside a cell called an **ascus**. There are generally eight spores to an ascus, lined up like peas in a pod. The ascus has a lid at the tip, which opens to release the spores. In the other major group, the **basidiomycetes**, the spores — usually four — develop on the apex of a special cell called a **basidium**. At maturity, each spore pops off at its point of attachment.

In the cup fungi, the asci (plural of ascus) line the inner surface of a cuplike structure. Among the morels, the asci coat the surface of the wrinkled or pitted cap. The spore-bearing surface of the basidiomycetes is more intricate. The basidia line the surface of teeth, branches, ridges, pores, gills, or hollow saclike structures. These are all means of increasing the surface area in order to pack as many spores as possible onto the fruiting body of the fungus.

WHAT FUNGI EAT

Whereas plants are producers and animals consumers, the fungi are the planet's decomposers and cleanup crew, breaking down and recycling every type of organic material. Without the fungi (and bacteria), this planet would be piled high with the remains of trees, plants, and animals. Fungi decompose wood in two ways. The white rot fungi digest both cellulose and lignin, the two main cell wall components of plants. The wood is left white and spongy. The brown rot fungi cannot digest the lignin; they leave the wood brown, harder, and crumbly.

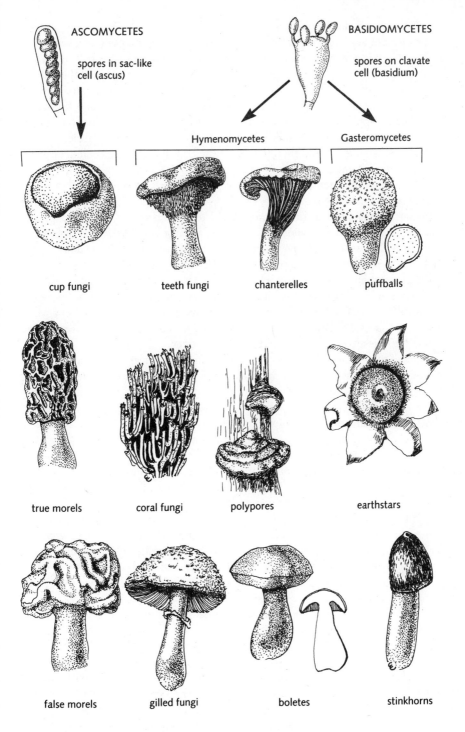

The major groups of fleshy fungi.

This form of nourishment is called **saprophytic** (from the Greek, *sapros,* meaning rotten, and *phyton,* meaning plant). Fungi feed by sending out masses of hyphal threads that secrete digestive enzymes onto their food. The digested breakdown products are then absorbed, much as plant roots absorb nutrients from the soil. We are all familiar with fungi of this sort. Merely open a neglected refrigerator. You will often find greenish colonies of molds upon forgotten leftovers. The appetites of the various saprophytic fungi are quite indiscriminate. They consume not only bread, fruit, vegetables, and other foods, but also leather, paper, lumber, fabric, feathers, dead carcasses, dung, and anything else organic. Their destruction of human goods can be monumental.

In addition to attacking dead and decaying material, fungi are also parasitic, preying upon living organisms. The fungal diseases of man range from such prosaic skin ailments as ringworm and athlete's foot to serious lung diseases with fancy names like coccidioidomycosis and blastomycosis. The fungal diseases of plants are no less important, causing losses of hundreds of millions of dollars when they destroy agricultural crops. The great famine of 1846 in Ireland resulted from the devastation of the potato crop by the potato blight, *Phytophthora infestans.* Tens of thousands of lives were lost. Rusts, smuts, rots, and scabs are other descriptive names for fungal diseases of wheat, oats, corn, potatoes, apples, and other agricultural products. The Dutch elm disease and the chestnut blight are fungal epidemics that have destroyed two of America's favorite trees.

Some fungi attack living insects. These **entomopathogenic** fungi may offer an alternative means of controlling insect pests. *Entomophthora muscae* commonly infects flies in the autumn. The fungus grows within the living fly, eventually filling the entire body cavity with a mass of hyphae. As the fly's internal organs and nervous system are slowly digested, it behaves erratically. Just before death the fly lands upon a smooth surface and becomes attached in place. The fly is now a lifeless container of fungi. The hyphae continue growing in the dead fly, pushing apart the abdominal segments of the fly. The minute fruiting bodies with their spores protrude through the body wall. Then the spores are shot off like bullets, forming a halo of spores surrounding the fly.

A few fungi have developed an unusual predatory way of life, preying upon small nematode worms. The fungal hyphae have sticky knobs like the sundew plant's, which stick to passing worms. In other cases, the hyphae form ringlike lassos. When a nematode inadvertently enters the fungal loop, the cells instantly swell up, squeezing and trapping the worm like a boa constrictor. The hyphae then penetrate the worm's body, release digestive enzymes, and consume their victim.

Not all the activities of fungi are detrimental. Quietly going on beneath the soil, unknown and unappreciated by most of us, is a symbiotic relationship between plants and fungi. Almost all green plants have their roots surrounded or penetrated by fungal hyphae. The fungus benefits by extracting nutrients, such as sugars and starch, from the plant's roots. The plant benefits because of the vast mycelial network that amplifies the plant's root system. This enables more efficient uptake of water and nutrients, such as phosphorus. This fungus-root symbiosis is called a **mycorrhizal association.** The majority of our food crops, economically important trees such as oak, pine, hickory, and beech, as well as nearly every weed and shrub, are involved in this mutualistic relationship. Many attempts at reforestation have failed because tree seedlings were planted that lacked their necessary fungal partners. Most orchids will not even germinate unless they are invaded by a mycorrhizal fungus.

THE LIFE CYCLE OF FUNGI

A mushroom begins its life cycle when a male and female spore germinate, sending out strands of hyphal threads. If hyphae from the two sexes meet, they fuse, giving rise to new hyphal cells containing nuclei from both cells. A mycelium develops that contains the genetic material from both parents. Eventually tiny buds develop in the mycelial tangle. These grow into the fruiting bodies, or mushrooms.

The random union of the male and female hyphae is the key feature of this means of sexual reproduction. To increase the likelihood of a union, the fungi have evolved several adaptations. Fungi can produce billions of wind-blown spores. Some of the large puffballs may produce trillions of spores. Even so, the chance that two spores of the opposite sex will germinate, find one another, and fuse their hyphae is obviously minuscule. If even a small fraction of all the spores produced mushrooms, the earth would be knee-deep in fungi.

Some fungi rely on other means of dispersing their spores. The fetid stinkhorn fungi have spores embedded in a greenish slimy mass at the end of a stalk. The mushroom's odor of carrion and dung attracts flies, slugs, and beetles, which walk over the slime, eating it, and getting it stuck upon their legs. The gooey mass is removed in a matter of hours. The spores, impervious to digestion, are dispersed by the insects as they defecate or wipe their spore-laden feet.

The most bizarre example of spore dispersal concerns the truffle, the famous European fungal delicacy that leads a subterranean existence. In order to locate the fungus, truffle hunters use pigs, which locate the underground truffles and then begin to tear up the ground in a frenzy. How can sows locate truffles three feet below the ground, and why all the excitement? Truffles contain a steroidal chemical identical to that produced by boars. Within their testicles, boars synthesize a sexual attractant, called a **pheromone**, which is transferred to the salivary gland through the bloodstream. During the mating period, the salivating boars release the pheromone, attracting the females. The porcine passion for truffles results from the sows' ardent search for subterranean boars.

Is this merely a chemical coincidence specific to pigs? Not at all. The same steroid is produced by other animals. Burrowing rodents are fond of truffles, and probably locate them by these special odors. The fungus is eaten, and the spores pass through their gastrointestinal tracts unharmed. The spores may even grow better packaged in a fertile ball of dung.

As for the human fondness for truffles, I can only offer the following facts. The truffle compound, with the unseductive name of 5a-androst-16-en-3a-ol, is synthesized in the testes of human males and is secreted by the sweat glands in their armpits. A study was done in which pictures of normally dressed women were shown to volunteers, some of whom were unknowingly exposed to the compound during the viewing. The volunteers were asked to rate the pictures for beauty. Those who were exposed to the pheromone consistently gave the pictures higher scores for attractiveness.

MUSHROOM TOXINS

All of us have probably been warned of the horrible toxicity of mushrooms. Perhaps we have even been cautioned not to touch a mushroom for fear of being poisoned. In fact, of the 5,000 varieties of fungi in the United States, only about 100 are poisonous. Of these, only two are known to have caused fatalities in this country. No mushroom can harm you by your picking it up. Worldwide, there are only 20 deaths from mushroom poisonings each year. Plants are far worse culprits than fungi, causing about ten times as many poisonings.

There are seven groups of poisons — the amanitins, monomethylhydrazine, psilocybin, ibotenic acid, muscimol, coprine, muscarine, and a group of unidentified toxins. The first two groups, amanitins and monomethylhydrazine, can be deadly.

The amanitin toxins are found in the Death Cap or Destroying Angel. These are lovely white mushrooms in the genus *Amanita*. A small brown mushroom, called *Galerina*, which grows on wood, is the other source of this toxin. The False Morel (*Gyromitra esculenta*) contains the other lethal toxin, monomethylhydrazine. Both of these toxins can destroy the cells of the liver and kidney. These mushrooms must be avoided. Anyone considering collecting mushrooms for food should learn to recognize these fungi.

Some toxins primarily affect the central nervous system, so these mushrooms are often eaten for their hallucinogenic effects. In this category are *Psilocybe* and *Panaeolus* mushrooms, which contain psilocybin; certain *Amanita* mushrooms contain ibotenic acid and muscimol.

Coprine by itself is not really a toxin. However, when consumed with alcohol, it causes nausea, vomiting, sweating, and other unpleasant symptoms. It acts by preventing the breakdown of alcohol in the body so that toxic by-products of alcohol metabolism build up in the blood. Its action is similar to that of Antabuse®, a drug used to treat alcoholism.

Muscarine affects the autonomic nervous system, causing perspiration, salivation, tearing, blurred vision, cramps, and diarrhea. The culprits are little brown mushrooms, mostly in the genus *Inocybe*.

The final group of toxic fungi consists of a hodgepodge of poorly studied mushrooms. All we really know is that most of these toxins are not particularly dangerous, generally causing a short bout of nausea, vomiting, and diarrhea. The chemistry of these toxins is mostly unknown.

With regard to collecting mushrooms for eating, this introduction to mushroom natural history cannot possibly give you enough expertise to enable you to gather a meal. After several weeks of collecting and observing, you should be able to recognize a half-dozen distinctive edible fungi that will not be confused with poisonous varieties. However, to learn to identify fungi, it is best to go collecting with an expert. In any case, remember these rules:

1. There are no rules for identifying all poisonous mushrooms. It is not true that a poisonous mushroom will darken a silver spoon or a garlic clove placed in the cooking pot. All the many other "rules" and old wives' tales have no basis in fact.

2. Do not eat any mushroom you cannot positively identify.

3. Eat only a small amount of any species you have not tried before, and keep a few fresh specimens in your refrigerator for identification, just in case.

4. Remember, wise mushroom hunters have a saying, "There are bold mycologists and there are old mycologists, but there are no old, bold mycologists."

A few of the better edible mushrooms for beginners are discussed and illustrated in Chapter 17.

Mushrooms as food for animals

Although they are mostly water (between 70 and 94 percent), mushrooms are actually quite nutritious. They have about as many calories as fruits and vegetables, and they contain carbohydrates, proteins, and fat. However, it is difficult to eat enough to get a nourishing meal. Perhaps red squirrels understand this shortcoming because they dehydrate their fungi. They collect mushrooms in the fall, placing them in the forks of tree branches to dry. Later they cache them in leaf nests or in the hollows of trees for winter use.

Squirrels are not our only mushroom connoisseurs. Opossums, bandicoots, wombats, shrews, baboons, armadillos, rabbits, mice, skunks, and deer are a few of the animals that eat fungi. A U.S. Forest Service study in South Carolina found that 95 percent of the deer were eating mushrooms, and that 80 percent of their diets were fungi at certain times of the year.

As a research biologist, I wondered whether animals could distinguish poisonous from edible species. Dozens of animals eat fungi, yet no one knows whether animals are poisoned by fungi in the wild. Therefore, I conducted a few experiments with opossums. I fed them bite-sized morsels of dozens of different mushrooms and recorded their preferences. In general the mushrooms that I found tasty, they also liked. The exception came one day when I was feeding them *Amanita muscaria,* an hallucinogenic species. All my opossums eagerly consumed every *Amanita muscaria* tidbit I fed them. Then, half an hour later, I was sadly surprised to find that my subjects had become ill and were vomiting. However, they all soon recovered. The next day, I offered them *Amanita muscaria* once again. This time they refused. This was the crucial test, since it proved that animals (or at least opossums) can learn to distinguish poisonous from edible species. Even a year later, several of the opossums remembered their unpleasant experience and would not eat the *Amanita* mushroom.

There is evidence that some animals are immune to certain mushroom toxins, but my experiments proved that animals can be poisoned. In the wild, animals tend to be quite cautious about novel foods they encounter. Deer judiciously sample new plants in small amounts as if to assess the food for any delayed ill-effects. This way they may avoid eating larger amounts that could be lethal, and they can learn from their mistakes.

ACTIVITIES

How to observe and identify mushrooms

Spend time out in the moist woodlands several days after heavy rains. Try to find representatives of each of the major groups of fungi. Learn to identify the differences between the agarics, boletes, stinkhorns, earthstars, puffballs, coral fungi, morels, and cup fungi. Then look at individual mushrooms in greater detail in order to identify some of the distinctive, easily recognized species within each group.

HOW TO LOOK AT A MUSHROOM

Mushrooms are much more difficult to identify than flowers; in fact, even experts cannot identify many mushrooms without examining them under the microscope. Plants have characteristic leaf shapes and floral types, with specific numbers and arrangements of the petals, sepals, anthers, and pistils. The colors of the flowers are relatively constant and distinctive. Mushrooms often cannot be identified simply by referring to a picture in a field guide. No guide includes all the fungi, and many mushrooms have look-alikes. Therefore, in order to identify a specimen, you must examine at it very carefully and gather as much information as you can.

A stinkhorn fungus.

What are the characteristics to observe? Before you snatch the mushroom from the ground, just look at it. Where is it growing? Is it on the ground, on a tree stump, on dung, or perhaps growing out of another mushroom? Is it growing in a cluster or singly? Make note of the habitat and the type of terrain. Is the mushroom growing among pine trees or hardwoods? Some mushrooms form mycorrhizal associations with a single species of tree, an important clue for identification. For example, *Gyrodon merulioides* will only be found near ash trees.

Now dig up the entire mushroom, being careful to include the base. Some mushrooms, such as deadly poisonous *Amanitas* have a bulbous cuplike base. *Collybia radicata* has a long rootlike stalk that may extend several inches into the ground.

Next, concentrate on the details of the cap. Always look at several mushrooms of different ages, since the mushroom changes as it grows. The **cap**, also called the **pileus**, may be conic or funnel-shaped or a dozen shapes in between. Its surface may be dry or wet or sticky. It may be covered with scales or patches of hairs or granules. The margin of the pileus may be straight or incurved or upturned.

Sometimes the cap has a particular odor or may change color when the flesh is injured. Some mushrooms have a distinctive taste. Whenever I mention this aspect of mushroom identification, I am greeted by cries of horror. It is safe to taste a bit of mushroom on the tip of your tongue and then spit it out, if you are sure you are not sampling the deadly *Amanitas* or the little brown *Galerinas*.

Now look at the underside of the mushroom. Does it have **gills**, like the mushrooms you buy at the market, or are there **pores** or tiny **teeth** present? If the mushroom has gills, they may be decurrent (extending partway down the stalk), adnate (attached to the stalk), or free from the stalk. The gills may be close together or widely spaced.

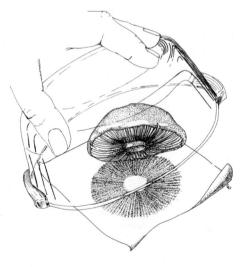

How to make a spore print.

The stalk, or **stipe**, may be short or long, hollow or solid, rubbery or brittle, and variably textured. Is it attached in the center of the mushroom or is it eccentric? Partway down the stalk a ring or **annulus** may be present. At the bottom of the stalk, there may be a distinctive bulb or **volva**.

One final detail of great importance is the character of the spores. Although individual spores are microscopic and invisible, a mass of millions together has a definite color. A spore print will let you see the spore color. Take a mushroom and cut off the stem. Place the cap, gill-side or pore-side down, on a piece of white paper, and cover it with a bowl. After several hours, sufficient numbers of spores will have been released to reveal a deposit on the paper. The print will be a shade of white, brown, green, pink, or black, and will show the pattern of the radiating gills or pores. I keep a collection of spore prints on 3 × 5-inch index cards, carefully labeled with the mushroom name, locality, and date. The powdery spores are easily smudged, so you may want to gently spray the spore print with clear lacquer or the fixative that artists use to spray their drawings. The microscopic structure of a spore is one of the most distinctive and beautiful features of a mushroom. It is well worth the effort to examine spores under a microscope at a magnification of 400 or more. They may be oval, round, or angular in shape, and they often have exquisitely ornamented surfaces.

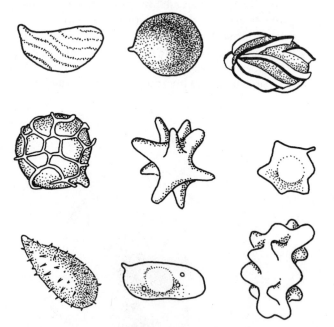

Examples of the many different spore shapes as seen under the microscope (enlarged more than 1,000 times).

After you have been examining mushrooms for a while, you will begin to appreciate all the minute details that you never noticed at first. Each detail is a clue to the mushroom's identity, and all the characteristics taken together contribute to the mushroom's unique portrait. Every one of us immediately recognizes our brother or sister. But if I asked you to describe this sibling, you probably could not come up with a description accurate enough to allow a stranger to recognize him or her. You recognize your brother instantly because you know what he looks like; you have a mental image in your mind. After a while you begin to know mushrooms this way—a crucial detail here, a detail there, all add up to a positive identification. The whole process goes on unconsciously, and then you suddenly come up with a name, such as *Strobilomyces floccopus,* the old man of the woods. All the details of mushroom identification are learned gradually through experience and reading. Remember, however, that even the best field guides include only a fraction of the mushroom species of a region. The best way to learn the names of fungi is to go collecting with people who know the mushrooms of an area well, and to carry one or two well-illustrated field guides. Many towns have mushroom clubs that go out on weekly forays during the year.

Keeping a field notebook will sharpen your powers of observation. I have a standard form that I fill out for each new mushroom I find.

Name (if known) _____
Location _____ Date _____
Associated Vegetation _____
Substrate (wood, ground, etc.) _____
Growth (clustered, single) _____
Cap: Shape _____
      Size _____
      Color _____
      Texture _____
      Odor & Taste _____
Gills: Color _____
      Attachment _____
Stem: Shape _____
      Size _____
      Ring _____
      Texture _____
      Base _____

Flowers can be pressed and mounted on sheets of paper, but there is no good way to make a mushroom collection. The only fungi that preserve well are the woody bracket fungi that dry without changing their shape. Other fungi can be dried, but they lose their colors and shrivel up. Specimens can be placed in a food dehydrator or in a drying oven made from a metal box that is equipped with a light bulb as a heating source. Mushrooms dried this way will last forever, but they are more useful as a reference collection for microscopic features than for demonstrating what the fungus looked like in real life. I keep a collection of spore prints carefully labeled in envelopes. This allows me to compare any unknown spore deposit with the identified specimens I have on file. My mushroom collection consists of hundreds of photographs. Those with artistic inclinations may find that fungi make ideal nature subjects for watercolor paintings.

REFERENCES AND SUGGESTIONS FOR FURTHER READING

Lincoff, G.H. 1981. *The Audubon Society Field Guide to North American Mushrooms.* Knopf, New York.

Maugh, T.H.,II. 1982. The scent makes sense. *Science* 215: 1224.

Miller, O.K.,Jr. 1972. *Mushrooms of North America.* Dutton, New York.

Pacioni, G. 1981. *Simon and Schuster's Guide to Mushrooms.* Simon and Schuster, New York.

Rolfe, R.T., and Rolfe, F.W. 1974. *The Romance of the Fungus World.* Dover, New York.

16

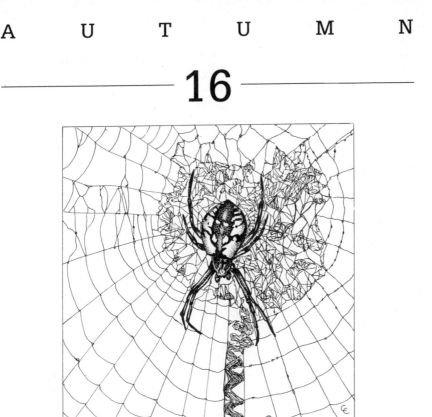

Scrutinizing Spiders

AT TIMES, the most difficult aspect of being a naturalist is finding the organism you wish to study. Not so with spiders. They are ubiquitous. For a city-dweller, only cockroaches are more accessible and appropriate subjects for study. Spiders abound in the rubble of empty city lots, along the hallways of dark subway stations, and even in kitchens on the top floors of luxurious apartment buildings. As I sit here writing, I can see cobwebs under my desk and up in the corners of the ceiling. My bookshelf has a few wisps of silk, along with an outgrown spider skin, molted to make way for a larger, more comfortable integument. Mine may not be the cleanest of homes, but I would be willing to bet that I could find spiders in anyone's house.

Daddy-long-legs spiders (family **Pholcidae**) inhabit cellars and basements, hanging upside down in loose irregular webs they have assembled in dark corners. When alarmed, they vibrate their webs in defense, shaking everything so violently that they appear as a blur. The same technique entangles prey that wanders into their lair. The mother spider protectively cradles the egg sac in her jaws and may continue to carry the writhing ball of hatched spiderlings until they disperse. Do not confuse these spiders with the harvestmen, found outdoors scurrying over vegetation with their stiltlike legs. They are also called daddy-long-legs, but they are not spiders. They have a compact oval body, which is not separated into two parts as in spiders. Harvestmen belong to a related order, **Opiliones**.

I can usually find a few cobweb weavers, or combfooted spiders (family **Theridiidae**), in any home. Although the black widow is a member of the family, our common household residents (in the genera *Achaearanea* and *Steatoda*) are harmless. They build a chaotic cobweb, the bane of fastidious housewives, and seat themselves in its center or hide in a crevice at the edge of the web. Although I find it difficult to believe, our common house resident *Achaearanea tepidariorum*, less than a half-inch long, has reportedly subdued small mice in its tangled snare. Perhaps I should trade in my cats.

Jumping spiders (family **Salticidae**) can be found anywhere in the house, on window sills in the bright sunlight, behind cabinets and picture frames, or pacing along the ceilings. Like miniature cats, they spend their lives stalking their prey and pouncing upon it. I welcome their presence, preferring to share my home with a few jumping spiders than to be plagued by house flies, carpet beetles, and cockroaches.

Outdoors in the suburbs or countryside, you risk squashing spiders with every step you take. At times a field may have more than 40 spiders per square foot. (That is nearly 2,000,000 spiders to an acre!) I shudder imagining the number of innocent spiders I kill every time I am out in the field.

The ubiquity of spiders can only thrill an ardent naturalist. Most people will have nothing to do with them, being afraid to approach even to stomp on them or pulverize them with a broom. Only a handful of my acquaintances has ever picked up a spider or examined one closely.

One goal of this chapter is to assuage the irrational and unfounded fear of spiders. Of the thousands of species of spiders in the United States, only two are dangerous. The widows (genus *Latrodectus*) include the black widows and northern widows, found throughout most of the United States. Their bite can cause severe abdominal pain, salivation, and profuse sweating. After several agonizing days, the victim usually recovers. The brown recluse spider (genus *Loxosceles*) gives a bite that often develops into a large, slow-healing, ulcerated wound. In addition to these two well-known villains, there are a few lesser offenders. Most commonly encountered is *Cheiracanthium mildei*, a small whitish-yellow spider (0.4 in., or 10 mm long), which was introduced into the New England area from the Mediterranean about 30 years ago. It is now common in houses in southern Canada and throughout the United States. *Cheiracanthium's* bite is painful and is sometimes accompanied by systemic complaints, such as fever, for about a day. Occasionally there is some destruction of the tissues (necrosis) around the bite. Nonetheless, most spiders will not bite even when coaxed, and the fangs of the majority cannot even break through the skin. The bites of the larger species typically cause localized pain for a few minutes, hours at the most, and perhaps some redness and swelling, no worse than a wasp sting.

Whenever the topic of spiders arises, people invariably tell me of the spider bites they have received. Leading them on, I always ask for a detailed description of the culprit. I always get the same reply, "Well, I didn't actually see the spider, but I'm sure it was a spider bite." I suppose it is human nature. After all, consider how much more sympathy one receives for a spider bite than for the bite of a bedbug, a flea, or a horsefly. No amount of arguing has ever convinced one of these individuals that they were bitten by anything other than a dangerous spider.

I have handled thousands of spiders, including black widows, and have been bitten just once, by *Cheiracanthium mildei*, discussed above. I was leaning against a tree in the summer, without a shirt on, reading a book, when I felt a sharp jab in my back. I jumped forward, turned around quickly, and there at the base of the tree, twitching in agony, was a small spider. When I squashed it against my back, it bit in self-defense. My pain subsided in two or three minutes and itched like a mosquito bite for several days. The poor spider died.

Spiders are shy, like nearly all animals big or small, fleeing pursuers whenever possible. When held or squeezed, a spider will try to bite, but even the most poisonous of spiders can be allowed to walk over your skin. Ambling along undisturbed, they are completely unaware of your presence.

ACTIVITIES

Collecting spiders

Spiders can be collected anywhere. They live underwater in air-filled domes made of silk, and on the cliffs of Mount Everest at an altitude of 22,000 feet. Spiders have been found floating through the air on wisps of silk 10,000 feet above the land. Any diligent naturalist can find dozens of species under stones and logs, beneath loose bark, in the leaf litter, and on vegetation. One New York City high school student found over 100 species on Staten Island.

You can begin your search with a survey of your home. To capture any house-mates you encounter, place a wide-mouthed jar beneath them and slowly come at them from below. Most spiders fold their legs and drop when disturbed, landing right in your jar. Place the cover on top and you have your prey.

A greater variety of spiders can be collected in the field. Use a butterfly net to sweep through vegetation. After several passes through the brush, the net will be filled with spiders, insects, and bits of leaves and flowers. The spiders can be coaxed into vials, or even picked up with your fingers. The tinier species are best collected by touching them gently with a finger moistened with saliva. If you object to sticking your finger in your mouth, a camel's-hair brush moistened with a bit of water is a more refined collecting technique. The spider will adhere to the brush and can then be transferred gently to a vial. Be sure to put each specimen into a separate container (or else you may arrive home with one fat spider).

To obtain variety, you need to know the habits of different spiders. Many species abound in the leaf litter of the forest floor. Handfuls of this debris can be placed in a coarse sieve (having about one-half inch spacing), and the spiders can be shaken

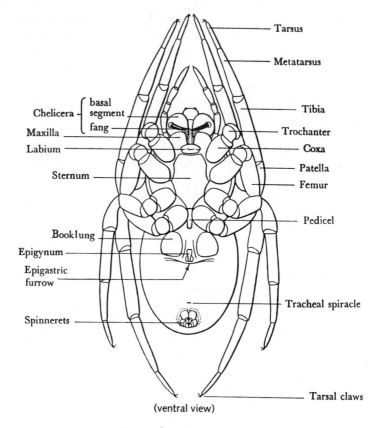

Tarsus

Metatarsus

Chelicera — basal segment

fang

Maxilla

Labium

Sternum

Booklung

Epigynum

Epigastric furrow

Spinnerets

Tibia

Trochanter

Coxa

Patella

Femur

Pedicel

Tracheal spiracle

Tarsal claws

(ventral view)

External anatomy of a spider.

and sifted onto a white bedsheet. A convenient sieve is a French fryer, which you can buy in a cooking supply store. (I would not advise trying to explain to the salesman what you plan to do with it.)

Wolf spiders (family **Lycosidae**) and jumping spiders run along the ground. Bury a tin can flush with the surface, and fill it with a few inches of water to which a few drops of detergent have been added. Spiders will fall into the soapy water and drown. Obviously this method is only useful for increasing your collection of preserved specimens.

Collecting at night is a real adventure. Take a flashlight or, even better, a headlamp, so both hands will be free. Many orb weavers hide during the day, but can be seen resting at the hub or repairing their webs at night. Wolf spiders will be your most spectacular nighttime quarry. Their large eyes appear as greenish, glowing dots, reflecting the light of your headlamp. They tend to remain motionless in the light beam and can be slowly approached and captured in a net. You may even be lucky enough to find a female wolf spider carrying young on her back. In the darkness you will see hundreds of tiny eyes shining near the mother's larger eyes.

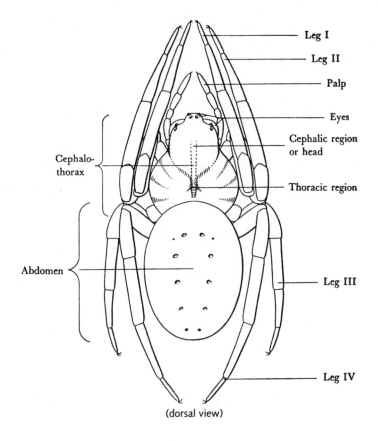

Leg I

Leg II

Palp

Eyes

Cephalic region
or head

Cephalo-
thorax

Thoracic region

Abdomen

Leg III

Leg IV

(dorsal view)

Preserving and identifying spiders

A few hours of collecting will yield a bewildering array of specimens. With over 3,000 species in North America, only experts can identify them all. Your initial goal should be to recognize the more common families and their representatives. The best way to begin is to make a collection and to learn the basics of spider anatomy.

Spiders are preserved by dropping them into 70 percent rubbing (isopropyl) alcohol, obtained in the drugstore. Place several specimens of each species in a separate vial, carefully labeled with the locality, habitat, date, and collector. I type the collection data on small labels cut from 3 × 5-inch index cards. The labels can also be hand-written with india ink or pencil, then placed in the vial with the spiders.

To identify spiders, you will need to become familiar with their external anatomy. A stereomicroscope provides the best view, but a 10x magnifier will suffice. Examine one of your preserved specimens. The spider's body consists of two parts, the **cephalothorax** and the **abdomen**. The cephalothorax, meaning head and thorax, is covered on top with a hardened shield or **carapace**. In front are the eyes (usually eight). Their arrangement is important in identifying families. Four pairs of legs, with two or three claws at their ends, are attached to the underside of the cephalothorax. The jaws, or **chelicerae**, are tipped by hollow fangs.

The abdomen is attached to the cephalothorax by a narrow waist, or **pedicel**. The abdomen is often a soft saclike structure, but it may be ornamented with brightly colored spines, hairs, and projections. Dimples on the upper surface mark the attachment of internal muscles. The underside has openings for two types of respiratory structures, the **booklungs** and the **tracheae**. Nearby are the sexual structures, the **epigynum** and **epigastric furrow**, and at the tip of the abdomen are silk **spinnerets**. The numbers, shapes, colors, and positions of all these anatomical details are used to identify spiders. For the more distinctive families, such as the jumping spiders, you may need to look only at the arrangement of the eyes. However, to classify other spiders, you may find yourself peering down the barrel of a microscope into a miniature, unknown landscape. In this world, numbers of tarsal claws, patterns of teeth on the chelicerae, placement of the tracheal spiracles, the height of spiny tubercles, relative lengths of bristles and spurs, and the peculiar curves of the epigynum take on a vital importance. Once you have entered this unknown territory, you will need to refer to one of the spider references to guide you on your journey.

The care and feeding of spiders

Spiders are simple to care for. Nearly any container makes an acceptable home. Clear plastic boxes are ideal. You can drill a few small air holes, or you can heat a pin over the stove until it is red hot, then melt holes in the plastic. If you cannot find a clear plastic box, a cardboard box will do, covered with a pane of glass or clear plastic kitchen wrap held in place with a rubber band. Cages like these provide a big open arena, allowing you to observe easily the spider's behavior. For keeping spiders that build orb webs, I prefer a different setup, described below, that allows better viewing and manipulation of the web.

Spiders need food and water. A few insects once a week will keep a spider healthy. Flies, crickets, or cockroaches are fine. Drop them into the cage and watch how each kind of spider catches its prey. Water is provided by moistening a ball of cotton about the size of a marble and placing it in the corner of the cage. A thirsty spider will suck the water from the wet cotton. That is all it takes to keep a spider happy.

Studying and observing common spiders

JUMPING SPIDERS

Jumping spiders do not build a web to capture their prey. They are the panthers of the spider world, silently stalking their prey, approaching closely, then pouncing at the final moment. The family name, **Salticidae**, is from Latin, meaning leap. These acrobats have no regard for gravity, sometimes taking seemingly reckless leaps through space to catch a flying insect. They are not at risk of falling, however.

Like rock climbers tied into a safety rope, salticids anchor themselves before each vault. Watch carefully before a spider dives for its prey, and you will see it briefly touch its spinnerets to the ground, wiggling them like little fingers. The spider has fastened a bit of silk to the substrate. If it misses its mark, it will be left dangling by a silken lifeline paid out during the jump.

The salticids are among the nimblest of spiders, difficult to catch without a net, and capable of leaping distances more than 40 times their own length when pursued. Unlike the myopic orb weavers, which rely chiefly upon their perception of vibrations, the jumping spiders have excellent vision, among the best of all invertebrates. They have two huge front eyes and can perceive a clear image a foot away. They use their vision not only for hunting, but also when courting a mate. The males are particularly gorgeous, often adorned with iridescent scales and with cuffs of hairs on the front legs. One of our commonest species is *Phidippus audax*. The male has striking black-and-white markings and brilliant green iridescent chelicerae. During his mating display, he waves his front legs, wiggles his abdomen, and hops about excitedly, trying to attract the female's attention. Jumping spiders will mate in captivity. The female makes a silk cocoon for her eggs and guards them tenaciously. In time, dozens of spiderlings will hatch. Cannibalistic, they must be placed in separate containers and fed fruit flies, aphids, or other minute insects until they can capture larger prey.

I was surprised to discover that jumping spiders have distinct feeding preferences. Despite voracious appetites, salticids are gourmets with discriminating tastes. You can see for yourself. Begin by starving a jumping spider for several days, but be sure to supply it with water. Do not worry about killing your spider; they can live for weeks without food. Next, capture as many different insects as you can, each about the size of your spider or smaller. With tweezers, gently grab an insect and slowly approach the spider in its cage. When it notices a wiggling leg or antenna, the spider will turn toward its prey, become alert, and approach. Do not make any sudden movements. The spider will pounce and grab the prey, paralyzing it with a single bite. Carefully withdraw the tweezers. Now observe the spider's behavior. If it likes the insect, it will begin to feed, injecting digestive juices into the victim's body through its fangs and sucking up the resulting liquefied soup. The spider then will chew the insect, crushing its hard exoskeleton into a pulp, leaving only the tough head capsule and legs recognizable.

However, if your spider does not care for the dainty morsel you offer, its behavior will be quite different. When a particularly distasteful insect is attacked, the spider immediately drops it and drags its chelicerae on the ground, apparently trying to clean them off. Sometimes it appears that the spider cannot make up its mind. It wanders about its cage hanging onto its prey but refusing to chew. After a while, the insect will be dropped, dead but uneaten.

To make a proper scientific study of *Phidippus*'s feeding preferences, make careful notes on which insects are eaten, how long it takes to eat each one, and what feeding behaviors you observe. Use several different *Phidippus* to see if the response to a particular species of insect is consistent. Remember that, after several insects, your spider will become satiated, so the last insect you present may be rejected simply because the spider is no longer hungry.

The reason that spiders are so finicky is that many insects do not taste good. They exude repulsive chemicals from tiny glands scattered over their bodies, or they have repellent substances circulating in their blood. Just as we engage in chemical warfare to repel mosquitoes and black flies, insects use chemical defenses to save their lives.

ORB WEAVERS

Although spiders build webs of many shapes, when we think of a spider's web, we generally have in mind the image of a perfectly engineered symmetric orb. These are mainly the work of the orb-weavers (family **Araneidae**), although a few other rather obscure families (**Theridiosomatidae, Tetragnathidae,** and **Uloboridae**) also practice the art. Several hundred Araneids occur in North America, but my favorites are the black-and-yellow Argiope and the banded Argiope, because of their bright colors and large size. They are common throughout much of the United States. In the Northeast, I find them in weedy fields throughout the summer.

For orb weavers, the web is their whole world. When disturbed, they may drop to the ground, but otherwise they stay on their web or in a small retreat off in one corner. They have poor vision and perceive the world mainly as a series of web vibrations. That they can easily distinguish a struggling insect from other disturbances you can induce by wiggling a stick among the silken threads.

When an insect does land in the sticky orb, the spider turns and quickly runs toward the commotion. A larger captive tangled in the threads is turned by the spider's front legs, like a pig on a spit, and swathed in broad silk sheets drawn out by the hind legs. The prey, wrapped like a mummy, is then bitten and carried to the hub to be consumed.

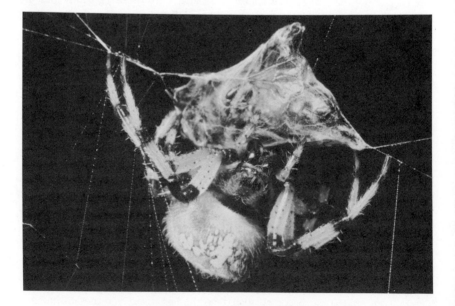

An orb weaver spider with its prey wrapped in silk.

Argiope webs, more than a foot across, are easily studied. I prefer to set up a special home for these spiders. I make a square frame out of coathanger wire, or use an empty picture frame. I attach this to a narrow base in a large pan of water, and release the spider on the frame. The spider's new home is like a castle surrounded by a moat, except that the object is to keep the occupant in, rather than the enemies out. It usually works, although an occasional spider sometimes manages to escape. The advantage of this setup is that it allows an unobstructed view of the spider as it makes its web within the frame. The orb can easily be manipulated, photographed, and removed intact. For feeding, or between observations, you may wish to place the frame in a large cardboard box fitted with cellophane windows.

Once the spider has settled down in its new home, you can begin some fascinating experiments and observations. It is always best to begin by watching normal behavior in order to have a basis for comparison. Then you can appreciate any variations induced by your experimental manipulations.

How is a web constructed? Unless you are a very early riser, you will need to change your sleeping habits to observe some spiders spin. The large orbs of *Argiope* are usually built at dawn. However, *Micrathena* builds later in the morning, and *Neoscona arabesca* spins its webs in the evening, around four or five o'clock. The sequence of events is as follows: First, the upper cross-bridge is laid down. Usually the spider lets out a strand of silk in the breeze. If it sticks to something, the spider tightens the line, attaches it at her end, and ventures across the bridge. Additional reinforcing lines are laid down over the original. The spider then goes to the center of the bridge, attaches a line to one of the cross-threads, and lowers herself. When the spider lands, this line is pulled taut and attached, forming a "Y," which makes up the three primary radii of the web. The spider then climbs back up this thread to where the "Y" forks. This is the central hub of the orb. Lines are attached from the hub to the periphery, forming additional radii. After the radii are constructed, the hub may be strengthened with a meshwork of silk. Next a widely spaced temporary spiral is laid down from the inside outward.

Up until now all the threads have been dry. When the spider finishes the temporary spiral, she turns around and begins rolling up the old nonsticky spiral as she lays down a more closely spaced spiral of viscid threads. After about an hour, the web is complete.

This is the merest outline of the spider's complex behavior. A moment's thought raises many questions. How does the spider measure distances and tension during web construction? Does each spider of the same species build an identical web? How variable is an individual's web from day to day? Are the webs of mature spiders the same as those of younger individuals?

Some of these questions can be easily explored at home by watching spiders, taking careful notes, and comparing the structure of different webs. Many orb weavers spin a new web almost every night or early morning. The main foundation lines are kept intact, but new radii and spirals are laid down. You can remove the entire web each day and let the spider build a new one. Each new web that the spider builds becomes part of the record of your studies.

The easiest and most accurate technique for preserving the web is photography. Carefully remove the spider from its web, taking care not to break any threads.

*A spider web photographed by
the method described in the text.*

Because the strands are nearly invisible, they need to be highlighted. You can gently spray the web with white paint or with an aerosol can of foot powder (such as Desenex®). Cornstarch is another favorite. Place it in an old sock and pat it gently to produce a cloud of powder that will gently settle on the web. Now illuminate the web from the side, and place it in front of a background of black velvet or a board painted flat black. Tape a small card to the frame, labeled with a letter indicating the date, the conditions of the web-building, and which individual spider made the web. Include a dark one-inch line on the card for scale. I photograph each web with a 35mm camera. Slides of each web can be projected onto a screen.

You can also preserve the actual web. Spray it lightly with white paint and let it dry. Then spray a black sheet of cardboard with a can of clear spray paint. While the sheet is still tacky, gently touch it to the web. If you are careful, the entire web will stick to the cardboard. You may need to have an assistant glue a few of the radii in place before you attempt to move the sheet. The technique is a bit tricky; it takes practice to get the whole web without breaking a few radii and distorting the web.

Once you know the structure of a normal web, you can begin making some experimental manipulations. Some of the following experiments may seem a bit heartless, but they are traditional for scientists who study spider and insect behavior. By watching spiders build webs, you may have guessed that spiders make measurements as they probe with their legs. You can test this hypothesis by amputating a leg and observing the effect on the web structure. Remove one front leg by gently pulling with a tweezers. The wound seals almost instantly, and the spider can be returned to its empty frame without any postoperative care. If you are worrying about your mutilated spider, it may console you to know that most immature spiders will regrow lost legs during subsequent molts. When the spider builds a new web, can you detect any differences? Does the removal of a hind leg have the same effect?

You can test the role of vision in web-building by covering the spider's eyes with black paint. You will need a steady hand, a very fine brush, and some magnification, but, with a bit of practice, you should be able to paint the eyes without injuring the spider or gumming up its whole head.

Another series of experiments involves manipulating the web, rather than the spider. Does gravity affect the shape of the web? During web-building, rotate the web 90 degrees, or tip it slightly from its vertical orientation. Does this have any effect? Can a spider detect subtle changes made in its web? Single strands can be cut from the web by heating a needle with a match and touching it to the strand. What happens if you remove a radius? Will the spider repair the damage?

Scientists have tested the effect of drugs on spider web-building. The hallucinogens (LSD, marijuana, mescaline, and psilocybin) have been tried, as well as dozens of other compounds, such as amphetamines, caffeine, strychnine, Valium®, ether, and carbon monoxide. Most drugs adversely affect the spider's spinning, resulting in more irregular, smaller, or less frequently constructed webs. However, spiders under the influence of LSD build webs with more regularly placed radii and spirals, while amphetamine-drugged spiders spin their webs more frequently and make them larger.

Experiments like these are simple to perform. The only difficulty is in drugging your spider. First, let the spider build a normal web as a control, and get a photographic record of it. Then, deprive the spider of water for a few days to make it thirsty. Prepare your experimental drug. You can try coffee, which contains caffeine, a bit of a Valium tablet dissolved in water, or some wine. (Valium is a tranquilizer, and can only be obtained by prescription. However, since it is one of the most widely prescribed drugs in the United States, you should have little difficulty finding someone to give you a portion of a single pill.) Get a tiny droplet of the drug on the tip of a needle, and slowly bring it into contact with the jaws of the spider. If it is thirsty, it will drink. An uncooperative spider that flees can be held, and a drop of the liquid can be applied to its jaws. Blot off the excess solution with a napkin after a minute or two.

Gently place the spider on its frame and let it spin a new web. If the spider spins abnormally, make a record of the changes, wait a few days for the drug to wear off, and let the spider spin another web. If it has recovered, the new web should be normal once again.

From here, you are on your own. By now you should be amicably acquainted with one of nature's most fascinating performers. Despite its minute size and pinhead-sized brain, the spider has an extraordinary behavioral repertoire, capable of keeping our own minds active for a lifetime.

REFERENCES AND SUGGESTIONS FOR FURTHER READING

Bristowe, W.S. 1958. *The World of Spiders*. Collins, London.

Fabre, J.H. 1915. *The Life of the Spider.* Dodd, Mead, New York.

Gertsch, W.J., Jr. 1979. *American Spiders.* Van Nostrand Reinhold, New York.

Kaston, B.J., and Kaston, E. 1953. *How to Know the Spiders*. Wm. C. Brown, Dubuque, Iowa.

Levi, H.W., and Levi, L.R. 1968. *Spiders and Their Kin*. Golden Press, New York.

Shear, W. (ed.) 1986. *Spider Webs and Spider Behavior.* Stanford University Press, Stanford, California.

Strong, C.L. December 1972. The joys of culturing spiders and investigating their webs. *Scientific American* 227: 108–111.

Witt, P.N., and Reed, C.F. 1965. Spider-web building. *Science* 149: 1190–1197.

17

Feasting in the Fields

AN ADDED BENEFIT of being a naturalist is knowing where and when to gather the best wild edibles. I can tell you where to find morel mushrooms early in the spring, and which old oak stumps always host a large cluster of sulfur shelf fungi late in the fall. I know a black walnut tree deep in the woods with hundreds of nuts, and a cool spot near a swamp where the bushes are sagging with their load of highbush blueberries.

I feel on more intimate terms with the woods when I can walk along, naming and describing the plants and animals as friends I have known for many years. The forests can be intimidating to those who are not on a "first-name basis" with the plants and creatures around them; every plant is perceived as potentially poisonous and every insect may wield a painful stinger. However, for those of us who are familiar with its inhabitants, the woodlands are a refuge and a solace. In addition to their exquisite beauty, they offer a wealth of edible treasures—spices, fruits, tubers, teas, and nuts.

Ancient man was a hunter and gatherer, spending most of his time foraging in order to survive. Supermarkets have relieved us of that necessity. We now have more time for learning and recreation, and many of us have chosen to spend our leisure in the fields, relearning some of the traditional ways in which our ancestors used the land around them.

THE PLEASURE OF FORAGING FOR WILD EDIBLES

My friends and relatives will be the first to emphasize that my wild food recipes have not always been epicurean delights. On the other hand, my gourmet dinners often feature a sampling of exotic mushroom hors d'oeuvres, sauteed wild vegetables, and freshly picked berries.

Fortunately, the pleasure of foraging for wild foods does not depend solely on the outcome of the dinner. Gathering wild edibles is its own reward. I delight in spending a day in the fields. Each autumn I roam the woods with groups of avid mushroom hunters. Carrying our wicker baskets and field guides, we learn the names and key features of common fungi. We always stop along the way for other discoveries — red efts, fungus-eating slugs, beetles, garter snakes, ferns, and weathered bones.

Although it is simpler to go to the market, wild foods offer some unusual taste experiences, and are generally as nutritious as cultivated produce. For those on a limited budget, you cannot beat the price.

There is the challenge of trying to make a meal out of what you bring home. Although it is unlikely that you will ever have to survive on what you can gather, it is gratifying to know that it is possible.

However, before we head for the woodlands to reap our harvest, just a few words of caution concerning poisonous plants. Collecting wild edibles is perfectly safe provided you are careful. There are thousands of plants and mushrooms in the United States; only a few are dangerous. Fatalities are extremely rare — about two deaths are reported a year.

Before eating any plant, be sure you can identify it with certainty. Make sure all its features fit the description in a field guide. If in doubt, throw it out. Some edible plants have toxic look-alikes. Particular culprits are members of the Pea family and the Lily family. Mushrooms and plants in the Carrot family are difficult to identify, and errors can be fatal. Start by learning the key features of plant families, and use these as the framework and foundation of your knowledge about plants.

Portions of plants can be toxic, although other parts are edible. Vines and sprouts of commercial potatoes can be lethal. Mayapple fruit is delicious, but the rest of the plant is highly poisonous. Also, some plants are edible when young but bitter or toxic when mature. Some species are poisonous raw, but edible when cooked. Do not experiment haphazardly. Refer to one of the books listed below and abide by its suggestions.

Do not assume a plant is edible if an animal has eaten it. Each animal has a unique physiology. Lethal mushrooms are consumed by some animals without ill-effects. There is no foolproof test for determining whether a plant or mushroom is edible or poisonous. You must learn the identity of each plant individually.

COMMON TOXIC PLANTS

Name	Toxic Portion
American yew	whole plant, except red pulp around seed
azalea	leaves, honey from flower nectar
baneberry	all parts, especially berries
black locust	seeds, leaves
bloodroot	all portions
blue flag	rootstocks
buckthorn	berries, bark
buttercup	whole plant
castor bean	seeds
clematis	whole plant
elderberry	whole plant, except flowers, ripe berries
false hellebore	whole plant
fool's parsley	whole plant
horsechestnut	seeds, twigs
jack-in-the-pulpit	whole plant
jimsonweed	whole plant
laurel	leaves, honey from flower nectar
mayapple	whole plant, except ripe fruit
nightshade	whole plant
poison hemlock	whole plant
pokeweed	roots, berries, mature leaves, and stems
rhododendron	leaves, honey from flower nectar
wisteria	whole plant

Your best health insurance is to learn the few poisonous plants in your region. You would also be wise to be able to recognize the common plants that cause skin rashes when handled. These include poison ivy, oak, and sumac, nettles, eyebane, trumpet creeper, and wild parsnip.

These warnings are not meant to discourage anyone, or to detract from the joy of eating wild foods. There is no need to fear being accidentally poisoned. If you use a little common sense, your forays will always have a happy ending.

ACTIVITIES

This section presents a sampling of my favorite recipes. It is just a hint of the gastronomic possibilities that can be prepared from the hundreds of edible plants and fungi growing throughout the United States. For more comprehensive coverage, use one of the field guides listed below, and venture out into the fields to gather your own wild edibles.

Sumac lemonade

I often offer a cold, refreshing glass of sumac lemonade on a hot August day. Someone always responds with the same quick query, "But isn't sumac poisonous?" Yes, poison sumac is poisonous, but the other sumacs are not. Furthermore, confusing the two would be quite difficult. Poison sumac has loose bunches of *white* berries. The edible sumacs have dense clusters of brilliant red berries (see illustration on page 185).

Sumacs grow as bushes or small trees 4 to 15 feet (1.2 to 4.6 m) high in fields, clearings, and along roadsides throughout much of the United States. Driving along in the country, you cannot miss the large stands displaying their torch-shaped clusters of scarlet berries. There are several common species. Each has compound leaves with 11 to 31 leaflets arranged opposite each other on the leafstalk. Staghorn sumac is a fuzzy plant with hairy twigs and a thick covering of red velvet on the berries. As you would expect, smooth sumac lacks these hairs. Dwarf sumac is a shorter species, slightly fuzzy and easily recognized by the winglike projections between the leaflets. In the West, one finds squaw bush sumac. Its compound leaves have only 3 leaflets, and there are fewer berries in each cluster. All the sumacs are **dioecious**, which means that the male and female flowers are borne on separate plants. We are after the female plants whose flowers mature into the fruits.

The berries remain on the plant all winter, providing an important food supply for wildlife when other more desirable foods are scarce. Sometimes in the North, grouse, pheasant, wild turkey, cardinals, common crows, and starlings rely on sumac to survive the winter. Cottontail rabbits feed on the bark and fruit, and white-tail deer browse the twigs and foliage.

The fruit of the red-berried sumacs is rich in malic acid, the same acid that flavors tart or unripe apples. The hard summer rains wash the soluble acid from the surface of the fruit, so you must collect the berries early. I always sample a patch before I collect, sucking on a few berries to measure the malic acid content. If they are puckeringly sour, I gather a bushelful by breaking off each cluster at the base.

At home, place all the berries in a bowl of cold water. Rub and mix the berries with your hands, breaking up the clusters to dissolve the acid. Always use cold water. Although hot water may work faster, it leaches out tannic acid in stems and berries, making the resultant brew offensively bitter. After a few minutes, the water will be colored a beautiful pink. To remove the debris and berries, strain the whole mixture through a fine-meshed cloth into a large jug. If it is too sour, add more water. Then add sugar to taste, and serve chilled. Unlike other fruit juices, pink sumac lemonade will keep for a week or two in the refrigerator without losing its original flavor. The American Indians gathered great quantities of the fruit, which they dried for use in winter. I freeze concentrated juice and serve hot sumac lemonade on snowy evenings.

The versatile cattail

The familiar cattail, denizen of wet areas throughout the country, is a year-round storehouse of food. Nearly every portion of the plant—young shoots, immature flower spikes, pollen, rootstocks, and sprouts — can be served as a nutritious and tasty dish. This perennial plant has shallow branching rootstocks up to one-inch (2.5 cm) thick, which form an intertwining, ropelike mat just below the mud. Numerous stalks develop from the roots, creating dense stands of cattails in swamps, marshes, and in the shallow water along the margins of ponds and lakes.

The cattail is easily recognized by its brown sausage-shaped flower spike, and its narrow parallel-veined leaves. It may reach a height of 12 feet (3.6 m). The curious flower spike is a compact cylindrical mass of hundreds of flowers, green at first, then turning brown. In late fall and winter, the mass breaks apart releasing cottony windblown seeds. Directly above these female flowers, is a fluffier spike of male flowers, which also encircle the stalk. This multitude of stamens produces golden pollen, then withers and falls, leaving that portion of the stalk bare.

Cattail

As the plant matures through the seasons, a succession of different portions can be gathered. Cattail sprouts are delicious to eat in the earliest spring, before they have even broken through the water's surface. These bulblike sprouts can be gathered from the leading end of the roots. After peeling, they can be boiled or sautéed in butter.

In early spring when the leaves are a foot or two long, break the stems off at the root. Stripping the leaves reveals a crisp white core, which can be eaten raw or boiled like asparagus. In the late spring, the immature female flower spikes are still green and firm. Cut them from the stalk, remove their papery sheath, and boil them for a few minutes in salted water. Served with butter and eaten like corn on the cob, they make a delicious wild vegetable.

A few weeks later, the flower spikes will be too mature to eat as they become dry and brown. Now the male flowers will put forth copious amounts of powdery golden pollen. By bending the flower spikes into a bag, you can shake off cupfuls of pollen in a few minutes. Mixed with equal parts of wheat flower, this unique flour makes dazzling yellow pancakes or muffins.

In the late fall, the roots of many perennial plants, including the cattail, begin to store starch in preparation for next year's growth. From this time until very early spring, a pure white flour can be prepared from the roots. Collect a batch of rootstocks and thoroughly wash off the mud under running water. Peel off the outer covering to expose the white inner core. Crush these cleaned roots in a bowl of cold water to separate the starch from the fibers. Let the starch settle, pour off the water, and rinse again. Repeating the washing process several times will leave you with a nutritious white flour, which can be used wet, or can be dried for storage and later use.

No other plant provides such a varied and delicious menu. Euell Gibbons, the maestro of wild edibles, called cattails the "supermarket of the swamps."

A taste of fungi

Mushrooms are my favorite wild edibles. They appear magically in great quantities each fall, and their flavor far surpasses that of supermarket mushrooms. I relish their tantalizing mystique and diabolical reputation; my friends are often both excited and somewhat apprehensive to have dinner prepared with wild fungi. They erroneously believe that collecting mushrooms for the table is a dangerous affair. It simply is not so. Even a novice need not worry if he chooses a few easily identified fungi. The four best choices for beginners are the giant puffball, shaggy mane, sulfur shelf, and morel. These fungi are as foolproof as any, except those bought in the supermarket. After reading Chapter 15, A Glimpse at Fungi, and learning more

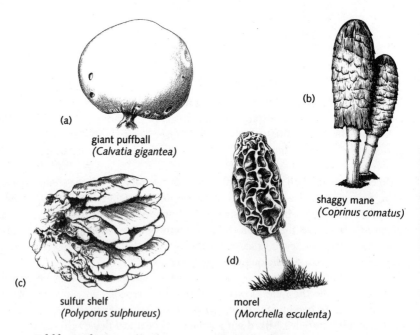

(a)
giant puffball
(*Calvatia gigantea*)

(b)

shaggy mane
(*Coprinus comatus*)

(c)

sulfur shelf
(*Polyporus sulphureus*)

(d)

morel
(*Morchella esculenta*)

Edible mushrooms. (a) The giant puffball. (b) Shaggy mane. (c) The brilliant yellow and orange sulfur shelf. (d) The morel. (Not shown to scale.)

about mushrooms from a field guide, the more experienced mushroom hunter may wish to experiment cautiously with other species.

THE GIANT PUFFBALL

The giant puffball is a smooth, globular fungus growing directly from the ground without a stalk. It can be the size of a basketball or larger, making a single fruiting body a complete meal for many. These puffballs are found in rich soil, such as well-fertilized lawns, barnyards, and cow pastures. The fruiting body should be picked when the flesh is pure white; the overly mature fungus becomes soft, bitter, and yellowish-brown inside. At an even later stage, its thick skin breaks open, exposing a powdery mass of black spores.

All white-fleshed puffballs are edible; there is only one rule of caution. Make sure you eat only those that are uniformly white inside. A toxic mushroom can masquerade as a puffball when in its very early "button" stage. Before a mushroom is mature, it lacks a stem and appears as a little round nubbin poking through the soil. However, if you slice the look-alike open longitudinally, you will discover a rudimentary stalk and gills. In addition, there are a few species of much smaller toxic puffballs that are blackish inside, and must be avoided.

For this fungus, my favorite recipe is Puffball Parmigiana. In place of the veal, slice the puffball into half inch "steaks" and discard the tough outer skin. Dip the puffball slabs into a batter of egg beaten with a few tablespoons of milk, then into a bowl of seasoned bread crumbs mixed with grated Parmesan cheese. Sauté in butter until crisp (about two minutes on each side), and cover with tomato sauce. Scrumptious!

SHAGGY MANES

The name describes these mushrooms perfectly. Along with the accompanying picture, the description is practically complete. You need only one other detail to make your identification certain. The shaggy mane is in the Inky Cap family, so named because the fungus dissolves into a black inky liquid as it grows old. This enzymatic process of self-digestion, called **deliquescence**, is characteristic of this group.

Shaggy manes grow in scattered colonies on lawns, roadsides, and waste places. Most often you will find them in all stages of development, from buttons to dripping black masses, a feature that aids in identification. Gather the young specimens, and use them quickly before they start to deliquesce.

Shaggy manes can be sautéed in butter with a touch of garlic, salt, and pepper. Sear them quickly over a high flame, since they liquefy when cooked slowly. The black sauce that forms is delicious, and you can take advantage of this natural process with the following recipe: Chop the mushrooms into one-inch pieces and sauté slowly over a low flame, to produce more liquid. Mix the resulting juices and mushroom morsels with enough spiced bread crumbs to soak up the liquid. Place in a one- or two-inch layer in a casserole dish and bake for 15 minutes. Just before serving, sprinkle a shallow layer of dry bread crumbs on the surface, add a bit of melted butter, and broil until the topping is crisp.

SULFUR SHELF

The sulfur shelf is sometimes called the chicken mushroom because of its light meaty flavor. Finding this treasure makes a day in the field an unsurpassed success. Look for it growing on dead or injured hardwoods and conifers where it forms multiple layers of broad yellow to orange brackets whose undersides have tiny pores. You cannot mistake this fungus for any other. At times huge sections of a trunk will be covered, permitting you to collect 20 pounds or more of the fungus. Furthermore, sulfur shelf grows on the same tree year after year, so each fall I make my rounds to reap another harvest.

I eat only the tender edges of the sulfur shelf; the flesh towards the center of the bracket becomes fibrous and bitter with age. Cut off the supple edges in the field, and leave the rest of the fungus intact. In the kitchen, slice these edge portions about one-fourth-inch thick, and sauté in butter for a few minutes.

MORELS

Morels are among the most delicious and sought-after fungi. Mycologists, aware of the demand and its lucrative potential, have made numerous attempts to cultivate the fungus. Spores germinate readily in the laboratory and grow into a cottony mat of intermingled mycelial threads. However, this primordial mass of fungal tissue has resisted every effort to make it fruit. Thus, morel lovers are forced to pay exorbitant prices for *morilles à la crème* in fancy French restaurants, or must head for the fields in search of their own. Morels can be difficult to find, and the tradition among successful morel hunters is to jealously guard the location of their collecting spots.

I am often asked where one finds morels. My list of collecting spots includes a rich, cool woodland along a stream, a moist, low-lying deciduous forest among ferns and may apples, and, of all places, a wood-mulched flower bed in downtown San Diego in December. Professional mycologists suggest oak ridges, old apple orchards, burned areas, and woodlands with tulip trees, poplars, ash, oak, beech, maple, or pine.

If I cannot tell you exactly where to find morels, at least I can tell you when. Morels fruit only in spring. In the Northeast, wander widely between mid-April and mid-May. Depending on the climate, you may find them as late as June in other parts of the country.

Morels are unlike other mushrooms. Deep pits and ridges give the cap an irregular honeycombed texture. The only mushrooms you are likely to confuse with these are the sometimes-toxic false morels. However, their cap is convoluted with folds and wrinkles, like a brain, and hangs skirtlike from its attachment at the top of the stalk. The morel's cap has no free border, but is attached directly to the stalk. Furthermore, the two mushrooms grow at different times of the year. If you think you have found a morel in the summer, leave it alone; it is probably one of the false morels.

As for morel recipes, any dish that emphasizes mushrooms is fine for morels. I prefer them sautéed by themselves in order to appreciate the mushroom's unique flavor.

After trying a few of these recipes, I am sure you will be converted to the cult of mycophagy. You may never eat a store-bought mushroom again.

COMMON EDIBLE PLANTS OF THE UNITED STATES

Name	Edible Portion	Use	Season of Availability
arrowhead	tubers	potato substitute	fall to spring
chicory	roasted roots	coffee substitute	fall to spring
choke cherry	fruit	jams, jellies	late summer
common milk-weed	young shoots, young pods	cooked vegetable	summer
dandelion	leaves, buds	salad, potherb	early spring
elderberry	berries	jelly, pie filling	late summer
groundnut	tubers	potato substitute	year-round
hawthorn	fruit	jams, jellies	fall
Japanese knot-weed	young shoots	cooked vegetable	spring
Jerusalem artichoke	tubers	potato substitute	fall
jewelweed	leaves, stems	potherb	summer
lamb's quarters	leaves	potherb	late spring
mayapple	fully ripe fruit	fresh or cooked fruit	late summer
mint	leaves	tea, spice	summer
nettle	young shoots, leaves*	potherb	spring
oak	ground, boiled acorns	flour substitute	fall
ostrich fern	young fronds (fiddleheads)	cooked vegetable	spring
pokeweed	young green shoots	cooked vegetable	spring
rose	fruit (hips)	jam	late summer
Solomon's seal	rootstocks	potato substitute	year-round
viburnum	fruit	nibble, cooked fruit, jelly	summer, fall
wild ginger	roots	spice	year-round
wild mustard	leaves	potherb, salad	spring
wintergreen	leaves, berries	tea, trail nibble	summer, fall
wood sorrel	leaves	salad	summer

* Handle with gloves before cooking!

REFERENCES AND SUGGESTIONS FOR FURTHER READING

Fernald, Merritt L., Kinsey, Alfred C., and Rollins, Reed C. 1958. *Edible Wild Plants of Eastern North America*. Harper & Row, New York.

Gibbons, Euell. 1969. *Stalking the Wild Asparagus*. McKay, New York.

Kingsbury, John M. 1964. *Poisonous Plants of the United States and Canada*. Prentice-Hall, New Jersey.

Lampe, Kenneth F., and McCann, Mary A. 1985. *AMA Handbook of Poisonous and Injurious Plants*. American Medical Association, Chicago.

Peterson, Lee. 1978. *A Field Guide to Wild Edible Plants of Eastern and Central North America*. Houghton Mifflin, Boston.

18

Autumn Color and Falling Leaves

EACH AUTUMN, leaves undergo a dramatic change of color, and then begin to fall. We've all witnessed this metamorphosis, and have marveled at its beauty. If you have ever wondered what accounts for all these autumn transformations, you have not been alone in your inquiries. In 1899, the botanist E. Overton described his important series of experiments on the autumn coloration of plants. Now, nearly 90 years later, the process is better understood. Many of the leaf pigments involved in the autumn foliage display have been isolated and analyzed. We understand better how weather, sunlight, and nutrition affect the color and intensity of the leaves. Although nature has not yet revealed all her secrets, we can appreciate many aspects of the intricate physiological changes that occur in trees each fall.

LEAF PIGMENTS

Leaves contain several pigments, in varying amounts, that change through the seasons. These chemical substances color the leaves, flowers, roots, and stems of the plant. The most important are the **chlorophylls**, from the Greek for green (*chloros*) and leaf (*phyllon*). These are the green leaf pigments with which we are all familiar. There are two types, *a* and *b,* packed into microscopic structures called **chloroplasts**, located in plant cells. Photosynthesis takes place within the chloroplasts. In the process, energy from the sunlight is trapped by chlorophyll, and it fuels the reaction by which carbon dioxide and water are converted to carbohydrates, such as sugar molecules.

A second category of pigments is the **carotenoids**. They are yellow or orange and derive their name from the Latin word, *carota,* meaning carrot. The carotenoids come in two varieties: the **carotenes**, which are usually orange, and the **xanthophylls** (from the Greek, *xanthos,* yellow-brown + *phyllon,* leaf), which are yellow. The carotenoid pigments are commonly found in the chloroplasts, along with the chlorophylls. Here they function as accessory pigments that trap wavelengths of light the chlorophylls cannot absorb. This enables the plants to absorb and utilize sunlight more efficiently. Sometimes carotenoids are present alone, in structures similar to the chloroplasts. These **chromoplasts** are responsible for the yellow coloration of certain flowers, ripe fruits, and many autumn leaves.

In addition to the green, yellow, and orange pigments, reddish-colored leaves contain **anthocyanins** (from the Greek, *anthos,* flower + *kyanos,* dark blue). This group of pigments got its name from **cyanin**, the first flower pigment to be studied over 100 years ago when it was extracted from blue cornflowers (bachelor's-buttons). The color of the anthocyanins ranges from deep red to brilliant blue, depending upon the acidity of the solution. In an acidic medium they are red, changing to violet in neutral solutions, and then to blue in an alkaline environment. Nature is versatile in its use of anthocyanins, using the same compound to produce a range of colors merely by varying the acidity of the cell sap. For example, the same cyanin which colors blue cornflowers is responsible for the dark red color of roses.

The pigments responsible for the color of autumn leaves are the raw materials in nature's palette. We must discover how they are blended to create a dazzling fall display.

THE YELLOWS AND GOLDS

In order for a leaf to stay green, the overpowering chlorophyll pigment must constantly be synthesized to replace the amounts that are slowly destroyed each day. However, in the autumn, the metabolism of the leaf slows down and less chlorophyll is produced. In addition, the rate of chlorophyll breakdown increases. The net result is a loss of the leaf's green pigment.

PLANT PIGMENTS

Anthocyanins

Vegetables and Fruits	Flowers	Leaves
turnip	aster	red maple
radish	geranium	sumac
beet	coleus	some oaks
grape	tulip	dogwood
plum	hyacinth	black gum
cherry	begonia	Euonymus
red cabbage	rose	hawthorn
blueberry	peony	

Carotenoids

Vegetables and Fruits	Flowers	Leaves
sweet potato	daffodil	poplar
squash	tulip	sycamore
carrot	marigold	birch
spinach	crocus	beech
broccoli	chrysanthemum	aspen
corn		hickory
		elm

This allows the carotenoids to shine. They have been there all the time, but only now do we get a chance to see them as the chlorophyll fades. These yellow pigments are more stable than the greens, and they remain after the chlorophyll is gone. The balance between carotenes and xanthophylls determines the precise shade of yellow. The carotenes create an orange hue, whereas xanthophylls produce a lighter yellow coloration.

Substances called tannins may also be present in the leaf. They are the bitter compounds responsible for the astringent taste of certain teas, and of unripe fruits such as persimmons and plums. They are most abundant in the cell walls, serving as chemical defenses against hungry insects and plant diseases caused by bacteria or fungi. In leaves, they modify the color of the carotenoids, producing a golden tone. The dingy brown color of oaks in late fall is the result of their high concentration of tannins.

THE REDS

Whereas the yellows and oranges were there all along, obscured by the overwhelming presence of chlorophyll, the development of red tones has a more complicated origin. Red anthocyanin pigments are newly synthesized at about the same time the chlorophyll is disappearing. The yellow carotenoid pigments may be present as well, but they are masked by the reds.

Plants that develop red hues in the autumn, are not devoid of anthocyanins earlier in the year; it is just that the amount of these pigments greatly increases if the proper conditions exist in the fall. That is why each autumn display is different, a surprise that depends upon a particular juxtaposition of weather conditions and other factors.

The formation of anthocyanins is stimulated by the accumulation of sugars in the plant tissues. In the autumn, several factors favor the production and mainte-nance of high sugar concentrations in the leaves. Light intensities remain high, stimulating the photosynthetic production of sugar by leaf tissues. You can observe examples of the effect of sunlight quite easily. The foliage of red maples, for example, is often brilliant red on the side of the tree that receives more sunlight and yellow on the shaded side. Look carefully at individual leaves. Where two leaves overlap, the lower leaf will often show the distinct colored "shadow" of the upper leaf, corresponding to the shaded and sunlight portions.

Cool night temperatures below 45° F (7° C) help slow down the movement of sugars to other parts of the tree, allowing them to accumulate in the leaf. Colder weather reduces the tree's metabolism so that less sugar is consumed. Contrary to popular belief, early, hard frosts do not promote greater development of autumn pigments. Rather, they have an adverse effect by injuring or killing the leaves before the pigments have reached their maximum production.

The foliage coloration differs in nearby areas because of different levels of minerals and nutrients in the soil. Excess nitrogen is believed to inhibit pigment development because the sugars that would normally be used for pigment forma-tion are diverted to pathways in which nitrogen is used to form proteins. Deficien-cies of nitrogen, phosphorus, and magnesium are associated with red anthocyanin formation. Farmers and gardeners are aware that premature red coloration of a tree's lower leaves may indicate inadequate levels of these elements.

Controversy exists over the effect of water. Drought can cause premature color-ation of the leaves, but a dry autumn diminishes the brilliance of the foliage, causing leaves to die and fall prematurely. Such displays tend to be more drab and brownish, suggesting a poor development of the anthocyanins.

A final factor that affects pigment development is disease. Diseased trees and individual branches show both premature and more intense coloration, the result of interrupted movement of sugars or alterations in mineral and water absorption caused by damage to the roots or conducting system.

FALLING LEAVES AND DEVELOPING BUDS

In addition to the obvious color changes in the leaves, other inconspicuous devel-opments are taking place. During this period of leaf senescence, as chlorophyll production slows down, a microscopic layer of weak, thin-walled cells forms at the base of the leaf. This separation, or **abscission layer**, prevents the sugars produced within the leaves from being transported to the rest of the tree. The sugars trapped in the leaf are used to synthesize red anthocyanins. The abscission layer also marks the spot where the leaf will fall.

The abscission of leaves is affected by factors such as a lack of adequate water, low temperature, reduced light intensity, and a decrease in the length of the day. In the autumn, these environmental factors influence the level of a growth hormone, auxin, in the leaf. Normally, auxins in the plant regulate cell growth, affecting the elongation of shoots, the growth of roots, and the development of fruit. Auxins are responsible for the bending of a seedling toward the light (**phototropism**), which was described as early as 1880 by Charles Darwin. Many years later, demonstrations proved that diminished auxin production also causes leaves to drop.

As the season advances, the cells in the separation layer become drier and disintegrate, through the action of enzymes. The leaf now clings tenuously to the tree. Blowing winds, the shrinkage of the leaf stalk on dry warm days, the crash of raindrops, or the formation of ice crystals within the abscission layer finally wrench the leaf from the stem. The tree has a special mechanism for sealing its wounds, preventing the loss of sap. A layer of cork, which had previously developed below the abscission layer, seals the leaf scar.

WHY TREES LOSE THEIR LEAVES

Why should a tree lose its leaves? In the winter, the leaves cannot perform their function of producing food by photosynthesis. With freezing temperatures, all the water is locked up in the frozen ground, and plant metabolism cannot function in subfreezing temperatures. Heavy snow piling upon the broad-leaved foliage would snap the tree's branches. The cold, drying winds would tear and shred the leaves and steal their moisture.

Trees have evolved a very efficient system of discarding their leaves when they aren't needed, replacing them each spring. The leaves that have fallen are not wasted. Decomposition by microorganisms frees minerals and nutrients, which seep into the soil and are reabsorbed by the tree.

ACTIVITIES

Recording the sequence of changes in the autumn foliage

Make a chart of the sequence of changes in the autumn foliage. Beginning in early September and continuing until the last leaf falls, note when each tree first begins to change its colors. Record your information on a weekly basis. These data will be more instructive if you keep track of the minimum and maximum temperature, and the amount of rainfall each week. If you have the patience to do this over several years, you will begin to understand how the weather affects the changing foliage colors.

THE AUTUMN FOLIAGE SEQUENCE IN THE NORTHEAST	
Species	Color
Early (late September)	
red maple	bright red or orange
white ash	maroon, rust, or greenish-red
staghorn sumac	brilliant orange, then red
Middle (early to mid-October)	
hickory	intense yellow
black birch	yellow
beech	yellow to brown
tupelo	intense dark red
sugar maple	bright orange, turning yellow
aspen	various shades of yellow
sassafras	pinkish orange, becoming yellow
maple-leaved viburnum	purplish, maroon
Late (sometimes until November)	
red oak	variable, reddish-brown
black oak	variable, yellowish-brown
white oak	fades purple to brown
Norway maple	bright yellow
wild cherry	yellow

Keep records for several different areas near your home, such as a swamp and an exposed hilltop. Trees in swampy areas may turn color earlier as the cool air settles on these low-lying regions. A weekly series of photographs taken at the identical spot will dramatically illustrate the sequence of changes. You might want to keep track of an individual tree, perhaps a large sugar maple or a red oak. Be sure to label all your charts and photographs with the date and locality so that you can refer back to your data in subsequent years.

Visualizing leaf pigments

FILTER PAPER CHROMATOGRAPHY

Chromatography, meaning "color writing," is a technique used to separate different kinds of molecules. It was devised to separate chloroplast pigments, but now many variations of the technique are used to separate substances, whether they are colored or not.

The simplest way to demonstrate paper chromatography is to perform the following kitchen experiment. Take a few drops of different food colorings and mix them until you have a dark solution. Take a paper napkin and cut out a long, thin strip. Place a single drop of your blackish dye on the strip, about an inch from one end. Using Scotch® tape or a paper clip, suspend the paper strip carefully in a glass filled with about half an inch of water, without letting it touch the sides of the glass. Only the very end of the strip should be in the water. The water will begin to rise up the napkin by capillary action and carry the food colors along with it. Let the water reach the top of the paper. Notice how different pigments travel at different rates, forming bands of individual colors.

Why does this happen? Each pigment molecule is a different size and has a different electric charge. Thus, each pigment in the solution has a different affinity for the water and for the paper napkin. Some pigments have little attraction for the paper and move quickly along with the water as it rises up the strip. Other pigments are attracted more to the paper, being bound to it more tightly, and moving more slowly up the strip. The result is a simple, yet elegant method for separating different types of molecules.

Try variations of this experiment, using different solvents or mixtures of solvents to alter the degree of separation of the pigments. Try different proportions of rubbing alcohol and water. Also try different pigments, such as felt-tipped markers or ball-point pen ink.

In the laboratory, a few refinements of the technique yield tidier results. Instead of napkins, we use filter paper. It absorbs solvents better and has a more uniform structure. Instead of water, we use a variety of solvents, such as acetone, methyl alcohol, and ether, since some molecules, such as carotenoids, are insoluble in water.

SEPARATION OF LEAF PIGMENTS BY CHROMATOGRAPHY

First, we need a source of chloroplast leaf pigments. Spinach leaves work well. Put a handful of chopped leaves into a glass kitchen blender, and add about half a cup of acetone to dissolve the pigments. (Acetone can be purchased in hardware stores, in the section with turpentine and paint thinners.) Do not breathe the fumes! Blend for a few minutes, then pour the liquid into a cup or beaker. Strain the solution to get rid of the bits of plant material. The solution will be a deep green color. It is a mixture of two chlorophyll pigments, *a* and *b*, and carotenoids. While you have this solution, shine a high intensity light, such as that from a slide projector, through the solution. Look at it from the side, and it will appear deep red, not green. The red color is caused by the fluorescence of chlorophyll *a*. All the pigments in the solution absorb the light, but ultimately most of the light energy is transferred to the chlorophyll *a*, which emits the energy as red light. This same phenomenon happens in the living chloroplasts and is part of the efficient system whereby the sun's light energy is captured and used in photosynthesis.

We can now return to our chromatography experiment. Pour a small amount of the pigment solution into a beaker so that there is about a half-inch on the bottom. Suspend a filter paper strip in the solution. Allow at least a half-hour for the solvent and pigments to move up the strip.

You will see distinct color bands form. Yellow-green chlorophyll *b* is bound most tightly to the filter paper and forms the lowermost band. Next is the dark blue-green band of chlorophyll *a*. The carotenoids travel upward faster, forming a bright yellow band.

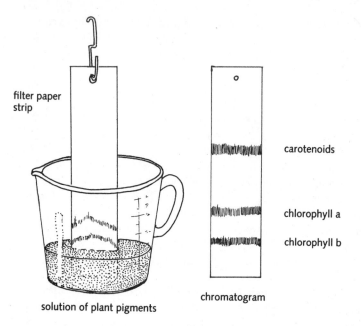

filter paper strip

carotenoids

chlorophyll a

chlorophyll b

chromatogram

solution of plant pigments

How to separate leaf pigments by using paper chromatography.

Repeat this experiment with different plants at different times of the year to obtain a distinctive "signature" for each plant. The chromatography strips tend to fade in the light, so keep them covered, or make a drawing of your filter paper chromatogram with colored pencils.

EXTRACTING ANTHOCYANIN PIGMENTS FROM PLANTS

The anthocyanin pigments are soluble in water, making them easy to extract. Slice a cupful of red cabbage and place it in a Pyrex® beaker. Cover the chopped cabbage with water and heat it until it almost boils, stirring until the liquid is a deep red color. Strain to get rid of the bits of plant tissue. You now have a solution of anthocyanin pigment.

Remember that a single anthocyanin pigment can take on any of a number of different shades from red to blue depending upon the acidity of the cell sap in the vacuoles. We can demonstrate this with the following experiment: Pour a small amount of your anthocyanin extract into two dishes. Add some acid to one. Vinegar is a good household source of acetic acid. Put a drop at a time of the vinegar into the extract until it changes color. Baking soda is alkaline. Add some baking soda, a bit at a time, to the other dish. Compare the colors. You can reverse the color change by adding acid or alkaline to the solutions.

Try other leaves, such as red-leaved coleus, red beets, and red maple leaves in autumn. Are all these pigments water soluble? Do they all show a color transformation when the acidity of the solution is altered? You can make **indicator** papers that tell you whether a solution is acidic or basic by soaking some filter paper in your red cabbage extract, drying the paper, and cutting it up into little strips. Litmus paper indicator is made this way, using a pigment obtained from lichens.

REFERENCES AND SUGGESTIONS FOR FURTHER READING

Machlis, L., and Torrey, J.G. 1956. *Plants in Action: A Laboratory Manual of Plant Physiology.* W.H. Freeman, San Francisco.

Meyer, B.S.; Anderson, D.B.; and Bohning, R.H. 1960. *Introduction to Plant Physiology.* Van Nostrand, New York.

Meyer, B.S.; Anderson, D.B.; and Swanson, C.A. 1955. *Laboratory Plant Physiology,* 3d ed. Van Nostrand, New York.

Onslow, M.W. 1925. *The Anthocyanin Pigments of Plants,* 2d ed. Cambridge University Press, London.

Overton, E. 1899. Experiments on the autumn colouring of plants. *Nature* 59: 296.

Walker, R.B. 1983. Why leaves change color in autumn. *University of Washington Arboretum Bulletin* 46: 28–30.

19

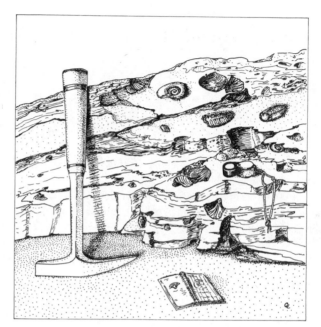

Fossils: Stories in Stone

THREE HUNDRED AND FIFTY million years ago a catastrophic storm wreaked havoc over the land. Torrents of water, heavily laden with silt, poured into the shallow seas, suffocating and covering schools of fish. Thousands died and were quickly covered with thick layers of sediments. In the muck, the lack of oxygen hindered their decomposition. Instead of rotting and falling apart, the fish remained relatively intact. Microorganisms eventually consumed most of the fishes' soft parts, but scales, bones, and teeth were more resistant, and remained.

As the years passed, more and more sediments accumulated on the bottom of the sea. Intermittently over the centuries, further flash floods led to other accumulations of organisms, and further deposits of silt. However, the ocean basin did not fill up with these sediments. It gradually subsided, keeping pace with the accumulation of sediments. Over the course of millions of years, the mud and sand reached thicknesses of up to 40,000 feet (12 km). Deep beneath the earth's surface, these sedimentary layers consolidated into shale and sandstone, preserving the marine inhabitants. Eventually, these strata were uplifted, and eroded. Streams carved channels in the soft rock. Water seeped into the stone, alternately freezing and thawing, prying apart layers of the rock. Finally an alert naturalist walked along a road cut for a new highway and spied a fossil fish in a stone recently freed from the hillside by a spring thaw. Had he come a month sooner, or later, he might never have found the treasure that now occupies a spot on a shelf at home.

Fossils are the preserved remains of plants and animals that died long ago. These stony remnants are crucial clues for piecing together the history of life on earth. The fossil record is our geologic history book. Reading these stories in stone, the naturalist can take an imaginary journey through time to view the world's ancient flora and fauna.

The story is fascinating, but often difficult to read. Paleontologists who spend their lives perusing the fossil record are keen detectives in following diaphanous threads of evidence. They have learned to decipher a story written in an obscure language. The movement of continents, the warping of the earth's crust, and millennia of erosion make the story difficult to read. In addition, the record of life on earth has not always been carefully preserved. Conditions have to be just right for fossilization to occur. Of all the organisms that ever died, only the merest fraction are fossilized, and of these fossils, only a few are ever discovered. Layers of fossil-bearing rocks, miles thick, were exposed eons ago and destroyed by erosion. Other fossils are ruined deep within the earth whenever immense heat and pressure convert the fossiliferous strata into metamorphic rocks. Still other fossils lie trapped thousands of feet below the surface in a stony tomb that man will never open.

As a result, the fossil record reveals only a smattering of the life that existed. For the most part, the book that paleontologists read is ragged, torn, and watermarked, with many pages missing and unintelligible. These gaps must be filled in by intelligent speculation.

HOW FOSSILS FORM

As a general rule, only the hard parts of an organism — shells, bones, and other skeletal structures — are preserved as fossils. These usually consist of calcium carbonate, calcium phosphate, silica, or chitin. Corals, molluscs, and many other marine organisms have calcareous shells of finely crystallized calcium carbonate. **Chitin** is a material that makes up the exoskeletons of insects, shrimps, crabs, and the extinct trilobites. It is a tough polysaccharide similar in structure to the cellulose of wood. The hard portion of bone is similar to the mineral **hydroxyapatite**, a form of calcium phosphate. **Silica**, the major ingredient of glass and sand, is the most resistant mineral found in organisms, making up the hard parts of certain protozoans, sponges, and microscopic plants called **diatoms**. The remaining soft portions of plants and animals are usually lost, except under special conditions.

The most abundant fossils are shells from shallow marine waters. In some cases, the original shells may persist unaltered. However, these sedimentary layers are

Era	Period	Epoch MILLIONS OF YEARS	Description

The geological time scale.

generally porous, allowing water to percolate through the strata to the buried shells. If the water is acidic, the shells will dissolve, leaving a hollow cavity or mold. Either the open cavity remains, as in much of the Devonian mudstone of eastern New York, Pennsylvania, and New Jersey, or the hollow space is obliterated when the strata settle and compress. A third possibility is that a mineral solution, such as silica, lime, or iron, will seep into the empty cavity and precipitate out, forming a cast of the mold. In each of these cases, the surface structure of the shell persists, allowing identification of the organism.

Other organisms become fossilized when buried under more specialized circumstances. In the sandstone beds of the Harrison formation in Nebraska, great haphazard accumulations of bones were discovered, the remains of giant pigs, small rhinoceroses, and clawed ungulates. The "dinosaur quarries" in the Morrison formation of the Rocky Mountain states have yielded similar jumbles of bones. Over 10,000 bones from seven dinosaur species were uncovered in one "dig" in Utah. It is hypothesized that the animals died after inadvertently wandering into an area of quicksand. The carcasses decomposed, the bones disarticulated, and were fossilized in disorganized accumulations.

Once an organism is buried, processes may occur that result in the alteration of its chemical structure. This process of **petrification**, or **petrifaction**, preserves the organism's internal structure. Most of us have seen examples of petrified wood from the Colorado plateau, sliced and polished with beautiful colors and incredible detail of the wood's original structure. These fossils formed when dead logs washed into rivers and were buried in the sand. Alkaline waters with dissolved silica seeped through the sediments and came into contact with the logs. As they decayed, they released carbon dioxide, which dissolved in the water, forming carbonic acid. This neutralized the alkaline water, and the silica precipitated out of solution. Slowly, the cellulose of the wood was replaced, molecule for molecule, by the silica. Sometimes the chemical substitution was so perfect that the growth rings and wood cells were preserved in minute detail. If various metal oxides, such as iron, copper, and manganese, were present, the petrified wood became stained in rainbow colors.

Other organisms become fossilized by petrifaction. The lime of corals and ammonite shells can be replaced by iron. Percolating waters, saturated with sulfur and iron, come into contact with these buried animals and precipitate as the mineral iron **pyrite**, lustrous fool's gold.

Carbonization is another process that preserves fine structural detail. When leaves fall into stagnant oxygen-poor waters of swamps, they may not decay. Covered with silt and eventually subjected to heat and pressure, most of the organic material of the leaf is released as methane, water, and carbon dioxide. What remains is a thin film of carbon, showing the imprint and venation of the leaf. Insects and fish have been preserved the same way.

In rare circumstances, organisms are preserved unaltered, providing an even better picture of the organism as it lived. Wooly mammoths roamed the frigid Siberian plains 25,000 years ago. They have been found frozen in the ice, in such perfect condition that their flesh was still red, so fresh that one animal was partly eaten by wild dogs before an expedition salvaged its thawing remains.

In Los Angeles, California, at the La Brea tar pits, remains of thousands of saber-toothed tigers and other Pleistocene animals have been recovered. These animals were abundant 15,000 years ago. They apparently died by wandering into sticky oil seeps exposed on the surface. Attempting to attack stranded animals, carnivorous tigers, wolves, and lions became victims of the oozy black tar.

On a smaller scale is the perfect preservation of insects in amber. This ancient resin, exuded from pine trees, held any tiny insect that encountered the sticky substance. When they were completely surrounded and shut off from the air, these creatures did not decompose. Their hard chitinous exoskeletons are so well preserved that they can be examined in detail under the microscope.

COMMON FOSSIL ORGANISMS

Paleontologists have been able to correlate the age of sedimentary rocks with the fossils of particular strata. Thus, if we know the age of a rock formation, we know what type of fossils we can expect to find. Similarly, since many plants and animals lived only in certain intervals of time, knowledge of fossils allows us to date the rocks in which they are found. For example, rocks near my home were laid down in the Devonian period, 370 million years ago. In this area of New York, one can find abundant evidence of the fossil invertebrates — brachiopods (lamp shells), clams, snails, trilobites, corals, and crinoids (sea lilies). These animals inhabited an enormous shallow sea that covered most of North America during the Paleozoic era between 570 and 225 million years ago. These same marine animals can be found in many regions of the country. The following is a brief description of some of these organisms.

Protozoans (meaning first animals) are a primitive group of mostly microscopic, single-celled animals. Two protozoan orders, **Foraminifera** and **Radiolaria**, are common as fossils because they secrete hard shells. Both groups are extremely abundant in the oceans today. Foraminiferans have calcareous shells that sink to the ocean bottom when the organisms die. Much of the limestone and chalk found on earth was formed from extensive deposits of foraminiferan shells. At great ocean depths (15,000 feet or more), the increased carbon dioxide content of the water tends to dissolve these shells, so the bottom ooze there consists mainly of silica-ceous radiolarian shells. These are very ancient organisms. Foraminiferan fossils date back to the Cambrian period; radiolarians are older yet, occurring in Precambrian rocks. Under the microscope, foraminiferans look like tiny snails. The skeletons of the radiolarians are delicately spined latticeworks of glassy silica. Each is an exquisitely detailed masterpiece, more ornate than the finest cut crystal.

The sponges are the simplest multicellular animals. Their saclike bodies are perforated by numerous pores, hence their scientific name, **Porifera**. Water is drawn into the sponge through the pores, and microscopic particles of food are extracted. The excess water is then expelled through the opening in the top of the sponge. Sponges have three body layers. The middle layer secretes a framework of spicules to support the organism. These spicules, composed of silica or calcium carbonate, are the durable structures that become fossilized.

Corals belong to a group called the **Coelenterates**, meaning hollow intestine. This refers to their saclike body, which acts as both mouth and intestine. Stinging tentacles surround this opening, capturing and drawing food in, where it is digested. These organisms have a simple structure, lacking the respiratory, circula-

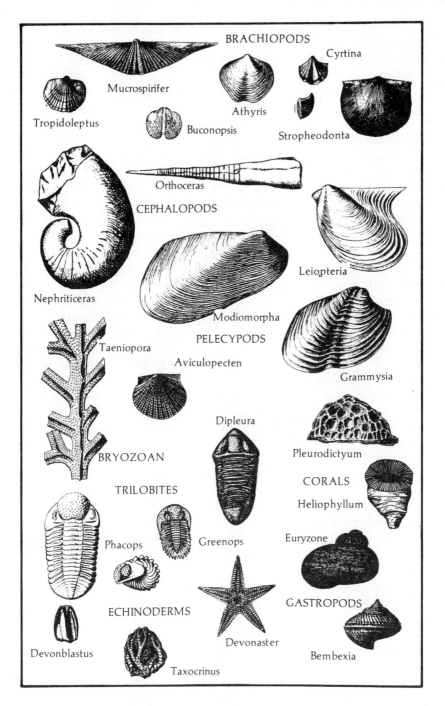

Representative Hamilton Group fossils of New York State, dating to the mid-Devonian period (approximately 370 million years ago). (All fossils are approximately one-half life-size.)

tory, and excretory systems of more advanced animals. Their soft bodies are not preserved, but they secrete a supporting skeleton of calcium carbonate. Entire tropical islands are made up of their remains.

Bryozoans, or moss animals, are so named because their colonies are often flattened, fanlike, and branched, resembling a primitive plant. Each individual grows in a tiny cup called a **zooecium**, composed of horn or lime. Although they superficially resemble corals, Bryozoans are more complex, having nervous and muscular systems, and a U-shaped intestine.

The remaining groups are familiar fossils. **Brachiopods**, or lamp shells, resemble clams. However, unlike clams, their shells are made of two unequal valves. Thirty thousand fossil forms are known, making them among the most common Paleozoic fossils. Today only 200 species are living.

The **Molluscs** include snails, clams, squids, octopuses, and nautiluses. The members of the group have a similar internal structure, but variable external appearance. The snails (**gastropods**) have a head with tentacles, eyes, and a rasping filelike tongue, the **radula**. The coiled shell consists of a single piece. The bivalved molluscs (**pelecypods**) include clams, oysters, and mussels. Unlike the snails, they lack a head. The two similar-shaped valves are opened by large adductor muscles, exposing siphons that draw in water containing microscopic food particles.

The **Cephalopods** (squid, octopuses, and nautiluses) barely resemble the other molluscs. The living forms have a well-developed head, eyes, and tentacles. Many of the fossil forms had straight, uncoiled shells. The fossil ammonites resemble present-day nautiluses.

Trilobites are extinct marine arthropods. Their bodies had three major divisions, of which the thorax had three lobed segments, giving this group its name. They lived on the sea bottom as scavengers or predators. Their jointed bodies allowed them to curl up in defense so that only their hard dorsal shield was exposed. Many fossils are found in this coiled position. Vision in trilobites varied among the species. Some had large faceted eyes, while a few genera were apparently blind. This is an extremely ancient group, dating back to Cambrian times, the earliest time from which fossils are commonly found.

Echinoderms are a phylum of animals that includes starfish, sea urchins, sea cucumbers, and crinoids (sea lilies). They have a radially symmetric body, divided into five parts. Their bodies are covered with calcareous plates or spines, which preserve well as fossils. The sea lilies are the oldest and most primitive echinoderms. They look like flowers, attached to the substrate by a long stalk, and with a calyx of feathery arms surrounding the mouth. Most commonly, one finds only the disk-shaped columnals that make up the stalk.

ACTIVITIES

Collecting fossils

Sedimentary rocks found throughout most of the United States are often rich in fossils. They are formed from hardened, accumulated sediments, such as clays on lake bottoms, sandy ocean shores, lime muds, salt precipitates from saline lakes, and coarse gravels deposited by floods.

Other types of rocks rarely contain fossils. Scattered areas in the West have igneous rocks formed from molten magma of volcanic origin. In portions of New England, the Appalachians, and the Rocky Mountains, one finds mostly metamorphic rocks. These were originally igneous or sedimentary rocks that were subjected to pressures and temperatures that altered and recrystallized the rock.

Fossil collecting is a treasure hunt. If you search widely and carefully, you are bound to find fossils. Fresh exposures of rock are best for collecting. Here the fossils will not be worn and weathered. Blasting and excavation sites for highways, railroads, and buildings are excellent sources. Slate, shale, and limestone quarries often contain abundant fossils. Be sure to obtain permission before collecting in these areas. In addition to these artificial exposures, search at natural outcroppings. As rocks are broken free from cliffs and riverbeds, new strata are constantly being exposed.

Information on collecting areas can be obtained from field guides to specific regions. Detailed geologic maps, prepared by state geologic surveys, can be obtained from local government offices. The U.S. Geologic Survey and the Superintendent of Documents, both in Washington, D.C., offer maps and publications about geology.

EQUIPMENT

Tools for fossil collecting are simple. A well-prepared collector may take along a backpack full of equipment, but in many cases a hammer is all that is needed. The following is a complete list of gear.

1. Clothing: Sturdy field clothing and durable hiking boots.

2. Hammers: A geology or stonemason's hammer, with a square, blunt end and a chisel-ended head. Small sledge-hammers, and crowbars can be useful.

3. Chisels: Tempered steel chisels in a variety of sizes.

4. Protective Gear: Always wear safety glasses. Smashing rocks send splinters flying at incredible speeds. They seem to have a predilection for the eyes. Wearing a pair of leather gloves will save you from blistered hands after a day of pounding stones. If you are working at the base of a cliff, a hardhat may prevent a headache or worse.

5. Packing and labeling materials: Wrap your finds in newspaper, and label them carefully with the exact location where the fossil was found, including its position within the stratum.

6. Notebook and pencils: Take detailed notes on the location of the site and the nature of the rock beds. Drawings and photographs of the strata are useful.

7. Maps: Road maps, topographic maps, and other geologic maps allow you to identify your collecting site and will help you find your way back to the exact spot months later, when your memory has begun to fail.

8. Miscellaneous items: A hand lens (10x) to examine details of small fossils, a hand broom to dust off debris and rock powder, a quick-drying glue for repairing specimens that did not come free as you had planned, and a tape measure for specifying the exact location of a fossil within the stratum.

Preparing specimens

Most often, the only preparation needed is to trim the extra rock matrix from around the fossil. If the fossiliferous rock is a thin slab, carefully score the surface with three or four straight lines that frame the fossil, but leave a generous margin for error. Set the scored line on the straight edge of a larger rock, fossil side up, and hit the overhanging portion of the slab gently. If the score is deep enough, the rock will split neatly along the line. With thicker rocks, it is more difficult, but remember that it is better to take home an intact fossil in a big rock than a shattered fossil in a few smaller stones.

At home, wash the fossil with water and a scrub brush, if it is not too fragile. Bits of matrix attached to the fossil can be picked off with a fine chisel, a needle, or a dentist's old tools. Sometimes power tools are handy, especially the small hand-held, high-speed grinders sold for hobby work. They have a variety of drill bits and grinding wheels. Be careful, however. It is much easier to ruin a prize specimen with a power tool than by slowly and painstakingly working by hand.

Some fossils need protection, especially if the matrix is crumbly, or if the fossil is particularly delicate. A clear plastic coating will help keep the matrix intact. Dissolve a cement, such as Duco®, in some acetone or toluene, and paint it on the fossil. (These solvents are available in hardware stores.) Many fossils covered with a dingy film of stone powder will seem to come alive when coated with a clear plastic aerosol spray, available at hardware or art supply stores.

Occasionally, a limestone matrix surrounds casts of silicified fossils. These fossils can be freed from the rock by dissolving the matrix with acid. Always experiment with an expendable fragment first; many fossils are calcium carbonate and will dissolve in acid. Goodbye fossil! Vinegar, a 5 percent solution of acetic acid, works fine. When you immerse the fossiliferous rock in the vinegar, bubbles of carbon dioxide will form as the surrounding limestone dissolves. Within a few hours to a few days, the matrix will dissolve, freeing fossils perfect in all their details. If you become impatient, you can try hydrochloric acid, which is much stronger. A commercial grade called muriatic acid is sold in hardware stores. Use it diluted tenfold, being careful not to get any on your skin or in your eyes — it will burn.

Organizing your collection

Unless a fossil is carefully labeled, it will have little scientific value. Each specimen should be numbered, with a label glued on the fossil or written directly on the rock with india ink. (Paint a dot of white enamel on the specimen, allow it to dry, and write the number on the spot.) In a notebook or on a file card, record the fossil's number, the exact location where the fossil was found, the date of the find, and the collector's name. If known, include the name of the fossil and the age of the rock formation in which it was found. Your collection will be best displayed in a series of shallow drawers, with each fossil in a separate cardboard box.

REFERENCES AND SUGGESTIONS FOR FURTHER READING

Eardley, A.J. 1965. *General College Geology*. Harper & Row, New York.

Rhodes, Frank H.T.; Zim, Herbert S.; and Shaffer, Paul R. 1962. *Fossils: A Guide to Prehistoric Life*. Golden Press, New York.

Thompson, Ida. 1982. *The Audubon Society Field Guide to North American Fossils*. Knopf, New York.

Weinman, Paul L. 1976. *An Introduction to Invertebrate Fossils of New York*. Educational Leaflet no. 19. State Museum, University of the State of New York, Albany, New York.

Explorations of Snowflakes

THE MENTION OF SNOWFLAKES brings to mind tiny, shimmering crystals of ice in exquisite six-sided feathery patterns. The basic hexagonal symmetry is a reflection of the way water molecules arrange themselves in the crystalline structure of ice. However, examination of snow will reveal a far greater diversity of snow crystal forms than six-sided stars. Snow has been classified into ten different crystalline forms, including flat plates, long needles, fat columns, and, of course, the familiar stellar dendrites we know as snowflakes.

What is a snowflake? How is it formed? What determines the shape of snow crystals? Why are they symmetrical? Is it true that no two snowflakes are alike? We'll explore these questions, keeping in mind that despite years of study, the answers are still incomplete. We'll also learn to make a permanent snowflake collection for study.

First, a bit of terminology. Scientists reserve the word snowflake for a cluster of several individual snow crystals. The largest snow crystals may be 0.6 inches (1.5 cm) across, whereas the largest snowflakes — consisting of a cottony mass of many crystals — may be as large as two inches (5 cm). In common usage, these two terms are often used interchangeably.

You have probably heard that no two snowflakes are alike. Can this be so? Considering the unimaginable number of snowflakes that have fallen, it is difficult to believe that there have never been two alike. I came across the following data: "About 600 cubic miles of snow cover the Northern Hemisphere, and in every cubic foot of the fluffy stuff there are about 18 million snow crystals." A bit of multiplication will show that this enormous pile of snow contains 600 × 5,280 × 5,280 × 5,280 × 18,000,000 snow crystals — about 1,589,737,882,000,000,000,000 — more than the number of stars in our galaxy. Or consider this calculation: A typical snow crystal weighs one-millionth of a gram. If the average amount of snow that forms on earth each year is equivalent to a layer of liquid one and two-tenths inches (3 cm) deep, then over the past 3 billion years, 100,000,000,000,000,000,000,000,000,000,000,000,000 snowflakes have formed. That is a lot of snow crystals, a total weight more than 50 times that of the earth. One may understandably argue that two of these snowflakes must certainly have been alike. On the other hand, each snow crystal contains about a quintillion water molecules, and these molecules can be arranged in countless numbers of ways. Of course, no one can prove it, but it is quite likely that every snow crystal is unique. We do not expect two people to look exactly alike, even "identical" twins. We therefore should not expect two snow crystals to be alike. Each has a unique history, arising from subtle variations in temperature and humidity encountered during its development, factors that could never be duplicated exactly.

HOW SNOW CRYSTALS GROW

Snow crystals are born in clouds tens of thousands of feet in the air. They begin as a microscopic particle of frozen water upon which more water molecules accumulate. To understand the manner in which the initial ice particle forms, we must first discuss some of the processes that take place as warm, moist air rises and cools.

Water vapor refers to microscopic water molecules suspended in the air. The amount of vapor that air can hold depends upon the air temperature. As air cools, it cannot hold as much water vapor so the vapor condenses, forming a cloud of water droplets or ice. Condensation of water vapor, however, requires more than cool, moist air. In order for a water droplet to form, it needs something to form upon, a **condensation nucleus**. Condensation nuclei are microscopic impurities in the air, such as dust, sea salt, or soil particles, about 0.00004 inches (1 micron) in diameter. That is about one-eighth the size of a red blood cell. Such condensation nuclei are fairly common, numbering about 10 to 10,000 per cubic centimeter of air.

Once a water droplet has formed around one of these condensation nuclei, to freeze it still requires another type of impurity, a **freezing nucleus**. Freezing nuclei are rarer; 0.06 cubic inches (1 cc) of air may only contain ten active nuclei at 14° F (−10° C). But as air gets colder, active freezing nuclei are more common. While only one in a million water droplets freeze at 14° F (−10° C), one in a thousand freezes at − 22° F (−30° C); at − 40° F (− 40° C), all the droplets will freeze spontaneously.

Now we have a basis for understanding how a cloud of water droplets or ice forms. Warm, moist air rises, expands, and in so doing cools. The air becomes saturated with water vapor, and condenses into a cloud. If the temperature is below freezing, the cloud will consist of both microscopic ice crystals and supercooled water droplets that have not encountered a freezing nucleus. In this environment a snow crystal forms.

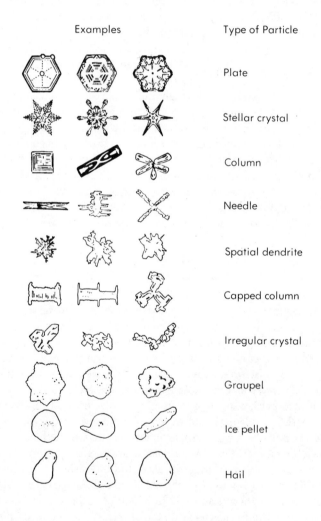

Examples	Type of Particle
	Plate
	Stellar crystal
	Column
	Needle
	Spatial dendrite
	Capped column
	Irregular crystal
	Graupel
	Ice pellet
	Hail

The international classification of the ten basic forms of ice crystals.

WHAT DETERMINES THE SHAPE OF SNOW CRYSTALS?

An international classification of snow crystals places individual snow particles in one of the following ten categories: hexagonal plates, stellar crystals, hexagonal columns, needles, spatial dendrites, capped columns, irregular particles, graupel, sleet, and hail. The crystalline structure, or **lattice**, of ice establishes the underlying hexagonal symmetry, but what determines whether the crystal grows as a long, thin hexagonal column or needle, a simple, flat hexagonal plate, or a delicate stellar crystal with intricate arms?

Atmospheric measurements as well as laboratory experiments have demonstrated that the particular form of a snow crystal is determined almost entirely by the temperature in which it forms. As the atmospheric temperature decreases from freezing to − 40° F (− 40° C), first planar crystals form, then needlelike crystals, planar ones again, and back to needles. The amount of water vapor in the air also affects the crystal shape. Consider droplets of water suspended in the atmosphere. Water molecules are constantly exchanged on the surface of the drop. If the

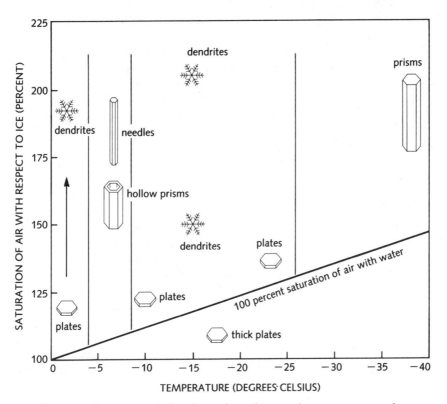

The type of snow crystal that forms depends upon the temperature and the amount of water vapor in the air. High water-vapor content results in more exaggerated crystal types: dendrites rather than plates, and long, thin needles instead of short, thick ones.

number of molecules leaving the drop equals the number going onto the drop, the air is said to be saturated with respect to the drop. If the air temperature cools, the number of water molecules condensing on the drop increases, and the air is said to be supersaturated with water. Under conditions such as these, when the water vapor content of the air is high, the rate of growth of a snow crystal increases, making it more complex or exaggerated in its form. Hexagonal columns become longer and more needlelike. Plates become larger, thinner, and more dendritic. These lacy patterns result from the way in which water diffuses to the hexagonal plates. With greater moisture content in the air, the corners of a plate grow faster than the sides, and develop branches. These branches subdivide further, resulting in a typical feathery snowflake pattern.

Thus, stellar dendrites form under a very specific set of circumstances: temperatures of about 5° F (−15° C), with a high degree of supersaturation. Needle-shaped crystals are also fastidious in their temperature requirements (18° to 25° F or −8° to −4° C), but form over a wide range of air-moisture content. Hexagonal plates develop under colder conditions (about −4° F, or −20° C) in drier air.

SNOW CRYSTAL SYMMETRY

Even a cursory examination of snow crystals reveals beautiful symmetry. Snowflakes in nature may not be nearly as symmetrical as the paper cutouts we find in store window displays at Christmas time, but symmetry is the rule among all crystals. Since each of the snowflake's six arms grows independently, why should a snow crystal grow so uniformly? Several explanations have been proposed. First, each portion of the crystal tends to be exposed to nearly identical atmospheric conditions, and thus each grows in the same manner.

Another theory suggests that there may be forces acting on the snow crystal that allow each arm to "know" what the others are doing. The following explanation has been offered: As a snow crystal drifts gently to earth, it vibrates, just as a string or the surface of a drum vibrates when struck. A vibrating object has certain regions, called anti-nodes, which undergo wide swings of movement, while other regions, the nodes, are relatively motionless. A growing crystal is in a dynamic state, constantly bombarded by water vapor molecules, some of which adhere to the developing crystal. In this delicate equilibrium, water molecules are less likely to adhere to regions in motion, and more likely to adhere to the quiet nodal areas. When molecules adhere to a particular region on one arm, this introduces a damping action on the vibrations, which is transmitted to the corresponding positions on the other five arms. Molecules arrive and adhere easily to the other arms in precisely the same positions as on the first arm. Thus, what happens on one arm tends to be repeated on the others, resulting in symmetric growth, despite the independence of each arm.

FACTORS CHANGING THE FORM OF SNOW CRYSTALS

As a crystal increases in size and begins to fall through a cloud, it may pass into an area of quite different temperature and water saturation. Updrafts, similarly, may carry crystals to different regions. If hexagonal needles ascend to cooler regions of about 5° F (−15° C), capped columns may form. These delicate crystals are called **tsuzumi** crystals, named for a Japanese drum of similar shape.

One of the most common changes that snow crystals undergo is **riming**. When a crystal forms within a cloud of supercooled water droplets, there are two ways in which the growing crystal may acquire water. In the vapor deposition mode, the water vapor molecules surrounding the droplets are gradually transferred, molecule by molecule, to the ice crystal. As small crystals gently fall, minute supercooled water droplets evaporate, and water molecules diffuse symmetrically to the crystal lattice. However, as the crystal grows larger, water droplets may not have time to evaporate completely and avoid collisions with the snow crystal. When a supercooled water droplet hits a snow crystal, it instantly freezes to its surface. The frozen droplet is called **rime**. As crystals rime, they fall faster, and accumulate rime more rapidly in an accelerating process. In contrast, when a crystal grows by water vapor deposition, water molecules are gradually added to its sides, increasing air resistence. During riming, a crystal collects ice mostly on the underside exposed to the droplets as it falls. This begins to obliterate the crystal symmetry, until finally a large deposit of rime may obscure the underlying form of the crystal. What is left is a crusty pellet of **graupel**.

A crystal that accumulates a light coat of rime may then fall into an area of smaller water droplets, where vapor deposition may again occur. An intricate crystal type, called a **spatial dendrite**, forms. Riming deposits ice haphazardly onto the snow crystal, and creates new orientations of the crystal lattice. The specks of rime become sites for new crystal growth, from which fernlike arms extend outward in many directions.

Other changes occur during a snowstorm. The intricate arms of stellar crystals may become interlocked or broken in turbulent winds. The detached crystal fragments continue to grow and collect rime. Careful examination of unbroken stellar dendrites will reveal some with fewer than six arms. These crystals began their life as tsuzumi crystals with a very short column between the two plates. When the end plates are less than 0.004 inches (0.1 mm) apart, the competition for crystal growth between the two plates becomes so intense that one end plate develops a few of the six arms, and the opposite end plate develops the remainder. When these very short tsuzumi crystals strike the ground or collide with other crystals, the two end plates may break apart, resulting in a crystal with fewer than six arms. However, as with normal stellar crystals, the angle between the arms is always a multiple of 60 degrees.

ACTIVITIES

Studying and preserving snowflakes

One can easily observe the details of snowflake structure in his own backyard. Take a piece of black velvet or black cardboard that is thoroughly chilled, and allow snowflakes to fall upon the surface. Here they can be examined with the naked eye, or, preferably, with a small hand lens of about 10x. Notice the type of crystal forms present during a storm. Is there a single type, or do needles, stellar dendrites, and hexagonal plates all occur at once? Does the type of snow crystal change as a storm progresses? Does a bitter midwinter blizzard yield a different snowflake fauna from a brief spring squall?

The finer details of individual snow crystals require study under higher magnification. The best method is to examine the crystals under a microscope. Take the microscope into a protected area, such as a garage, and allow it to cool below freezing. Let some snowflakes fall upon your black velvet. Being careful to avoid drafts that will whisk away your prized specimens, take your catch into a well-lit sheltered spot out of the wind. Quickly examine the crystals with a magnifying glass. When a promising one is found, transfer it ever so gently to a chilled microscope slide by touching it gently with a dampened toothpick. It will adhere and can be placed on the slide. Without breathing on the crystals, or allowing the warmth of your fingers to heat the slide, place the crystal under the microscope for viewing. Before your eyes will be revealed the symmetry and intricacy of crystalline ice. Convince yourself that each crystal is unique. Note the overall symmetry, as well as the slight imperfections of each flake. Under the microscope, what appeared to the naked eye as a uniform surface is now seen as a far more detailed landscape. The crystal is riddled with ridges, grooves, and cavities.

In 1885, a man named Wilson A. Bentley was studying snowflakes in this manner. Toward the end of the 19th century, the advent of the camera gave a new impetus to snowflake lovers. Working in a small shed on a hillside farm in Jericho, Vermont, Bentley pioneered snow crystal photography. In the bitter cold of Northeast blizzards, he worked alone, passionately examining snowflake after snowflake. His equipment was primitive by today's standards — a bulky studio camera attached to a microscope. Wearing hat, gloves, and a long black coat, he photographed thousands of snow crystals. His persistence and skill are revealed in a collection of ice crystal portraits published in 1931. Most of the photographs in his book are examples of perfect crystals, gleaned from years of painstaking search and selection.

A hardy, warmly dressed nature lover can continue Bentley's quest, spending chilly winters outdoors exploring the microcosm in a snowstorm. New developments have made snowflake study a less grueling endeavor. In the 1940's a scientist by the name of Vincent J. Schaefer discovered how to preserve snowflakes in the form of perfect plastic casts. His technique is simple, allowing those of us who chill easily to study snowflakes more comfortably in the warmth of our living rooms.

By embedding a snow crystal in a thin layer of liquid plastic and allowing it to harden, you can create an exact replica of the crystal's external structure. There are several variations to Schaefer's basic technique. The easiest is to use a clear plastic aerosol spray, available in any hardware store. Chill the can outdoors in the subfreezing weather. Then take a microscope slide or a pane of clean window glass, and give it a light coating of the lacquer. Allow the snowflakes to fall upon the sprayed glass. Because the spray is below freezing temperature, the crystals landing in the wet spray will not melt. They will become embedded in the clear lacquer, and as the solvents in the spray slowly evaporate, the lacquer will dry around the crystal, leaving a perfect cast. Be sure to leave the pane of glass outdoors, but out of the snowfall, until the spray is completely dry. The snowflake is trapped within,

(a)

(b)

Photographs of snowflakes by Wilson A. Bentley. (a) Intricate stellar dendrites usually form at lower altitudes where the air is relatively warm (5° F, or −15° C) and has a high water-vapor content. (b) Hexagonal plates generally form at higher altitudes in colder air with less water vapor.

Photograph of a plastic snowflake replica, prepared as described in the text.

but it will evaporate slowly through the thin layer of plastic. After several hours, the replicas can be brought indoors for leisurely examination by the warmth of the fireplace.

I collect my snowflakes on 2 × 2-inch glass slides obtained in photo supply stores. These slides fit directly into a slide projector, allowing the images of the crystals to be projected, greatly magnified, on the screen. For detailed examination and photomicrography, I view my icy jewels under the microscope.

If you wish to make a collection of perfect single crystals, a variation of this technique is recommended. A Plexiglas® solution makes better replicas than does plastic spray. Obtain some chloroform, ethylene dichloride, or acetone, and some chips of Plexiglas broken from a larger sheet. You can obtain these supplies from a pharmacy and a hardware store. Make a 1 percent Plexiglas solution by dissolving 1 gram of Plexiglas chips in 100 milliliters of the solvent in a wide-mouthed jar with a tight cover. When the Plexiglas has dissolved, place it outdoors in the cold. When you are ready to capture your snowflakes, dip a glass rod or a toothpick into the solution, and place a single droplet on a chilled glass slide. Very gently touch the moist rod to an individual snow crystal selected from your black velvet background. It will adhere to the rod and can be carefully transferred to the drop of Plexiglas solution on the slide. In moments, the solvent will evaporate, leaving a perfect cast of the crystal. For larger flakes and thickly rimed crystals, a stronger 2 percent solution is recommended.

Preparing a collection of snow crystals is an engrossing wintertime activity. A set of snowflake replicas can be prepared in a few hours, yet will last a lifetime. Next July, when the salty sweat is streaming down your hot forehead, retreat to your study. Pull out your snowflake collection, and dream of those cool winter evenings when the icy stars were falling from the heavens.

REFERENCES AND SUGGESTIONS FOR FURTHER READING

Bentley, W.A., and Humphreys, W.J. 1962. *Snow Crystals*. Dover, New York.

Knight, C., and Knight, N. January 1973. Snow Crystal. *Scientific American* 228: 100–107.

LaChapelle, E.R. 1969. *Field Guide to Snow Crystals*. University of Washington Press, Seattle.

Mason, B.J. 1957. *The Physics of Clouds*. Oxford University Press, London.

Nakaya, U. 1954. *Snow Crystals: Natural and Artificial*. Harvard University Press, Cambridge.

Perla, R.I. and Martinelli, M., Jr. 1975. *Avalanche Handbook*. Agriculture Handbook no. 489, U.S. Department of Agriculture, U.S. Government Printing Office, Washington, D.C.

Tolansky, S. 1958. Symmetry of snow crystals. *Nature* 181: 256–257.

21

Blowing Winds and Drifting Snow

SHAPING SNOW into intricate drifted formations, the biting winds of winter are nature's sculptor. Whereas man's creations emanate from images in the artist's mind, snowdrifts are designed by wind and snow obeying the laws of physics. The results are equally artistic, and are often on a much grander scale than is possible for mere human beings. Nature's work may cover entire mountainsides with gracefully curved crests and crevasses carved of snow and ice. The finished works are left to melt away slowly, or may come crashing down the hillside.

INTERACTIONS BETWEEN WIND AND SNOW

Windblown snow on a flat and featureless terrain is not very interesting. The obstacles in the path of the wind are what produce patterns of air currents, and also produce drifting snow. These barriers cause the wind to speed up in some places and to slow down in others, just as wind flowing over an airplane wing speeds up as it courses over the wing, then slows down beyond it. The airflow over a surface creates swirling eddies, or vortices, when the wind encounters slopes, trees, hedges, fences, or boulders. The shapes of snowdrifts are determined by the wind speed, the shape of the obstacles, and the character of the snow. On this field trip we will venture out after a snowstorm to learn how the wind has sculpted snowdrifts.

Snow is lifted and carried off when the wind speed exceeds a certain critical value between 11 and 22 MPH (18 to 36 km/hr). Loose, freshly fallen snow will start to drift with lighter winds than wet or older snow that has been compacted by the wind. The shape of the obstacle is the main factor that determines the shape of the snowdrift.

Consider the wind traveling over a small ridge on an otherwise level area. As the wind rises over the ridge, it accelerates. The air reaches its maximum velocity above the crest, then decelerates on the leeward, or downwind, side of the ridge. The steepness of the ridge determines the wind's acceleration and deceleration. These changes in wind velocity as air flows over the ridge result in a characteristic pattern of snow deposition. Snow is carried from regions where the air is accelerated, and is redeposited in regions where the air slows down. At the ridge crest, a cornice forms. This sharply curved accumulation of snow forms near the peak of obstacles, as a result of the swirling patterns of wind flow at the crest. Large cornices look like huge ocean waves, frozen in their liquid motion.

Massive cornices, extending over 45 feet (14 m) upward and outward, often form on the ridge crests of mountains. Successive layers accumulating with each snowfall can be a hazard to the unwary skier or traveler who ventures out onto the precarious, cantilevered edge. Occasionally, these large cornices may break off and

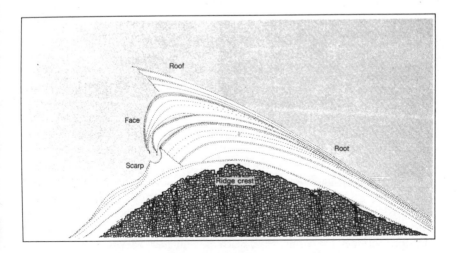

The basic structure of a snow cornice

trigger snowslides, or avalanches. To prevent potential disasters, ski patrols routinely knock off small cornices with their skis, and destroy larger ones with explosives.

Avalanches form on slopes when the accumulating snow can no longer adhere to the surface or to itself, and begins to slide. Snow varies greatly in its **cohesion**, the ability to stick to itself. We all know that wet snow makes better snowballs than light, dry snow. The difference is its greater cohesion. Air temperature, the shape of .the snow crystals, the age of the snow, and its wetness affect cohesion. Loose, dry, freshly fallen snow may fail to cling to slopes steeper than 30 to 40 degrees. The steepness of the slope is then said to exceed the **angle of repose** of the snow.

There are two different types of snowslides, loose-snow avalanches and slab avalanches. Loose-snow avalanches rarely cause damage. These occur when a small mass of snow, often no larger than a baseball, slips out of position on the slope and triggers a slide. A disturbance, such as snow falling from a tree, or a passing skier, may dislodge snow tenuously held in place on the slope. Once freed, it begins to slide and dislodges more snow in its path. The process continues, creating an avalanche. Such snowslides often begin at one point on a slope, spread out more broadly as they progress, and result in an inverted V-shaped scar on the snow slope. Most loose-snow avalanches fall as innocuous masses called **sluffs**. However, wet, slushy snow may have an angle of repose of as little as 15 degrees, and may easily break free from the rest of the snowpack. This heavier snow has caused destructive loose-snow avalanches in the Pacific coastal ranges. Even seemingly harmless sluffs can knock down skiers, breaking legs and sending people over cliffs.

Slab avalanches are triggered by a different process. As snow ages, ice crystals become compacted and cemented together. Layers accumulate with each successive snowfall and cling tightly to steep mountainsides. Such layers occasionally fracture, releasing slabs larger than a football field (1,000 to 100,000 square feet in area; 93 to 9,300 square meters). As the moving slab hurtles down the slope, it breaks up into smaller blocks; it may dislodge 100 times the original amount of snow. Slab avalanches may attain speeds of 200 MPH (320 km/hr), sweeping everything from their paths. A slide of dry snow may rush ahead of the avalanche, generating a huge cloud of snow and a blast of air that can move at speeds of over 60 MPH (100 km/hr), destroying doors and roofs. The accompanying avalanche, exerting pressures exceeding ten tons per square foot (100,000 kg per square meter), easily uproots stands of trees and moves reinforced-concrete buildings.

Let's consider a few simple cases of snowdrift patterns. As the wind rises over a long wall or solid fence, it speeds up and forms an eddy on both sides of the barrier (shown by curved arrows in the figure). In these two regions of more rapid, turbulent air flow, snow does not accumulate. It is deposited on either side, where the wind speed is below that critical value required for drifting. Thus drifts with sharp-edged cornices develop on both sides of the wall. These drifts themselves alter the shape of the barrier, and hence the pattern of airflow and eddies. If drifting continues, the cornices may reach the wall itself, enclosing hollow pockets of air, ending the process of snow accumulation. At this point the drift has a smooth streamlined outline, and is said to be saturated.

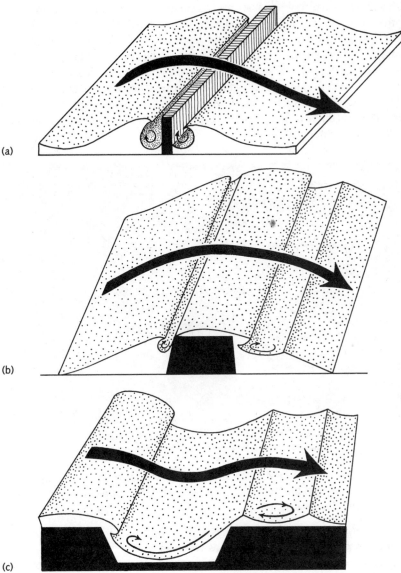

The shapes of snowdrifts near various barriers and obstacles. (a) A long barrier, such as a fence or wall, perpendicular to the wind. (b) Drifts around an embankment with steep sides. (c) Drifts near a depression, such as a roadcut bounded by steep sides. Arrows indicate air flow patterns.

In many areas that encounter heavy winter storms, snow fences are placed in strategic locations, upwind of an area to be protected, in an attempt to diminish heavy accumulations of snow on major roadways. I was surprised that these snow fences are not solid structures but are rather flimsy devices made of wood slats, with wide spaces in between. I assumed economic considerations to be responsible for the cheap construction. It seemed likely that such porous barriers would be far less efficient than a more sturdy solid fence. Quite the contrary. Air blowing through open snow fences causes the eddy area to be larger, and to extend farther downwind as the porosity increases. Surprisingly, a fence with a porosity of 50 percent results in the largest drift, which captures and deposits the greatest amount of blowing snow. It has also been shown that the downwind length of the drift is about 15 times the height of the fence, compared with only 10 times the height of the fence for a solid wall.

A snow fence, showing the downwind accumulation of snow. The roadway is off to the left, not visible in the photograph. The predominant wind direction is from the upper right to the lower left.

Based upon what we have just learned, try to visualize the airflow patterns around other types of barriers, such as roadcuts, and embankments of varying steepness. You might even wish to perform some outdoor experiments of your own before reading on and looking at the illustrations.

Steep barriers favor the development of larger drifts with delicate cornices. Areas such as roadcuts can be a constant nuisance for snowplows, which may have to continually remove accumulating snowdrifts that form for days after a snowstorm.

Smaller obstacles, such as rounded boulders lying on level ground, produce a slightly more complex drift. Because the boulder is as wide as it is tall, the airflow pattern around its edges is as important in determining the shape of the drift as the airflow over the top. Previously we considered only long barriers and concerned ourselves with the airflow over, rather than around, the obstacle. Air rushing past the sides of the boulder also speeds up, scooping out pockets of snow and leaving a small drift on the leeward side. If the boulder is even narrower than that shown in the figure, the two scoops may meet on the leeward side and obliterate the lee drift. Scoops are also seen around the edges of snow fences and are common at the corners of houses, where the winds rush around the building.

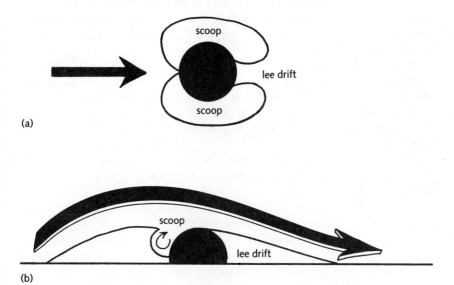

(a)

(b)

Top view (a) and side view (b) of scoops and lee drifts around a boulder. Arrows indicate air flow patterns.

It can be seen that a little knowledge of aerodynamics helps us understand the structure and beauty of nature's wintertime sculpture. We may have the opportunity to put this knowledge to a practical use. Should you ever have the opportunity to plan a driveway or walkway, you will know that any fence or hedge should be placed far enough away so that drifts do not form right on the roadway. It's certainly more enjoyable to spend the winter outdoors observing snowdrifts than shoveling them away!

ACTIVITIES

Creating a miniature avalanche

You can make a model loose-snow avalanche that demonstrates some of the factors that trigger snowslides. Instead of snow, use very fine sand, the kind sold in pet stores for the bottom of a fishtank. For the mountainside, get a pane of glass about two feet square. Lay the glass pane on a flat surface, and, using a sifter, gently sift a fine, even layer of sand onto the glass, simulating a snowfall. Next, carefully raise one end of the glass, and rest it on some convenient support. Continue raising the end until a few grains of sand start to slip. You will be approaching the critical angle of repose for the sand. Measure this angle with a protractor. At this angle, the layer of sand has enough friction to cling to the smooth surface of the glass, and to the neighboring sand grains as well. If you raise the glass to a steeper angle, the sand will slide down all at once, and you will have to begin again.

With the sand in place on the slope, take a pinch of sand and drop it onto the layer. If the sand was at its critical angle of repose, this slight disturbance will be enough to trigger an avalanche. If not, drop a few more pinches of sand, or raise the slope gently to a steeper angle and try again.

When the slide occurs, each grain of sand rolls down the slope and bumps a few of its neighbors. If these grains are tenuously held in place, they will be knocked loose, hitting others. In seconds, the whole process "snowballs," sending increasing numbers of sand grains careening down the slope. The result will be a long, triangular-shaped area that is swept free of sand. This is characteristic of loose-snow avalanches.

If you use a surface rougher than glass — wood, for example — you will find that the sand has a much steeper angle of repose. In the setup that I used, the undisturbed sand rested at an angle of 45 degrees. Try using different substrates, and measure the angle for each. Try varying the characteristics of the "snow." Wet the sand lightly with a spray bottle before raising the slope. You should be able to raise the incline higher without causing a slide. The dampened sand may hold together to such an extent that you cannot trigger a loose-snow avalanche. The sand may break free as a cohesive unit, sliding down the slope as a slab avalanche. Try using different types of "snow," such as coarse sand, sugar, or salt. Each has its own texture and cohesiveness, which will affect the type of avalanche it produces.

Experimenting with snowdrifts

You can explore the growth and form of snowdrifts in your own neighborhood. You can either wander around until you find an area where snowdrifts have formed, or, what's more interesting, find a level area and construct your own ridges, hills, and other obstacles to create your own snow-drifts. Since I use a woodstove in winter, I always have a supply of logs on hand. They are useful building blocks for a variety of snow fences and barriers. By constructing your own obstacles, you can experiment more freely, varying the height, the steepness, and the length of the obstacles you build.

REFERENCES AND SUGGESTIONS FOR FURTHER READING

LaChapelle, E.R. February 1966. The control of snow avalanches. *Scientific American*. 215: 92–101.

Pedgley, D.E. 1967. The shapes of snowdrifts. *Weather* 22: 42–48.

Perla, R.I., and Martinelli, M., Jr. 1975. *Avalanche Handbook*. Agriculture Handbook no. 489, U.S. Department of Agriculture, U.S. Government Printing Office, Washington, D.C.

22

Unraveling the Mysteries
of Skeletons

THERE'S SOMETHING FASCINATING about bones. Patients are fascinated by their x-ray pictures; kids delight in dressing as skeletons on Halloween. Perhaps the attraction is that bones are concealed inside your body, yet are so evident. You cannot see them, but just squeeze an arm or a finger, and you know they are there. This is not so of your kidneys or liver. Unless these organs malfunction, one rarely thinks of them.

This innate passion for bones can be seen in my collection of animal skulls, toes, hips, legs, and other body parts that decorate my living-room shelves. I'm always thrilled to find another bone. A sun-bleached seagull skull with its gently curved surfaces and myriad orifices is an engineering marvel, a sculptural masterpiece, and a mystery. How does each bone's structure relate to its particular function?

What is it about the leg of a mole that makes it suited to dig rather than run? What gives bone the strength it needs to support the weight of an elephant?

Lifeless as they may be, bones are lovely objects that can tell us much about how an animal lives. In this chapter, we'll learn about the structure and function of bones, and how to prepare an animal skeleton for display.

SOME FACTS ABOUT BONES AND SKELETONS

Once an animal reaches an appreciable size, it needs some sort of framework to support itself. On land, small creatures, like worms, slugs, and caterpillars, can get away without a rigid skeleton, and in the water, floating animals can be even larger without requiring supports. However, once a critical size is reached, a land animal will collapse under its own weight, unless it is content with a bloblike structure and the slithering locomotion epitomized by the slug.

Nature has come up with two major solutions to the problem of support, the **endoskeleton** and the **exoskeleton**. Vertebrate animals — cats, bats, frogs, fish, eagles, lizards, and all the rest — have internal skeletons (endoskeletons). Arthropods — insects, spiders, crabs, etc. — have evolved external skeletons.

Both endoskeletons and exoskeletons are hard, jointed structures, with the muscles arranged so that each end of the muscle is attached to a different portion of the skeleton. When a muscle contracts, the joint bends, permitting movement. Both types of skeletons are reasonable solutions to the problems of locomotion and support, but each has advantages and disadvantages.

Exoskeletons are practical only for small animals, so gigantic man-eating cockroaches are found only in grade-B science-fiction movies. In order to grow, an arthropod needs to molt. Its unyielding skeleton imprisons its body and won't permit it to expand, so the animal must cast off its old constricting shell, and replace it with a new larger shell. For large animals, this exchange would be impossible, because the moment the supportive armor was relinquished, the animal would collapse under its own weight. The buoyancy of an underwater existence permits arthropods, such as king crabs, to reach sizes impossible on land.

A large exoskeleton is also more easily punctured than is a small one. Larger, heavier animals exert greater forces on their body surfaces, and the exoskeleton would soon be scratched and notched to such an extent that it would buckle and crack. In order to achieve the necessary strength to avoid being fractured, an exoskeleton would have to be prohibitively thick, bulky, and cumbersome.

In the final analysis, it turns out that exoskeletons and endoskeletons are about equally effective for small animals, and that exoskeletons are probably superior for very small ones. For large animals, an endoskeleton is required. This is precisely what we find in nature. The smallest mammals, the shrews, are about the same size as the largest insects.

Regardless of type, a skeleton's main functions are the same. The skeleton supports an animal and maintains its body shape. The skeleton also provides attachments for muscles. When your biceps contracts, it needs something rigid to pull against in order to flex your arm. Bones form pivots and levers that enable muscles to do useful work. The skeleton also provides protection for the body's fragile internal structures. The heart, lung, kidneys, spleen, and liver are protected by the rib cage. The spinal cord is safe within the vertebral canal, and the brain is encased in the hard, bony chamber of the skull. Like a trembling bowl of Jell-o®, the brain could not survive the violent motions of the head without being wrapped in the protective cradle of the skull. Just imagine the forces involved when two male bighorn sheep crash heads in combat.

The unique structure of bone gives it its great strength and rigidity. Bones are a composite material consisting of two substances, mineral crystals and organic fibers. The marriage of these two components imparts remarkable properties.

The mineral portion of bone consists of needle-shaped crystals of **hydroxyapatite**, a form of calcium phosphate. They surround and impregnate **collagen** fibers. These fibers are protein chains, coiled around one another like strands of rope.

In order not to break, bones must resist two kinds of forces, **compression** and **tension**. Compression squashes an object, while tension tries to pull it apart. Pillars are made to withstand compression. Guy wires and ropes support objects by being placed under tension.

Organic fibers are strong in tension but buckle when compressed because of their fibrous nature. Mineral crystals can withstand great compressive forces but are weak in tension. Bone is strong because it is a composite material that combines the strengths of both of its components. For the same reason, builders reinforce concrete, which is excellent for compression, with internally placed steel rods, which deal with tension.

The results are astounding. Bone can withstand a compression of 24,000 pounds per square inch (1,690 kg/cm²). More than 150 men would have to stand on a one-inch cube of bone to crush it. That is eight times the strength of concrete. Do bones need to be that strong? For normal activity, bones are stronger than necessary, but running, jumping, and falling can exert tremendous forces. One might also consider the weight that large animals must support. The dinosaur Aptosaurus weighed 30 tons (27,000 kg). When it lifted one hind foot to walk, it has been estimated that the other foot had to support 20 tons!

THE SKULL

With a little familiarity, one can tell the identity of an animal just by looking at the skull. In fact, a specialist can identify mammalian skulls by examining a single molar tooth.

The mammalian skull is made up of about 30 separate bones, and its shape is governed by the functions it must perform. The skull houses the brain. It carries special sense organs—the nose, the eyes, and the ears. As the entrance to the digestive system, the skull contains the mouth, jaws, and teeth. Through the nose, it provides a passageway for oxygen to the lungs. The design of the skull takes into account all of these factors.

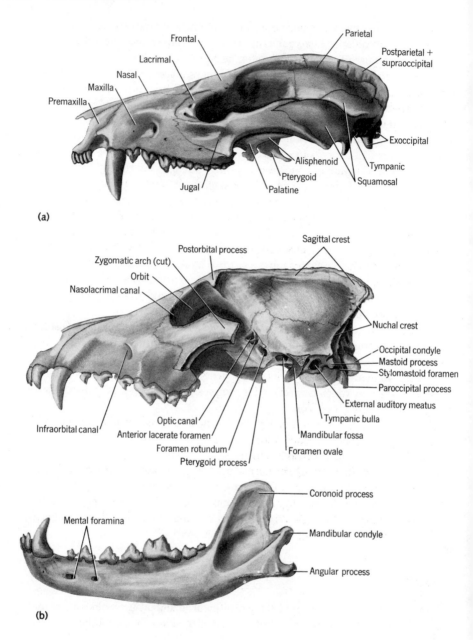

(a)

(b)

Some features of the mammalian skull. (a) Opossum. (b) Wolf. The foramina and canals transmit nerves, blood vessels, and ducts. The other labeled structures refer to bones and other prominent bony features. From Analysis of Vertebrate Structure, 2d En., M. Hildebrand, copyright © 1982 by John Wiley & Sons, New York, pp. 141, 143. Reprinted by permission.

The posterior portion of the skull is a container that encloses and cushions the brain. Portions of 12 bones develop in response to the outward pressure of the enlarging brain. In monkeys and man, the brain cavity is large and bulbous, housing the copious cerebral hemispheres. Compare this with the much smaller brain case of a primitive marsupial, the opossum. Even more incredible is the minute brain cavity of the alligator, a few thimblefuls of neurons controlling a massive creature.

Besides the brain, the jaws and muscles of chewing have the greatest effect on the form of the skull. The herbivores that nibble, gnaw, and grind their plant food have much different requirements from carnivores, which use their teeth and jaws to grab, stab, and slice their prey. This difference is clearly reflected in the jaw structure. In herbivores, a muscle called the **masseter** is most prominent, with its attachments from the **zygomatic arch** down to the lower jaw (**mandible**). Rabbits and deer, which spend their time grinding vegetation, have a deep, broad surface on their mandibles to accommodate their large masseters. In carnivores the most important jaw muscle is the **temporal**. This muscle is attached from the posterior skull to the coronoid process of the mandible. The large **sagittal crest** of the dog provides additional surface area for the attachment of this muscle.

The orbits are bony cavities that accommodate and protect the eyes and the muscles moving them. The **tympanic bullae** are rounded bony capsules that help protect and enclose the middle ear with its three bony **ossicles**, the eardrum, and the organs of hearing and equilibrium.

For most mammals, with their well-developed sense of smell, the nasal passages strongly influence the shape of the skull. They are deep passageways, starting at the nostrils and extending back into the skull. Their length is greater than one usually imagines, and is best appreciated by peering into the nasal passages of a dog's skull. The nasal passages have two functions, that of smell and that of moistening, warming, and filtering incoming air.

In summary, we find that the size and shape of particular bony regions reflect the form and function of the structures they enclose and the muscles that require surfaces for attachment. These same principles apply elsewhere in the skeleton.

TEETH

Dentine, enamel, and **cement** are the three materials that make up teeth. Each tooth has an exposed part or **crown,** covered by enamel, the hardest tissue in the body. Below this is the dentine, a bony substance, softer than cement but harder than true bone. The root of the tooth below the gums is fixed in a socket by cement, the softest of the three constituents.

Most mammals have four kinds of teeth. The **incisors,** in front, are adapted for securing, holding, or cutting food. In carnivores the incisors are simple spikes, but they are more specialized among the herbivores. The characteristic rodent incisor is designed as a self-sharpening knife. The enamel on the front edge is much thicker than on the back. As the animal continually gnaws its tough food, the back edge wears away more easily, always leaving a sharp narrow edge in front. To replace what is lost, these incisors continually grow out from the base.

The **canines** are the long fanglike teeth of carnivores, used to stab and kill prey, and for fighting. They are absent in rodents.

Next are the cheek teeth, the **premolars** and the **molars**. The premolars and molars of carnivores are designed to shear tough skin and tendons, and to crush bones. In the herbivores, such as rabbits and horses, molars are more complicated, being specially adapted to act like millstones to grind vegetation. They have tall, broad surfaces, and the enamel is folded up and down, forming peaks and valleys. Cement lies in between these enamel folds, and as the teeth wear down from eating hard grasses mixed with bits of gritty soil, the enamel, dentine, and cement wear away at different rates. This differential wear maintains a rough grinding surface.

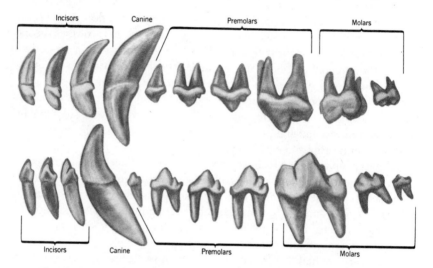

The four kinds of teeth in the upper and lower jaws of the dog. From Analysis of Vertebrate Structure, 2d Ed., M. Hildebrand, copyright © 1982 by John Wiley & Sons, New York, p. 114. Reprinted by permission.

Because the function of teeth in different animals is so specialized, we find considerable variation in the numbers of each type. This helps us to identify an unknown skull. All the teeth collectively form the dentition, and their number can be expressed by a **dental formula**, a shorthand way of describing the numbers of each type of tooth in the upper and lower jaw.

The dental formula of the opossum is as follows:

$$I \frac{5-5}{4-4} \quad C \frac{1-1}{1-1} \quad P \frac{3-3}{3-3} \quad M \frac{4-4}{4-4} = \frac{26}{24} = 50$$

The symbols, I, C, P, and M refer to incisors, canines, premolars, and molars, respectively. What this formula means is that there are 26 teeth in the upper jaw, 5 incisors, 1 canine, 3 premolars, and 4 molars on each side. The lower jaw is the same except that there are 4 incisors on each side rather than 5. With a total of 50 teeth, the only North American mammal with this dentition is the opossum. In more complicated cases, different mammals may have the same number but different types of teeth.

A LOOK AT OTHER PARTS OF THE SKELETON

Examining other portions of the skeleton will give us further opportunities to understand why bones are shaped the way they are. Important functions of the long bones of the arms and legs are to provide strength and leverage for muscles.

One of the guiding principles of nature is economy. The skeleton is designed to provide maximum strength with the minimum amount of material. This saves on weight, bulk, and the need to nourish excess bone. Consider taking a fixed amount of bone to make a leg. We could construct a small-diameter solid cylinder, or a hollow cylinder of larger diameter. The hollow cylinder will be better able to support a given weight. This explains the hollow shafts of the long bones in the legs and arms. We are all familiar with this principle in nature and everyday life. Table legs, lamp bases, stems of grasses, weeds, and bamboo are all hollow tubes.

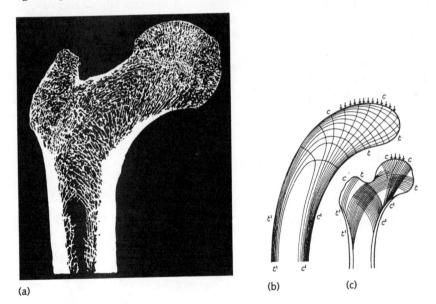

(a)

(b)   (c)

(a) Longitudinal section of a human femur showing the bony spicules, or trabeculae, which reinforce the bone along the major lines of stress. The trabeculae follow lines similar to the lines of internal stress in a crane. (b) The head of a Fairbairn crane. (c) Diagrammatic view of the head of a femur (cc¹ compression lines; tt¹ tension lines; arrows indicate the placement of a load).

Bones are not merely uniform hollow cylinders, however. This is clearly demonstrated by taking a longitudinal section of a femur. First, notice how the bone is thicker toward the midportion of the shaft. All cylinders, including bones, are more likely to buckle and break at their centers, so this area is reinforced with extra material. At the ends of the bones, many different forces are acting, making a simple tubular structure inadequate. Rather than make the ends of the bones completely solid and overly bulky, a meshwork of bony spicules, called **trabeculae**, is used to reinforce the ends of the bones, following the major lines of stress.

Engineers use the same principle to strengthen their structures. There is the story of the great engineer Culmann of Zurich who, in 1866, visited the laboratory of his friend, Meyer, while the anatomist was examining a section of bone. Culmann, who was designing a new type of crane, immediately perceived that the arrangement of bony trabeculae perfectly matched the lines of stress to which the bone was subjected. Noting the similar manner in which both structures were being reinforced, he reportedly exclaimed, "That's my crane."

Now, let us look at the form and function of an entire limb by comparing the legs of a deer and a mole. Each is adapted for different functions. One animal is a swift runner, the other a powerful digger. Even if a mole were the size of a deer, these differences in function could be read in the shape of the bones.

Deer and horses are runners designed for speed. Their leg bones are lengthened and made less bulky by the fusion and elimination of bones. Like a ballerina's, the leg is made effectively longer by standing on the tips of the toes.

Animals such as armadillos, badgers, and moles have limbs designed for digging, equipped with strong, heavy bones and powerful claws. Each bone has broad extensions to act as long lever arms for the attachment of strong digging muscles. One of the best examples is the long **olecranon** ("funny bone" of the elbow), which provides leverage for the triceps as the mole tunnels through the earth. The mole's hand is built as a wide spade.

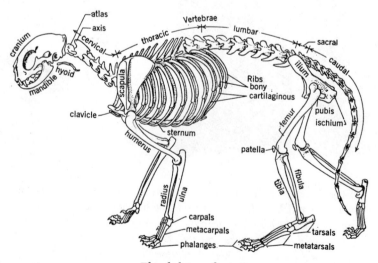

The skeleton of a cat.

All the aspects of the skeleton, from the tiniest bony spicule within a toe to the features of an entire limb, are adapted for an animal's specific survival tasks. By carefully examining an animal's bones, we can read the story of that animal's life.

ACTIVITIES

To fully appreciate the preceding discussion, one needs to have the bones in hand. Any description I can give of the intricate scroll-like arrangement of the nasal turbinates of a dog cannot compare with a glimpse of the real thing. I therefore hope that this deficiency will serve as a potent incentive for you to start your own skeleton collection. Although some readers may be put off by the thought of these activities, those of you with a keen interest will surely wish to venture on.

Needless to say, in order to begin, you will need some specimens. Perhaps the easiest place to start is at the supermarket, with a chicken. Animals killed on the road are also a readily available source of material. As a child, I wandered the highways near my home gathering skunks, opossums, and raccoons that had not been too flattened by the onrushing traffic. My two cats provide me with an occasional meadow vole, white-footed mouse, shrew, or mole. At times I stumble across an animal in the woods.

Preparing skeletons for study

There are several methods of preparing skeletons. The simplest is maceration. Using a pair of gloves and a sharp knife, skin the animal. Place it in a covered container filled with water, and allow it to decompose. By bacterial action, all the muscles and soft structures will be digested, leaving the bones at the bottom of the vessel. After a month or so, depending upon the temperature, strain the foul-smelling liquid through a piece of fine screen to make sure you do not lose any of the small bones. Working outdoors, wash the bones in a few changes of water, and use an old toothbrush to scrub off any remaining bits of flesh. If the bones are greasy, soak them in ammonia for a day or two. (For really greasy bones, kerosene is a better degreasing agent but be careful about breathing the fumes, and especially about keeping everything away from flames.) Finally, bleach the skeleton overnight in a solution of hydrogen peroxide, available in pharmacies. (Household laundry bleach will also work, but use a dilute solution so the bones do not become crumbly.) This method has the advantage of requiring the least effort to get a perfectly clean set of separate bones. The disadvantage is the offensive odor. However, if you macerate in a 2 to 5 percent solution of potassium or sodium hydroxide, there will be little odor, and the bones will not need to be degreased.

For skulls, I prefer maceration. I simply put the skull in a jar of water, close it up, and put it on the shelf for a month or so. In adult animals, the skull bones are all fused, so the skull does not fall apart. I only have to be careful not to lose any of the animal's teeth. I would not recommend this method for immature animals or delicate animals like snakes, shrews, or bats. All you end up with is a heap of tiny bones. For a larger animal, such as a dog or cat, this method is an ideal way to learn skeletal anatomy. The bones are big enough to handle, and, with the help of a textbook diagram, you can glue each bone in its proper place, teaching yourself anatomy as you go along. For gluing, I have found that Duco® cement works best. (I can remember one sad-looking rat skeleton that slumped to the ground on a hot, humid summer day after being glued together with "Brand X" cement.)

To mount your skeleton, insert a wire through the opening in the vertebrae to support the back, and use wooden dowels to support the hips and the front legs. The finished skeleton can be glued to a wooden base, and will be a beautiful and instructive specimen. I usually spray the bones with clear enamel so they will not become dirty.

After years of macerating skeletons, I learned that you can let beetles do most of the work for you. Dermestid beetles feed on dead animals, dried stored foods, carpets, upholstery, and even museum specimens. They can be found in almost any home, hence their common name, carpet beetles. The voracious feeders are the immature larvae, although the adult beetles feed as well.

You can most easily find the beetles on road-killed carcasses during the summer. You can also put a dried carcass into an open cardboard box, and leave it outdoors to attract beetles. The dermestids come when the carcass is dry and hard, like leather. At this point, the carcass does not smell particularly offensive. Using gloves, pick it up and shake it out over a few sheets of newspaper, letting the dermestids fall out. Get both the larvae and the adults. The larvae will begin to work for you right away, and the adults will start to lay eggs, keeping the process going.

To prepare a skeleton with beetles, completely skin the animal, taking special care to remove the fur from around the toes, lips, ears, and nose. Using scissors, a scalpel, or a razor blade, remove as much of the big muscles of the arms and legs as possible, taking care not to cut any bones. Open the abdomen to remove all the internal organs.

Now the specimen should be thoroughly dried. In a hot, dry climate, you can put the animal out in the sun for a day or two, being careful to protect it from any wild animals or pets. (An old wire cage works fine.) In more humid regions, dry the carcass by propping an old hair drier near the animal, changing its position every hour or so. The advantage of this technique is that you can arrange the animal in a lifelike position while it is still wet, using blocks or wood or clay to prop it up.

You then put the carcass into a container with the beetles, and let them feast. They will begin to eat all the dried muscles, then start to consume the tougher structures, like the ligaments and tendons. By carefully monitoring the process, you can remove the specimen just before it falls apart. Enough of the ligaments will be left intact to keep the skeleton in one piece. Of course, toes, ribs, or even a leg may fall off, but most of the skeleton will stay together. You can briefly soak the preparation in some ammonia and then peroxide, as you did with the macerated bones. If you are careful, you will have only a minimal amount of regluing to do. I have used this method to prepare snakes with hundreds of ribs, bats with their delicate fingers, and the tiniest of shrews.

The disadvantages of this method are that the skeletons are never quite as clean as with maceration. You have to leave some ligaments attached, and that obscures some of the detail of the articulations. You also cannot bleach and degrease the skeleton as well, or it will tend to fall apart. Maintaining a beetle colony has its pros and cons. Dermestids like warmth and darkness. The beetles will quickly eat through cardboard, so you need to house them in a wooden or metal box. If you have the space, and can find one, an old refrigerator is ideal. Turn it on its side, and cut a small hole in one end to insert a 60-watt bulb for warmth. Put a metal partition inside to keep part of the interior dark. The beetles are as voracious as piranhas, so once you have started a colony, you will be a slave to their appetites. It is best to keep the colony in the garage, away from your other biological specimens. Many an insect collection, even in museums, has been ruined by hungry dermestids.

If you do not want to get involved with maintaining a dermestid colony, you can do as I usually do. I collect a few beetles in late spring and keep them in an old fish tank, covered with a pane of glass. In the summer it is generally warm enough to keep the colony flourishing. I periodically place dried chicken necks in the colony so the beetles will not starve. These can be obtained cheaply at the grocery store. I put each specimen I am cleaning into a separate plastic box inside the tank because the beetles get quite active, jostling around delicate animals and mixing up the bones.

These are the basics of skeletal preparation. I realize that, for some, this may be an aspect of nature that is difficult to stomach. However, fascinating natural history can be learned through studying animal anatomy. If you have an aversion to dissecting wild animals, begin your studies at the dinner table, examining the chicken bones. You will soon be captivated as you try to unravel the mysteries of bones.

REFERENCES AND SUGGESTIONS FOR FURTHER READING

Burt, W.H. 1964. *A Field Guide to the Mammals.* Houghton Mifflin, Boston.

Currey, J.D. 1970. *Animal Skeletons.* Edward Arnold, London.

Hildebrand, M. 1968. *Anatomical Preparations.* University of California Press, Berkeley.

———. 1982. *Analysis of Vertebrate Structure.* John Wiley & Sons, New York.

Thompson, D.W. 1952. *On Growth and Form.* Cambridge University Press, Cambridge.

Young, J.Z. 1981. *The Life of Mammals,* 3d ed. Oxford University Press, London.

23

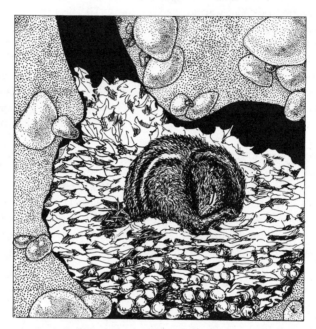

Coping with the Cold

AS THE EARTH ROTATES around the sun, the seasons slowly progress. With winter's approach, the earth's inclination on its axis brings weaker sunshine, shorter days, and colder weather. In the Northern Hemisphere, plants and animals encounter a period of constant subfreezing temperatures, and desiccating winds. Trees drop their leaves, and plants wither. The lush green vegetation that once fed hordes of insects and hungry rodents is now dry and stiff. Falling rains and flowing water become imprisoned as ice. Plants and animals have difficulty surviving in this wintry world. They were not designed for such conditions; life's delicate physiological processes were meant to function in a medium of liquid water. As temperatures plunge, ice crystals form inside the body's delicate cells. They act as tiny daggers, stabbing their way through cell membranes, bursting them like pins popping balloons. As ice forms from the water in our cells and is frozen out of solution, the remaining salts become so concentrated that life processes go awry and cells die.

When the tomatoes in the garden are hit by a hard frost, they become mushy and ruined upon thawing. Also, if one is not careful, fingers and toes get frostbitten and gangrenous in winter's icy climate.

Of all the environmental extremes on our planet, only the hot desert can compare with winter for the hardships it presents. Nonetheless, through eons of evolution, life has learned to survive in nearly every nook and cranny on earth.

HOW ORGANISMS DEAL WITH WINTER

Keeping warm

To survive freezing temperatures, organisms have several options. One approach is to maintain the body temperature by generating heat, then insulating the body against excessive loss. However, for some organisms, the heating bill is too high. They let their body temperature fall, but they resist freezing, or tolerate its effects. Each approach involves balancing costs and benefits, different for each species. Thus, each organism arrives at its own unique solution to the problems of winter. An organism's behavioral adaptations, its structural modifications, and its physiological ploys are the weapons wielded in this war against winter. As wintertime naturalists, we will observe some of the battles.

With the approach of winter, we unpack our cedar closets and take our sweaters out of mothballs. Country folk busily preserve their harvests of vegetables and fruits. Woodland mammals — field mice, meadow voles, muskrats, foxes, rabbits, deer, and others — are also busy, making preparations that allow them to remain active all winter. They shed their thinner summer coats for thicker, more insulating apparel. Birds put on their winter plumage. In the fall these hardy creatures have been feverishly building up stores of body fat, and some, like field mice and red squirrels, have been furiously stockpiling nuts and berries.

Most mammals and birds maintain a relatively constant body temperature, even when the environmental temperature fluctuates widely. Such animals are said to be **homeothermic**, or warm-blooded. This enables them to stay active and to exploit cold environments. However, the approach is not always practical.

Among warm-blooded animals, there is a relationship between body size and metabolism. The smaller the animal, the faster its metabolism. The smallest mammals, the shrews, weigh little more than one-tenth of an ounce (3 g). They are slaves to their appetites. To maintain their metabolic rate, they must eat nearly their own body weight in food each day, and they will starve to death in hours if deprived of food.

In winter, animals suffer enormous heat losses; food to fuel their physiological ovens is scarce. Many animals, finding it impossible to maintain an elevated body temperature under cold conditions, allow their body temperature to fall to a cool, but safe, range. Animals such as frogs, toads, lizards, and snakes are cold-blooded, or **poikilothermic**, which means that their body temperature is variable, rising and falling with that of their surroundings. When it becomes too cold to function, these cold-blooded animals are reduced to a stuporous state of inactivity. They wait out the winter, slaves to the environmental temperature.

Most mammals are active all winter, yet some retreat into burrows to sleep during severe cold spells. Only a few truly hibernate, such as bats, woodchucks, raccoons, chipmunks, and jumping mice. The bears become dormant, but their lethargy does not become as profound as that of the true hibernators. They are easily awakened, and their body temperature decreases only a few degrees.

By a quirk of fate and evolution, only the honey bees, among all insects, have managed to maintain an elevated body temperature all winter long. They have a unique means of surviving winter — clustering. Coordinated behavioral and physiological adaptations permit a colony of thousands of bees to keep warm. Heat production, and the prevention of its dissipation, are the key features of honey bee strategy.

As soon as the nest temperature dips below about 64° F (18° C), the colony's inhabitants pack together into a carefully structured, compact ball. The outer mantle of the cluster consists of several layers of densely packed bees, oriented with their heads inward. This blanket of bees insulates the others within. Bees in the core of the cluster are loosely packed, with room to spread their wings, crawl about, feed on honey, and even raise young.

These behaviors are complemented by physiological mechanisms that generate enormous amounts of heat. Even a resting bee generates some heat, but by revving up its flight muscles, a bee can increase heat production 25-fold. In brief bursts of one to five minutes, groups of bees in the cluster's center periodically vibrate their powerful flight muscles, generating thoracic temperatures of up to 100° F (38° C). Even when the outdoor temperature plummets to −20° F (−29° C), the bees remain snug and warm in the center, with a minimum of 50° F (10° C) at the periphery. It is crucial that the bees in the core maintain a temperature of at least 64° F (18° C). Below that point the bees cannot activate their flight muscles.

Despite being shielded within a well-insulated tree cavity, and despite the relative inactivity of overwintering bees, this strategy is quite costly. A colony must store 40 pounds (18 kg) of honey to survive the winter. For some animals, such a price is too extravagant. Many birds opt to flee winter's hardships with annual southbound migrations, since flight makes long-distance travel practical.

Another alternative is hibernation. Except for the honey bees, most other small invertebrates — insects, spiders, centipedes, and sowbugs — hibernate. So do reptiles, amphibians, and some mammals. In this comatose, nearly lifeless state, all metabolic processes stagnate. Food requirements diminish, allowing the animal to live off fat reserves built up in the fall. Heart rate and breathing slow down to such

WINTER ACTIVITIES OF COMMON NORTH AMERICAN MAMMALS			
Name	Activity	Home	Winter Food
bat	hibernates	caves, tree cavities, attics	none while hibernating
bear	dormant	dens in caves, hollow trees	none while dormant

WINTER ACTIVITIES *(continued)*

Name	Activity	Home	Winter Food
beaver	active	dens of branches in ponds and streams	twigs, branches
common mole	active	underground tunnels	insects, small invertebrates
common shrew	active	tunnels in leaf litter, under snow and logs	insects, small invertebrates
cottontail rabbit	active	underground burrows	twigs, buds, bark
Eastern chipmunk	hibernates	underground burrows	none while hibernating
field mouse	active	grass-lined nests on the ground	grain, grass, tree bark
flying squirrel	active	tree cavities, bird boxes	seeds, nuts
gray squirrel	active	nests of leaves and twigs in trees	acorns, nuts (hickory, walnut, beech)
jumping mouse	hibernates	grass-lined nests underground	none while hibernating
muskrat	active	mounds of mud and vegetation in ponds	roots, stalks of marsh plants
opossum	active[a]	underground burrows	insects, small animals, carrion, berries
porcupine	active	underground burrows	inner bark, twigs
raccoon	hibernates[b]	tree cavities	corn, berries, fish, mammals, birds, insects
red fox	active	underground burrows	mice, birds, rabbits
red squirrel	active[a]	tree cavities, leaf nests in trees	seeds, nuts, fungi
skunk	active[a]	underground burrows	insects, mice, crayfish, birds, grain
star-nosed mole	active	tunnels in bogs, marshes, stream banks	aquatic insects
white-footed mouse	active	grass-lined nests in tree hollows, bird nests	seeds, nuts
woodchuck	hibernates	underground burrows	none while hibernating

[a] Dormant in extreme cold.
[b] Irregular hibernator, often active in cold weather.

an extent that only careful observation reveals any life. A squirrel's heart pounds at 350 beats per minute in summer but may dawdle imperceptibly at 5 beats per minute while the squirrel is hibernating.

Surviving freezing

An entirely different strategy for coping with the cold is to allow the body temperature to plummet. Animals can either resist freezing solid, or they can tolerate the effects of ice formation within their bodies. Most animals are killed by freezing, and must rely on freeze resistance.

Water freezes by forming crystals around impurities or upon preexisting ice, which act as seeds upon which ice crystals grow. However, very pure water can be supercooled to $-40°$ F $(-40°$ C) without freezing. The addition of certain chemicals to water also enhances supercooling.

Insects supercool without freezing, using both these methods. In late fall, many insects stop feeding, empty their guts, and rid themselves of potentially lethal impurities around which ice crystals could form. Insects also synthesize **glycerol**, a chemical similar to the ethylene glycol we add to our car radiators. Glycerol enhances supercooling, and also acts as an antifreeze, lowering the temperature at which water freezes. In the hibernating stages of certain braconid wasps, the insect may be 25 percent glycerol. At this concentration, the freezing point of the insect's body fluids is $5°$ F $(-15°$ C), far below the freezing point of water, but still not good enough for the temperatures of icy northern winters. The additional supercooling effect of glycerol gives the insect the extra protection it needs to be chilled to $-50°$ F $(-46°$ C) without freezing solid.

In a supercooled state, an animal is poised between life and death. Cunners are small, edible wrasse fish inhabiting the rocky shores of New England. The adults flee the shallow coastal waters in winter when the saltwater temperature gets close to its freezing point ($28°$ F, or $-2°$ C). The juveniles remain in sandy burrows in a torpid, supercooled state. If such a fish is touched with a piece of ice, it quickly freezes solid and dies. The crystalline structure of the ice provides the framework upon which the entire supercooled fish congeals.

A few insects can tolerate ice formation, provided it is restricted to the fluids surrounding the body's cells. These are mostly the caterpillars and pupae of moths and butterflies that hibernate in extremely cold climates. Some flies, wasps, and beetles can also survive freezing, but even in these animals, intracellular ice formation can be lethal.

Studies have shown that these insects take the paradoxical approach of actively promoting freezing. They synthesize proteins, which act as nucleating agents, to ensure the growth of ice crystals at relatively high freezing temperatures. Supercooling is inhibited, allowing ice to form around the cells, but not within them.

This is the gamut of winter activity levels. Most mammals and birds maintain a normal body temperature. Clustering bees and hibernating animals let their temperature fall to a cool but still safe range, far above the freezing point of water. The invertebrates abandon temperature regulation completely, but survive icy body temperatures lethal to other animals.

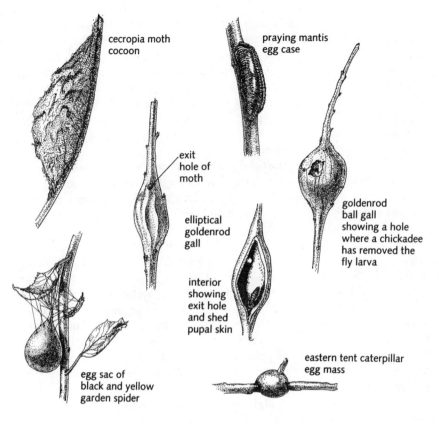

cecropia moth cocoon

praying mantis egg case

exit hole of moth

elliptical goldenrod gall

goldenrod ball gall showing a hole where a chickadee has removed the fly larva

interior showing exit hole and shed pupal skin

egg sac of black and yellow garden spider

eastern tent caterpillar egg mass

Signs of common invertebrate animals found in winter.

ACTIVITIES

Collecting winter creatures and observing their survival adaptations

Many adult insects and spiders mate in the fall and die shortly thereafter. The fate of the next generation depends upon the survival of the eggs, which are deposited during the female's final hours. Many of these egg cases are easy to spot once the winter winds have stripped the foliage from the plants and trees. They are packaged in carefully constructed wrappers, which feel the chill of winter but are impervious to rains and desiccating winds. These are the real killers. The packaging may also keep out predators.

In recent years, gypsy moths have plagued the Northeast. The female moth does not fly or eat. She emerges from her pupal case and crawls a short distance away. She summons the male by emitting a sex attractant, called a pheromone, which is carried off in the breeze. He flies upwind to find her, they mate, and she lays her eggs.

The egg masses are ideally designed for northern winters. From 100 to over 700 eggs are glued to tree trunks, under loose bark, and on stone walls. The hard, shiny eggs are overlaid with a feltlike covering of yellow-brown hairs taken from the female's abdomen. Once the eggs are deposited, the female has served her purpose in life, and she soon dies, often clinging to her eggs. Despite the impending harsh winter, the eggs do not wait for spring to develop. By the time winter arrives, each egg contains a fully formed caterpillar, awaiting the warmth of spring. In exposed areas, the eggs may die if the temperature is persistently below −20° F (−29° C), but such temperatures are unusual.

Tent caterpillar eggs are most often found on cherry and apple trees. The eggs are neatly packed side by side in a band encircling the twig. The entire egg mass receives a varnishy waterproof coating. By May, the caterpillars have eaten their way out of the egg case and have begun to build their familiar tents of silk in the crotches of branches.

Praying mantis egg cases can be found in fields on the dried stems of plants. The egg mass is deposited as a brown foam that hardens into a material resembling Styrofoam®. The minute eggs, the shape of rice grains but smaller, are embedded within the thick bubbly froth. This tough case would imprison the young mantids, were it not for cleverly designed escape exits that the female builds. Carefully take a longitudinal slice or a cross-section through the egg mass, and you will see that the inner chamber of eggs communicates with the outside world through a series of thin slits with partially overlapping flaps. The hatching mantids can crawl out these narrow passageways, yet the flaps act as one-way valves to prevent water and predators from getting in.

Of all the egg cases you are likely to find on a winter walk, the most intricately constructed is that of the black and yellow garden spider. The pear-shaped egg case, about an inch in diameter (2.5 cm), is held in place by silken guy wires attached to the surrounding vegetation. In the fall the case is placed off to one side of the web, but when you stumble upon it in winter, all traces of the spider and her web will have disappeared. With a fine scissors, cut open the layers of the sac. The extremely tough brown outer covering has a crackly, parchmentlike texture, impervious to rain or snow. Beneath this layer is a thick fluffy blanket of loosely woven rusty brown or yellowish brown silk. If you part this flossy wadding, the eggs will still not be evident. The final layer, a thin satiny white fabric, envelops nearly 1,000 orange eggs. Inspecting the egg sac, one can only marvel at the hours of energetic spinning required to fashion this exquisite winter home. However, even more marvelous than observing the finished product is watching its construction, but that must wait until next fall.

Overwintering insect larvae can be found without difficulty. Many wood-boring beetles spend several years in this stage, chewing tunnels through living or dead trees. Let a well-rotted log warm up in the basement of your home, and then slowly break it apart with a screwdriver or a hammer and chisel. A meticulous search through the log should reveal many beetle larvae, as well as overwintering adults. Wasp queens, bees, centipedes, millipedes, ants, and cockroaches are other insects that spend their winters beneath the bark of rotted logs or within their spongy interior.

The fluffy cattails of the swamps harbor a tiny caterpillar, a specialist feeder, found only within the cottony seedheads of this plant. The female cattail moths lay their eggs on the developing flowerheads. The young caterpillars feed on the cattails all summer long. In the fall when the mature flowers have developed into the familiar tubular seedheads, the larvae prepare for winter. Normally the swift, violent winds would tear the plumed seeds from the stalk, dispersing them throughout the swamp, but seedheads infested with caterpillars tenaciously refuse to be scattered. The caterpillars energetically lay down trails of silk, which bind the downy seeds into a mass. Their winter home and food supply remain intact. The seedheads persist into June, only partially exploded, while the caterpillars continue their final spring feedings before pupating. All through the winter and spring, the half-inch (1.3 cm), white- and brown-striped caterpillars can be collected from the cattail fluff. The last batch of cattails I gathered yielded an additional surprise when dozens of minute wasps emerged in May. These ichneumonid wasps had parasitized the caterpillars.

Winter is the best time to search for the large cocoons of the beautiful giant silk moths. The cecropia moth cocoon is found attached to the host plant — cherry, plum, apple, maple, birch, or willow. Polyphemus caterpillars prefer oak, hickory, and elm. Promethea cocoons can be found wrapped in a dried leaf of spicebush, sassafras, tulip tree, or wild cherry. The gorgeous green luna moth pupates on the ground, a short distance from its host tree. These cocoons can be gathered in the winter. To keep the moths from emerging in the middle of the winter and to prevent the cocoons from drying out, keep them in screened cages outdoors, allowing the moths to emerge naturally in the spring.

The nest of a deer mouse made by adding material to an abandoned bird's nest. Inside the nest were numerous gnawed cherry pits, and mouse scats.

Of course, this is merely a sampling of the many invertebrates that can be found by diligently perusing the fields in winter. In your searches you will also encounter the homes and resting places of larger animals. Deer mice nest in woodpiles, under boards and in abandoned bird nests. The winding tunnels of meadow voles can be found in most fields. Flying squirrels live in tree hollows and bird boxes. Look for the sloppy leaf and twig nests of gray squirrels high in the trees. Bats can be found hibernating in caves and in cold attics. In winter, finding living creatures is a challenge, but with a little effort, your jaunts to the field will be well rewarded.

HOW COMMON INSECTS OVERWINTER

Name	Overwintering Stage	Where Found
aphid	egg	on tree bark
bald-faced hornet	fertile queen	cavity in a rotted log
cabbage butterfly	pupa	exposed chrysalis in leaf litter
cecropia moth	pupa	cocoon attached to a twig
centipede	adult, immature	leaf litter, beneath stones, in rotted logs
Eastern tent caterpillar	egg	encircling twigs
field cricket	nymph	beneath stones
firefly	larva	underground
ground beetle	adult	leaf litter, beneath stones
gypsy moth	egg	on tree bark
Junebug	adult	underground
katydid	egg	on leaves
lacewing	adult	in woodpiles, tree bark, crevices
long-horned beetle	larva	in tunnels made in wood
luna moth	pupa	cocoon between leaves on the ground
millipede	adult, immature	leaf litter, beneath stones, in rotted logs
mosquito	adult female	cellars, caves, hollows of trees
mourning cloak butterfly	adult	under tree bark, in leaf litter
paper wasp	fertile queen	cavity in a rotted log
snail	adult, immature	leaf litter, beneath stones, in rotted logs
snow flea (springtail)	adult	leaf litter, active on snow on warm days
spider	adult, immature, egg	leaf litter, beneath stones, in rotted logs
tiger beetle	larva	underground
viceroy butterfly	larva	in a rolled-up leaf

HOW COMMON INSECTS OVERWINTER *(continued)*		
Name	Overwintering Stage	Where Found
whirligig beetle	adult	in the mud on the bottom of ponds
wood cockroach	nymph	in rotted logs
wood lice (sowbug, pillbug)	adult, immature	leaf litter, beneath stones, in rotted logs
wooly bear (Isabella moth)	larva	leaf litter

REFERENCES AND SUGGESTIONS FOR FURTHER READING

Block, W. 1982. Cold hardiness in invertebrate poikilotherms. *Comparative Biochemistry and Physiology.* 73A: 581–593.

Burt, W.H. 1952. *A Field Guide to the Mammals.* Houghton Mifflin, Boston.

Chapman, R.F. 1971. *The Insects: Structure and Function.* Elsevier, New York.

DeVries, A.L. 1982. Biological antifreeze agents in coldwater fishes. *Comparative Biochemistry and Physiology.* 73A: 627–640.

Martin, A.S.; Zim, H.S.; and Nelson, A. L. 1961. *American Wildlife and Plants.* Dover, New York.

Morgan, A.H. 1939. *Field Book of Animals in Winter.* Putnam, New York.

Seeley, T.D. 1985. *Honeybee Ecology: A Study of Adaptation in Social Life.* Princeton University Press, New Jersey.

Stokes, D.W., and Stokes, L.Q. 1986. *A Guide to Animal Tracking and Behavior.* Little, Brown, Boston.

Whitaker, J.O., Jr. 1980. *The Audubon Society Field Guide to North American Mammals.* Knopf, New York.

24

Under the Night Sky: Sights Beyond Our Solar System

A CURIOUS NATURALIST has no difficulty in finding subjects for study 24 hours a day, all year round. On a frigid evening in the midst of winter, when few living creatures stir outdoors, look up into the sky and try to grasp the "big picture." Forget for a moment the earth, which cradles a restless mass of living creatures. Tonight, look at our planet as a sphere of whirling stone, one of many in a solar system, in turn but one of many in a starry galaxy, which is also but one of many galaxies in the universe. We will take an imaginary voyage to sights beyond the solar system.

Earthbound naturalists are accustomed to observing things that fit neatly in the palm of the hand: flies and frogs and flowers. Coping with the stars will require a new outlook. We will make observations to unimaginable distances, and use our imaginations to arrive at a better understanding of our place in the universe.

THE MOTION OF THE EARTH AND SOME OF ITS CONSEQUENCES

Rotation of the earth on its axis

To understand how things appear beyond our planet, we must first understand the motions of the earth. We know that the earth rotates on its axis as it travels in its orbit around the sun. However, how many of us have thought about the consequences of these motions, and have imagined how things would be if the earth moved differently?

Of all the earth's motions, rotation on its axis has the most immediate effect. Every day the earth rotates once on its axis. As a result, an observer experiences day and night as he alternately rotates in and out of the sun's light.

We do not feel the earth's motion. Paradoxically, we are reminded of it only by observing the apparent motion of the sun and stars. An observer standing on earth perceives himself as stationary, while the sun and the stars appear to rise in the east and move west as the day progresses. In fact, it is the earth that is turning, counterclockwise on its axis, in a direction opposite to the stars' apparent motion. The simplest means of picturing the motion of the stars is to imagine that they are all pasted onto an enormous globe, the **celestial sphere**, and we are inside, at the center. As the celestial sphere turns (or we turn inside of it), we see the stars move across the heavens.

We perceive the stars in patterns or constellations on the celestial sphere. However, the constellations are not real groupings of stars, just illusions based upon the perspective of our vantage point on earth. Seen from a different spot in the universe, the stars would form quite different patterns. Stars that seem close together may or may not be neighbors. **Castor** and **Pollux**, the two bright stars in **Gemini** (The Twins), are indeed close neighbors, a mere dozen light-years apart (a light-year is the distance light travels in one year, or six million million miles). In contrast, **Rigel** and **Betelgeuse**, the two brightest stars in **Orion** (The Hunter), are very far apart. Reddish Betelgeuse in Orion's left shoulder is 300 light-years away, while Rigel, the bluish-white star in the right foot, is over 200 light-years more distant.

Despite its illusory nature, the concept of the celestial sphere is quite useful for finding one's way about the universe. It serves as a means of locating a particular star and communicating that information to others. For this purpose, we have a system of celestial coordinates, analogous to latitude and longitude on the earth. The celestial sphere is merely another globe, surrounding the earth. The axis of the celestial sphere is the extension into space of the earth's axis. This axis goes through the North Pole on earth and very close to **Polaris**, the pole star in space.

The earth's circles of latitude, or parallels, measure distances north or south from the equator. On the celestial sphere, they are called **parallels of declination**. Midway between the north and south celestial poles, the celestial equator divides the sky into northern and southern celestial hemispheres. The declination of the celestial equator is zero, just as the latitude of the earth's equator is zero. The declinations of the north and south celestial poles are $+90$ degrees and -90 degrees, respectively.

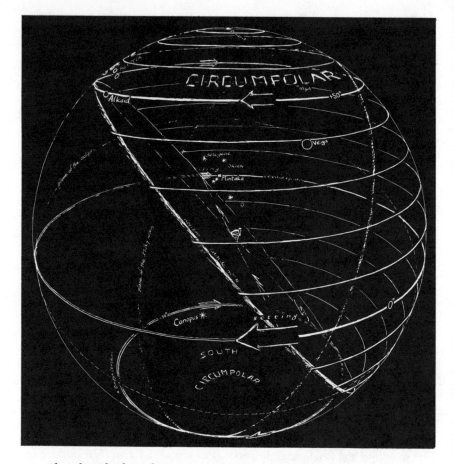

The celestial sphere showing several stars and parallels of declination. An observer is sitting on earth at latitude 40° north. His horizon is inclined at an angle of 50° with that of the celestial equator. Notice that the Big Dipper, and all the northern stars whose declination is greater than 50, never dip below the horizon to set. These are the circumpolar stars, present in the sky always, although half the time they cannot be seen because of daylight.

If the stars streaked rapidly across the sky, you would better appreciate the parallels of declination. You would see each star tracing a circle representing its parallel of declination. However, unless you were standing at the North Pole, these circles would appear inclined with respect to your horizon, so that the height, or altitude, of the star would change during the night.

To visualize these circles of declination, we can aim a camera at Polaris, with its shutter opened for several hours. This time-exposure photograph will show the stars rotating around the north celestial pole. Another way to visualize the celestial sphere is to watch the motions of stars located at key points on the sphere. **Orion**'s belt and the center of **Aquila** (The Eagle) are close to the celestial equator. Watch the progression of these stars through the night as they trace the celestial equator, dividing the celestial sphere into northern and southern celestial hemispheres.

Just as a city on earth is specified by its latitude and longitude, to pinpoint a star's location we need another angular measurement in addition to declination. Longitude on the earth is arbitrarily designated as a certain number of degrees east or west from Greenwich, England, chosen for historical reasons. **Right Ascension** (R.A.), the equivalent of longitude on the celestial sphere, is measured east and west from a point in constellation **Pisces** (The Fishes). As with longitude, it is an arbitrary, though specific, point. The celestial sphere is divided into 24 segments, or **hour circles**. Instead of being measured in degrees, right ascension is measured in hours, minutes, and seconds. This convention is used because time and the angular measurement, right ascension, are interrelated; a star rises and moves across the sky at a rate of 15 degrees per hour because the earth rotates 360 degrees in 24 hours ($360 \div 24 = 15$). Thus, to specify the location of a star, such as Sirius, one gives its right ascension and declination: R.A. 6h 41m Dec. $-16°$ 35′.

What if the earth rotated on a different schedule? For example, the moon rotates on its axis once for each revolution around the earth. As a result, one side of the moon permanently faces the earth. (It may help to visualize this if you mark a spot on a ball and move it around you in a circle as you slowly rotate the spot on the ball's axis.) If the earth's period of rotation on its axis equaled its period of revolution around the sun (i.e, one rotation in a year), the consequences would be disastrous. Half the planet would be permanently bathed in sunlight, the other half forever cold and dark. If the earth did not rotate at all, the situation would hardly be better. At any one spot, half the year would be day and half the year night.

The earth's orbit around the sun

The second great motion of the earth is its revolution around the sun. The earth and the other planets orbit the sun in nearly the same plane. If we extend this plane, called the **ecliptic**, off into space to where it intersects the celestial equator, it will slice through a band of 12 constellations, the **zodiac**, the familiar constellations of the 12 astrological signs. The zodiac is important because it is the background against which we view the paths of the planets, the moon, and the sun. As we look beyond a planet or the moon, they appear to lie within one of the constellations of the zodiac. By learning these 12 constellations, we will be able to spot the planets as starlike objects moving within the zodiac.

We now have two planes that divide the celestial sphere into huge hemispheres. Do not confuse the plane of the ecliptic with that of the celestial equator. One is based upon the earth's equator, the other upon the plane of the earth's orbit. They are not the same, but are tilted 23-1/2 degrees with respect to each other. This seemingly trivial fact has enormous consequences; the tilt is responsible for the change of seasons and for differences in day-length during the year.

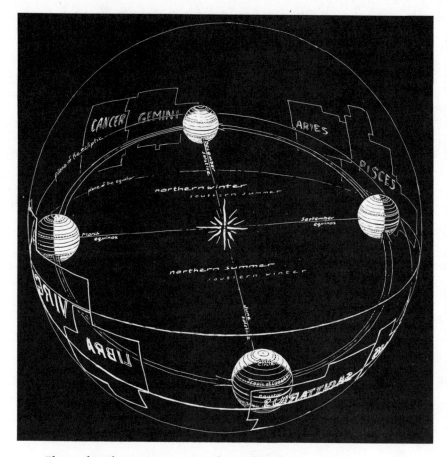

The earth's tilt on its axis causes the yearly cycle of seasons as the earth orbits around the sun in the plane of the ecliptic. The Northern Hemisphere leans toward the sun in summer and away from the sun in winter. In the background is the celestial sphere, with 8 of the 12 regions of the zodiac constellations indicated.

Activities: a tour of our galaxy

Equipment for stargazing

Star maps and star wheels

You do not need very much equipment for stargazing. Most important is a star chart to help you find your way around the galaxy. All field guides have charts showing the constellations at different times of the year. A star wheel is a fancier map, consisting of a disc upon which the constellations are printed. Superimposed is another disc, which has a window. On one, the dates are marked, and on the other the time of day. By rotating the wheels to line up the correct date and time, you can see which portion of the sky is currently visible. Although most star wheels show less detail than individual star maps, they present a convenient overall view of the heavens.

Many of the brightest stars have common names, often Arabic in origin. Most of the others are labeled with Greek letters, usually in order of brightness. For example, **Alpha Centauri** is the brightest star in the constellation **Centaurus** (The Centaur). When stargazing, it is best to illuminate your star map only with a red light because bright light makes your eyes less sensitive. (You can cover a flashlight with a piece of red cellophane.)

On a chart, the brightness of objects is indicated by circles of different sizes, corresponding to a scale of **magnitudes** used by astronomers. Since celestial objects span an enormous range of brightnesses, the magnitude scale is set up logarithmically; a difference of five magnitudes is a 100-fold factor in intensity. This means that a star of the first magnitude is about 2.5 times as bright as one of the second magnitude, or $2.5 \times 2.5 = 6.25$ times as bright as a star of the third

THE TWENTY BRIGHTEST STARS IN THE SKY			
Name	Constellation	Magnitude	Distance (light years)
Sirius	Canis Major (The Great Dog)	−1.4	9
Canopus[a]	Carina (The Keel)	−0.7	181
Alpha Centauri[a]	Centaurus (The Centaur)	−0.3	4
Arcturus	Boötes (The Herdsman)	−0.1	36
Vega	Lyra (The Lyre)	0.0	26
Capella	Auriga (The Charioteer)	0.1	46
Rigel	Orion (The Hunter)	0.1	880
Procyon	Canis Minor (The Small Dog)	0.4	11
Achernar[a]	Eridani (The River Eridanus)	0.5	114
Beta Centauri[a]	Centaurus (The Centaur)	0.6	424
Altair	Aquila (The Eagle)	0.8	16
Betelgeuse	Orion (The Hunter)	0.8	586
Aldebaran	Taurus (The Bull)	0.9	68
Alpha Crucis[a]	Crux (The Southern Cross)	0.9	424
Spica	Virgo (The Virgin)	1.0	212
Antares	Scorpius (The Scorpion)	1.0	424
Pollux	Gemini (The Twins)	1.2	35
Fomalhaut	Piscis Austrinus (The Southern Fish)	1.2	23
Deneb	Cygnus (The Swan)	1.3	1630
Beta Crucis[a]	Crux (The Southern Cross)	1.3	261

[a] Not visible at latitude 40° north.

magnitude. Also notice that the dimmer the star, the greater the magnitude. The brightest stars have magnitudes of zero or negative numbers. The sun's magnitude is −27; the full moon's is −13; Venus can be as bright as − 4, and the brightest star, Sirius, is −1.4. With the naked eye we can see a star as faint as sixth magnitude. With binoculars, ninth-magnitude objects are visible.

As with terrestrial travel, it is convenient to have a yardstick with which to make measurements. When stargazing, we do not measure actual distances, but angles separating celestial objects. Two stars are said to be a certain number of degrees apart. On a sheet of paper, angles are measured with a protractor, and are divided into degrees, minutes, and seconds, with 60 seconds to a minute and 60 minutes to a degree. In the sky, one uses a sextant for accurate measurements. However, we can estimate angular distances without any equipment. From the zenith directly overhead to the horizon is 90 degrees. A fist at arm's length appears about 10 degrees wide, and a finger's width about 2 degrees. The full moon and the sun are each only a half-degree (30 minutes). Sometimes these measurements can be deceiving. You will probably be surprised to find that a dime held at arm's length is several times the diameter of the moon.

BINOCULARS

You can easily occupy yourself for weeks observing the sky with the naked eye, but the heavens become magnificent through binoculars or a small telescope. How do you choose a pair of binoculars for stargazing or animal study? The optical characteristics of binoculars are described by two numbers such as 7 × 50. The first number indicates the magnification, usually between 6- and 12-power. Just as important is the second number, which indicates the diameter of the objective lenses in millimeters (the lenses farthest from the eye). The larger the objective, the better the light-gathering power of your instrument. This is precisely what we need for stargazing, the ability to see dim objects and to distinguish them clearly from other nearby objects. A measure of the light-gathering power of binoculars is called the **Relative Light Efficiency** (RLE). This is calculated by dividing the diameter of the objective in millimeters by the square of the magnification. For a 7 × 50 pair of binoculars this equals 50/(7 × 7) or about 1. The higher the RLE, the brighter the image. An RLE of 1 will enable you to see objects as faint as ninth magnitude, 16 times dimmer than possible with the unaided eye. Such binoculars will reveal distant star clusters and the moons of Jupiter. (Binoculars 7 × 35 or 9 × 40 are fine for bird-watching. Their RLE is only half that of the 7 × 50's, but bird-watching is a daylight activity.)

The other useful property of binoculars is their ability to resolve fine details, such as the rings of Saturn, or two stars that appear close together. This property is also a function of the diameter of the objective. With a good pair of binoculars, you should be able to distinguish two stars as individual points when they are only one minute apart. That is three times the ability of the naked eye.

Slight vibrations are magnified greatly with binoculars. It will be much more convenient to mount your binoculars on a sturdy tripod. Most binoculars do not have a mounting screw to attach the binoculars to the tripod base. However, you can improvise an arrangement with rubber bands or tape. Regardless of what you use to observe the stars, proper viewing conditions are essential. Clouds, smog, and city lights will obscure a lot of detail. The dim objects listed in the table as being visible with the naked eye are only visible under optimal conditions.

Star-hopping through the night sky

On the earth we find our way around by learning a few landmarks and their locations. In a new city we may use a street map. Soon we can find our way from place to place. Similarly, we will orient ourselves in the night sky by star-hopping through the celestial sphere, learning a few constellations at a time, and following

The major constellations of the Northern Hemisphere, showing the approximate locations of the celestial objects listed in the table on page 260. The arrows from the Big Dipper in the constellation Ursa Major are guideposts for star-hopping from one constellation to the next, as described in the text.

25 INTERESTING CELESTIAL OBJECTS TO SEE WITH THE NAKED EYE OR BINOCULARS

	DOUBLE STARS	Constellation	Angular Distance Between the Stars (in minutes of arc)	Magnitudes
1	Mizar, Alcor	Ursa Major	11.8	2.1, 4.0[n]
2	Giedi (Alpha Capricorni)	Capricorn	6.3	4.6, 3.8[n]
3	Alpha Librae	Libra	3.9	2.8, 5.2[n]
4	Epsilon Lyrae	Lyre	3.5	5.1, 4.4[n]
	GLOBULAR CLUSTERS		Distance lt-yr	
5	M4[a]	Scorpius	7,200	5.2[b]
6	M15	Pegasus	34,000	6.0[b]
7	Omega Centauri	Centaurus	17,000	3.7[n]
8	M3	Canes Venatici	35,000	6.4[b]
9	Great Cluster (M13)	Hercules	21,000	5.7[n]
10	M22	Sagittarius	10,000	6.2[b]
11	M55	Sagittarius	20,000	6.7[b]
	OPEN CLUSTERS			
12	Pleiades (M45)	Taurus	541	1.6[n]
13	Hyades	Taurus	130	4.0[n]
14	Perseus Double Cluster	Perseus	7,000/8,000	4.4[n]/4.7[n]
15	Trapezium	Orion	1,300	5.0[n]
16	Praesepe (Beehive) (M44)	Cancer	590	3.7[n]
17	M7	Scorpius	800	5.0[b]
18	M35	Gemini	2,800	5.3[b]
19	M11	Scutum	5,600	6.3[b]
	NEBULAE			
20	Great Nebula (M42)	Orion	300	4.0[n]
21	Trifid Nebula (M20)	Sagittarius	3,500	6.9[b]
22	Lagoon Nebula (M8)	Sagittarius	5,100	6.8[b]
23	Horseshoe Nebula (M17)	Sagittarius	3,000	7.0[b]
	GALAXIES			
24	Andromeda (M31)	Andromeda	2,100,000	4.8[n]
25	M33	Triangulum	2,400,000	6.7[b]

[a] Celestial objects designated by a prefix letter M are Messier objects, named by Charles Messier who compiled a catalog of nebulae, galaxies, and star clusters from 1784–1786. These objects are often referred to by their Messier numbers in field guides and astronomical books, so these designations are used along with the common name if one exists.
[b] Visible with binoculars.
[n] Visible with the naked eye.

our voyage on a star chart. At each latitude in the United States, the observer sees a different view of the skies. The following discussion applies specifically to 40 degrees north, the latitude that passes across the middle of the nation, but it is applicable to the entire country.

The **Big Dipper**, part of the constellation **Ursa Major** (The Big Bear), is the best place to start. For most of us in the United States, at a latitude of 40 degrees north or above, the Dipper is always visible at night. Those stars whose declination is far enough north are called the north circumpolar stars because they rotate around Polaris, the North Star, and never dip below the horizon to set. **Merak** and **Dubhe** are the pointers in the bowl of the Dipper, at the end opposite from the handle. A line joining these two stars and extending northward five times the distance between them will land you just about at Polaris. This is the last star in the handle of the **Little Dipper**, or **Ursa Minor** (The Little Bear). A third circumpolar constellation is **Cassiopeia** (The Queen), shaped like a "W" or an "M" depending upon the season. She is on the opposite side of Polaris, roughly the same distance from the North Star as the Big Dipper.

Once we leave the circumpolar stars, the constellations we visit will be most easily seen in particular seasons. Remember that the celestial sphere makes one revolution a day, so each of our constellations will cross the sky at some time during the day. However, during certain seasons, a particular constellation will pass overhead during daylight and cannot be seen. Other constellations will be visible only very late at night. Orion, for example, our most prominent "winter" constellation, can be seen in the summer if you are willing to do your stargazing at four o'clock in the morning.

To locate the major winter constellations, we will again start star-hopping from our familiar guidepost, the Big Dipper. This time use the two stars in the bottom of the bowl (**Phecda** and **Merak**) to point away from the handle. About seven lengths the distance between them, you will come to Castor and Pollux, the two bright stars in Gemini (The Twins). Continuing in the same direction, you will find Orion (The Hunter), with its two brightest stars, Rigel and Betelgeuse. Midway between them are three stars, sometimes called the **3 Marys**. They make up Orion's belt, and point downward at an angle to the southeast, to the brightest star, **Sirius**, in the constellation **Canis Major** (The Great Dog). Following the 3 Marys in the other direction brings you to **Taurus** (The Bull) with its bright star **Aldebaran**.

We can use the Big Dipper once again to star-hop to the spring constellations. This time, use the two stars in the Dipper's bowl closest to the handle (**Megrez** and **Phecda**). Follow them southward until you come to the bright star **Regulus** in the foot of **Leo** (The Lion). The front part of Leo forms a conspicuous sickle, or backward "?" with Regulus as its dot.

Following the curve of the Dipper's handle away from the bowl, you can "Arc to Arcturus and spike to Spica." **Arcturus** in **Bootes** (The Herdsman) is an orange star, the fourth brightest in the sky. Continue in the same curved arc, and you will arrive at **Spica**, a bluish star in **Virgo** (The Virgin).

The highlight of the summer is the **Summer Triangle** formed by **Deneb**, **Vega**, and **Altair**, the three brightest stars in **Cygnus** (The Swan), **Lyra** (The Lyre), and **Aquila** (The Eagle). It does not have the status of a constellation, but is called an asterism. You can find the Summer Triangle by using the stars in the Dipper's bowl closest to the handle. However, instead of pointing downward toward Leo, head in the other direction across the sky. Depending upon how much you veer off course, you will run into Vega or Deneb. The Summer Triangle is such a conspicuous asterism that you will soon pick it right out without needing to star hop to find it.

Scorpius lives up to its name, looking like a scorpion with pincers and a recurved tail. One bright star near the head is distinctly reddish, making it possible to confuse it with Mars, which is sometimes nearby. For this reason, the star was named **Antares** (Ant-Ares) meaning "Rival of Mars."

In the Autumn, **Pegasus** (The Winged Horse) comes into view. The **Great Square** of Pegasus, formed by four of its brightest stars, is one of the prominent asterisms in the heavens. A line drawn from Polaris to the last star in Cassiopeia's "W" and beyond passes through two of the stars in the Square. **Andromeda** (The Chained Lady) is to the east of Pegasus, with one of the stars in the Square forming her head.

Sightseeing in the celestial sphere

Besides the constellations, other heavenly objects provide fascinating viewing. For the following tour of the universe, you will need a detailed road map to find the precise locations of the sights at a particular season and time of the year. Refer to one of the field guides listed at the end of the chapter. To best appreciate the scenery, do not forget your binoculars.

THE MILKY WAY

The universe contains millions of galaxies. Our solar system is embedded in the edge of one of them. Our galaxy is a flattened disc of billions of stars, called the **Milky Way**, or just the **Galaxy**. Its shape is a flattened disc 100,000 light-years across, with spiral arms extending out into space. Toward the center it has a bulging nucleus 10,000 light-years thick, more densely packed with stars. Surrounding the disk is a halo containing scattered clusters of stars. Our solar system is off to one edge of the Galaxy, about two-thirds of the way out from the hub.

Every star that we can see with the naked eye belongs to the Milky Way. Looking up at right angles out of the Galaxy, we see fewer stars than when we look within the plane of the Milky Way. In winter, our view is toward the outer edge of the Galaxy where there are fewer stars, but on summer nights we look in the opposite direction, toward the center. These myriad stars appear as a milky band of light, with the individual stars too faint to distinguish. The best view of the Milky Way is on clear summer nights, far from city lights. It passes through the Summer Triangle and Cassiopeia.

MULTIPLE STARS, CLUSTERS, AND NEBULAE

Some stars appear to be single entities, but on closer examination prove to be two or more stars. In some cases, the two stars are along the same line of sight, but, in fact, they are far apart with no real "connection." In contrast to these **optical doubles** are **physical doubles**, or **binaries**. Such stars are gravitationally bound, traveling together through space, orbiting around a common center. Multiple groups of triplets and quadruplets are also common. These star systems make wonderful objects to observe. You can test your visual acuity and the resolution of your binoculars by trying to distinguish the individual stars. The most famous naked-eye double is in the Big Dipper. **Mizar**, the second star in from the end of the handle, has a faint companion, **Alcor**. This optical double was called the **Horse and Rider** by the American Indians. The magnitudes of the two stars are 2.1 and 4.0. The stars are 12 minutes of arc apart, easily within the resolving ability of the naked eye. **Epsilon Lyrae** is a double star, located next to Vega in the constellation Lyra. It provides a sensitive test of visual acuity. The two stars are separated by 3.5 minutes of arc, just a bit greater than the limit of our eyes (3 minutes). Examine these stars on a clear night. Actually each of the stars also has a companion, forming a "double double." However they are a mere 2 seconds of arc apart, beyond the limit of binoculars. Refer to the table of interesting celestial objects for a list of progressively closer double stars to test the limits of your eyes and binoculars.

Within our galaxy some stars occur in clusters. There are two types: globular and open clusters. They are faint objects and provide a challenge to find. Most require binoculars.

Globular clusters are aggregations of hundreds of thousands of stars concentrated toward the center, and bound together by a common gravitational system. They are enormous distances from the earth, the nearest about 10,000 light-years away. In size, they are 20 to 1,000 light-years in diameter. Many of the globular clusters are slightly ellipsoidal in shape, indicating that they probably rotate. The globular clusters mostly occur out of the plane of the Milky Way, in a region called the galactic halo located over the bulge in the galaxy's center. Their stars are old, having formed early in the evolution of the Milky Way when it was condensing from vast clouds of intergalactic material. On clear nights, **M13**, the **Great Cluster** in Hercules, is just visible to the naked eye as a fuzzy dot. The cluster consists of over 100,000 stars over 21,000 light-years away.

Open clusters are loose aggregations of tens or hundreds of stars. These are second-generation stars, formed in part from debris of older exploded stars after the original galaxy was created. The open clusters are found in the plane of the Galaxy. Several open clusters are visible to the naked eye, but they are gorgeous objects through binoculars. You will be surprised at the difference in the number of stars you can see with and without binoculars. **Hyades** is the nearest open cluster, making up the head of Taurus (The Bull). The **Pleiades**, or the **Seven Sisters**, is the most famous cluster, with six stars visible to the naked eye, and many more with binoculars. The **Double Cluster** in **Perseus** and the **Beehive** in **Cancer** (The Crab) are also visible without binoculars.

In the vast, unimaginable spaces between the stars are particles of gas and dust, forming clouds called **diffuse nebulae**. They consist mostly of hydrogen, but sometimes include helium, oxygen, carbon dioxide, water, and other simple compounds. These nebulae have no light of their own but depend on nearby stars to illuminate them. A few are bright enough to be seen with the unaided eye or binoculars.

OTHER GALAXIES

The last stop on our tour of the heavens takes us out of our galaxy to another, Andromeda, 2,100,000 light-years away. It is the farthest object visible to the naked eye, a fuzzy smudge of the fifth magnitude. Only a large telescope can resolve the Andromeda galaxy into individual stars. The star map shows its location in the constellation of the same name.

When you look at all these sights with the naked eye, they appear more or less similar, spots of light emanating from a point in space. However, keep in mind that you are seeing completely different kinds of objects. The star Albeireo is really two; the Great Nebula in Orion is a gigantic cloud of dust; the Hercules cluster contains thousands of stars; and the Andromeda galaxy, with billions of stars, is larger than the Milky Way.

REFERENCES AND SUGGESTIONS FOR FURTHER READING

Brown, Peter Lancaster. 1972. *Astronomy in Color.* Macmillan, New York.

Chartrand, Mark R., III. 1982. *Skyguide: A Field Guide for Amateur Astronomers.* Golden Press, New York.

Menzel, Donald H. 1964. *A Field Guide to the Stars and Planets.* Houghton Mifflin, Boston.

Ottewell, Guy. 1985. *The Astronomical Companion.* Guy Ottewell, Furman University, Greenville, South Carolina.

Rey, H.A. 1970. *The Stars: A New Way to See Them.* Houghton Mifflin, Boston.

Appendix A

Common names and scientific names of organisms mentioned in this book

IT IS DIFFICULT to imagine the enormous variety of living organisms that exist. There are nearly 300,000 species of flowering plants, over 25,000 kinds of fungi, and over 1,000,000 animals. With so many different organisms, each one does not have a unique common name. Often many related species share a single common name. In some cases the entire family has the same common name. In the following table, when the genus name is listed followed by "sp." (meaning species; plural, "spp."), this indicates that there are several species with the same common name in the genus. Sometimes the genus name is used as the common name. Specific scientific names are given when reference was made to a particular species, or for common examples of the organism discussed in the text.

PLANTS

agrimony	*Agrimonia sp.*	beech	*Fagus sp.*
ailanthus, tree of heaven	*Ailanthus altissima*	beggar's tick	*Bidens sp.*
		begonia	*Begonia*
alfalfa	*Medicago sativa*	birdfoot trefoil	*Lotus corniculatus*
anthurium	*Anthurium*	bitter cherry	*Prunus emarginata*
apple	*Malus sp.*	black birch (sweet birch)	*Betula lenta*
arrowhead	*Sagittaria sp.*		
aster	*Aster sp.*	black cherry	*Prunus serotina*
autumn crocus	*Colchicum autumnale*	black gum (sour gum, tupelo)	*Nyssa sylvatica*
avens	*Geum sp.*	black locust	*Robinia pseudoacacia*
azalea	*Rhododendron sp.*		
balsam fir	*Abies balsamea*	black walnut	*Juglans nigra*
baneberry	*Actaea sp.*	blackberry	*Rubus sp.*
barrel cactus	*Echinocactus wislizeni*	bloodroot	*Sanguinaria canadensis*
basswood (linden)	*Tilia americana*	blue flag	*Iris versicolor*
bayberry	*Myrica cerifera*	boneset	*Eupatorium perfoliatum*
bearberry	*Arctostaphylos uva-ursi*	boxelder	*Acer negundo*

broom	*Cytisus scoparius*	false hellebore	*Veratrum viride*
buckthorn	*Rhamnus purshiana*	fleabane	*Erigeron sp.*
		fool's parsley	*Aethusa cynapium*
bur clover	*Medicago denticulata*	foxglove	*Digitalis purpurea, D. lanata*
burdock	*Arctium minus*	geranium	*Geranium sp.*
buttercups	*Ranunculus sp.*	goat's beard	*Tragopogon pratensis*
Calabar bean	*Physostigma venenosum*	goldenrod	*Solidago sp.*
caladium	*Caladium sp.*	grape	*Vitis sp.*
California poppy	*Eschscholtzia californica*	greenbrier, catbrier	*Smilax rotundifolia*
		groundnut	*Apios americana*
calla	*Calla sp.*	gumweed	*Grindelia sp.*
candelilla	*Euphorbia antisyphylitica*	hackberry	*Celtis occidentalis*
		hawthorn	*Crataegus sp.*
castor bean	*Ricinus communis*	hepatica, liverleaf	*Hepatica acutiloba*
catalpa	*Catalpa sp.*	hickory	*Carya sp.*
cattail	*Typha sp.*	honeysuckle	*Lonicera sp.*
chicory	*Cichorium intybus*	horse chestnut	*Aesculus hippocastanum*
choke cherry	*Prunus virginiana*		
chrysanthemum	*Chrysanthemum*	hyacinth	*Hyacinthus*
cinchona	*Cinchona sp.*	ironwood,	*Carpinus*
clematis	*Clematis sp.*	musclewood	*caroliniana*
coca	*Erythroxylon coca*	Jack-in-the-pulpit	*Arisaema triphyllum*
cocklebur	*Xanthium strumarium*		
		Japanese	*Polygonum*
coconut palm	*Cocos nucifera*	knotweed	*cuspidatum*
coleus	*Coleus sp.*	Jerusalem	*Helianthus*
cornflower, bachelor's button	*Centaurea cyanus*	artichoke	*tuberosus*
		jewelweed	*Impatiens capensis*
		jimsonweed	*Datura stramonium*
cranberry	*Vaccinium macrocarpon*	lady's slipper	*Cypripedium sp.*
		lamb's quarters,	*Chenopodium*
cranesbill	*Geranium sp.*	pigweed	*album*
crocus	*Crocus vernus*	laurel	*Kalmia sp.*
daffodil	*Narcissus pseudo-narcissus*	lords-and-ladies	*Arum maculatum*
		lousewort,	*Pedicularis*
dandelion	*Taraxacum offininale*	wood-betony	*canadensis*
		lupine	*Lupinus sp.*
diffenbachia	*Diffenbachia sp.*	Madagascar	*Catharanthus*
dock	*Rumex crispus*	periwinkle	*roseus*
dogwood	*Cornus sp.*	maple-leaved	*Viburnum*
doveweed	*Croton texensis*	viburnum	*acerifolium*
Dutchman's breeches	*Dicentra cucullaria*	marigold	*Tagetes sp.*
		mayapple	*Podophyllum peltatum*
dwarf mistletoe	*Arceuthobium sp.*	mesquite	*Prosopis sp.*
eastern hemlock	*Tsuga canadensis*	Mexican yam	*Dioscorea sp.*
eastern white pine	*Pinus strobus*	milk-vetch	*Astragalus canadensis*
elderberry	*Sambucus canadensis*		
elm	*Ulmus sp.*	milkweed	*Asclepias sp.*
enchanter's nightshade	*Circaea alpina*	mint	*Mentha sp.*
		motherwort	*Leonurus cardiaca*
euonymus	*Euonymus sp.*	mountain laurel	*Kalmia latifolia*
evening primrose	*Oenothera hookeri*	mullein	*Verbascum thapsus*

mustard	*Brassica sp.*
nettle	*Urtica dioica*
night-flowering catchfly	*Silene noctiflora*
nightshade	*Solanum nigrum*
Norway maple	*Acer platanoides*
oak	*Quercus sp.*
Ohio buckeye	*Aesculus glabra*
old man cactus	*Cephalocereus senilis*
opium poppy	*Papaver somniferum*
orchis	*Orchis sp.*
ostrich fern	*Matteuccia Struthiopteris*
peony	*Paeonia sp.*
philodendron	*Philodendron sp.*
pin cherry	*Prunus pensylvanica*
pinyon pine	*Pinus edulis*
plantain	*Plantago psyllium*
poison hemlock	*Conium maculatum*
pokeweed	*Phytolacca americana*
poplar	*Populus sp.*
purple loosestrife	*Lythrum salicaria*
pussy willow	*Salix discolor*
raspberry	*Rubus sp.*
red maple	*Acer rubrum*
red oak	*Quercus rubra*
rhododendron	*Rhododendron sp.*
rosary pea	*Abrus precatorius*
Russian tumbleweed	*Salsola kali*
sage	*Salvia sp.*
sagebrush, wormwood	*Artemisia sp.*
salt cedar, tamarisk	*Tamarix sp.*
sassafras	*Sassafras albidum*
skunk cabbage	*Symplocarpus foetidus*
slippery elm	*Ulmus rubra*
Solomon's seal	*Polygonatum biflorum*
spring cress, bittercress	*Cardamine sp.*
spruce	*Picea sp.*
squirrel corn	*Dicentra canadensis*

staghorn sumac	*Rhus typhina*
sticky currant	*Ribes viscosissimum*
stinking groundsel	*Senecio viscosus*
storksbill	*Erodium cicutarium*
sugar maple	*Acer saccharum*
swamp azalea, swamp-honeysuckle	*Rhododendron viscosum*
sweet cicely	*Osmorhiza claytoni*
sycamore	*Platanus occidentalis*
thimbleweed	*Anemone virginiana*
thistle	*Cirsium ochrocentrum*
tiger lily	*Lilium tigrinum*
tobacco	*Nicotiana sp.*
trillium	*Trillium sp.*
tulip	*Tulipa sp.*
tulip tree	*Liriodendron tulipifera*
twinflower	*Linnaea borealis*
twinleaf	*Jeffersonia diphylla*
vetch	*Vicia sp.*
violet	*Viola sp.*
virgin's bower	*Clematis virginiana*
voodoo lily	*Sauromatum guttatum*
water lily	*Nymphaea odorata*
water plantain	*Alisma triviale*
white ash	*Fraxinus americana*
white cedar	*Thuja occidentalis*
white horsenettle	*Solanum elaegnifolium*
white oak	*Quercus alba*
wild bergamot	*Monarda fistulosa*
wild carrot, Queen Anne's lace	*Daucus carota*
wild ginger	*Asarum canadense*
wild rose	*Rosa sp.*
wisteria	*Wisteria sp.*
wood sage	*Teucrium sp.*
wood sorrel	*Oxalis montana*
woundwort	*Stachys palustris*
yew	*Taxus canadensis*

FUNGI

ash bolete	*Gyrodon merulioides*
death cap, destroying angel	*Amanita virosa, A. phalloides*

false morel	*Gyromitra sp.*
fly agaric	*Amanita muscaria*
Galerina	*Galerina sp.*
giant puffball	*Calvatia gigantea*
Inocybe	*Inocybe sp.*
morel	*Morchella sp.*
old man of the woods	*Strobilomyces floccopus*

Paneolus	*Paneolus sp.*
potato blight	*Phytophthora infestans*
Psilocybe	*Psilocybe sp.*
shaggy mane	*Coprinus conatus*
sulfur shelf	*Polyporus sulphureus*

INSECTS

alderfly	family Sialidae
American cockroach	*Periplaneta americana*
aphid	*Aphis nerii*
backswimmer	family Notonectidae
bald-faced hornet	*Vespula maculata*
bedbug	*Cimex lectularius*
black carpet beetle	*Attagenus unicolor*
black fly	family Simuliidae
blister beetle	*Epicauta sp.*
bloodworm (midge larva)	family Chironomidae
bluebottle fly	*Calliphoria vomitoria, Lucilia caesar*
bombardier beetle	*Brachinus sp.*
booklouse	*Liposcelis divinatorius*
brown lacewing	*Hemerobius sp.*
brown-banded cockroach	*Supella supellectilium*
bumble bee	*Bombus sp.*
cabbage butterfly	*Pieris rapae*
caddisfly	order TRICHOPTERA
carpenter ant	*Camponotus sp.*
carpenter bee	*Xylocopa sp.*
carpet beetle	*Anthrenus scrophulariae*
case-making clothes moth	*Tinea pellionella*
cat flea	*Ctenocephalides felis*
caterpillar hunter beetle	*Calasoma sp.*
cattail moth	*Lymnaecia phragmitella*
cecropia moth	*Hyalophora cecropia*
clearwing moth	*Sanninoidea exitiosa*

cluster fly	*Pollenia rudis*
confused flour beetle	*Tribolium confusum*
crane fly	family Tipulidae
crawling water beetle	family Haliplidae
ctenucha moth	*Ctenucha sp.*
cuckoo bumble bee	*Psithyrus sp.*
damselfly	order ODONATA, suborder ZYGOPTERA
darkling beetle	*Eleodes sp.*
dobsonfly	*Corydalus cornutus*
dog flea	*Ctenocephalides canis*
dragonfly	order ODONATA, suborder ANISOPTERA
drugstore beetle	*Stegobium paniceum*
earwig	*Forficula auricularia*
eastern tent caterpillar	*Malacosoma americana*
evergreen bagworm	*Thyridopteryx ephemeraeformis*
face fly	*Musca autumnalis*
field ant	*Lasius neoniger*
field cricket	*Gryllus pennsylvanicus*
firebrat	*Thermobia domestica*
firefly	*Photinus sp.*
frit fly	family Chloropidae
fruit fly	*Drosophila sp.*
furniture beetle	*Anobium punctatum*
gall gnat	family Cecidomyiidae
geometrid moth	*Caripeta piniata*
geometrid moth	*Synchlora sp.*

geometrid stick caterpillar	*Prochoerodes transversata*	milkweed beetle	*Tetraopes tetraophthalmus*
German cockroach	*Blatella germanica*	milkweed tiger moth	*Euchchaetias egle*
giant water bug	*Belostoma sp.*		
goldenrod ball gall fly	*Eurosta sp.*	monarch butterfly	*Danaus plexippus*
goldenrod elliptical gall moth	*Gnorimoschema gallaesolidaginis*	mosquito	family Culicidae (*Culex, Aedes, Mansonia spp.*)
green lacewing	family Chrysopidae	moth fly	*Psychoda alternata*
		mountain midge	*Deuterophlebia sp.*
greenbottle fly	*Phaenicia sericata*	mourning cloak butterfly	*Nymphalis antiopa*
ground beetle	family Carabidae		
gypsy moth	*Porthetria dispar*	mud dauber	*Sceliphron caementarium*
hairstreak butterfly	*Satyrium sp., Strymon sp.*	net-winged midge	*Blepharocera sp.*
hawkmoth, sphinx moth	*Sphinx sp.*	noctuid moth	*Catocala ilia*
		oriental cockroach	*Blatta orientalis*
hide beetle	*Dermestes maculatus*	paper wasp	*Polistes sp.*
honey bee	*Apis mellifera*	pharaoh ant	*Monomorium pharaonis*
house cricket	*Acheta domesticus*	phymatid bug	*Phymata fasciata*
house fly	*Musca domestica*	pomace fly	family Drosophilidae
human flea	*Pulex irritans*		
Indian meal moth	*Plodia interpunctella*	powder-post beetle	*Lyctus sp.*
Io moth	*Automeris io*	praying mantis	*Tenodera aridifolia sinensis*
junebug	*Phyllophaga sp.*		
katydid	*Pterophylla sp.*	predaceous diving beetle	*Dytiscus sp.*
ladybug	*Coccinella sp.*	prometheus moth	*Callosamia promethea*
larder beetle	*Dermestes lardarius*	punky (biting midge)	family Ceratopogonidae
large milkweed bug	*Oncopeltus fasciatus*	rat-tailed maggot	*Eristalis tenax*
lesser house fly	*Fannia canicularis*	riffle beetle	*Elmis sp.*
lily-leaf caterpillar	*Nymphala sp.*	robber fly	*Laphria sacrator*
little black ant	*Monomorium minimum*	saw-toothed grain beetle	*Oryzaephilus surinamensis*
locust borer	*Megacyllene robiniae*	sawfly	*Neodiprion sp.*
long-horned beetle	family Cerambycidae	shore fly	family Ephydridae
		silverfish	*Lepisma saccharina*
long-horned leaf beetle	*Donacia sp.*	skipper	*Polites sp.*
lubber grasshopper	*Romalea microptera*	small milkweed bug	*Lygaeus kalmii*
luna moth	*Actias luna*	snow flea	*Achorutes nivicolus*
maple leaf cutter caterpillar	*Paraclemensia acerifoliella*	spider wasp	*Anoplius marginalis*
mayfly	order EPHEMEROPTERA	stink bug	*Euschistus servus, Nezara viridula*
Mediterranean flour moth	*Anagasta kuehniella*	stonefly	order PLECOPTERA
midge	family Chironomidae	swallowtail	*Papilio sp.*
		syrphid fly, flower fly	*Eristalis tenax, Syrphus torvus*

tachinid fly	*Pararchytas decisus*	water-penny beetle	*Psephenus herricki*
termite	*Reticulitermes flavipes*	waterscorpion	*Ranatra sp., Nepa sp.*
tiger beetle	family Cicindelidae	webbing clothes moth	*Tineola biselliella*
tiger swallowtail	*Pterourus glaucus*	whirligig beetle	*Dineutes*
tortoise beetle	*Cassida pallidula*		*americanus*
treehopper	*Thelia sp.*	wood cockroach	*Parcoblatta*
underwing moth	*Catocala sp.*		*pennsylvanica*
viceroy	*Limenites archippus*	wooly bear	*Isia isabella*
walking stick	family Phasmatidae	(Isabella moth)	
		yellowjacket	*Vespula sp.,*
water boatman	family Corixidae		*Dolichovespula*
water scavenger beetle	*Hydrophilus sp.*		*sp.*

SPIDERS

banded Argiope	*Argiope trifasciata*	jumping spider	family Salticidae (*Phidippus audax*)
black and yellow garden spider	*Argiope aurantia*		
black widow	*Latrodectus mactans*	Micrathena	*Micrathena sp.*
		Neoscona	*Neoscona sp.*
cobweb weaver	family Theridiidae (*Achaearanea sp., Steatoda sp.*)	northern widow	*Latrodectus variolus*
		orb weaver spider	family Araneidae
crab spider	*Misumena vatia*	sac spider	*Cheiracanthium mildei*
daddy-long-legs spider	*Pholcus sp.*		
		thick-jawed spider	*Pachygnatha brevis*
		wolf spider	family Lycosidae

OTHER INVERTEBRATES

earthworm	*Lumbricus terrestris, Allolobophora rosea*	polydesmid millipede	*Apheloria corrugata*
		roundworm	*Ascaris lumbricoides*
glomerid millipede	*Glomeris marginata*	scabies (itch mite)	*Sarcoptes scabiei*
		slug	*Arion sp., Limax maximus*
hair follicle mite	*Demodex folliculorum*		
		tapeworm	*Taenia sp., Diphyllobothrium latum*
harvestman, daddy-long-legs	*Phalangium opilio*		
hookworm	*Necator americanus, Ancylostoma duodenale*	whipscorpion (vinegaroon)	*Mastigoproctus giganteus*
		whipworm	*Trichuris trichiura*
		wood louse	order ISOPODA
lithobiid centipede	*Lithobius sp.*	(pillbug,	
pinworm	*Enterobius vernicularis*	sowbug)	

REPTILES AND AMPHIBIANS

blue-spotted salamander	*Ambystoma laterale*	northwestern salamander	*Ambystoma gracile*
flatwoods salamander	*Ambystoma cingulatum*	ringed salamander	*Ambystoma annulatum*
horned toad	*Phrynosoma sp.*	small-mouth salamander	*Ambystoma texanum*
Jefferson's salamander	*Ambystoma jeffersonianum*	spadefoot toad	*Scaphiopus couchi*
long-toed salamander	*Ambystoma macrodactylum*	spotted salamander	*Ambystoma maculatum*
Mabee's salamander	*Ambystoma mabeei*	spring peeper	*Hyla crucifer*
marbled salamander	*Ambystoma opacum*	talpid salamander	*Ambystoma talpoideum*
		tiger salamander	*Ambystoma tigrinum*

BIRDS

albatross	*Diomedea sp.*	common scoter	*Oidemia nigra*
American goldfinch	*Spinus tristis*	domestic pigeon (rock dove)	*Columba livia*
American redstart	*Setophaga ruticilla*	downy woodpecker	*Dendrocopos pubescens*
American widgeon	*Mareca americana*	eastern bluebird	*Sialia sialis*
American woodcock	*Philohela minor*	eastern kingbird	*Tyrannus tyrannus*
arctic tern	*Sterna paradisaea*	eastern phoebe	*Sayornis phoebe*
Baltimore oriole	*Icterus galbula*	evening grosbeak	*Hesperiphona vespertina*
barn swallow	*Hirundo rustica*		
black-capped chickadee	*Parus atricapillus*	field sparrow	*Spizella pusilla*
		golden-winged warbler	*Vermivora chrysoptera*
black-headed grosbeak	*Pheucticus melanocephalus*	great blue heron	*Ardea herodias*
blackpoll warbler	*Dendroica striata*	great horned owl	*Bubo virginianus*
blue jay	*Cyanocitta cristata*	hairy woodpecker	*Dendrocopos villosus*
bobolink	*Dolichonyx oryzivorous*	hermit thrush	*Hylocichla guttata*
bohemian waxwing	*Bombycilla garrulus*	horned lark	*Eremophila alpestris*
brown creeper	*Certhia familiaris*	house sparrow	*Passer domesticus*
cactus wren	*Campylorhynchus brunneicapillus*	house wren	*Troglodytes aedon*
		indigo bunting	*Passerina cyanea*
Canada goose	*Branta canadensis*	Kentucky warbler	*Oporornis formosus*
cardinal	*Richmondena cardinalis*	lesser yellowlegs	*Totanus flavipes*
catbird	*Dumetella carolinensis*	long-billed marsh wren	*Telmatodytes palustris*
cedar waxwing	*Bombycilla cedrorum*	magnolia warbler	*Dendroica magnolia*
chimney swift	*Chaetura pelagica*	mockingbird	*Mimus polyglottos*
common crow	*Corvus brachyrhynchos*	mourning dove	*Zenaidura macroura*
common grackle	*Quiscalus quiscula*	myrtle warbler	*Dendroica coronata*

nighthawk — *Chordeiles minor*
pine warbler — *Dendroica pinus*
pintail — *Anas acuta*
purple finch — *Carpodacus purpureus*
red-tailed hawk — *Buteo jamaicensis*
red-winged blackbird — *Agelaius phoeniceus*
redhead duck — *Aythya americana*
redpoll — *Acanthis flammea*
ring-necked pheasant — *Phasianus colchicus*
roadrunner — *Geococcyx californianus*
robin — *Turdus migratorius*
rose-breasted grosbeak — *Pheucticus ludovicianus*
Ross' goose — *Chen rossii*
ruby-throated hummingbird — *Archilochus colubris*
ruffed grouse — *Bonasa umbellus*
rufous hummingbird — *Selasphorus rufus*
rufous-sided towhee — *Pipilo erythrophthalmus*
scarlet tanager — *Piranga olivacea*
scrub jay — *Aphelocoma coerulescens*

slate-colored junco — *Junco hyemalis*
snowy owl — *Nyctea scandiaca*
song sparrow — *Melospiza melodia*
starling — *Sturnus vulgaris*
Stellar's jay — *Cyanocitta stelleri*
tree swallow — *Iridoprocne bicolor*
tufted titmouse — *Parus bicolor*
western tanager — *Piranga ludoviciana*
whip-poor-will — *Caprimulgus vociferus*
white-breasted nuthatch — *Sitta carolinensis*
white-throated sparrow — *Zonotrichia albicollis*
Wilson's warbler — *Wilsonia pusilla*
wood thrush — *Hylocichla mustelina*
worm-eating warbler — *Helmitheros vermivorous*
yellow warbler — *Dendroica petechia*
yellow-bellied sapsucker — *Sphyrapicus varius*
yellow-shafted flicker — *Colaptes auratus*
yellowthroat — *Geothlypis trichas*

MAMMALS

armadillo — *Dasypus novemcinctus*
badger — *Taxidea taxus*
beaver — *Castor canadensis*
bighorn sheep — *Ovis canadensis*
black bear — *Ursus americanus*
bobcat — *Felis rufus*
buffalo (bison) — *Bison bison*
caribou — *Rangifer caribou*
cougar (mountain lion) — *Felis concolor*
coyote — *Canis latrans*
desert kangaroo rat — *Dipodomys deserti*
eastern chipmunk — *Tamias striatus*
eastern cottontail rabbit — *Sylvilagus floridanus*
eastern mole — *Scalopus aquaticus*
elk — *Cervus canadensis*
gray squirrel — *Sciurus carolinensis*
jumping mouse — *Zapus sp.*
lynx — *Lynx canadensis*
meadow vole — *Microtus pennsylvanicus*

moose — *Alces alces*
mountain goat — *Oreamnos americanus*
mule deer — *Odocoileus hemionus*
muskrat — *Ondatra zibethica*
northern flying squirrel — *Glaucomys sabrinus*
opossum — *Didelphis virginianus*
porcupine — *Erethizon dorsatum*
raccoon — *Procyon lotor*
red fox — *Vulpes vulpes*
red squirrel — *Tamiasciurus hudsonicus*
short-tailed shrew — *Blarina brevicauda*
star-nosed mole — *Condylura cristata*
striped skunk — *Mephitis mephitis*
white-footed mouse — *Peromyscus leucopus*
whitetail deer — *Odocoileus virginianus*
wolf — *Canis lupus*
woodchuck — *Marmota monax*

Appendix B

Sources of Equipment and Supplies

MUCH OF THE EQUIPMENT that a naturalist needs can be homemade or purchased in local pharmacies and hardware stores. For most purposes, instruments such as razor blades and tweezers serve as well as fancier, more expensive scalpels and forceps. However, as you add to your field equipment and expand your home laboratory, you will want to purchase some instruments and supplies. The following supply houses offer a complete line of science materials including microscopes, binoculars, magnifying glasses, glassware, dissecting equipment, scales, chemicals, and display boxes. They publish beautiful color catalogs with offerings to tempt any naturalist.

Carolina Biological Supply Company
2700 York Road
Burlington, NC 27215
(800-547-1733)

Connecticut Valley Biological Supply Company
82 Valley Road
South Hampton, MA 01073

Edmund Scientific
101 E. Gloucester Pike
Barrington, NJ 08007
(609-573-6250)

Fisher Scientific
52 Fadem Road
Springfield, NJ 07081

Ward's Natural Science Establishment
5100 West Henrietta Road
Box 92912
Rochester, NY 14692
(800-962-2660)

Index

Abdomen, spider, 177, 178
Abscesses, herbal medicines, 77
Abscission, autumn leaves, 198, 199
Adaptation
  aquatic insects, 68-69
  desert life, 106
  see also Cold adaptations
Age, skunk cabbage, 11
Ajoene, 76
Albatross, migration, 25
Alfalfa, 92-93
Amanita (death cap) mushroom, 166, 167
Amanitin, 166
Amber, 208
Ambystoma. See Mole salamanders (*Ambystoma*)
Amphibians
  common and scientific names, listed, 271
  development, 20-21
Amputation, spiders, 183
Anoplura, 57
Antabuse®, 166
Anthers, 83, 84, 91, 94
Anthocyanins, autumn leaves, 196-198, 202-203
Anti-cancer agents, 76
Antlers, whitetail deer, 128, 129, 134-135
  cf. horns, 128
Ants, 50, 53, 101-103, 121-122, 147
  seed dispersal, 152, 153
Aphids, 121

Aposematism, 141
Aquarium, setting up, 70-71
Aquatic insects, 60-73
  advantages, 61
  aquarium, setting up, 70-71
  breathing, 63, 66-68
  adaptations, listed by species, 68-69
  collecting, 70
  collophore, 62
  common species, pictured, 64-65
  egg laying, 63
  locomotion, 61
  observation, 72
  surface tension, 62, 71
Araneidae, 180
Arctic tern, migration, 26, 27
Aristophanes, 76
Aristotle, 23, 76
Artemisinin, 75
Arthropods, 51, 232
Artiodactyla, 128
Arum family, skunk cabbage, 8-9, 12
Asclepias. See Milkweed (*Asclepias*)
Ascomycetes cf. basidiomycetes, 162, 163
Ascus, 162, 163
Asterism, 262
Atmospheric water uptake, desert life, 111
Autohemorrhage, 143
Autotoxicity, chemical defenses, invertebrates, 143-144
Autotrophs cf. heterotrophs, 100

Autumn leaves, 195–203
  changes, recording sequences,
    199–200
  falling, 198–199
  pigments, 196, 197
    anthocyanins, 196–198, 202–203
    carotenoids, 196–198, 201–202
    chlorophylls, 196–198, 201–202
    listed, 197
    tannin, 197
    visualizing, filter paper chroma-
      tography, 200–203
    xanthophylls, 196, 197
  reds, 197–198
  yellows and golds, 196–197
Auxin, 199
Avalanches
  creating, 229–230
  loose-snow cf. slab, 226
Axis, earth's
  rotation on, 253–255
  tilt, 256
Axolotl, 16

Backswimmer, 65, 67, 68, 72
Banding, bird, migration, 25–27
Barbs, seeds, 152, 157, 159
Barn swallows, migration, 25
Basidiomycetes cf. ascomycetes, 162,
  163
Basidium, 162, 163
Batesian mimicry, 122, 142
Bedbug, 50, 52
Bee beard, 41–42
Beekeepers, 38–41
Bees. *See* Honey bees
Beesmoker, 39
Beetles
  bombardier, 140, 143, 144
  carpet, 50–52
  darkling, 106–107, 112, 144
  dermestid, 51, 147
    skeleton preparation, 240–241
  diving, 65, 67, 68, 72
  ground, 139
  saw-toothed grain-, 50, 52
  water penny, 65, 69
  whirligig, 62, 65, 68, 69, 72, 251
Bee veil, 39, 40

Behavior
  adaptation, 106
  camouflage/mimicry, 119
Belladonna, 76
Bentley, Wilson A., 220–221
Bernoulli's law, 151
Big Dipper (Ursa Major), 254, 259,
  261–263
Binocular microscope, 57
Binoculars, 132
  stargazing, 258–259, 260, 262–263
Biological compasses, bird migration,
  24
Bird dropping mimicry, moths, 120–122
Birdfoot trefoil, 91–93, 157
Birds
  common and scientific names,
    listed, 271–272
  number of species, 31
  permanent U.S. residents, listed, 29
Birds, migration, 22–34, 244
  advantages of, 23
  albatross, 25
  arctic tern, 26, 27
  banding studies, 25–27
  barn swallows, 25
  bird-watching, spring migrants,
    28–31
  Canada geese, 27–28, 31
  characteristics listed, New York, 30
  early beliefs, 23
  flyways, 31–33
  hummingbird, 22–23
  mechanisms, 24–25
  moon-watching, 33
  wood thrush, 26
Black widow spider, 174
Blake, William, 3
Blastomere, 21
Blastula, 21
Blinds, whitetail deer observation, 132
Blow fly, 44
Blue-bottle fly, 46, 53, 58
Blue jay, 97, 142
Bombardier beetles, 140, 143, 144
Bones. *See* Skeletons
Booklouse, 50, 52
Booklungs, spider, 178
Brachiopods, fossils, 210
Breeding, mole salamanders, 15–20

Brown recluse spider, 174
Browsing, whitetail deer, 131
Bryozoans, fossils, 210
Butterfly
  monarch, 97, 101, 102, 103, 142, 144
  tiger swallowtail, 121, 122
  viceroy, 97, 142, 250

Cactus, 107–109
Caddisfly, 63, 65, 69, 72
Calliphoridae, 46
Calyx, 83, 84, 90, 94
Camels, 110
Camera, 123–124
Camouflage and mimicry, 117–126,
    138
  Batesian mimicry, 122, 142
  behavior, 119
  bird dropping mimicry, moths,
    120–122
  contrasting stripes, 119
  countershading, 120
  disruptive coloration, 118
  eyespots, 121, 122
  insects, listed, 122
  leaf mimicry, 120, 122
  photography, close-up, 123–125
  shadows, 119–120
  underwing (catocala) moth, 119,
    122
  whip-poor-will, 118, 119
Canada geese, migration, 27–28, 31
Cancer drugs, 76
Candelilla, 107
Cap, mushrooms, 169
Carabidae, 139
Carapace, spider, 177
Carbonization, fossils, 207
Cardiac glycosides, milkweed, 97, 142
Carotenoids, autumn leaves, 196–198,
    201–202
Carpels (pistils), 83, 84, 88, 89
Carpet beetle, 50–52
Casts, plastic, snowflakes, 220, 222
Cat skeleton, 238
Caterpillar
  monarch, 97, 101, 102, 103, 142, 144
  swallowtail, 140–141, 144
  tent, 248, 250

tiger swallowtail, 121, 122
Catocala (underwing) moth, camou-
    flage/mimicry, 119, 122
Cattail, 188–190
Cattail moth, 249
Celestial objects, listed, 260
Celestial sphere, 253–255, 262
Cellulose, brown rot cf. white rot
    fungi, 162
Cement, teeth, 235
Cephalopods, fossils, 210
Cephalothorax, spider, 177, 178
Cerci, cockroaches, 48
Cervidae, 128
Chemical defenses. *See* Defenses,
    chemical, invertebrates
Chestnut blight, 164
Chitin, 107, 204
Chlorophylls, autumn leaves, 196–198,
    201–202
Chloroplast, 196
Chromatography, filter paper, autumn
    leaf pigments, 200–203
Chromoplasts, 196
Cinchona bark, 75
Cloaca, mole salamanders, 17
Clothes moth, 50–52
Cluster fly, 44, 47, 53, 58
Clusters, globular and open, 260, 263
Coats, whitetail deer, 129
Cocaine, 76
Cockroaches, 47–49, 52
  diet, 49
  life cycle, 49
Cocoons, winter creatures, 247, 249
Coelenterates, fossils, 208
Cold adaptations, 242–251
  cold-blooded animals, 243
  collecting winter creatures, 247–251
  hibernations, 244–246
  honey bee, clustering, 244, 246
  keeping warm, 243–246
  mammals, common, 244–245
  overwintering, insects, 250–251
  surviving freezing, 246
  warm-blooded animals, 243
Cold-blooded animals (poikilotherms),
    243
Cold remedies, herbal, 79, 81
Coleoptera, 55, 72

Collecting
fossils, 212
insects, 145–147
aquatic, 70
plants, 81–83
spiders, 175–176
winter creatures, 247–251
Collembola, 57, 72
Collophore, aquatic insects, 62
Color, flowers, 88
Common names, 1–2, 53–57
jimsonweed, multiple names, 1
listed, with scientific names,
265–272
Compasses, biological, bird migration,
24
Constellations, 253, 255, 257, 259–263
Big Dipper (Ursa Major), 254, 259,
261–263
and bird migration, 24
map, 259
Zodiac, 255
see also Stargazing
Contrasting stripes, 119
Coprine, 166
Corals, fossils, 208
Corolla, flower, 83, 84, 89, 90
Corona, milkweed pollination, 98
Corpusculum, milkweed pollination,
98, 100
Countershading, 120
Crab spider, 102–103
Cretaceous period, 87
Cricket, 50, 52
Croton bug, 49
Crown, 235
Cunners (wrasse fish), 246
Cyanide, released by polydesmid
millipedes, 139, 143, 144

Daddy-long-legs, 12, 173–174
Damselfly, 64, 69, 72
Darkling beetles, 106–107, 112, 144
Darwin, Charles, 86–87, 199
Death cap mushroom (*Amanita*), 166,
167
Declination, parallels of, 253–254
Deer. *See* Whitetail deer
Deer mouse nest, 249, 250

Defenses, chemical, invertebrates,
138–147
aposematism, 141
autotoxicity, 143–144
economy of use, 140–141
insect collecting, 145–147
listed, 144
Müllerian mimicry, 141
observing, 145
odors, 139
origin, 141–142
osmeterium (scent gland), 140
sticky substances, 139
swallowtail caterpillar, 140–141, 144
venom, 138
whip scorpions, 139, 144
see also Camouflage and mimicry
Deliquescence, 191
Dental formula, 236–237
Dentine, 235
Depth of field, photography, 125
Dermaptera, 55
Dermestid beetles, 51, 147
skeleton preparation, 240–241
Desert life, 105–116
adaptations, 106
cactus, 107–109
estivation, frogs, 111–112
evaporation, 106–108
surface area:volume ratio,
107–108
excretory loss, conserving, 109–110
insect, dissection, 112–115
maximizing water gain, 110–111
plant stomata, 109, 115–116
respiratory losses, 108–109
water balance, 106
Destroying angel (*Amanita*) mushroom, 166, 167
Devonian, 206, 209
Diabetes, herbal medicines, Zuni
Indians, 78
Diatoms, 205
Diet
cockroaches, 49
mole salamanders, 17
whitetail deer, 130–131
Digestive system
desert insects, 115
whitetail deer, 128

Digitalis, 75, 76
Dioscorides, 76
Diptera, 54, 55, 58, 73
Disease transmission, flies, 45–47
Disruptive coloration, 118
Diving beetle, 65, 67, 68, 72
Doctrine of signatures, 78
Dogbane, 75
Double stars, 262–263
Dragonflies, 63, 64, 68, 69, 72
Drug effects, spiders, 183; *see also*
    Herbal medicines
Dutch elm disease, 164
Dytiscidae, 61

Earth's motion, 253–256
  axis
    rotation on, 253–255
    tilt, 256
  orbit around sun, 255
  parallels of declination, 253–254
  photography, time-exposure,
    254–255
Earthworm, 47
Earwig, 50–52, 144
Ebers papyrus, 76
Echinoderms, fossils, 210
Ecliptic, 255
Edible plants, 185–194
  cattail, 188–190
  common, listed, 193
  poisonous plants, 186–187
    listed, 187
  sumac lemonade, 188
  see also under Fungi/mushrooms
Eggs
  aquatic insects, laying, 63
  flies, deposition on skunk cabbage,
    12–13
  mole salamanders, 15, 17–20
    protection from predators, 18
  winter creatures, 247–248
    cases, 248
Elaiosomes, seed dispersal, 152–153
Elytra, 67, 72, 107, 113
Enamel, tooth, 235
Endoskeleton cf. exoskeleton, 232
Entomopathogenic fungi, 164

Ephedrine, 75, 79
Ephemeroptera, 56, 72
Ephydridae, 61
Equipment and supplies, sources, 273
Estivation, frogs, 111–112
Evaporation, 106–108
  surface area:volume ratio,
    107–108
Evolution, flowers, 87
Excretory water loss, minimizing,
    desert life, 109–110
Exoskeleton cf. endoskeleton, 232
Explosion mechanism, flowers
  pollen, 93–95
  seed dispersal, 153, 154
Eyespots, 121, 122

Fabre, Jean Henri, ix
Face fly, 44, 46, 53, 58
False morel, 166
Feeding, house fly, 45
Femur, 237
A Field Guide to the Insects (Borror
    and White), 58
Field trip, checklist, 4
Filament, 83, 84
Filter paper chromatography, autumn
    leaves, 200–203
Firebrats, 49, 52
Fleas, 53
Flies, 43–47, 51, 53, 58, 73
  blow, 44
  caddis-, 63, 65, 69, 72
  cluster, 44, 47, 53, 58
  damsel-, 64, 69, 72
  egg deposition, skunk cabbage,
    12–13
  face, 44, 46, 53, 58
  green- and blue-bottle,
    46, 53, 58
  house, 44–46, 53, 54, 58
    life cycle, 44
  identifying, 58
  lesser house, 44, 46, 53
  may-, 64, 67, 69, 72
  moth, 51
  stone-, 64, 69, 70, 72
  syrphid, 64

Flowers
  anatomy, 83–84
  anthers, 83, 84, 91, 94
  calyx, 83, 84, 90
  carpels (pistils), 83, 84, 88, 89
  corolla, 83, 84, 89, 90
  filament, 83, 84
  milkweed pollination, 97–99
  nectaries, 83, 91
  ovary, 83, 84
  ovule, 83, 89
  perianth, 83
  petals, 83, 84, 88–90
    keel, 91–93
    standard (banner), 91
  pollinia, 88, 98–100
  sepals, 83, 84
  stamens, 83, 84, 88, 92, 93, 98
  stigma, 83, 84, 89, 92, 94, 98
  style, 83, 84
  see also under Pollination by insects
Flyways, migration, 31–33
Foliage. *See* Autumn leaves
Follicle, 157
Food web, 100
Fossils, 204–213
  collecting, 210–212
    equipment, 211
    specimen preparation, 212
  common organisms, 208–210
  formation, 204–208
  geologic time scale, 206
Foxglove, 75, 76
Freezing, surviving, 246
Frogs, estivation, 111–112
Fruit, definition, 156
Fungi/mushrooms, 161–172
  ascomycetes cf. basidiomycetes,
    162–163
  brown rot cf. white rot, 162
    saprophytic, 164
  common and scientific names,
    listed, 267–268
  edible, 166–167, 186, 190–193
    morels, 190, 192–193
    puffball, 190, 191
    shaggy manes, 190, 191
    sulfur shelf, 190, 192
  entomopathogenic (predaceous), 164
  as food for animals, 167–168

  hyphae, 162, 164, 165
  identification, 168–171
  mycelium, 162, 164, 165
  mycorrhizal association, 164–165,
    169
  parasitic, 164
  pictured, 163
  poisonous, 166–167
  reproduction and life cycle, 162,
    165–166
  spores, 162, 164, 165
Funny bone (olecranon), 238

Galaxies
  Milky Way, 262, 263, 264
  other, listed, 257
Galen, 75
Galloping tracks, whitetail deer, 134
Garlic, 76
Geese, Canada, migration, 27–28, 31
Genus, 2, 53–57
Gills
  aquatic insects
    physical, 67
    tracheal, 67, 69
  fungi and mushrooms, 169
Glands
  chemical defenses, invertebrates, 143
  reproductive, whitetail deer, 129
  scent, 140
Globular clusters, 260, 263
Glues, defensive
  invertebrates, 139
  plants, 90
Glycerol, surviving freezing, 246
Glycosides, cardiac, milkweed, 97, 142
Gonorrhea, 77–78
Graupel, snowflakes, 219
Green-bottle fly, 46, 53, 58
Ground beetles, 139
Gypsy moths, 247, 250
Gyrinidae, 61

Hallucinogens, 166, 167, 183
Harvestmen, 12, 174
Heat production, skunk cabbage, 8–9
Heinrich, Bernd, 119
Hemiptera, 55, 72
Hemoglobin, aquatic insects, 68, 69

Herbal medicines, 74–85
  cold remedies, 79, 81
  collecting plants, 81–83
    identification, 83
    plant press, 82
  common plants, listed, 80
  fallacies, 77–81
    abscesses, 77
    doctrine of signatures, 78
  flower anatomy, 83–84
  plant-derived drugs, listed, 76
  quackery, 79
  why plants make drugs, 81
  Zuni Indians, 77, 78, 81
    diabetes, 78
Herpes, 79
Heterotrophs cf. autotrophs, 100
Hibernation, 244–246
Hippocrates, 76
Hitchhikers, seeds, 152, 157, 159
Homeotherms, 243
Home range, whitetail deer, 130–131
Homoptera, 56, 57
Honey bees, 35–36, 94, 99
  dissection, 113
  drone, 36
  honey production, 35
  honey stomach, 36
  pollination, 88–94
  queen, 35
  scouts, 37
  skunk cabbage, 11
  swarm, observing, 36–42
    attire, behavior, and equipment,
      39–40
    bee beard, 41–42
    division of labor, 41
    dry swarms, 39–40
    importance of experience, 38
    locating, 38
    marking bees, 40
    rain, 39–41
    size, 40
    structure, 40–41
  waggle dance, 37–38
  winter survival, clustering,
    244, 246
  worker, 35–37
Hooks, seeds, 152, 157, 159
Horns cf. antlers, whitetail deer, 128

House fly (*Musca domestica*), 44–46,
    53, 54, 58
  life cycle, 44
Household insects, listed, 52–53
Houseplants cf. skunk cabbage, 9, 12
Hummingbird, 101–103
  migration, 22–23
Hydrophobicity, 62
Hydroxyapatite, 233
Hymenoptera, 56
Hyphae, fungi and mushrooms, 162,
    164, 165

Indians, Zuni, herbal medicines, 77,
    78, 81
Inedibility, advertising (aposematism),
    141
Infrasound and bird migration, 24
Insects
  camouflage/mimicry, 122
  collecting, 145–147
    arrangement and care of collec-
      tion, 147
    chemical defenses, 145–147
    killing jars, 145–146
    pinning and labeling specimens,
      145–147
    spreading board, 145, 146
  common and scientific names,
    listed, 268–270
  dissection, 112–115
  household, listed, 52–53
  overwintering, 250–251
  proboscis, 90, 99
  see also Aquatic insects; Pollination
    by insects; specific insects
Iodine deficiency, neoteny, mole
    salamanders, 16
Ireland, potato famine, 164
Iron pyrite, 207
Isoptera, 56

Jewelweed, 89, 94–95, 157, 193
Jimsonweed, multiple names, 1
Jumping spiders, 174, 176, 178–180

Kahun papyrus, 74
Killing jars, 145–146
Knutson, Roger, 8

Labium, 72
La Brea tar pits, 207
Lacewing, green, 121–122
Larvae, mole salamanders, 16, 17, 21
Latex, milkweed, 97, 102
Leaf mimicry, 120, 122
Leaves. *See* Autumn leaves
Leg amputation, spiders, 183
Lepidoptera, 55, 73
Lesser house fly, 44, 46, 53
Life cycle
  cockroaches, 49
  fungi and mushrooms, 162, 165–166
    spores, 162, 164, 165
  house fly, 44
  mole salamanders, 15–16
Lighting, photography, 125
Light, polarized, and bird migration, 24
Light-year, 253
Lignin, brown rot cf. white rot fungi, 162
Lincoln, Frederick, 31
Linnaeus, Carolus, 53
Litmus paper, 203
Locomotion, aquatic insects, 61
Lords and ladies, 9
Lycosidae, 176

Maceration, skeleton preparation, 239
Magnetic field, earth's, and bird migration, 24
Magnetite and bird migration, 24
Magnitudes, stars, 257–258
Malaria, 75
Malic acid, 188
Mallophaga, 57
Mammals
  common and scientific names, listed, 272
  winter activities, 244–245
  see also Whitetail deer
Mammoth, wooly, 207
Mandible, 235
Masseter, 235
Mating, mole salamanders, 15–20
Mayfly, 64, 67, 69, 72
Measurement system, 2
Mecoptera, 56

Medicines. *See* Herbal medicines
Microscopes, 57–58, 72
  binocular (dissecting), 57
  snowflakes, 220
  stereo-, 57, 58, 113
  spiders, 177
Migration, breeding, mole salamander, 15–20; *see also* Birds, migration
Milkweed (*Asclepias*), 96–104, 142, 156
  cardiac glycosides, 97, 142
  crab spider, 102–103
  latex (milk), poison, 97, 102
  nighttime, 102, 104
  pollination, 97–99
    flower, 98
  rhizome (root), 96
  visitors to, 100–104
    listed with activities, 103
Milkweed bug, 101–103, 144
Millipedes, polydesmid, cyanide released by, 139, 143, 144
Milt (sperm), 17, 20
Mimicry. *See* Camouflage and mimicry
Mole salamanders (*Ambystoma*), 14–21
  amphibian development, 20–21
  breeding migrations and mating behavior, 15–20
    observing, 19–20
  diet, 17
  eggs, 15–20
    protection from predators, 18
  larvae, 16, 17, 21
  life cycle, 15–16
  neoteny, iodine deficiency, 16
  species, number and distribution, 15, 18–19
    listed, and breeding period, 18–19
Molluscs, fossils, 210
Monarch caterpillar and butterfly, 97, 101, 102, 103, 142, 144
Monomethylhydrazine, 166
Morels, 190, 192–193
  false, 166
Mortality, whitetail deer, 129
Mosquitoes, 63, 66, 68
Moth fly, 51
Moths, 73
  bird dropping mimicry, 120–122
  clothes, 50–52

gypsy, 247, 250
underwing (catocala), camouflage/
    mimicry, 119, 122
Mounting, skeleton, 240
Mouse, deer, nest, 249, 250
Mule deer, 127
Müllerian mimicry, chemical defenses,
    invertebrates, 141
Muscarine, 166
Muscidae, 46, 54
Muscles, masseter and temporal, 235
Mushrooms. *See* Fungi/mushrooms
Mycelium, fungi, 162, 164, 165
Mycophobia, 161
Mycorrhizal association, fungi,
    164–165, 169

Names, common and scientific, 1–2,
    53-57
    listed, 265–272
Naturalist, 3
    responsibilities, 4–5
Nebulae, 260, 262–263
Nectaries, 83, 91
Nectar theft, 89–90, 94–95
Neoteny, iodine deficiency, mole
    salamanders, 16
Nest, deer mouse, 249, 250
Neuroptera, 56, 72
New York state
    bird migration, 30
    fossils, 209
Nuptial dance, mole salamanders,
    16–17
Nymphs, cockroaches, 49

Observing
    chemical defenses, invertebrates, 145
    milkweed
        pollination, 100
        visitors to, 100–104
    seed dispersal, 156–159
    snowflakes, 219–223
    whitetail deer, 131–133
Odonata, 56, 72
Odor
    defensive, invertebrates, 139
    flowers, 89

skunk cabbage, 9
Olecranon (funny bone), 238
Ootheca, cockroaches, 48
Open clusters, 260, 263
Opiliones, 174
Opium, 76
Opossum, skull, 234
Orb weavers, spiders,
    178, 180–183
Orchids, 165
    pollination, 86–88
Orthoptera, 55
Osmeterium, 140
Ovary, 83, 84
Overton, E., 195
Overwintering, insects, 250–251
    house fly, 45
Ovule, 83, 89
Oxalate, 12

Parallels of declination, 253–254
Parasites
    fungi/mushrooms, 164
    human, 51
Pasteur, Louis, 76
Perianth, 83
Petals, 83, 84, 88–90
    keel, 91–93
    standard (banner), 91
Petrification (petrifaction), 207
Pheromones, 247
    fungi and mushrooms, 165–166
Pholcidae, 173
Photography
    camouflage/mimicry, 123–125
    close-up, 123–125
        camera, 123–124
        depth of field, 125
        lighting, 125
    snowflakes, 220–221
    spiders, 181–182
    time exposure, earth's motion,
        254–255
Phototropism, 199
Physical gill, aquatic insects, 67
Pine resins, 77
Pistils (carpels), 83, 84, 88, 89
Piston apparatus, flowers, pollen,
    91–93

Plant(s)
  common and scientific names,
    listed, 265–267
  medicinal. *See* Herbal medicines
  press, 82
  stomata, desert, 109, 115–116
Plaster casts, tracks, whitetail deer,
    135–137
Plastic casts, snowflakes, 220, 222
Plastron respiration, aquatic insects,
    67, 69
Plecoptera, 56, 72
Poikilotherms, 243
Poisonous fungi and mushrooms,
    166–167
Poisonous plants, 186–187
  listed, 187
Poisonous spiders, 174–175
Polarized light and bird migration, 24
Pollinarium, milkweed pollination,
    97–100
Pollination by insects, 86–95
  bees, 88–94
  exclusion of unwanted visitors,
    89–90
  flowers, 87–95
    color, 88
    evolution, 87
    explosion mechanism, 93–95
    odor, 89
    piston apparatus, 91–93
    structure, 88, 89
    see also Flowers
  nectar theft, 89–90, 94–95
  observing, 90–91
  orchids, 86–88
  pollen, 89, 91–93, 98
  self-fertilization vs. cross-pollina-
    tion, 86–87
  cf. wind, 87, 89
Pollinia, 88, 98–100
Polydesmid millipedes, cyanide
    released by, 139, 143, 144
Poppy, seed dispersal, 153
Porifera, fossils, 208
Porta, Giambattista, 78
Potato blight, 164
Praying mantis, 248
Predaceous fungi, 164

Proboscis, insect, 90, 99
  house fly, 45
Pronotum, cockroaches, 48
Protozoans, fossils, 208
Psilocybin, 166, 183
Psocoptera, 57
Ptilinum, house fly, 44
Puffball, 165, 190, 191
Pulvilli, house fly, 45
Puparium, house fly, 44

Quackery, herbal medicines, 79
Quinine, 75, 76
Quinones, 140, 143

Rain, honey bees, 39–41
Relative light efficiency, 258
Reproduction
  fungi/mushrooms, 162, 165–166
    spores, 162, 164, 165
  mole salamanders, 15–20
  whitetail deer, 129–130
Reptiles, common and scientific
    names, listed, 271
Reserpine, 75, 76
Respiration, aquatic insects, 63, 66–68
  plastron, 67, 69
  by species, 68–69
Respiratory water losses, desert life,
    108–109, 113, 114
Rhizome (root), milkweed, 96
Right Ascension, 255
Riming, snowflakes, 219
Roadkills, whitetail deer, 129
Roots
  desert life, 110
  milkweed, 96
  skunk cabbage, 10–11
Rose hips, 79

Salamander. *See* Mole salamanders
    (*Ambystoma*)
Salticidae, 174, 178–180
Salt shaker fruit, poppy, seed dis-
    persal, 153
Saprophytes, fungi, 164
Saw-toothed grain-beetle, 50, 52
Scent gland, 140
Schaefer, Vincent J., 220

Schizophora, 44
Scientific names, 1–2, 53–57
    genus and species, 2, 53–57
    listed, with common names, 265–272
Scorpions, 78
    whip (vinegaroons), 139, 144
Seed dispersal, 148–160
    air currents/wind, 150–151, 155, 156, 158–159
        lift, 151, 155
        samaras, 151, 155, 156, 159
    animals, 151–152, 157, 159
    ants, 152–153
    barbs and hooks (hitchhikers), 152, 157, 159
    common mechanisms, listed, 156–157
    difficulties, 149–150
    elaiosomes, 152, 153
    observation, 156–159
    self-dispersal, 153–154, 157
        explosive or shooting devices, 153, 154
        poppy, salt shaker fruit, 153
    surface area, 150, 156
    water, 151
Sepals, 83, 84
Shadows, camouflage, 119–120
Shaggy manes, 190, 191
Shelf fungi, sulfur, 190, 192
Shooting devices, seed dispersal, 153, 154
Shufeldt, R.W., 12
Shull, J. Marion, 11
Silica, 204
Silverfish, 49, 50, 52
Siphonoptera, 57
Skeletons, 231–241
    cat, 238
    endo- cf. exo-, 232
    femur, 237
    forces, compression and tension, 232, 237
    hollowness, 237–238
    preparation for study, 239–241
        dermestid beetles, 240–241
        maceration, 239
    skull, 233–235

teeth, 235–237
    whitetail deer, 134–135
Skulls, 233–235
Skunk cabbage, 7–13
    age, 11
    Arum family, 8–9, 12
        cf. house plants, 9, 12
    development, 9–11
    heat production, 8–9
    odor, 9
    roots, 10–11
    spadix, 8–11
    spathe, 8, 10, 12
    visitors to, 11–13
        listed, 12
Skunks, 141
Snake bite, 77
Snorkels, aquatic insects, 66
Snow drifts, wind and, 224–230
    avalanches
        creating, 229–230
        loose-snow cf. slab, 226
    snow cornice, 225
    snow fences, 227, 228
Snowflakes, 214–223
    classification, 216, 217
    graupel, 219
    growth, 215–216
        nucleus, condensation and freezing, 215
    observation and preservation, 219–223
    riming, 219
    shape determination, 217–218
    spatial dendrite, 219
    symmetry, 218
    tsuzumi crystals, 219
    uniqueness, 215
Soil, water absorption from, desert life, 110–111
Spadix, skunk cabbage, 8–11
Spathe, skunk cabbage, 8, 10, 12
Spatial dendrite, snowflakes, 219
Species, 2, 53–57
    numbers of, ix
Spermatophore, mole salamanders, 16–17, 20
Sperm (milt), mole salamanders, 17, 20

Spiders, 12, 173–184, 248, 250
  black widow, 174
  brown recluse, 174
  care and feeding, 176
  collecting, 175–176
  common and scientific names,
    listed, 270
  crab, 102–103
  drug effects, 183
  external anatomy, 176–178
  jumping, 174, 176, 178–180
  leg amputation, 183
  orb weavers, 178, 180–183
    web, 181–182
  photography, 181–182
  poisonous, 174–175
  preserving and identifying, 177–178
    stereomicroscope, 177
  wolf spiders, 176
Spinnerets, spider, 176, 178
Spiracles
  aquatic insects, 66, 69
  desert life, 108, 113
Sponges, fossils, 208
Spores, fungi, 162, 164, 165
  prints, 169–171
Spreading board, 145–146
Springtail, 64, 72
Stamens, 83, 84, 88, 92, 93, 98
Staphylococcus aureus, 77
Stargazing, 256–264
  binoculars, 258–259, 260, 263
  brightest stars, listed, 257
  celestial objects, listed, 260
  clusters, 262, 263
    globular and open, 260, 263
  double stars, 260, 262–263
  magnitudes, 257–258
  maps, 256–258
  Milky Way, 262, 263, 264
  nebulae, 262–263
  other galaxies, 260, 263–264
  star wheels, 256–258
  see also Constellations
Stars and bird migration, 24
Star wheels, 256–258
Stereomicroscopes, 57, 58, 113
Sticky substances, defensive
  invertebrates, 139
  plants, 90

Stigma, 83, 84, 89, 92, 94, 98
Stinkhorn, 168
Stomata, plant, desert life, 109, 115–116
Stonefly, 64, 69, 70, 72
Stripes, contrasting, 119
Style, 83, 84
Sulfur shelf fungi, 190, 192
Sumac
  lemonade, 188
  poison, 188
Sun, earth's orbit around, 255
Supercooling, surviving freezing, 246
Supplies and equipment, sources, 273
Surface area : volume ratio, 107–108
Surface tension, water
  aquatic insects, 62, 71
  seed dispersal, 151
Swallows, barn, migration, 25
Swallowtail caterpillar, 140–141, 144
Sweating, desert life, 110
Syphilis, 47–48, 77–78
Syrphid fly, 64

Taenidia, desert insects, 114
Tannin, autumn leaves, 197
Tarsi, house fly, 45
Taxonomy, 53–57
  key, 54–57
Teeth, 235–237
Temporal muscles, 235
Tennyson, Alfred Lord, 117
Tent caterpillar, 248, 250
Termite, 50, 52
Tern, arctic, migration, 26, 27
Theridiidae, 174
Thrush, wood, migration, 26
Thysanoptera, 56
Thysanura, 57
Tiger swallowtail caterpillar, 121, 122
Tobacco, 89
Trabeculae, 238
Tracheae
  aquatic insects, 66
  desert insects, 108, 113, 114
  spider, 178
Tracheal gills, aquatic insects, 67, 69
Tracheoles
  aquatic insects, 68
  desert insects, 108

Tracks and traces, whitetail deer, 133–135
  plaster casts, 135–137
Translator arms, milkweed pollination, 98–100
Tree blights, 164
Treefrog, camouflage/mimicry, 118
Trichoptera, 56, 72
Trilobites, fossils, 210
Truffles, 165
Tsuzumi crystals, snowflakes, 219
Turpentine, 77

Underwing (catocala) moth camouflage/mimicry, 119, 122
Urine, minimizing water losses, desert life, 109–110
Ursa Major (Big Dipper), 254, 259, 261–263

Valium®, 183
Vendors, equipment and supplies, 273
Venom, 138
Viceroy butterfly, 97, 142, 250
Vinegaroons, 139, 144
Virginia bluebell, 89, 94
Vitamin C, rose hips cf. synthetic, 79
Voodoo lilies, 9

Warm-blooded animals (homeotherms), 243
Water
  balance, desert life, 106
  gain, maximizing, desert life, 110–111
  seed dispersal, 151
  surface tension, 62, 71, 151
Water boatman, 65, 67, 68, 72
Water bug, 63, 65, 67, 68
Water penny beetle, 65, 69
Water scorpions, 65, 68

Water strider, 65, 71
Waxes, desert life, 107
Webs, spiders, 181–182
Whip-poor-will, camouflage/mimicry, 118–119
Whip scorpions, 139, 144
Whirligig beetle, 62, 65, 68, 69, 72, 251
Whitetail deer, 127–137
  antlers, 128–129, 134–135
    cf. horns, 128
  attracting, 135–136
  coats, 129
  digestive system, 128
  habits and behavior, 130–131
  observing, 131–133
  population and mortality, 129
  reproductive cycle and mating, 129–130
  tracks and traces, 133–135
    plaster casts, 135–137
Wind
  pollination, 87, 89
  seed dispersal, 150–151, 155, 156, 158–159
    lift, 151, 155
    samaras, 151, 155, 156, 159
  see also Snow drifts, wind and
Winter. *See* Cold adaptations
Withering, William, 75
Wolf, skull, 234
Wolf spiders, 176
Wood thrush, migration, 26
Wooly mammoth, 207
Wormwood, 75, 79, 81
Wrasse fish (cunners), 246

Xanthophylls, autumn leaves, 196, 197

Zodiac, 255
Zuni Indians, herbal medicines, 77, 78, 81